Hydrogen Energy

To the search for a sustainable energy future to which all the authors of this book are committed

Hydrogen Energy

Economic and Social Challenges

Edited by Paul Ekins

First published by Earthscan in the UK and USA in 2010

For a full list of publications please contact:
Earthscan
2 Park Square, Milton Park, Abingdon, Oxfordshire OX14 4RN
711 Third Avenue, New York, NY 10017

First issued in paperback 2015

Earthscan is an imprint of the Taylor & Francis Group, an informa business

Notices

Practitioners and researchers must always rely on their own experience and knowledge in evaluating and using any information, methods, compounds,or experiments described herein. In using such information or methods they should be mindful of their own safety and the safety of others, including parties for whom they have a professional responsibility.

Product or corporate names may be trademarks or registered trademarks, and are used only for identification and explanation without intent to infringe.

ISBN 13: 978-1-138-88125-9 (pbk)
ISBN 13: 978-1-8440-7680-2 (hbk)

Typeset by 4word Ltd, Bristol
Cover design by Clifford Hayes

The front cover image is a photo-montage created using illustration reference from iStock.com. The design is based on the logo of the UK Sustainable Hydrogen Energy Consortium (UKSHEC), one of the SUPERGEN consortia funded by the Engineering and Physical Sciences Research Council. The logo was designed by Dr Matthew T. J. Lodge of Oxford University, Chemistry Department, and is used with permission from UKSHEC.

A catalogue record for this book is available from the British Library

Library of Congress Cataloging-in-Publication Data

Hydrogen energy : economic and social challenges / edited by Paul Ekins. — 1st ed.
p. cm.
Includes bibliographical references and index.
ISBN 978-1-84407-680-2 (hardback)
1. Hydrogen as fuel—Economic aspects. I. Ekins, Paul.
TP359.H8H876 2010
665.8'1—dc22

2009028135

Contents

List of Figures, Tables and Boxes

Figures

Tables

Boxes

List of Contributors

Paolo Agnolucci is an environmental/energy economist with a strong analytical and statistical background. He holds a PhD in Economics from Birkbeck College, University of London. After working as environmental advisor for a corporate client and as consultant in the energy sector, he spent six years at the Policy Studies Institute, London. He is currently a Visiting Scholar in the Department of Land Economy, University of Cambridge, while working as a forecasting analyst in the energy industry. Paolo has authored several journal articles on renewable energy, hydrogen and fuel cells, and energy economics.

Nazmiye Balta-Ozkan has a PhD in Regional Planning from the University of Illinois at Urbana-Champaign. Currently she is a Senior Research Fellow at the Policy Studies Institute in London. Her research interests include modelling of energy systems and transitions, and analysis of how energy policy can contribute to regional development and planning.

Paul Bellaby is now Research Professor in Sociology, University of Salford. He took his first degree (1964) and PhD (1974) at Cambridge University and was successively Lecturer at Keele University (1968–89), Senior Lecturer at the University of East Anglia (1989–2000) and Reader, then Professor, at Salford (2000–). He has published widely in the sociologies of education, health and illness, risk and latterly sustainable energy, and has, of late, led or been part of major projects in the ESRC 'E-Society' and the EPSRC 'Supergen' programmes.

Simon Dresner is a research fellow in the Environment Group at the Policy Studies Institute. He has a PhD in Social and Economic Research on Technology from Edinburgh University. Simon's expertise is in the social and economic aspects of sustainability. His book *The Principles of Sustainability* was published by Earthscan in 2002 and a revised second edition was published in 2008. As well as his work on hydrogen in UKSHEC, Simon has done research on public attitudes to green taxes and their distributional effects, household energy, the interactions between different environmental policy instruments, sustainable development indicators and environmental risk.

Malcolm Eames has a DPhil in Science and Technology Policy Studies from Sussex University and is Professor of Low Carbon Research at the Welsh School of Architecture, Cardiff University. Over the last ten years Malcolm has participated in and led research and consultancy projects for a wide range of UK and European research funding bodies and government agencies. His current research interests span: hydrogen energy and the transition to a low carbon economy; energy and innovation policy; foresight and low carbon futures; socio-technical change, innovation and sustainability; participatory technology assessment; deliberative decision-making; and environmental justice.

Paul Ekins has a PhD in economics from the University of London and is a Co-Director of the UK Energy Research Centre. He has been Professor of Energy and Environment Policy at the Energy Institute, University College London, since August 2009, but during the research reported in this book was both Head of the Environment Group at the Policy Studies Institute and then Professor of Energy and Environment Policy at King's College London. He was a Member of the Royal Commission on Environmental Pollution from 2002 to 2008. His academic work focuses on the conditions and policies for achieving an environmentally sustainable economy, with a special focus on energy policy, innovation, the role of economic instruments, sustainability assessment and environment and trade.

Rob Flynn is Professor of Sociology at the University of Salford, Salford, UK. Previously he has researched and published widely in urban sociology, health service studies and medical sociology, focusing on the regulation of professionals and the impact of quasi-markets. More recently he has been carrying out research on public perceptions of risk, and public attitudes towards sustainable energy. Currently he is collaborating with other colleagues on deliberative methods and public engagement in emerging hydrogen energy technologies. With Paul Bellaby, he is co-editor of *Risk and the Public Acceptance of New Technologies* (2007, Palgrave-Macmillan).

Sam Hawkins has a BA in computer science and an MSc in sustainable development. He worked at the Policy Studies Institute, where he investigated the technical and economic characteristics of hydrogen as a energy vector. He has also worked promoting community renewable energy projects in Scotland, and assessing the technical barriers presented to small-scale hydro development by the Scottish electricity grid. He is currently studying for a PhD at Edinburgh University on the variability of wind power and the integration with electricity networks.

Andrew Hewitson was Research Associate at the Centre for Sustainable Urban and Regional Futures. Andrew holds undergraduate (1999) and postgraduate (2002) degrees from Leeds Metropolitan University and a doctorate from the

University of Hull (2006). His research work in SURF focused on the development of the hydrogen economy in international comparison.

Mike Hodson is Research Fellow at the Centre for Sustainable Urban and Regional Futures (SURF). He has degrees from Sheffield (1996), City University, London (1997), and his doctorate from Salford (2004). Mike's research interests focus on city-regional transitions to low-carbon economies, the ways in which this may or may not happen and understandings of the lessons to be learned from such processes. His many projects have principally addressed the relationships between sub-national territories and the reconfiguration of their key socio-technical infrastructures in a period of globalization, neoliberalization and in a context of the challenges posed by climate change and resource constraint.

Nick Hughes received a BA with Honours in Music from the University of Oxford, and an MSc in Environmental Technology from Imperial College London. For the last four years he has been undertaking research in the area of energy policy and low carbon energy technologies. As well as undertaking socioeconomic analysis and technological characterization of sustainable hydrogen technologies, he is involved in numerous energy system modelling and scenario development activities, and has contributed to the development of long-term electricity network scenarios for Ofgem and to the UKERC's Energy 2050 project.

Simon Marvin is Professor and Co-Director of SURF. He is an expert on the changing relations between neighbourhoods, cities, regions and infrastructure networks in a period of resource constraint, institutional restructuring and climate change. Simon's research has been funded by the ESRC, EPSRC, international research foundations, the European Commission, commercial funders, and many public agencies. His research has examined how the urban, city-regional and regional policy agendas are understood by government departments within Whitehall, regions and cities. Simon is a co-author of three internationally leading books on cities and infrastructure.

William McDowall is a Research Associate at the National Round Table on the Environment and the Economy in Canada, and Associate Member of Sustainability Solutions Group Workers' Co-operative, a Canadian consulting firm. He was previously a Research Fellow at the Policy Studies Institute in London, and Policy Associate at the University of British Columbia's Centre for Health and Environment Research. His research interests focus on climate change and energy policy, innovation, and the use of research evidence in policy-making.

Miriam Ricci is currently a Research Fellow at the Centre for Transport & Society at the University of the West of England, Bristol. Until June 2009 she was a Post Doctoral Research Fellow at the Institute for Social, Cultural & Policy Research at the University of Salford. During her PhD, she held a Marie Curie Doctoral Fellowship at the Manchester Institute of Innovation Research. Her main research interests are in social studies of science, technology and innovation, more specifically around sustainability, energy and climate change. Her work on hydrogen energy has included analysis of scientific risk assessment, stakeholders' representations and public perceptions of hydrogen. She is also interested in the theory and practice of public engagement with energy and environmental issues.

Neil Strachan received his PhD in Engineering and Public Policy from Carnegie Mellon University in 2000 and is an interdisciplinary energy economist. Currently he is a Senior Research Fellow at King's College London. His research interests focus on energy-environment-economic modelling, scenarios and transitions pathways, and energy technology diffusion.

Julia Tomei has a BSc in Biology from the University of Leeds and an MSc in Environmental Technology from Imperial College London. Since 2006, she has worked as a Research Associate and her work has focused on two Supergen projects: UKSHEC, where she investigated public perceptions of and future demand for hydrogen energy; and Supergen Bioenergy, where she explored stakeholder perceptions of UK bioenergy and biofuels policy.
Julia is currently studying for a PhD at University College London on the socio-economic impacts of bioenergy production.

Acknowledgements

Most of this book (in fact, everything except Chapter 8) derives from research carried out over the four years 2003–07, during Phase 1 of the UK Sustainable Hydrogen Energy Consortium (UKSHEC 1), one of a number of so-called SUPERGEN (Sustainable Power Generation and Supply) consortia funded by the UK's Engineering and Physical Sciences Research Council (EPSRC), under the UK Research Councils' Energy programme. The working papers produced by the social science component of UKSHEC 1, which underlie much of the substance of this book, may be found at http://www.psi.org.uk/ukshec/. The second phase of research under UKSHEC (UKSHEC 2) will continue until 2012, and outputs may be accessed at http://www.uk-shec.org.uk/. Our principal grateful acknowledgement is to the EPSRC for funding the research, without which this book would not have existed.

The work on which Chapter 8 is based was funded by Brunel Research in Enterprise, Innovation, Sustainability and Ethics (BRESE) at Brunel Business School, Brunel University, and is gratefully acknowledged.

Many other people also helped with the research, of course, most notably those who gave of their time to answer the questions, give the interviews and complete the surveys which provide much of the substance of the research. Individuals we would gratefully like to acknowledge for their input are Kerry-Ann Adamson of Fuel Cell Today for insights into fuel cell markets, Kirthi Roberts, for his early advice and insights into the fuel cell community in Vancouver, and Geert van der Vossen for help with identifying interviewees there. Of course, in all cases our conclusions, and any errors, are our own and not theirs.

Thanks are also due to Dr Matthew T. J. Lodge of Oxford University, Chemistry Department, who designed the UKSHEC logo, on which the book's cover design is based.

Finally, a number of the chapters in this book are modifications (sometimes quite extensive) of papers which have already appeared in the academic literature. These papers include:

Chapter 2
Agnolucci, P. and Ekins, P. (2007) 'Technological Transitions and Strategic Niche Management: The Case of the Hydrogen Economy', *International Journal of Environmental Technology and Management*, vol 7, nos 5/6, pp644–671

Chapter 3
Ekins, P. and Hughes, N. (2009) 'The Prospects for a Hydrogen Economy (1): Hydrogen Futures', *Technology Analysis and Strategic Management*, vol 21, no 7, pp783–803

Chapter 7
Hodson, M., Marvin, S. and Hewitson, A. (2008) 'Constructing a typology of H2 in cities and regions: An international review', *International Journal of Hydrogen Energy*, vol 33, Issue 6, March 2008, pp1619–1629

Chapter 12
Ekins, P. and Hughes, N. (2009) 'The Prospects for a Hydrogen Economy (2): Hydrogen Transitions', *Technology Analysis and Strategic Management*, vol 22, no 1, pp1–17

The authors would like to thank the original publishers for their permission to reprint this revised material here.

List of Acronyms and Abbreviations

2WH	Two-wheeled vehicles
AC	Alternating current
AD	Anaerobic digestion
AFC	Alkaline Fuel Cell
APU	Auxiliary Power Unit
Bar	Unit of pressure: equivalent to 0.1MPa
BC	British Columbia
BERR	Department for Business, Enterprise, and Regulatory Reform (UK Government Department, renamed Department for Business, Innovation and Skills (BIS) in June 2009)
CCS	Carbon capture and sequestration
CG	Coal gasification
CHP	Combined heat and power
CO	Carbon monoxide
CO_2	Carbon dioxide
CNG	Compressed natural gas
CTFCA	Canadian Transportation Fuel Cell Alliance
CUTE	Clean Urban Transport for Europe
DGTREN	Directorate-General Energy and Transport
DM	Deliberative Mapping
DMFC	Direct Methanol Fuel Cell
DOE	Department of Energy (United States)
DTI	Department of Trade and Industry (former UK Government Department)
EIHP 2	European Integrated Hydrogen Project 2
ERDF	European Regional Development Funding
ESCO	Energy Service Company
EU	European Union
FC	Fuel cell
FCV	Fuel cell vehicle
GH_2	Gaseous hydrogen

GHG	Greenhouse gas
GIS	Geographical information system
GLA	Greater London Authority
H_2	Hydrogen
H2EA	Hydrogen Early Adopters Program (in Canada)
HFCCC	Hydrogen and Fuel Cells Co-ordination Committee
HGVs	Heavy goods vehicles
HNEI	Hawaii Natural Energy Institute
HVI	Hydrogen Valley Initiative
IC	Industry Canada
ICE	Internal combustion engine
ICEV	Internal combustion engine vehicle
IFCI	Institute for Fuel Cell Innovation
LGVs	Light goods vehicles
LH_2	Liquefied hydrogen
LHP	London Hydrogen Partnership
LNG	Liquefied natural gas
MARKAL	Market Allocation (model)
MCFC	Molten Carbonate Fuel Cell
MNC	Multinational Company
MPa	Megapascal (1,000,000 Pascals). Unit of pressure.
NGCC	Natural gas combined cycle
NGO	Non-governmental organizations
NRC	National Research Council (United States)
NRCan	Natural Resources Canada
OECD	Organization for Economic Co-operation and Development
PAFC	Phosphoric Acid Fuel Cell
PEM	Polymer Electrolyte Membrane, or Proton Exchange Membrane
PEMFC	Proton Exchange (or Polymer Electrolyte) Membrane Fuel Cell
PEwfH2	Public Engagement with future Hydrogen Infrastructure for Transport
PJ	Peta (10^{16}) joule
PPP	Public–Private Partnership
PSA	Pressure Swing Adsorption
R&D	Research and development
RDA	Regional Development Agency
RD & D	Research, development and demonstration
SDTC	Sustainable Development Technology Canada
SMR	Steam methane reforming
SNM	Strategic niche management
SOFC	Solid Oxide Fuel Cell
SPE	Solid Polymer Electrolyte
ST	Socio-technical
TTW	Travel to Work
UK	United Kingdom

UKSHEC	United Kingdom Sustainable Hydrogen Energy Consortium
UKSHEC 1	The first phase of research of UKSHEC, 2003–07
US	United States
US DOE	United States Department of Energy
V2G	Vehicles-to-Grid
VFCVP	Vancouver Fuel Cell Vehicle Partnership
WEPA	Western Economic Partnership Agreement
WTP	Willingness to Pay

1
Introduction and Overview

Paul Ekins

Introduction

In their early days, new energy technologies tend to be hailed in extravagant terms as single-bullet solutions to multifarious human problems. Hydrogen is no exception to this, and has been welcomed by some as the ultimate solution to the problems of energy security, climate change and air pollution (Rifkin, 2002). There has also been more scholarly work published over the last decade or so (e.g. Padró and Putsche, 1999;NRC and NAE, 2004; Ogden et al, 2004; Hisschemöller et al, 2006; Solomon and Banerjee, 2006 and other papers in this Special Issue of *Energy Policy*) on the possibility and desirability of a 'hydrogen economy', the costs that might be involved, and how such an economy might come about.

Hydrogen's desirability relates mainly to the challenges of pollution (especially climate-change related, but also local pollution) and energy security that current reliance on fossil fuels as the industrial world's primary energy source has created. This book explores from first principles why and how 'a hydrogen economy' might come about, and identifies the main conditions that will need to be met for this to happen.

There has been a number of attempts to define the hydrogen economy (Dutton, 2002; POST, 2002; Rifkin, 2002). For POST, the hydrogen economy was seen as entailing a 'widespread and diverse production and use of hydrogen' (POST, 2002: p1). In the more ambitious visions for hydrogen, it is used as a fuel for all forms of transport, for heat and for electricity generation (see Rifkin, 2002). As concerns related to industrial societies' widespread reliance on fossil fuels – reducing carbon dioxide emissions, confronting air pollution and securing (national) energy supply – have increased, so has interest in the idea of a hydrogen economy.

The definition of a hydrogen economy used here is simply a (national) economic system in which hydrogen is the energy carrier that delivers 'a substantial fraction of the nation's energy-based goods and services' (NRC and NAE, 2004: p11). It would obviously be possible for the concept of a hydrogen economy to apply at a sub-national level, but the term as used here implies a certain scale that would not be satisfied by purely very local applications. As will become clear throughout this book, there is not a single view of what might constitute a hydrogen economy, but a range of possibilities as to precisely what hydrogen-related technologies, in different combinations, a hydrogen economy might include.

The current, largely fossil-fuel based, energy system in industrial countries is mature, pervasive, reasonably efficient in its satisfaction of a wide range of demands for energy services (heat, light, power, mobility), and has an extensive infrastructure which is long-lasting and has been developed over many years with very large investments. For the hydrogen economy to come about, there will need to be an extensive transition away from the fossil-fuel economy and its associated energy system.

The nature of an energy system

An energy system in an industrial country, schematically illustrated in Figure 1.1, is absolutely crucial to its functioning and is comprised of multiple sophisticated technologies in complex and continuous interactions with each other. The technologies should not be understood simply as engineering devices. Certainly they often contain engineering of a high order, but the physical components of an energy system are embedded in social and economic structures and institutions which crucially influence how they are used and how they develop.

Very briefly to describe the main pathways of Figure 1.1, the energy system may be seen to process natural resources (e.g. crude oil, uranium, wind) into energy carriers, or fuels (e.g. petrol, electricity, hydrogen), to provide the energy source for devices which will provide desired energy services to final consumers. Energy services may be one of four kinds: heat, light, (electric) power, and mobility. Power, in particular, is used to provide a very wide range of services through an enormous range of machines and appliances, ranging from factory equipment to information and communication technologies and home entertainment.

All energy carriers ultimately derive from the environment. A whole technological chain converts the environmental resources into useful fuels, which are then fed into energy demand technologies to produce the energy services required. Hydrogen, the production of which can be carried out through a number of technologies, as will be seen in Chapter 3, is one possible fuel output from this system, which can be used in a number of energy demand technologies.

The kinds of changes in the energy system that would be required for hydrogen to play a major role as an energy carrier are fundamental and

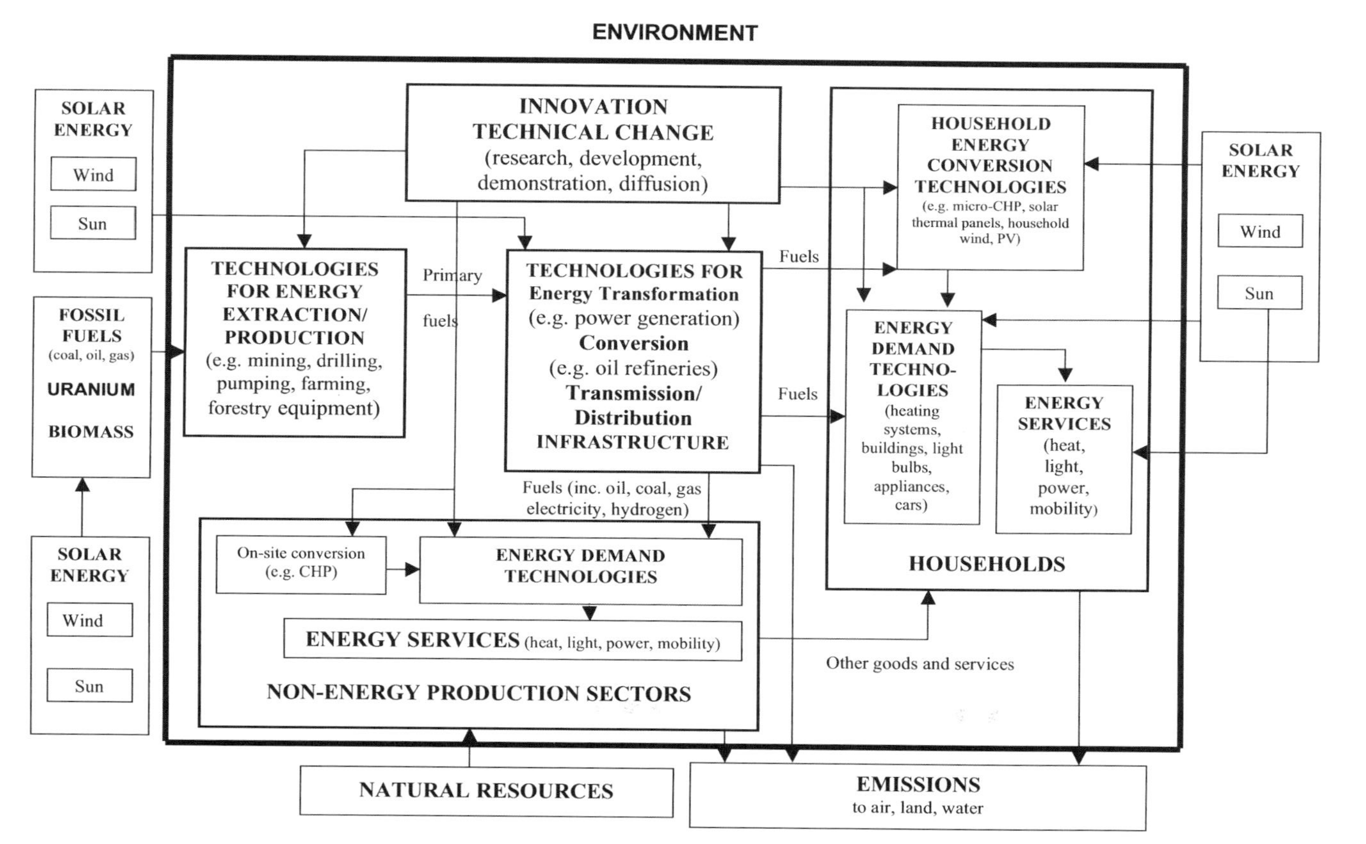

Figure 1.1 *Schematic illustration of an energy system*

far-reaching. At present, hydrogen is a negligible component of the energy system. Eighty-seven per cent of current hydrogen use is for fertilizer manufacturing and refining (Maddy et al, 2003: p29), that is, it is not part of mainstream energy demand at all. For there to be a 'hydrogen economy', enormous technical innovation and change will need to take place in respect of all the kinds of technology (hydrogen production, storage, transport and end-use application) identified in Chapter 3. This will require very large investments over long periods. One of the purposes of this book is to identify who might make the investments that could lead to a transition to a hydrogen economy, and why.

Most fundamental technological changes in developed industrial societies have come about through the operation of markets. Producers have used new technologies to develop new ways of producing and delivering goods and services of superior functionality or quality, or lower cost, or all of these. Consumers have bought these goods and services for these reasons. However, even in such cases, the development, deployment and diffusion of new technologies is far from straightforward, and there has been much study as to why and how certain technological developments become established, and others do not, even when they do not seem to be so different in terms of market advantages.

For a transition to a hydrogen economy to occur through the operation of market forces, hydrogen technologies must compete effectively with fossil fuels and other alternatives to them. In particular, 'devices that use hydrogen (e.g. fuel cells) must compete successfully with devices that use competing fuels (e.g. hybrid propulsion systems)' and 'hydrogen must compete successfully with electricity and secondary fuels (e.g. gasoline, diesel fuel and methanol)' (NRC and NAE 2004: p17). This book identifies some of the main contexts for this competition, and the principal conditions which hydrogen will have to satisfy if it is to prevail.

In respect of hydrogen technologies, which are reviewed in some detail in Chapter 3, the evidence suggests that their current market advantages over incumbent and developing technologies with which they are in competition are rather few. The interest in these technologies is driven almost entirely by public interest considerations: depending on how hydrogen is produced, it may promote energy security and result in lower carbon emissions than the use of fossil fuels, and it has no harmful emissions at its point of use. Private consumers have not historically been motivated to trade off conventional consumer benefits, such as functionality, quality or cost, for such public interest considerations, which gives public policy a crucial role in promoting hydrogen technologies, as will be seen.

As will become apparent, hydrogen technologies are currently very far from fulfilling the competitive imperatives cited from the NRC and NAE report above, and there is no literature that suggests that the hydrogen economy will come to exist in the foreseeable future, if ever, without substantial and long-term public support. Even with the political will to give that support, the nature of what is being attempted should not be underestimated. It is unprecedented. Writing about the US, NRC and NAE (2004: p17) state:

> *In no prior case has the government attempted to promote the replacement of an entire, mature, networked energy infrastructure before market forces did the job. The magnitude of the change required if a meaningful fraction of the U.S. energy system is to shift to hydrogen exceeds by a wide margin that of previous transitions in which the government has intervened.*

The same would be true for other industrialized countries.

Overview

This book explores how a transition to a hydrogen economy might come about. Its theoretical starting point is the literature on technological transitions and strategic niche management, which is the subject of Chapter 2. This makes clear that a technological transition of the kind envisaged is far more than just a change in the physical technologies employed in the energy system, important though this change is. The point is that such a change cannot and will not come about unless it is accompanied by parallel changes in the economic and social systems, which both facilitate the technological changes and make them both economically viable and socially acceptable.

Chapter 3 works through the many different technological possibilities for producing, storing, transporting and distributing and using hydrogen, discussing both the characteristics of the different technologies and estimates that have been made of their costs. Some of this material is quite technical, but understanding it is fundamental to an appreciation later in the book of what a large-scale transition to hydrogen in the future might involve.

Whereas Chapter 3 is focused mainly on the engineering and cost aspects of hydrogen technologies, Chapter 4 explores hydrogen applications more from a market and consumer point of view. Why should people want to use hydrogen technologies? What do they offer from a private consumer perspective? The answers to these questions will greatly influence the extent to which a transition to a hydrogen economy might be driven by markets, or will need to be largely brought about through public policy.

Having by this stage established what hydrogen technologies are and how they might be used, Chapter 5 returns to the theme of technological transitions that was introduced in Chapter 2, and maps out what such transitions might look like for hydrogen. The key point is that there is a number of possible transitions. Which of them comes about, if any, will depend on how the various technologies develop, and on the nature and level of public policy support. Two of the possible transitions are then modelled in some detail in Chapter 6, using a model of the whole energy system, which is essential to see how hydrogen might sit within it, and how it might compete with and displace, or itself be squeezed out by, other energy technologies. Extensions to the basic model explore the implications of changing the taxation of hydrogen, and of taking into account the spatial requirements of different kinds of hydrogen infrastructure.

The development of hydrogen technologies is very much an international affair, with global research partnerships involving the private and public sectors. While most of this book is about how these technologies might play out in the UK, a number of chapters also have a dimension of international applicability: Chapter 3 that describes the technologies, Chapter 4 that explores the markets, Chapter 5 that generates hydrogen transitions, Chapter 7 which is an international review of hydrogen experiments, demonstration projects and initiatives around the world, and Chapter 8.

Chapter 7 is also the first of three chapters which look in detail at the regional realities and motivations of hydrogen manifestations on the ground. It identifies seven different regional types of hydrogen initiatives, and explores their rationale, genesis and what it is hoped that each one will achieve. The differences are instructive as to the reasons why regional, rather than national, policy-makers might wish to establish hydrogen economies in the places where they live. Chapters 8 and 9 take as case studies and look in more depth at some of the 'hydrogen regions' identified in Chapter 7: Vancouver in Canada; and three different regions in the UK: London, Teesside and Wales. It becomes even clearer from these case studies that there is no single model or blueprint for 'rolling out' hydrogen at a regional level. To be successful, hydrogen developments must mesh with regional realities, aspirations and capabilities.

Both Chapters 10 and 11 move the focus of analysis and discussion to the interface between hydrogen technologies and the public. Chapter 10 explores what is known about the public risks posed by the widespread use of hydrogen as an energy carrier (as opposed to an industrial chemical). Its conclusion is that there are many gaps in knowledge and understanding in this area. Until both the social and technical components of hydrogen are more developed, these gaps will remain a ground for debate and possible opposition to hydrogen's more widespread deployment. Chapter 11 shows that, while public awareness about hydrogen technologies is still generally low, there is as yet little public concern about it, and widespread support for its development. However, it is clear that as people learn more about these technologies, they become more questioning, so that processes that enable them to engage with hydrogen developments to address their questions may be important in securing the positive public acceptance of hydrogen applications if and when they become ready for widespread diffusion.

Finally, Chapter 12 seeks to pull the threads of the book together, draw some conclusions and make some recommendations.

Firstly, under some assessments of possible technological developments up to 2050, hydrogen energy may enter the UK energy system by that date even without major public policy drivers. To achieve this, research funding and initial deployments must be successful in greatly driving down costs and improving performance across a range of hydrogen technologies.

However, it also seems clear that, for hydrogen energy to play a really significant role as an energy carrier in the UK economy, public policy will need to do more than fund research and development along with private investors, and will also need to go beyond strategic niche management. It will need to develop infrastructure, give generous incentives for the technologies to be deployed and used as well as developed, be regionally attuned to locally based needs and aspirations, and take the public along with the technology developers and policy experts who bring the hydrogen economy into being. This book is ultimately about giving the justifications for, and exploring the details around, these headline conclusions.

References

Dutton, G. (2002) *Hydrogen Energy Technology*, Tyndall Centre Working Paper No. 17, available at http://www.tyndall.ac.uk/publications/working_papers/working_papers.shtml (accessed 16 June 2009)

Hisschemöller, M., Bode, R. and van de Kerkhof, M. (2006) 'What Governs the Transition to a Sustainable Hydrogen Economy? Articulating the Relationship Between Technologies and Political Institutions', *Energy Policy*, vol 34, pp1227–1235

Maddy, J., Cherryman, S., Hawkes, F., Hawkes, D., Dinsdale, R., Guwy, A., Premier, G. and Cole, S. (2003) *Hydrogen 2003*, University of Glamorgan, Wales

NRC and NAE (National Research Council and National Academy of Engineering) (2004) *The Hydrogen Economy: Opportunities, Costs, Barriers, and R&D Needs*, The National Academies Press, Washington, DC, www.nap.edu

Ogden, J., Williams, R. and Larson, E. (2004) 'Societal Lifecycle Costs of Cars with Alternative Fuels/Engines', *Energy Policy*, vol 32, pp7–27

Padró, C. and Putsche, V. (1999) 'Survey of the Economics of Hydrogen Technologies', National Renewable Energy Laboratory, Colorado, available on http://www.nrel.gov/docs/fy99osti/27079.pdf

POST (Parliamentary Office of Science and Technology) (2002) *Prospects for a Hydrogen Economy*, POST, London

Rifkin, J. (2002) *The Hydrogen Economy: The Creation of the World-Wide Energy Web and the Redistribution of Power on Earth*, Polity Press, Oxford

Solomon, B. and Banerjee, A. (2006) 'A Global Survey of Hydrogen Energy Research, Development and Policy', *Energy Policy*, vol 34, pp781–792

2
Innovation and Technological Change

Paul Ekins

Theories of technological transitions

Oosterhuis and ten Brink (2006) note that new technologies, when they are successful in being applied and finding their way to the market, often follow a pattern in which the uptake starts at a low speed then accelerates, before slowing down again when the level of saturation approaches. This is reflected in the well-known logistic or S-curve (see Figure 2.1).

However, the scale of the innovation required for anything resembling a 'hydrogen economy' to develop goes far beyond the mere introduction of a new technology, and is more akin to what the innovation literature calls 'a technological transition'. This chapter sets the stage for a more detailed examination of hydrogen technologies by reviewing a number of theories of technological transition, given that some such process will be required for these technologies to become widely established.

Underlying all theories of technological transition is the insight that technologies do not exist in a vacuum. They are products of the social and economic context in which they were developed and which they subsequently help to shape. The idea of a technological transition therefore implies more than the substitution of one artefact for another. It implies a change from one techno-socio-economic system (or 'socio-technical configuration', as it is called below) to another, in a complex and pervasive series of processes that may leave little of society unaffected.

There is now an enormous literature on technological change and the broader concept of technological transition (a significant portion of this literature is reviewed in Geels, 2002a), only certain elements of which can be

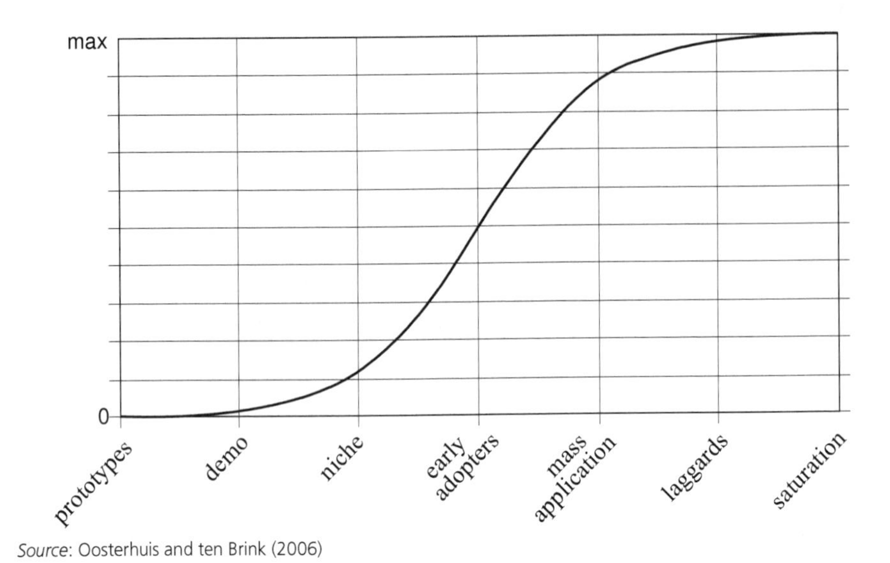

Source: Oosterhuis and ten Brink (2006)

Figure 2.1 *Stages in the introduction of a new technology: the S-curve*

highlighted here. The three which have been chosen seem to have special relevance for thinking about the possible transition to a hydrogen economy.

Technology-push and market-pull

One of the commonest descriptions of the way technologies are developed and diffused in society is in terms of 'technology-push/market-pull', as illustrated in Figure 2.2. This suggests that technologies are developed through basic and applied research and development (R&D), to demonstration and commercialization, and thereby diffused into society.

The first, pre-market phases of the process are described as 'technology push', because the principal drivers are the business and policy decisions, including government investment in R&D, and the activities and interests of scientists and engineers, that cause the technology to be developed. The commercialization and diffusion processes are much more driven by consumer demand-pull in the markets which have been targeted or into which the technologies will by then have penetrated to some extent. Clearly, as shown, both sets of drivers are present to some extent in all phases: even at the earliest phases of technology R&D, potential market demand is a major interest, and even during diffusion, research-driven technological change may occur. For the process to take place successfully, continuous learning from and feedback between these processes are required.

Each stage of the process may require, or be subject to, private investments or policy interventions (which may include government investments). At the R&D stages, at least for technologies which are thought to be of major potential public benefit, policy interventions are likely to be relatively important

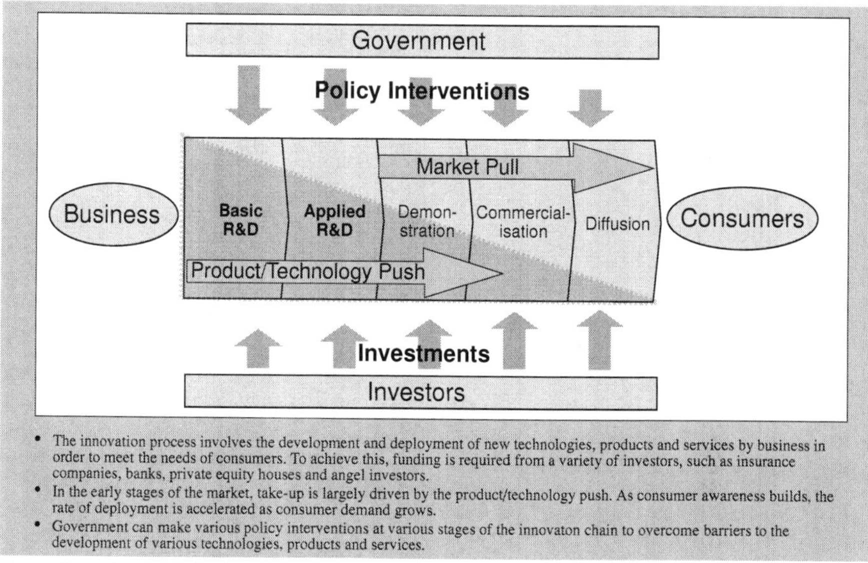

Source: Foxon (2003: p18), after Carbon Trust (2002)

Figure 2.2 *Roles of innovation chain actors*

(shown by the length of the arrows). From demonstration onwards, private investments are likely to be relatively important. However, especially for technologies of potential public benefit but uncertain market demand (of which hydrogen technologies may be a good example), it is likely that public support and policy interventions will be necessary both to help the technology from the demonstration to commercialization stages (a risky transition sometimes called the 'valley of death' (e.g. Wessner, 2005), because of the business casualties and the demise of potentially good ideas, technologies and innovations, which it often induces), and even right through to the diffusion stage.

The linear nature of the technology-push/market-pull model has been criticized by Kemp and Foxon (2007), who recommend instead the more interactive 'chain-linked' model developed by Kline and Rosenberg (1986), illustrated in Figure 2.3, in which research and knowledge creation take place throughout the innovation and product development, design and marketing stages. Such a model is certainly consistent with the recent investigation of the inter-relationship between propositional (basic scientific) and prescriptive (technical know-how) knowledge of Mokyr (2002).

While technology-push and market-pull may be important aspects of technological change, they contain no element of the social context in which such change is taking place, and therefore are clearly insufficient concepts by themselves to explain the much more widespread changes that are implied by the term 'technological transition'. This requires an approach which takes a much wider view of the social and economic system in which technologies are embedded, and which provide the context in which they thrive and decline.

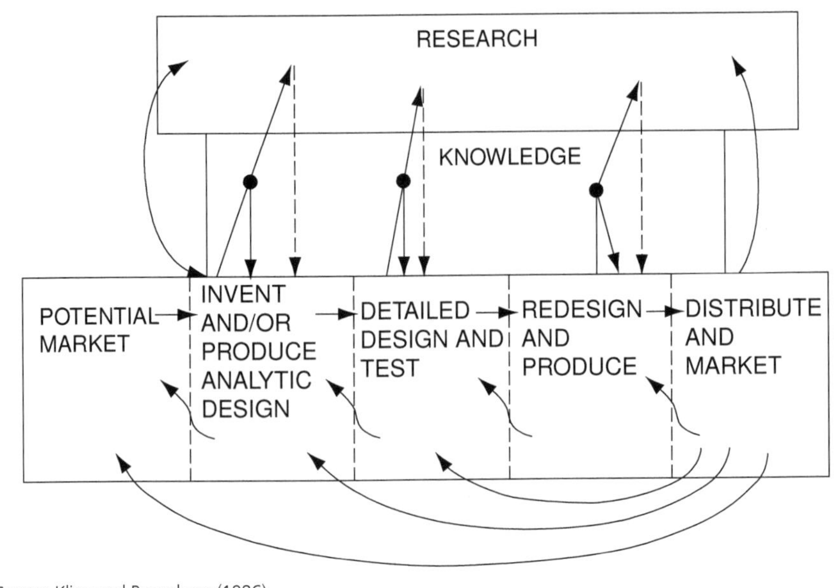

Source: Kline and Rosenberg (1986)

Figure 2.3 *A chain-linked model of the innovation process*

Co-evolution of social subsystems

Fundamental changes in technology are now understood to be processes that are rooted at the deepest level in the social contexts in which they occur. For example, the evolutionary approach to technological development adopted by Freeman and Louça (2001: p121) proposes that such development requires the co-evolution of five 'semi-autonomous' social subsystems: science, technology, economics, politics, culture. They are semi-autonomous because, although the five variables are linked and interact, they also have autonomous elements. Fundamental technological changes (such as the move to a hydrogen economy) are possible when, and only when, the co-evolutionary direction of change of all five variables is basically supportive of such change.

Freeman and Louça themselves do little to explore the implications of their insight into the necessary co-evolution of the five sub-systems. In the case of hydrogen it may be useful to expand the categories so that they embrace the **physical dimension**, which deals with the physical issues involved in the production/storage/distribution/end use of hydrogen, and the **socio-economic dimension**, which deals with the interests and drivers that push technical change along: entrepreneurs (and profits), consumers (and preferences), and public policy pressures.

The physical dimension has the following components:

- *Science:* the physically possible.
- *Technology:* the physical realization of the physically possible.

- *Infrastructure:* the physical (including technical) support and diffusion of the physical realization.

The socio-economic dimension has the following components:

- *Economics:* issues of allocation, distribution, competition.
- *Institutions:* legal, financial, regulatory, planning frameworks.
- *Political drivers:* social perceptions driving political priority (security of supply, environmental issues) and the planning system, and the policy instruments through which these perceptions are implemented.
- *Culture:* social perceptions driving social acceptability and consumer demand.

These categories help to clarify that the transition to a hydrogen economy will only begin in earnest when some combination of entrepreneurs, consumers and public policy pressures generates both the investment in science, technology and infrastructure that physically permits hydrogen to be a widely used energy carrier, and the economic, institutional and cultural conditions that make the widespread diffusion of hydrogen end-use applications economically competitive and institutionally and socially acceptable.

It has already been noted that the public policy pressures derive largely from a desire to reduce the pollution (in environmental economics, often referred to as 'negative externalities') and energy insecurity that are associated with fossil fuels. At present, these pressures are nothing like sufficient to drive the transition to a hydrogen economy, although it is of course possible that they could become so. The kinds of pressures that may come from economic actors – entrepreneurs and consumers – will be an important influence on the extent to which these market forces may help, or perhaps hinder, the pressure starting to come from public policy (see Chapter 4).

Socio-technical landscapes and regimes, and technological niches

Another (though not contradictory) approach to technological transitions, which informed much of the work in this area undertaken in UKSHEC 1, is taken by Geels (2002a, b), who adopts a three-tier 'multi-level perspective', the three levels of which are:

- the socio-technical landscape: material infrastructure and 'widely shared cultural beliefs, symbols and values that are hard to deviate from' (Geels, 2002a: p102);
- the socio-technical regime: the institutional and mental structures ('knowledge base, engineering practices, corporate governance structures, manufacturing processes and product characteristics'; Geels, 2002a: p98) that provide the framework for any pervasive technology; and

- the technological niche: spaces insulated from the competitive challenge from mainstream technologies, in which innovations can survive and, perhaps, develop.

Geels' concept of socio-technical regime is an extension of the 'technical regimes' discussed by Rip and Kemp (1998) and Nelson and Winter (1982). According to Geels (2002b: p1260), socio-technical regimes include not only the organizational and cognitive rules and routines adopted and followed by engineers and firms, but also the routines influencing the behaviour of 'users, policy-makers, social groups, suppliers, scientists and bankers etc.'. The stability and persistence of a regime, and the widespread recognition of its function and purpose, derives from the fact that there is coherence between the incentives, rules and routines of these different actors: 'The activities of these different groups are aligned and co-ordinated' (Geels, 2002b: p1259). Thus the socio-economic actors in the same regime share an overall common aim – the fulfilment of the regime function. Each actor in the regime has an incentive to cooperate, as they would be worse off if they took an action putting the existence of the regime at risk. Innovation under such circumstances, when it occurs, tends to be incremental and to result in improvements to (and reinforcement of) the existing regime, rather than a transition to a new regime. It is unlikely that hydrogen technologies will become established through such incremental processes.

It may not always be straightforward to demarcate clearly the boundaries between different socio-technical regimes, while some elements of one regime might also belong to another. Hughes (1987: p53) considered that a defining characteristic of technological systems is that they solve problems or fulfil goals, using whatever means are available and appropriate, where the problems have to do mostly with reordering the physical world in ways considered useful or desirable, at least by those designing or employing a technological system. More simply, Rip and Kemp (1998) define regimes as 'configurations that work', a definition which Geels (2002a) makes clear refers to fulfilment by a regime, in an economically and socially acceptable way, of a *function* that is considered useful or desirable by some actor in the regime. Geels (2002a:pp14–15) uses this idea to map the various elements and functions of the current socio-technical regime of road transportation, concluding:

> *Societal functions are fulfilled by socio-technical configurations, i.e. the interrelated set of technologies, distribution networks, regulation, infrastructure, symbolic meanings, techno-scientific knowledge, organisations, markets. Societal functions can be fulfilled because these heterogeneous aspects are linked and work together.*

This particular socio-technical regime is important in this context because road transportation is widely cited as a possible area of application for hydrogen. The complexity of the current regime indicates the scale of the challenge of creating an alternative regime involving hydrogen vehicles.

Identifying the main attribute of a regime as related to its functionality makes it easier to identify its core, if not precisely to delineate its boundaries: substantially different functions will be associated with different regimes (however, it is also clear that the functions defining a regime can evolve over time). Going beyond function, Geels (2002b: p1262) identifies the seven key dimensions of a socio-technical regime as:

- technology;
- user practices and application domains (markets);
- symbolic meaning of technology;
- infrastructure;
- industry structure;
- policy; and
- techno-scientific knowledge.

Although these dimensions change through their own internally generated impulses, they are also linked and co-evolve in the same way as Freeman and Louça's social subsystems, described above. The stability of the regime comes from the coherence of and linkages between the dimensions. Regime change may arise when this coherence or the linkages weaken.

Regime stability also derives from the process of technological 'lock-in', which Arthur (1988: p591) identified as deriving from five factors that, once they are operational in favour of a particular technology, tend to give it a competitive advantage which is increasingly difficult for competing technologies to counter. The five factors are:

- *Learning by using*, which accelerates technological improvement.
- *Network externalities* – the more widely a technology is used, the more applications are developed for it and the more useful it becomes.
- *Economies of scale*, which reduce the unit price.
- *Increasing informational returns*, linked to learning by using, whereby the increased numbers of users, knowing more about the technology, make it easier for others to learn about the technology.
- *Development of complementary technologies*, which both reinforce the position of the technology and make it more useful.

The concept of technological lock-in is often used to describe the persistence of sub-optimal technologies (the QWERTY keyboard is a frequently quoted example; see David, 1985), but these processes are actually characteristic of all successful technologies, sub-optimal or not. If there is to be a transition to the hydrogen economy, hydrogen technologies will need to be subject in large measure to all these processes.

There is also the issue of how broad a regime needs to be in order to qualify as such. Regimes may be seen to be 'nested' within each other. For example, Berkhout et al (2003: p 9) ask whether the fundamental shift in pesticide use brought about by the banning of DDT amounted to an agricultural regime change, or whether it left intact the wider regime of a chemical-intensive agriculture.

At a higher level than the regime, Geels' socio-technical (ST) landscape provides an external 'structure or context for interactions among actors' (Geels, 2002b: p1260) in a regime. This landscape contains a set of:

> *heterogeneous factors, such as oil prices, economic growth, wars, political coalitions, cultural and normative values and environmental problems. The landscape is an external structure or context for interactions of actors. While regimes refer to rules that enable and constrain activities within communities, the 'ST-landscape' refers to wider technology-*external *factors. (Geels, 2002b: p1260, emphasis in original)*

A similar definition describes landscapes as composed of:

> *background variables such as material infrastructure, political culture and coalitions, social values, worldviews and paradigms, the macro economy, demography and the natural environment, which channel transition processes and change themselves slowly in an autonomous way. (Kemp and Rotmans, 2001, cited in Berkhout et al, 2003: p6)*

The internal/external distinction between regimes and landscapes seems more useful than another distinction used by both Kemp and Rotmans and Geels, relating to speed of change: 'landscapes do change, but more slowly than regimes' (Geels, 2002: p1260). This is by no means obvious. The external factors which belong to landscapes can in fact change very quickly. Oil prices, which historically have been very volatile, are one example. Other examples are the geopolitical circumstances that can affect (perceptions of) energy security, and the political perceptions of the priority of an issue such as climate change. Changes in any or all three of these examples of landscape factors might be important in stimulating a technological transition towards hydrogen. Through these examples, it can be seen that changes in the socio-technical landscape can be the means whereby the stability and internal coherence of a socio-technical regime can be undermined.

Another distinction between the factors belonging to regimes or landscapes might be the extent to which they can be influenced by the socio-economic actors involved in the regime. Clearly, this varies among different actors. For example, the oil price can hardly be affected by individuals, but governments can have more effect. A rule of thumb for distinguishing between regime or landscape factors might be: if socio-economic actors can influence the direction, the timing or the rapidity of the change in a factor more than the extent to which they are influenced by it, this factor is likely to be part of the regime; in the opposite case that element will belong to the landscape. But the degree of influence is likely to vary for different actors and in different situations, so that it is not a hard and fast distinction. Such considerations suggest that, rather than being clearly differentiated, landscapes and regimes at different levels merge into each other by displaying some elements and characteristics in common, and others that are clearly differentiated, but all of which are subject to change.

In the final analysis, because of the wide-ranging nature of the concepts of socio-technical landscapes and regimes, it probably needs to be accepted that no taxonomy is likely to distinguish unambiguously between different regimes, and between the elements belonging to the regime and those belonging to the landscape. In any case, the concepts of regimes and landscapes by themselves cannot explain how hydrogen might progress from being the insignificant energy carrier it is at present, to becoming the defining energy characteristic of an economy. For this, the third element of Geels' multi-level perspective is also required: the concept of the niche.

The niche is in fact a longstanding theme in relation to the diffusion of innovations and technological change (see, for example, Wallace, 1995; Kemp et al, 1998; Foxon, 2003), with the literature identifying such issues as the importance or the size of the niche market, the technical and financial capabilities of suppliers, and stable investment conditions as key for successful diffusion. A number of potential niche markets for hydrogen technologies and hydrogen fuel cells are discussed in Chapter 4.

Adamson defines niche markets as 'small protected market[s] that a new disruptive innovation enters before it reaches the mass market' (Adamson, 2005: p343). Geels (2002a, b) seems to share that perception, seeing a fundamental property of niches as being that they 'act as "incubation rooms" for radical novelties', and offer some protection from normal market selection in the regime (Geels, 2002b: p1261). However, it is not clear why only disruptive innovations should inhabit niche markets, as seems to be implied by Adamson (2005). It seems quite possible for non-disruptive innovations also to be found in niche markets, although they may not have the potential to break into the mass market and may exist in their niche for a considerable period of time. Nor is it clear why technologies in niches need necessarily to be protected from competition with technologies in the mass market (they may contain valued functional characteristics that distinguish them from such technologies).

In Agnolucci and Ekins (2007), a theoretical framework was presented in which niche markets are more simply defined as small, focused and targetable portions of a larger market, comprising a group of actors whose needs for products or services to perform particular functions are not being addressed by mainstream providers. It was shown that niche markets may function as incubators for new technologies, and that this can occur in the absence of protection from market competition in the regime. The framework describes the way in which socio-economic actors decide on the adoption of technologies, and what factors can influence their choice. It shows that technology is produced by socio-economic actors making investments and behaving in other ways to secure the availability and diffusion of certain artefacts, because they perceive this to be in their interests. Then the three levels of Geels' multi-level perspective can be brought together to show how jointly they can explain technological transitions.

Geels' own perception of the interaction between landscapes, regimes and niches as a three-level process is shown in Figure 2.4 (Geels, 2002a: Figure 3.6, p110; Geels, 2005b: Figure 4, p452). Regimes are in the middle, affected by landscape developments (above) which create windows of opportunity (e.g. increasing concern about climate change) for niche development (below). The niches develop through learning (learning by doing, using and interacting) and by increased coordination between the different actors within the niche (e.g. through trade associations, supply chains, user–producer relationships, journals, academic partners, university courses etc.). Actors in niche markets are likely to relate more strongly to each other than with those in other parts of the regime. In fact, actors belonging to the same niche market share a stake in the same technology, while actors in the same regime have a common stake only in the fulfilment of the regime function. The learning and network development stimulate innovation and cost reduction.

In this way the niches can break into the mainstream by acquiring attributes which users want and value, and by reducing costs, although it should be remembered that, faced with this challenge, incumbent technologies will also innovate and develop (the 'sailing ship effect' – see Geels, 2002b: p1270). Thus, by the time, for example, hydrogen cars finally emerge into the marketplace, they will be competing with hybrid and conventional cars that are much improved in those areas where hydrogen is currently perceived to offer advantages (emissions, efficiency) over current models.

The normal processes of technological innovation and development, which may create new niches or expand old ones, are basically driven by the desire to develop new or improved functionalities or attributes which will cause users to switch to, or stay with, a particular technology. Geels (2002a: pp111–112) lists additional drivers of niche expansion as:

- internal technical problems in the existing regime, also called 'bottlenecks' (Rosenberg, 1976) or 'reverse salients' (Hughes, 1987);
- negative externalities, as already discussed above, which lead to policy interventions;
- changing user preferences;
- strategic and competitive games between producers;
- the availability of complementary technologies.

At present, the two principal drivers for hydrogen niche creation and expansion seem to be the negative externalities and insecurities (a 'bottleneck') of

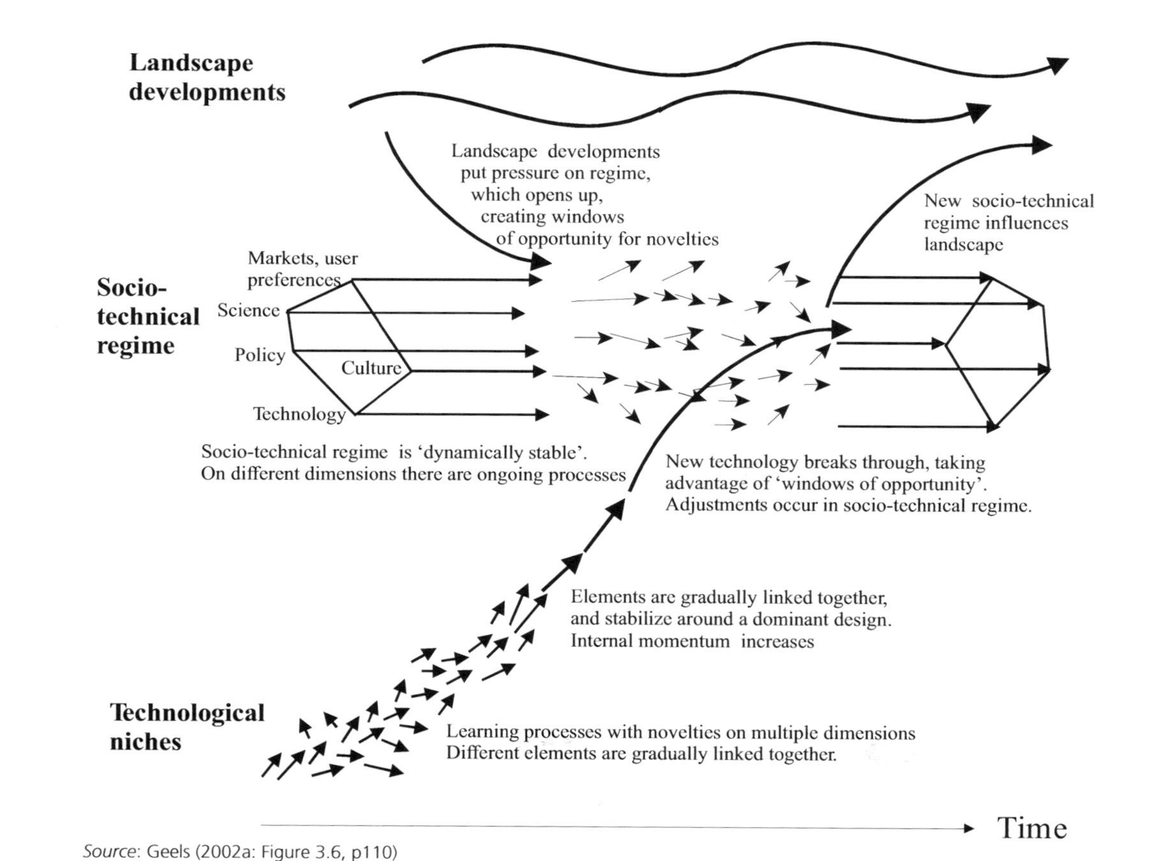

Source: Geels (2002a: Figure 3.6, p110)

Figure 2.4 *A dynamic multi-level perspective on transitions*

the incumbent fossil-fuel energy system, and the strategic and competitive games between major producers to develop a functional hydrogen alternative to it, rather than user preferences. It is still by no means clear whether these drivers will be strong enough to initiate a transition to a hydrogen economy.

For suppliers of future technologies involved in these strategic and competitive games, it is important to get a grasp of the likely size of future niche and mainstream markets by considering the effect of unfolding changes in the landscape and in the regimes on the expected adoption of technologies. Before committing to the development and eventual provision of a certain technology, suppliers will have to compare the attributes of current and future technologies, and their likely evaluation by users and policy-makers. An important difference for suppliers is that their future horizon will have to be much longer than that of users. Because they need to adopt a more strategic approach, the physical and socio-economic dimensions that affect technology transitions need to be characterized in a richer way.

In respect of the physical dimension, a supplier will have to consider how the likely evolution of technologies will influence their performance, and will have to evaluate the technological issues hindering a wider adoption of a certain technology, such as fuel cells, and how current scientific knowledge and capabilities might eventually solve these problems. In terms of infrastructure requirements, a supplier will have to consider issues related to the critical mass of actors who must be involved to facilitate the construction of the infrastructure needed to win customers. The transition from a niche to a mass market (essentially the diffusion process shown in Figure 2.1) is anything but straightforward. As already noted, the casualty rate among firms attempting this transition is so high as to lead to it being called the 'valley of death' (Wessner, 2005). It is for this reason that, where one of the main drivers for the transition is public benefit, rather than pure market demand, the transition may need public support.

It is in relation to the socio-economic dimension that landscape and regime issues can become really important for technology suppliers. Examples of economic factors that have to be considered relate to the profitability of different technologies, the existence of patents granted for intellectual property, competition with other suppliers, and the structure of the market of inputs and outputs. In terms of institutional factors, issues related to the likely future legal, financial, regulatory and planning systems are important. Regulations influence the competitiveness of new technologies through the burden imposed on potential adopters; some technologies can be hindered, while others helped by current or expected regulation. Technology suppliers will also have to take into account political drivers, that is, the objectives of current and future governments, as they will affect the policy instruments and institutional changes likely to be introduced in the future. For example, in the past, the policy driver to reduce local emissions from motor vehicles facilitated the diffusion of catalytic converters. Finally, a technology supplier also has to pay attention to cultural factors influencing potential adopters in the future and the rhetoric used by governments and other suppliers.

The dynamics of technological transitions

It is worth sketching the dynamics of technological transition, as outlined by Geels (2002a), in order to consider later to what extent various elements of hydrogen technologies may illustrate these dynamics. Geels (2002a: pp113ff) considers that innovation in a technological transition proceeds through four phases:

1. *Emergence of novelty in an existing regime and landscape.* Such emergence may be driven by the 'technology-push' forces identified in the text around Figure 2.2, in which basic and applied R&D are pursued by private firms or governments in anticipation of private returns or public benefits.
2. *Technical consolidation in market niches and development of new functionalities.* Once established in niches, choices will start to be made between the different technological options, in order to begin to benefit from the processes of technological 'lock-in' discussed above, without which no new technology will get established, so that a technological trajectory begins to emerge. At the same time, new functionalities will be developed for the technology to prepare for its expansion into new niches and thence into the mainstream socio-technical regime.
3. *Wide diffusion and breakthrough of the new technology in competition with the established regime.*
4. *Gradual replacement of the established regime and wider socio-economic changes.* Technological transitions take time as new functionalities emerge, cost:performance ratios improve, new skills are learned, new networks are formed and old investments are replaced.

During these processes the technology starts by occupying the niche(s) for which it was developed or which offer the most obvious fit, but gradually stretches the niches, through new design and functionalities, and occupies, or creates, new niches, processes accelerated by the co-evolution of complementary technologies.

The way these processes work out will be different depending on whether the existing socio-technical regime is stable and socio-economically deeply embedded, or unstable, characterized by internal problems and contradictions, or already in transition. In the former case, the 'technology-push' processes of basic and applied R&D will need to develop significant new functionalities or cost advantages, with little public support, for the new technology to break through. Given such development, however, breakthroughs can be rapid (as with, for example, mobile telephony). In the latter case, it may be that there are more opportunities for it to break into the mainstream and become established (one of Geels' (2002a) case studies, the transition from horse-drawn carriages to automobiles, is said to be of this type), or it may qualify for public support.

The context of current consideration of a hydrogen economy would seem to exhibit both these characteristics simultaneously. First, as noted earlier, the existing socio-technical regime of the fossil-fuel energy system is mature, deeply embedded in the industrial economy and society, and works reasonably efficiently to deliver an unprecedented range of energy services. At the same time it is causing very serious problems of pollution (especially climate change, but also local pollution) and energy insecurity. It is clear that in such circumstances public policy intervention and support for hydrogen technologies will be critical for their success, but it also shifts the focus of attention away from hydrogen itself towards the ways it is produced (which will need to be both clean and low-carbon).

Bringing about technological transitions

Most of the literature that discusses and analyses technological transitions, including that referenced above, takes a historical perspective. It analyses transitions that have taken place (e.g. Geels, 2002a: sailing ships to steam ships, propellers to jet engines in aviation, horse-drawn carriages to auto-mobiles; Freeman and Louça, 2001: the Kondratiev cycles, Table II.1, p141), and seeks to discern the reasons for them. For Freeman and Louça, as noted above, coherent co-evolutionary changes in five social subsystems (science, technology, economics, politics, culture) are required. In Geels' multi-level perspective (see Figure 2.4), there are three basic possibilities: the current socio-technical regime may evolve over time such that in retrospect the change is viewed as so significant as to comprise a transition to a new regime; changes in the landscape may bring about a transition; expansion of niches may bring about a transition. In reality, a change at any level will stimulate changes at the other levels. When these changes reinforce each other sufficiently (i.e. there is enough positive feedback), a transition will take place; when they stimulate an opposing reaction, the transition will not do so. When they produce both kinds of response, a definable transition may or may not result. One of the characteristics of a technological transition is that its outcome is rarely foreseen: 'Whenever a new technology is born, few see its ultimate place in society' (Ceruzzi, 1986: p196).

In contrast to such analysis, thinking about the hydrogen economy tends to be deeply prescriptive. As noted above, the hydrogen economy is seen as a potential solution to major challenges (mainly greenhouse gas emissions and energy insecurity) of the current socio-technical regime based on fossil fuels. The focus of discussion is not on *whether* a transition to a hydrogen economy will come about, but *how* it can be brought about, and what the economic and other implications of the transition might be.

This shifts the whole context of thinking from the analysis of technological transitions to what has come to be known as 'transition management', which 'seeks to direct the widening process of socio-technical change and stabilisation around a new regime. The objective for transition management is to steer bottom-up, niche-to-regime processes of transformation towards a pre-defined goal or "vision"' (Berkhout et al, 2003: p11). Berkhout et al (2003: pp25ff) have constructed a two-axis typology of 'transition contexts and transformation processes', depending on whether the change to the existing socio-economic regime is brought about using resources that are internal or external to it (the former likely to lead to more incremental and less structural change); and whether the change is intended, or is the largely autonomous outcome of historical processes. Eames and McDowall apply this framework to a consideration of possible hydrogen futures in Chapter 5. The stylized examples from the energy sector of each type of change given by Berkhout et al (2003) are:

- Internal/intended – endogenous renewal: e.g. scaling up of thermal generating plant, over the 20th century.
- Internal/autonomous – reorientation of trajectories: e.g. adoption of combined cycle gas turbines (CCGTs) for power generation in the UK in the 1990s.
- External/autonomous – emergent transformation: e.g. Kondratiev cycles.
- External/intended – purposive transition: e.g. power generation from nuclear fission or, more recently, renewables.

Of course, each of these examples involved or involves a different scale of transformation of the relevant socio-technical regime, and it might be argued that the adoption of CCGTs did not entail a regime change at all, and was instead just a technology change. Such an argument arises from the lack of definition of precisely what constitutes a socio-technical regime. It is also likely that those transitions involving external resources are likely to be more fundamental. In the context of hydrogen, there is little doubt that a transition to a hydrogen economy, as defined earlier, would constitute a transformation of the current socio-technical regime of energy supply and demand, and would be a purposive transition, according to the typology above (i.e. it will be intended rather than autonomous, and involve resources external to the current energy system). As noted in Chapter 1, it also constitutes a more ambitious social project than has ever yet been attempted in terms of changing the energy system.

Cost-reduction in the introduction of new technologies

It is frequently the case, and is certainly so for hydrogen technologies, that at first new technologies are substantially more expensive than the technologies with which they are competing. Any acceleration in uptake of these technologies, or moves up the S-curve of Figure 2.1, are usually due not only to the fact that the technology is becoming more widely known, but also to improvements and cost reductions occurring in the course of the diffusion process, through economies of scale and learning effects. Cost reductions as a function of the cumulative production (or sales) of a particular technology can be

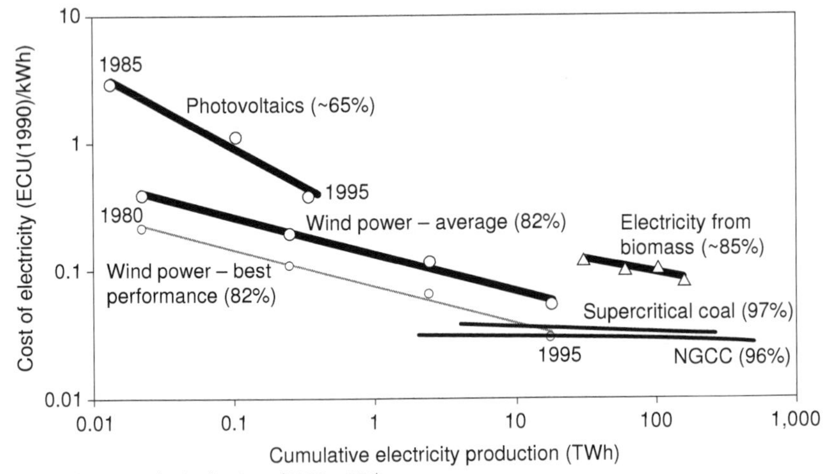

Source: IEA (2000: p21), cited in Stern (2007: p254)

Figure 2.5 *Evidence on learning rates in energy technologies*

represented by 'learning curves' or 'experience curves'. Figure 2.5 shows learning curves for a number of energy technologies. The 'learning rate' is the percentage cost reduction with each doubling of cumulative production or sales (e.g. the learning rate in Figure 2.5 for photovoltaics is ~35 per cent; the percentage in brackets denotes that after each doubling of cumulative production the cost of photovoltaics was ~65 per cent of the cost before it).

The cost reduction illustrated by learning curves may come from two fundamentally different sources:

- Gradual improvements of already existing technologies, which may not have the potential for dramatic cost reduction (an example in Figure 2.5 may be the natural gas combined cycle (NGCC) turbines).
- Innovations (or 'leap technologies') for technologies which are new and can compete with existing technologies in both efficiency (lower costs) and effectiveness (larger reduction potential).

This distinction is important, especially concerning the development of the reduction potential. As will be seen in Chapters 3 and 4, hydrogen technologies such as fuel cells are unlikely to become cost-competitive unless they can experience the substantial cost reductions associated with the latter, more radical kinds of innovation.

IEA (2000) assessed the potential of experience curves as tools to inform and strengthen energy technology policy. It stresses the importance of measures to encourage niche markets for new technologies as one of the most efficient ways for governments to provide learning opportunities. This leads in the next section to brief consideration of the main theoretical approach to transition management – strategic niche management – which paves the way to discussing later in the book its possible applicability to the transition to the hydrogen economy.

Strategic niche management

One of the principal approaches that has been put forward for transition management is strategic niche management (SNM). Indeed, the authors have even claimed that 'it may be the only feasible way to transform environmentally unsustainable regimes', although they accept that a regime shift may need in addition policies such as taxes and regulation (Kemp et al, 1998: p191).

The basic argument underlying advocacy of SNM is that technological regimes are deeply embedded and are unlikely to be changed purely by undifferentiated whole-system approaches such as carbon taxes (Kemp et al, 1998: p184), although such approaches may be complementary to SNM, as noted above. Because of user and market uncertainties, nor can a regime shift be centrally planned. Rather, the authors note that new technologies often get established in niches (very much conceived of as protected spaces) and advocate SNM as:

> *the creation, development and controlled phase-out of protected spaces for promoting the development and use of technologies by means of experimentation, with the aim of (1) learning about the desirability of the new technology and (2) enhancing the further development and the rate of application of the new technology. (ibid: p186)*

SNM involves five steps: 'the choice of technology, the selection of an experiment, the set-up of the experiment, scaling up the experiment and the breakdown of protection by means of policy' (ibid: p186).

The technology to be chosen must have social advantages, must have the potential for major technological and economic improvements, must be manageable and must have certain applications to which it is already well suited. The experiment is then set up in relation to these applications and the barriers to their expansion are then removed by appropriate public policy.

The whole process is fraught with uncertainty, from the initial choice of technology (it is unlikely on cost grounds that all potential technologies could be chosen, but very difficult to know at an early stage of development which has the most potential, and the risk exists of lock-in to an inappropriate early choice) to the identification of the barriers, which may relate to any or all of:

- the need for scientific and technological breakthroughs;
- the need for appropriate infrastructure and skills;
- inappropriate government policy or institutional structure;
- poor price/performance ratio;
- social and cultural perceptions and acceptability; and
- environmental effects.

As an example of SNM, Kemp et al (1998: p190) give the experiments with battery vehicles in the Netherlands in the early 1990s (although it may be pointed out that battery vehicles have existed at least as long as petrol-driven vehicles), which 'resulted in a much clearer picture of the potential of electric vehicles'. This may be so, but there is little evidence in the Netherlands or elsewhere that these experiments have even helped expand the niche for electric vehicles, let alone initiated a regime change of which they are the driving force. If this is the best example to date of SNM, then, as a means of transition management, it must be regarded as still unproved. The question then arises as to whether it might be a useful concept in the context of a purposive transition to a hydrogen economy. This question is revisited in Chapter 12, once it has become much clearer what hydrogen niches there are and what kinds of futures for hydrogen as an energy carrier they might help to create. First, however, it is necessary to explore in much more detail the precise nature and characteristics, technical and economic, of hydrogen technologies, to understand the kind of transformation of the energy system to which they might give rise.

References

Adamson, K.-A. (2005) 'Calculating the price trajectory of adoption of fuel cell vehicles', *International Journal of Hydrogen Energy*, vol 30, pp341–350

Adamson, K.-A. (2006) 'Fuel Cell Today Market Survey: Niche Transport', Part 1, August, *Fuel Cell Today*, site accessed 8 September 2006, http://www.fuelcelltoday.com/FuelCellToday/FCTFiles/FCTArticleFiles/Article_1113_Part%201%202006.pdf#search=%22Fuel%20Cells%3A%20niche%20market%20applications%20and%20design%20studies%22

Agnolucci, P. and Ekins, P. (2007) 'Technological Transitions and Strategic Niche Management: The Case of the Hydrogen Economy', *International Journal of Environmental Technology and Management*, vol 7, nos 5/6, pp644–671

Arthur, W. B. (1988) 'Competing Technologies: an Overview', in Dosi, G., Freeman, C., Silverberg, G. and Soete, L. (eds) *Technical Change and Economic Theory*, Frances Pinter, London, pp590–607

Berkhout, F., Smith, A. and Stirling, A. (2003) 'Socio-technological Regimes and Transition Contexts', Paper no 106, September, SPRU, University of Sussex, Brighton

Carbon Trust (2002) Submission to Energy White Paper Consultation Process, Carbon Trust, London

Ceruzzi, P. (1986) 'An Unforeseen Revolution: Computers and Expectations, 1935–1980', in Corn, J. (ed) (1986) *Imagining Tomorrow: History, Technology and the American Future*, MIT Press, Cambridge MA, pp188–201

David, P. (1985) 'Clio and the Economics of QWERTY', *American Economic Review*, vol 76, pp332–337

Foxon, T. (2003) *Inducing Innovation for a Low-Carbon Future: Drivers, Barriers and Policies*, a report for the Carbon Trust, July, Carbon Trust, London

Freeman, C. and Louça, F. (2001) *As Time Goes By*, Oxford University Press, Oxford

Geels, F. (2002a) *Understanding the Dynamics of Technological Transitions*, Twente University Press, Enschede NL, published in revised form as Geels (2005a)

Geels, F. (2002b) 'Technological transitions as evolutionary reconfiguration processes: a multi-level perspective and a case-study', *Research Policy*, vol 31, pp1257–1274

Geels, F. (2004) 'From sectoral systems of innovation to socio-technical systems: Insights about dynamics and change from sociology and institutional theory', *Research Policy*, vol 3, pp897–920

Geels, F. (2005a) *Technological Transitions and System Innovations: A Co-evolutionary and Socio-Technical Analysis*, Edward Elgar, Cheltenham

Geels, F. (2005b) 'The dynamics of transitions in socio-technical systems: a multi-level analysis of the transition pathway from horse-drawn carriages to automobiles (1860–1930)', *Technology Analysis and Strategic Management*, vol 17, no 4, December, pp445–476

Hisschemöller, M., Bode, R. and van de Kerkhof, M. (2006) 'What Governs the Transition to a Sustainable Hydrogen Economy? Articulating the Relationship Between Technologies and Political Institutions', *Energy Policy*, vol 34, pp1227–1235

Hughes, T. (1987) 'The evolution of large technological systems', in Bijker, W., Hughes T. and Pinch, T. (eds) (1987) *The Social Construction of Technological Systems: New Directions in the Sociology and History of Technology*, MIT Press, Cambridge MA, pp51–82

IEA (International Energy Agency) (2000) *Experience Curves for Energy Technology Policy*, IEA, Paris

Kemp, R. and Foxon, T. (2007) 'Eco-innovation from an innovation dynamics perspective', Deliverable 1 of MEI project, April, UNU-MERIT, Maastricht; for the MEI project, see http://www.merit.unu.edu/MEI/, accessed 11 June 2009

Kemp, R. and Rotmans, J. (2001) 'The management of the co-evolution of technical, environmental and social systems', international conference Towards Environmental Innovation Systems, Garmisch-Partenkirchen, September

Kemp, R., Schot, J. and Hoogma, R. (1998) 'Regime Shifts to Sustainability through Processes of Niche Formation: the Approach of Strategic Niche Management', *Technology Analysis and Strategic Management*, vol 10, pp175–196

Kline, S. J. and Rosenberg, N. (1986) 'An Overview of Innovation', in Landau, R. and Rosenberg, N. (eds) (1986) *The Positive Sum Strategy*, National Academic Press, Washington, DC

Maddy, J., Cherryman, S., Hawkes, F., Hawkes, D., Dinsdale, R., Guwy, A., Premier, G. and Cole, S. (2003) *Hydrogen 2003*, University of Glamorgan, Wales

Mokyr, J. (2002) *The Gifts of Athena: Historical Origins of the Knowledge Economy,* Princeton University Press, Woodstock (GB)

Nelson, R. and Winter, S. (1982) *An Evolutionary Theory of Economic Change*, Bellknap Press, Cambridge MA

Ogden, J., Williams, R. and Larson, E. (2004) 'Societal Lifecycle Costs of Cars with Alternative Fuels/Engines', *Energy Policy*, vol 32, pp7–27

Oosterhuis, F. and ten Brink, P. (2006) *Assessing innovation dynamics induced by environment policy: Findings from literature and analytical framework for the case studies*, The Institute for Environmental Studies (IVM), Vrije Universiteit, Amsterdam

Rip, A. and Kemp, R. (1998) 'Technological Change', in Rayner, S. and Malone, E. (eds) *Human Choice and Climate Change*, vol 2, Battelle Press, Columbus OH, pp327–399

Rosenberg, N. (1976) *Perspectives on Technology*, Cambridge University Press, Cambridge

Solomon, B. and Banerjee, A. (2006) 'A Global Survey of Hydrogen Energy Research, Development and Policy', *Energy Policy*, vol 34, pp781–792

Stern, N. (2007) *The Economics of Climate Change: the Stern Review*, Cambridge University Press, Cambridge

Wallace, D. (1995) *Environmental Policy and Industrial Innovation: Strategies in Europe, the US and Japan*, Earthscan, London

Wessner, C. (2005) 'Driving Innovations Across the "Valley of Death"', *Research-Technology Management,* vol 48, no 1, January–February 2005, pp 9–12

3
Hydrogen Technologies and Costs

Paul Ekins, Sam Hawkins and Nick Hughes

Introduction

Hydrogen (H_2) is often cited as the most common element in nature, but such citations do not always say that it is also reactive, and therefore in nature does not exist in elemental form, but needs to be produced from compounds that contain it. Where hydrogen is produced by fossil fuels (either through steam methane reforming (SMR) or through electrolysis where fossil fuels are the source of the electricity), carbon capture and storage (CCS) is necessary for the hydrogen to be considered a 'low-carbon' energy source.

Once produced, hydrogen may need to be either stored or distributed, or both. It may be stored or distributed as a gas or a liquid, or in the molecular structure of a variety of solid media. Means of distribution include pipelines (where it is a gas) and truck, rail and ship transport for hydrogen in all its forms.

Finally, hydrogen may be put to a range of final uses to satisfy the demand for energy services. Some of these involve hydrogen fuel cells (but note that not all fuel cells use hydrogen as their fuel), devices which convert hydrogen to electric power with high efficiency; some of them involve hydrogen being burned in turbines or internal combustion engines. A major category of end use is in vehicles, and one of the most active fields of research and development relates to fuel cell vehicles. Previously the possibility of 'reforming' conventional fuels into hydrogen on board the vehicle has been considered an attractive approach, particularly at an early or transitional stage in the roll-out of hydrogen technologies, as it obviates the need for on-board storage of hydrogen, and for hydrogen refuelling infrastructure. However, fuel cell vehicle prototypes have in recent years shown a decisive move away from on-board reforming, due to the significant additional complications the process adds to the vehicle (NRC and NAE, 2004), and an official 'no-go' decision has brought US Department of Energy (DoE) funding for on-board reforming research to a halt (DoE, 2004). The implication of this is that fuel cell vehicles will require hydrogen to be stored on board (either as a compressed gas, a liquid, or in a solid-state form), raising a number of specific technological problems relating to the performance of the vehicle concerned.

Padró and Putsche (1999) list and survey the economics of the technologies shown in Table 3.1, which include the key technologies which might be included in a hydrogen economy, however it might develop. The production technologies all have in common that they require energy to produce hydrogen, and then to store and distribute it. A key question for any production technology is whether the energy used in producing hydrogen might not be better used to satisfy the demand for energy services itself, and what the energy cost of producing hydrogen actually is for different technologies.

This chapter describes the main hydrogen production, distribution, storage and end-use technologies, with some of the main cost estimates that have been produced, as essential background to the subsequent chapters on how a hydrogen economy might develop.

Hydrogen production

This section, with information taken from Hawkins and Joffe (2006), where all the detailed references may be found, provides a summary review of four major hydrogen production pathways: steam methane reforming (SMR), coal gasification, biomass gasification or pyrolysis, and electrolysis, focusing on the technologies used and the hydrogen production costs. It also briefly covers anaerobic digestion of biomass, and describes some potential advances in small-scale electrolysis and microbial electrolysis (electrohydrogenesis). These production pathways do not cover all the possible routes to hydrogen. In

Table 3.1 *Technologies included in the survey by Padró and Putsche*

Hydrogen production	*Hydrogen transport*	*Hydrogen storage*	*Stationary power*	*Transportation applications*
Steam methane reforming (SMR) Non-catalytic partial oxidation Coal gasification Biomass gasification Biomass pyrolysis Electrolysis	Pipelines Truck transport Rail transport Ship transport	Compressed gas Liquefied gas Metal hydride Carbon-based Chemical hydrides	Proton exchange membrane fuel cells (PEMFC) Phosphoric acid fuel cells (PAFC) Solid oxide fuel cells (SOFC) Molten carbonate fuel cells (MCFC) Alkaline fuel cells (AFC) Gas turbine Stationary internal combustion engine	Hydrogen fuel cell vehicles Hydrogen internal combustion engines Hybrid vehicles Onboard storage Onboard reforming Refuelling options

Source: Padró and Putsche (1999: p1)

particular, a number of biological production routes through bacterial breakdown of biomass, and thermo-chemical cycles utilizing nuclear or concentrated solar heat, are not analysed. However, the routes presented here are commonly thought to be important, especially for the early stages of, or transitions to, a hydrogen economy. The four major production pathways reviewed are those with the most data available.

Many studies have looked at hydrogen production costs. However, assumptions vary between studies, and there are no agreed standards for analysis or reporting results, which makes comparison across studies difficult. Here costs are presented in US dollars, adjusted to a base year of 2000. Quantity of hydrogen is given in GJ, and production rate is given in MW. The 'size' or 'scale' of a hydrogen production plant refers to the production rate. Conversion factors are given in Table 3.2, which also includes comparisons with natural gas.

Where the costs of CO_2 capture have been reported, it usually refers only to the separation of CO_2 at the plant, and does not include the cost of CO_2 transport and sequestration. CO_2 sequestration specifically for the purpose of emissions reduction has not yet been demonstrated on a commercial scale, and its costs and long-term viability remain speculative. The cost and viability of CO_2 transport, which would require additional infrastructure, is also very uncertain and is likely to be very site-specific, depending on factors such as terrain and distance to a suitable sequestration site.

Overview of production technologies

Steam methane reforming (SMR) is widely used in the chemical and refining industries, and is currently considered the cheapest way of producing hydrogen. Reforming involves the reaction of desulphurized natural gas with high-temperature steam over a nickel-based catalyst. This produces syngas – mainly a mixture of hydrogen and carbon monoxide. The carbon monoxide is then converted to hydrogen and CO_2 via a water gas shift reaction, then high purity (up to 99.999 per cent) hydrogen is separated using pressure swing

Table 3.2 *Conversion factors for hydrogen and natural gas*

	Hydrogen (HHV)					**Natural gas (HHV)**				
	kg	*MJ*	*Nm³*	*kg/h*	*Nm³/h*	*kg*	*MJ*	*Nm³*	*kg/h*	*Nm³/h*
1 kg	1	142	11.1			1	28.1	1.41		
1 GJ	7.04	1,000	78.4			35.6	1,000	25.3		
1 MW				25.4	282				128	181

1GJ = 0.95 MMBtu = 277.8kWh

Key: HHV stands for 'high heating value'. Heating values express how much energy is released on combustion of a given quantity of fuel; for example, joules per kilogram, or Btu per gallon. A 'high heating value' includes the heat that can be obtained by condensing the water vapour produced by combustion. A 'low heating value' does not include this heat.

Nm^3 stands for 'normal cubic metres', and is the volume of a gas at standard temperature and (atmospheric) pressure

adsorption (PSA), with the remaining gas recycled or used as a fuel for the reforming process. Adding CO_2 capture depends on the design, but generally requires an additional CO_2 removal stage, based on physical or chemical absorption, before the PSA unit.

Coal gasification (CG) is an established commercial technology used in the chemical and refining industries, and increasingly for power generation. It involves the production of syngas (CO and H_2) from coal. Pulverized or slurried coal is exposed to steam and carefully controlled amounts of oxygen or air at high temperature (1,100–1,300°C) and high pressure (~6MPa). The use of pure oxygen over air ensures a concentrated syngas stream, making subsequent gas cleaning and separation much easier. The syngas can be used directly for electrical power generation, as a chemical feedstock for the production of synthetic chemicals and fuels (Fischer-Tropsch liquids), or for hydrogen production, when the syngas is chemically cleaned of hydrogen sulphide, coal ash and other impurities, before being fed to a water gas shift reactor, where carbon monoxide reacts with water to produce hydrogen and CO_2. CO_2 is removed either by an amine-based absorbent (such as Selexol) or by pressure swing adsorption (PSA). In commercial hydrogen production processes, CO_2 is usually vented to the atmosphere. At the time of the Hawkins and Joffe (2006) review, there were around 180 coal gasifiers in operation at 22 locations worldwide, with a further 22 planned. However, the CO_2 could also be captured and compressed for later sequestration, allowing coal gasification production routes to deliver low-carbon hydrogen. In discussions of carbon capture and storage (CCS) for electricity generating coal plants, the process described above is known as 'pre-combustion capture' – hydrogen is isolated from CO_2 through the PSA process and it is hydrogen which is combusted to generate electricity – as opposed to 'post-combustion capture', where electricity is generated from the combustion of the syngas, with the CO_2 removed at the 'end of pipe' from the flue gases. A large-scale project for the demonstration of pre-combustion CCS is being developed by the US DoE with a consortium of private partners under the banner of 'FutureGen' (FutureGen, 2009), and the recent announcement of four demonstration CCS plants to be built in the UK indicates that these would employ a mix of pre- and post-combustion capture technology (Miliband, 2009).

Biomass gasification and *pyrolysis* provide two ways to produce hydrogen from biomass. The processes can be adapted to a range of feedstocks, including dedicated fuel crops such as willow and switch grass, and biomass residues such as peanut shells and sugar cane waste. Different feedstocks may require different amounts of pre-treatment – drying, pelletizing, milling etc. Because the carbon in biomass has been captured from the atmosphere, and if the feedstock crops are regrown, then, once the energy inputs of fertilizer, harvesting, transport and any fossil fuel used in processing have been accounted for, the rest of the cycle is carbon neutral. Both techniques are followed by a reforming stage very similar to that used in steam methane reforming (SMR). Gasifiers may be heated indirectly (biomass is heated in the absence of oxygen by circulating hot sand into the gasification chamber) and directly (the heat for gasification is provided by allowing the partial oxidation of the biomass feed in pure oxygen inside the gasification chamber). With pyrolysis, biomass is rapidly heated in the absence of oxygen; the vapours are then condensed to form pyrolysis oil (also called bio-oil). This pyrolysis oil can later be used as a feedstock for hydrogen production, and is more easily stored and transported than raw biomass (it contains about five times the volumetric energy density of wood chips). Pyrolysis also generates non-condensable gases and char (carbon), which can be combusted to provide part of the energy for the process.

Anaerobic digestion (AD) of organic or other residual waste materials has also been considered as a possible route to hydrogen production. This process, in which microbial organisms break down organic material in the absence of oxygen, is well known for the production of 'biogas' composed largely of methane (Joffe, 2006). As for the above two processes therefore, a subsequent reforming stage would be required to produce hydrogen. Though it is possible to produce hydrogen directly from anaerobic digestion, the process is currently at an experimental stage, and is disadvantaged by low yields (Cooney et al, 2007).

Hydrogen can also be produced by the *electrolysis* of water, producing hydrogen at the cathode, and oxygen at the anode. The electrodes are separated by an ionic transfer membrane which allows a current to flow, while ensuring the gases accumulate in separate physical streams. Electrolysis is a process, not an energy source – energy must be provided from primary sources such as natural gas, coal, nuclear or renewables. There are two main types of electrolyser: conventional alkaline and proton exchange membrane, or polymer electrolyte membrane, both of which give it its commonly used acronym (PEM). Alkaline units usually use a solution of potassium hydroxide (KOH) as the electrolyte, due to its high conductivity. PEM electrolysers use a solid polymer electrolyte, and are essentially a PEM fuel cell operating in reverse. Alkaline electrolysers are a more mature technology than PEM electrolysers. They have lower capital costs, operate well (~80 per cent efficiency) across a broader range of current densities (and hence hydrogen outputs), and currently dominate the industrial market. PEM technology is less well developed, although it has been successful in some niche markets. It is more expensive and has lower efficiency at high current densities. However, it has some advantages: PEM units are smaller, have very high efficiency (>90 per cent) at low current densities, require less maintenance, do not require subsequent hydrogen drying, and are better suited to high-pressure electrolysis, which reduces substantially the energy needed for subsequent hydrogen compression. They also have more room for future improvement, and will benefit from the large amount of R&D going into PEM fuel cells. They are therefore generally seen as a promising future option for electrolysis and are the focus of much research.

Table 3.3 *Costs for various hydrogen production technologies*

Technology	*Cost range, US$(2000)/GJH$_2$*	*Additional cost of CO_2 capture*	*Comments*
SMR, large-scale (>100MW)	5.25–7.26	$7.26 cost increases to $8.59/GJ with CCS	Cost highly dependent on natural gas price. Transitional technology.
SMR, small-scale (<5MW)	11.50 (4.18MW)–40.40 (0.42MW)	Prohibitive (perhaps $31/GJ)	Cost highly dependent on natural gas price, plant size and purity of H_2 required.
Coal gasification (min.376MW)	5.4–6.8	Average of 11%	Coal price more stable and predictable than natural gas.
Biomass gasification (>10MW)	7.54–32.61 (av. 14.31)	Not given (with CCS technology, would become carbon negative)	Size ranges from 25 to 303MW and affects cost.
Biomass pyrolysis (>10MW)	6.19–14.98	Not given (with CCS technology would become carbon negative)	Size ranges from 36 to 150MW; cost reduced by sale of co-products.
Electrolysis, large-scale (>1MW)	11–75 (20–60 is preferred range)	Emissions (and CCS options) depend on source of electricity	Size ranges from 2 to 376MW, but little effect on cost; cost very dependent on assumed price of electricity.
Electrolysis, small-scale (<1MW)	28–133	Emissions (and CCS options) depend on source of electricity	Size ranges from 0.03 to 0.79MW, cost very size-dependent.

Overview of costs

Table 3.3 reproduces the range of costs in Hawkins and Joffe (2006), with relevant comments. Throughout their study, they emphasize the uncertain and contingent nature of their results – the studies reviewed make a wide range of different assumptions about current technologies and how they might develop – but the range of costs they thereby derive is nonetheless instructive. Key points from the table or the paper follow.

Economies of scale are particularly important in SMR: small-scale (forecourt) reformers produce hydrogen at about twice the cost of large-scale SMR. Hydrogen produced by CG has generally been more expensive than SMR, although CG is economical where gas is relatively expensive and coal relatively cheap. Since significant coal reserves exist in many areas of the world, and gas prices are increasing, it could become important for hydrogen production (Padró and Putsche, 1999), especially if it were successfully combined with large-scale carbon capture and storage. As indicated above, the extent to which hydrogen production may be linked to coal gasification with CCS could be strongly dependent on whether pre- or post-combustion CCS technologies are favoured following the next round of demonstration projects over the next few years.

It is apparent that costs from electrolysis are much higher than other routes such as (large-scale) SMR or coal gasification. Biomass gasification or pyrolysis with CCS would make the hydrogen carbon-negative, which could become economically attractive if carbon prices became very high, but no data was provided on this.

Promising developments in hydrogen production

The Hawkins and Joffe (2006) review summarized above focused on those hydrogen production technologies at a sufficient level of development to allow the collection and comparison of data. Exploration of novel hydrogen production methods is, of course, ongoing. While a comprehensive survey of such exploratory research is not attempted here, two examples are given to illustrate the continually emerging nature of the field, and the ever-present possibility of 'breakthrough' developments.

Small-scale electrolysis

A British-based company called ITM Power has been making increasingly positive claims about the cost reductions it is able to achieve in water electrolysis. As noted by Smith and Newborough (2004), the DoE's target for electrolyser unit costs by 2010 is $300/kW. ITM claims to have already slashed this to $164/kW. Their approach is based on the development of significantly lower-cost membrane materials, and the development of a 'one step' assembly process which greatly simplifies the electrolyser architecture and facilitates mass production (Smith and Newborough, 2004). Subsequent reports from ITM have revealed that the complete elimination of the platinum catalyst from the electrolyser has been another major factor in reducing costs. ITM claims that these developments make hydrogen produced from electrolysis a commercially competitive transport fuel, and the company intends to use the technology within a home electrolyser unit which it hopes to market imminently (ITM Power, 2009). The development of cost-effective small-scale electrolysers could potentially provide a significant turning point in the use of hydrogen, as it could allow hydrogen to be widely used without the need for major new infrastructure. However, when considering the prospects for 'home' electrolysers, it must be acknowledged that there could be serious questions for public acceptability to be answered. Public perceptions of hydrogen are discussed further in Chapter 11.

Electrohydrogenesis

A number of researchers (Cheng and Logan, 2007; Logan et al, 2008) have used a modified microbial fuel cell to catalyse protons and electrons released by bacteria within a biodegradable substrate, to produce hydrogen upon application of a small charge (0.2–0.8V) to the circuit. In the process, the bacteria consume the organic matter in the biomass material. According to Logan et al (2008), electrohydrogenesis will be able to achieve greater efficiencies than other biological hydrogen production processes – hydrogen yields have been reported close to 100 per cent of that contained in the original organic matter. The energy yield based on electrical input is many times greater than that of water electrolysis, Logan and colleagues reporting hydrogen energy output 288 per cent of that contained in the input electricity. Overall efficiencies, accounting for all energy inputs, have been reported of 64–82 per cent (Cheng and Logan, 2007). The process may also have a use in the treatment of waste water, reducing solids, which could lower sludge-handling costs. The input energy for the process compares favourably with that of current waste water treatment processes (Logan et al, 2008). As with water electrolysis, costs are still high, due to the use of platinum catalysts. However, Rozendal et al (2008) have recently demonstrated catalysis of the hydrogen evolution reaction (HER) using bacteria, and have produced 'biocathodes' to achieve this. This could potentially provide an attractive production stream for hydrogen through the use of waste products, with additional benefits for the waste management process.

Alternative hydrogen production routes – synthetic fuels

The above methods describe routes for the production of hydrogen (H_2) from other feedstocks, for use as an energy carrier. However, hydrogen could itself become a feedstock for the production of other fuels. Bossel et al (2005) argue strongly that the properties of liquefied or gaseous hydrogen make it unsuitable for use as a widespread fuel. Their primary argument is that in an effort to reduce carbon emissions, wherever possible the electricity grid will be expanded and technologies developed for the direct use of electricity (e.g. electric vehicles). However, they argue that for applications less amenable to direct use of electricity, there could be a role for hydrogen as a renewable energy carrier, if packaged within synthetic fuels such as methanol (CH_4O), ethanol (C_2H_6O) or octane (C_8H_{18}). Such fuels could be synthesized by combining hydrogen produced from renewable electrolysis with carbon derived from biomass, waste or CO_2 flue gases. Bossel et al (2005) highlight two particular advantages of such synthetic fuels compared to pure hydrogen. First, these synthetic fuels have physical properties which the authors consider to be ideal in an energy carrier – they are liquid fuels at ambient temperatures, which improves handling. Second, their volumetric energy density is far greater than liquefied or 80Mpa (800 bar)-compressed gaseous hydrogen.

Of the various synthetic fuels listed by Bossel et al, methanol has received particular attention. It can be combusted in conventional internal combustion engines, reformed to produce pure hydrogen, or used for the direct production of electricity in a direct methanol fuel cell (DMFC). As will be discussed in Chapter 4, the energy storage potential for DMFCs is being explored for portable electronics, as well as for certain niche transport applications. Methanol has been prominent in certain articulations of Iceland's vision for its future 'hydrogen economy' (Arnason and Sigfusson, 2000), though less so in more recent descriptions (Sigfusson, 2007). For further discussion of possible processes for the production of methanol from renewable hydrogen, see, for example, Galindo Cifre and Badr (2007).

Hydrogen storage

Hydrogen can be stored as a compressed gas, as a liquid, in a chemical compound, or physically held within structures such as metal hydrides or carbon nanofibres. Storage may be needed at different scales: on board vehicles, at filling stations, at production centres, and nationally as a strategic reserve. A major element of the cost of most of these storage modes (and a major consideration, in terms of their energy efficiency) is the energy required to get the hydrogen in and out of storage.

In this chapter, storage costs are in general expressed as a cost per unit of hydrogen stored (\$/kg H_2). This is useful when estimating how much storage might contribute to the final hydrogen price seen by the consumer, and also for assessing how the cost of storage compares with the cost of production. However, this metric can vary depending on the throughput of hydrogen over the course of the storage facility's economic lifetime: shorter storage times give higher throughput, and hence lower costs per unit of hydrogen stored.

In Hawkins (2006), from which the information and much of the description in this section is taken, costs (adjusted to year 2000 US dollars) have been given per kg H_2, rather than per GJ, since this appears most often in the literature, and avoids any confusion over higher and lower heating values. The principal primary source for Hawkins' data used a 22-year straight-line depreciation at a zero rate of return, to estimate the cost of the various technologies. Therefore, this represents a storage or transport cost, rather than a price which might be charged to a consumer.

Overview of technologies

Liquid hydrogen (LH_2) storage is currently used in industrial hydrogen demand centres such as refineries. It is produced in a central liquefaction plant, with typical production rates of 110–2,300kg LH_2/hour, and distributed to consumers by road tanker. Industrial consumer storage tanks typically have capacities between 110 and 5,300kg, while central liquefaction plants typically have over 100,000kg. NASA has the largest LH_2 tank in the world, which holds 228,000kg. Hydrogen's boiling point is very low: –253°C (20.3K), in comparison to natural gas, which is liquid at –160°C (113K). This means the equipment for LH_2 storage and handling is more expensive than for liquefied natural gas (LNG). Boil-off (evaporation) of LH_2 will always occur, no matter how well insulated the vessel is. Boil-off rates depend on the size (surface area to volume ratio) of the storage vessel, and range from 2 to 3 per cent per day for small portable containers down to 0.06 per cent per day for large vessels, with a typical rate being 0.1 per cent per day (Amos, 1998: p23). Boil-off gas can be used immediately, vented, reliquefied, or allowed to build up pressure within the storage vessel's specified limits.

Compressed gas storage is widely used in the refining and chemical industry, as well as being deployed in many current fuel cell vehicle prototypes. It requires less energy than liquefaction, and is easily scaled down. However, it suffers from low volumetric energy density and requires relatively costly storage tanks. Tanks storing hydrogen at 70MPa (700 bar) have been designed and fabricated. These high pressures achieve large reductions in volume for modest increases in weight and cost, but may require more costly filling arrangements. Also, there are some safety concerns about using highly pressurized gas storage on board domestic vehicles, and there is as yet no consensus about whether the level of safety is acceptable.

Bulk underground storage is widely used for crude oil and natural gas, and also for hydrogen in the chemical and refining industries. It relies on suitable geology, and requires a large cavern or porous chamber with impermeable cap rock above. Options include natural gas wells, aquifers, solution-mined salt caverns, and other man-made caverns. Hydrogen is extracted by using another fluid, for example, brine in the case of salt caverns, to displace it. The UK has an active H_2 storage site at Teesside, where salt caverns have the capacity for nearly 1,000 tonnes H_2 storage.

Hydrogen can be stored as the *chemical hydride* of such elements as calcium, magnesium or lithium, or in sodium borohydride. These have high volumetric (comparable to LH_2) and gravimetric energy densities, and have the advantage that hydrogen is readily liberated when they are exposed to water (hydrolysis). Some of the hydrogen is 'stored' in the hydride, and some is liberated from water in the reaction. Hydrides are stored as slurry with a mineral oil, effectively making them a liquid fuel which can be stored in most conventional tanks. The hydrolysis reaction is highly exothermic and needs to be carefully controlled – capturing this waste heat might be possible in a CHP application, but would be difficult on board a vehicle. Conversely, the regeneration process is highly endothermic, and is relatively inefficient and expensive. Used fuel (metal hydroxides) require high temperatures and large energy inputs, and must be returned to a central plant for regeneration. This would mean that if chemical hydrides were used for on-board vehicle storage, they would be regenerated 'off-board' (Satyapal et al, 2007), posing a different refuelling paradigm for vehicle users. For chemical hydrides, it is hard to differentiate the cost of 'storage' from the cost of production. Chemical hydride storage has been demonstrated at various scales, from portable battery replacement to vehicle power, and is available commercially in some power back-up devices.

Hydrogen can also be stored within a metallic lattice as a *metal hydride*. In contrast to chemical hydrides, absorption of hydrogen (hydriding) is exothermic and requires cooling, and releasing hydrogen (dehydriding) is endothermic and requires heating. The temperature at which hydrogen is released is a property of the hydride. Metal hydrides achieve high volumetric energy density (better than LH_2) at ambient temperatures and pressures. They are inherently safe, with no danger of catastrophic leaks or runaway reactions. However, they are very heavy, and have no economies of scale in terms of weight or cost. The high temperatures required for release of hydrogen (e.g. 300°C for magnesium hydride) could be problematic on board a vehicle, as would the poor kinetics (slow rate of release of hydrogen). More complex metal hydrides can improve hydrogen uptake and reduce desorption temperatures, though usually with reduced reversibility (Guo et al, 2008). With regard to their use in on-board vehicle storage, according to Satyapal et al (2007), in contrast to chemical hydrides, metal hydrides would not have to be removed from a vehicle for regeneration, but could be regenerated on board the vehicle, allowing a much more familiar refuelling paradigm. However, the poor kinetics would be likely to require long filling times when scaled up to vehicle applications (perhaps at least ten minutes, compared to the US DoE goal of five minutes (Satyapal et al, 2007)), which could be a problem for commercial vehicles. In addition, their sensitivity to impurities can degrade storage performance over time. Metal hydride storage has been demonstrated in applications where extra weight or limited range is not a problem. Hydrogen hydride storage canisters are commercially available for stationary power systems, and systems have been demonstrated in mine vehicles, tractors, buses and scooters. Hydride storage was recently tested in a modified Toyota Prius hybrid (H_2 combustion engine), achieving a driving range of 200 miles (compared with 600 with petrol), and requiring a filling time of eight minutes. Metal hydrides can be used for thermal compression, since the pressure at which hydrogen is released increases with temperature; and for purification, since impurities tend to be held within the metal (they can be flushed out at a higher temperature later). This means that hydrides could be used to perform combined storage, purification and compression, which would improve their economics.

Overview of costs and other characteristics of storage options

Table 3.4 (reproduced from Hawkins, 2006: Table 2.10) summarizes the advantages and disadvantages of different hydrogen storage technologies. The key determinants of cost are storage time, storage capacity and energy requirements. Storage time determines hydrogen throughput – shorter storage times mean higher throughput and hence lower costs per unit of hydrogen stored. Larger capacity storage can benefit from economies of scale, provided there are economies of scale in the underlying technology. Energy requirements are directly related to the amount of hydrogen stored, and therefore do not vary with storage time or capacity. To reduce the energy costs, the efficiency of storage would need to be increased, or a cheaper energy source utilized.

It is difficult to compare the cost of storage with the cost of hydrogen production, since both vary depending on the situation. However, storage costs presented here range from about \$0.12 to \$4/kg, depending on the technology. Hydrogen production costs from large-scale SMR or coal gasification, which are the cheapest routes to hydrogen, might be around \$1/kg. Therefore, storage costs range from being a minor component, if the cheapest technology and favourable conditions are assumed, to several times the cost of production, if cheap production is coupled with expensive storage. However, if hydrogen was produced from electrolysis, it might cost between \$4 and \$10, and storage is likely to be a minor (though still significant) component of hydrogen cost.

Table 3.4 *Characteristics of different hydrogen storage technologies*

	Bulk underground storage	*Liquid*	*Compressed gas*	*Metal hydrides*	*Chemical hydrides*
Advantages	Large capacities (millions kg)	Better energy density than compressed gas	Simple capital equipment (compressors)	Good volumetric energy density at ambient temperature and pressure	High-energy density
	Long times (months, years)	Low storage vessel costs	Modular	Safe – no risk of catastrophic leaks	Stable if kept away from water
	Lowest capital cost if suitable cavern exists	Strong economies of scale	Easily scaled down	Can also be used to purify and pressurize	Easy to store and transport
	Low O&M cost				
Disadvantages	Requires pre-existing caverns, otherwise more costly	Very low temperature (20K)	Low energy density	Heavy	Spent fuel requires recyling
	Not suitable for small amounts of short-term storage	High capital cost of liquefaction plant	Higher capital cost of tanks than liquid storage	High capital costs	Energy intensive manufacture
		Large energy requirement for liquefaction	Safety concerns for on-board storage	No economies of scale	Controlling some reactions is difficult
		Boil-off			High cost of manufacture
Suitable for	Large quantities of gas, or long-term storage	Large quantities of gas, long-term storage, or applications requiring liquid H_2	Small amounts of gas, short cycle times	Small quantities of gas	Applications where high-energy density is valued and primary energy available
Capacity (kg)	10,000–1,000,000	100–200,000	0–1,000	Weight, volume and expense limited 0–100	
Efficiency	85–95	70–80	85–90	85–90 (uncertain)	60–65**
Added cost to hydrogen $/kg*	$0.12–$0.30	$1.00–$1.50	$0.15–$0.60	$0.40–$4.0	$1.5–$2.5**
Major cost components	Energy (90%)	Energy (50%) Capital (50%)	Energy (25–50%), Tanks (25–75%)	Metal (95%)	Energy
Scaling Factor	1	0.6–0.65	0.80–0.95	1	1

* These figures depend on capacity and storage time, and it is difficult to give a single range
** Includes some energy and costs which would be regarded as production

Source: Hawkins (2006: Table 2.10, p21)

Figure 3.1, from the US DoE's Hydrogen Programme 2008 annual review, compares various hydrogen storage technologies to 2010 performance goals.

These performance goals are intended to serve as benchmarks towards still more stringent 2015 targets, which if attained would deliver equivalent energy storage performance to a conventional petrol tank on board an average family car. Considered in these terms, the performance of hydrogen storage materials appears to be highly problematic. The US National Academies' assessment that on-board hydrogen storage is 'a major stumbling block ... for the future of transportation use of fuel cells' (NRC and NAE, 2004) remains the case, and as Guo et al (2008) acknowledge, 'for onboard applications, the progresses so far are insufficient to meet all the practical targets for on-board hydrogen storage'. Neither is it clear, from reviews such as Guo et al (2008) and Satyapal et al (2007), where a breakthrough might be likely to come from. As opposed to research, for example, in fuel cells and electrolysis, where efforts are now being directed at particular aspects such as integrating stack components and reducing platinum loading, storage research appears to be still somewhat more exploratory and speculative. Some beneficial developments in metal hydrides have been achieved through the mechanical 'milling' of the materials, and through chemical 'doping' to modify hydride properties (Guo et al, 2008). Computer-based modelling of hybridizations between pairs of the various materials have suggested new compounds with improved qualities, offering a faster way of running through the myriad of possible combinations and selecting potential candidates (Guo et al, 2008; Satyapal, 2008). However, this process still requires the materials to be manufactured, before their performance in practice can be verified.

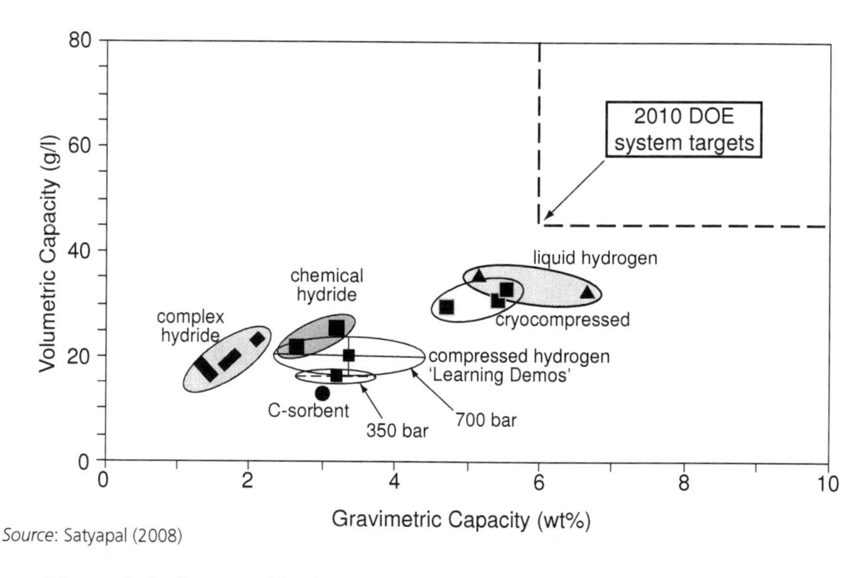

Source: Satyapal (2008)

Figure 3.1 *Status of hydrogen storage systems in 2008 compared with 2010 targets*

Nonetheless, it should be acknowledged that various factors could blur the apparently rigid boundaries of the 2010 target zone in Figure 3.1. First, on-board engineering solutions could extend the performance of storage materials, often through hybridization between technologies. Honda's fuel cell vehicle prototype, the FCX Clarity, is reported to have a range of 270 miles with a single tank of gaseous hydrogen – its range is extended by the use of electric batteries which capture regenerated energy from braking, as with hybrid electric vehicles (IHS, 2007). Mori and Hirose (2008) report on an experiment placing a metal hydride material inside a 35Mpa (350 bar) gaseous hydrogen storage tank. It is reported that this kind of hybridized approach extends the storage capacity of a normal gaseous storage tank by 2.5 times, and the tank can refill to 80 per cent capacity in five minutes. Second, it is not inconceivable that the vehicle market could segment more than is allowed for under the assumptions of the US DoE programme. Even if the performance targets are not met, given that 99 per cent of car journeys in the UK are under 100 miles (DfT, 2005), it may be that there could be an increased interest in owning a vehicle which had a much smaller range than current conventional vehicles, if it had other attractions (see Chapter 4). Third, it should be emphasized that the DoE targets are somewhat focused towards the use of hydrogen in road vehicles. However, there could be a range of other applications which could potentially use hydrogen, and for which different characteristics could be required from hydrogen storage. A range of applications is discussed later in this chapter.

Hydrogen transport/distribution

In addition to being stored, with associated cost, hydrogen must often be transported to its place of use. Clearly the means of transport will be closely related to the means of storage. Pipelines distribute compressed gas, and an extensive pipeline network will store a sizeable quantity of gas (the stored quantity can be increased by increasing the pipeline pressure). 'Tube trailers' deliver compressed gas, and road tankers liquid hydrogen. As with the previous section, much of the information and description in this section is taken from Hawkins (2006).

Overview of technologies

Hydrogen is delivered by *pipeline* in several areas of Europe, the US and Canada. The longest European pipeline is 400km long, from northern France to Belgium, while the UK has about 30km of hydrogen pipeline in the Tees Valley. It would not be possible to use the existing natural gas infrastructure in its current form to carry pure hydrogen, as it would induce cracking in steel pipelines, react with lubricants and seals, could require different compressors, and could permeate plastic pipelines. Modifications to the existing natural gas network to allow it to carry hydrogen would therefore have to be quite considerable. It has also been suggested that as an interim measure, hydrogen could be carried through the existing gas network in a mixture with natural gas (methane) (Cherryman et al, 2004) – the original gas infrastructure in the UK was developed to carry town gas, a mixture of hydrogen and carbon monoxide, derived from coal. However, it is not clear how much investment would be needed to allow the existing infrastructure to carry hydrogen or various grades of mixed methane and hydrogen. The costs of building hydrogen pipelines from scratch are in general considered to be higher than the costs of laying equivalent lengths of natural gas pipeline; for example, Ogden (1999) estimates total capital costs for hydrogen pipelines will be 40–50 per cent higher than those of natural gas pipelines. However, the costs are potentially highly variable, depending on the effects of economies of scale and learning by doing, as well as the fact that practical issues such as topography and planning consent can come to dominate costs for any kind of pipeline (Hughes, 2006). As well as transport, pipelines provide some storage capacity, since the pressure of gas in the pipeline can be increased above what is needed to meet the immediate demand.

Tube trailers or *trucks* are currently used to transport compressed hydrogen gas to smaller industrial customers, where LH_2 is not available or feasible. They consist of several steel cylinders mounted on a protective framework, and can carry 60–460kg at 20–60MPa (200–600 bar). A typical trailer might carry 300kg of hydrogen, which represents about 1 per cent of the total mass of the truck.

Liquid hydrogen (LH_2) delivery by *road tanker* is widely used in the chemical and refining industries, since more hydrogen can be delivered per vehicle than with tube trailers. Tank trucks can carry 400–4,000kg LH_2, a factor of ten more than tube trailers. LH_2 can also be carried by rail, in cylindrical tanks with capacities of around 9,000kg. Boil-off can be a problem, typically running at 0.30–0.6 per cent/day, although road deliveries taking more than one day would be very rare in the UK. Flash losses (rapid evaporation) when transferring from a high-pressure vessel to a lower pressure one can be high: 10–20 per cent, and possibly up to 50 per cent, although this can be reduced if LH_2 is transported at atmospheric pressure, although with presumably some loss in carrying capacity.

LH_2 could potentially be transported internationally by *ship tanker*, as is done increasingly for liquefied natural gas (LNG). No LH_2 tankers exist, but LNG tankers are being built with capacities of 145,000m^3 of LNG (equivalent to about 10 million kg H_2), and ships with capacities up to 240,000m^3 are under study. Canada is reported to have some designs for LH_2 ships carrying up to 14 million kg LH_2. Boil-off can be a problem, since journey times are longer. For large vessels, boil-off rates might be 0.2–0.4 per cent per day. Reliquefaction on board ship is currently not feasible, due to the large refrigeration plant needed, and boil-off in LNG ships is usually used to supplement fuel for the carriers. Clearly, if at a future point hydrogen was being used as a propulsion fuel for such ships, then boil-off could be reclaimed in a similar way.

Overview of hydrogen transport costs

Table 3.5 gives estimates of the cost of various hydrogen transport/distribution technologies. It can be seen that these estimates, like those for different storage technologies, differ by an order of magnitude, ranging from $0.1 to $2, and that the key variables that affect cost are the quantities transported (there are strong economies of scale) and, as would be expected, the transport distance. The most significant cost for LH_2 transport is the cost of liquefaction. This has been considered in the storage section, but must be included here if a fair comparison is to be made between transport and distribution options.

Comparing distribution costs with the cost of production is difficult, since both vary depending on the pathway and technology. The cheapest options for producing hydrogen (large-scale fossil fuel routes) might cost around $1/kg. The cheapest option of transporting hydrogen is by high-capacity pipeline, which can cost less than $0.1/kg over 100km. However, if hydrogen is liquefied and transported by road for several hundred kilometres, the cost is likely to be over $1/kg – possibly more than the cost of production. Hence transport can be a significant factor when analysing the cost of hydrogen.

Figure 3.2 indicates the relative cost-effectiveness of the different transport options over different distances with different throughputs. It should be emphasized that the diagram is indicative, and should not be read as a precise indication of the points at which switches between economically optimal distribution technologies would occur. Apart from the significant cost uncertainties already emphasized, the lines are further blurred by issues of topography, planning and long-term certainty of demand, and the nature of the end-use application. Nonetheless, the general point is instructive: costs are sensitive to both distance and capacity, but this affects the different technologies in different ways. Due to the relatively small incremental cost of installing higher-capacity (wider) pipelines, costs of pipelines do not rise greatly with increased capacity. This means that pipelines are likely to be the most cost-effective option at high throughput rates. On the other hand, pipeline costs are much more sensitive to distance, whereas truck deliveries can accommodate

Table 3.5 *Costs for various hydrogen transport/distribution technologies*

Technology	*Cost range, US$(2000)/ kg H_2/100km*	*Comments*
Pipeline (compressed gas)	0.1–1	Cost decreases with size of pipeline (flow-rate) and increases with distance
Tube-trailer (compressed gas)	0.5–2.0	Cost increases more than linearly with distance
Liquid (road)	0.3–0.5	Includes cost of liquefaction; cost increases more than linearly with distance
Liquid (ship)	1.8–2.0	Uncertain estimate because no ship for liquid H_2 yet built

Source: Hawkins (2006: Table 3.2, p32)

incrementally increasing distances with diminishing increases in cost. The lesser energy density of gaseous, compared to liquefied delivery, means that it would be preferred for small throughput rates and short distances – at higher distances the reduced transportation costs achieved by the greater quantities of hydrogen per truck justify the additional costs of liquefaction.

However, Figure 3.2 is based only on cost, not practical considerations. For example, delivering 500kg/h by tube trailer would require more than one truck delivery per hour. Various estimates suggest that tube trailer delivery is suitable up to capacities of up to about 13kg/h, and LH_2 trucks are suitable up to 1,000kg/h, while pipelines can deliver up to 100,000kg/h.

Also pipelines offer a storage and buffering capacity, and their useful lifetime is likely to be longer than their investment lifetime, so companies might see investments in pipelines as strategic. However, the high capital costs of pipelines makes investment less likely if the market for hydrogen is uncertain. Decisions on the mode of transport are also linked to the mode of storage; for example, if both the producer and consumer are using liquid storage, then it makes sense to transport hydrogen as a liquid.

Hydrogen Infrastructure

Production and large-scale storage facilities, and distribution equipment, are all part of what is sometimes termed hydrogen 'infrastructure', and it has been seen that they can all be important components of the cost of delivering hydrogen to end-users. Another important component of such infrastructure is the network of refuelling stations that will be required if hydrogen is to be widely used as a motor fuel. This issue is reviewed in detail by Agnolucci (2007a).

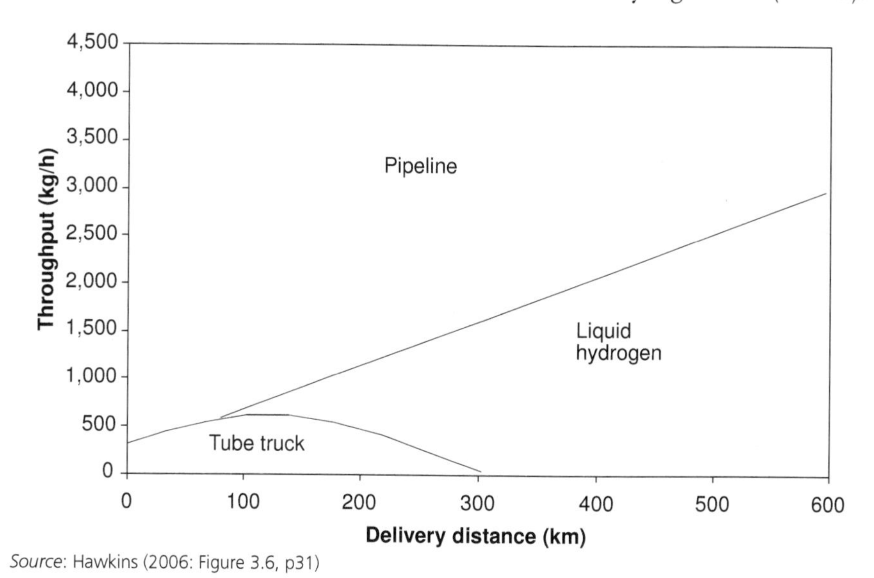

Source: Hawkins (2006: Figure 3.6, p31)

Figure 3.2 *Least-cost hydrogen transport options with distance and capacity*

The key issue in this regard is the chicken-and-egg problem that motorists are unlikely to buy hydrogen fuel cell vehicles (FCVs) until there is a well-developed network of filling stations, but energy companies will not provide filling stations until there is adequate demand for them from FCVs. The timing of the provision of this infrastructure could have a major influence on the cost of the delivered hydrogen – Agnolucci (2007a: p3539) reports that there is wide agreement in the literature that the extent of use of infrastructure, called the capacity factor, 'is the single most important factor influencing the price of hydrogen'. Agnolucci (2007a: p3531ff) has identified three approaches in the literature to tackle the issue of timing infrastructure provision.

Whole-system incremental approach

This envisages that hydrogen will gradually spread through the economy through a number of different routes, perhaps starting with portable power applications and then moving to stationary distributed power, buses and government fleet vehicles, and only then starting to service commercial and luxury passenger vehicles, followed by ordinary passenger vehicles. At each stage, an appropriately targeted infrastructure would be installed, with the gradual investment entailing a natural risk management strategy which keeps the capacity factor high and generates returns for investors prior to each new investment. In addition, provided that there were synergies between the various hydrogen applications, learning about one could spill over into cost-reductions for the next phase. However, few experts seem to share an opinion that use of hydrogen is likely to develop in this 'whole system' manner. Rather, the portable, stationary and automotive sectors are increasingly regarded as separate markets using different technologies (Hughes, 2006; and see Chapter 4).

Incremental approach

This approach focuses only on the transport sector, but again is incremental in nature, sequentially targeting different parts of the vehicle market in order to keep capacity factors on an investment relatively high and generating a return, before moving on to the next stage. Typically, it is envisaged that this approach would start with demonstration projects, then move on to providing hydrogen for vehicle fleets, and then to different segments of the private passenger vehicle market. Clearly, for this approach to work, FCVs would need to offer advantages for consumers in each phase of market development. While enthusiasts consider that FCVs offer advantages in relation to 'environmental performance, quiet operation, rapid acceleration from a standstill, potentially low maintenance requirements and greater design flexibility', and can generate electrical power for applications outside the vehicle, others question whether these benefits will be adequate to enable FCVs to expand their appeal beyond speciality markets (Agnolucci, 2006: p15; and see Chapter 4).

Step-change approach

Of course, one way of resolving the chicken-and-egg problem would be simply to provide large-scale infrastructure in advance of the wide use of FCVs, in the belief that this would follow (developments would be very unlikely to occur the other way round). There is some consensus in the literature that this would require the installation of around 10–15 per cent of the current number of filling stations over around a five-year period (Agnolucci, 2007a: p3534), and there has been considerable analysis of the optimal design of a hydrogen refuelling infrastructure of this kind.

The financial risk involved in a step-change approach is considerable – low-capacity factors can entail a price of hydrogen of over \$20/kg H_2 for an extended period in order to recoup costs, even though the long-term cost of H_2 with deep market penetration and high-capacity factors may be only around \$2.5/kg (Melaina, 2003).

Hydrogen end-use applications

While it is possible to burn hydrogen directly as a fuel (as in an internal combustion engine, as a direct replacement for petrol), most projections of widespread future hydrogen use envisage its use in fuel cells (FCs). There are four main areas of such applications: auxiliary power units, portable fuel cells, stationary power and FCVs. The brief descriptions of each of these areas that follow is followed in Chapter 4 by more detailed discussions of the market prospects for APUs, portable fuel cells and FCVs.

It is important to note that all of the potential fuel cell applications described below could use fuels other than hydrogen. Indeed, as is discussed in Chapter 4, many are already beginning to establish markets which do not entail the use of hydrogen. Whether developments in non-hydrogen fuel cells could stimulate later developments in hydrogen fuel cells through technology transfer is debatable, as also discussed in Chapter 4.

For clarity, it can be summarized that there are a number of different fuel cell designs, operating at either high temperatures (molten carbonate (MC) FCs and solid oxide (SO) FCs) or low temperatures (PEMFCs, phosphoric acid (PA) FCs, and alkaline (A) FCs). Those operating at high temperatures (MCFCs, SOFCs) (600–1,000°C) can reform hydrogen from other fuels internally (but will then produce carbon dioxide emissions), while PEMFCs, which operate at lower temperatures of around 80°C, require a source of pure hydrogen. At present, PAFCs are offered commercially in sizes of 20–200kW and MCFCs at sizes of 250kW and above. PEMFCs, with most prospects for technical development, are entering the market at 1–5kW and 75–250kW, and SOFCs are expected commercially at around 200kW. AFCs are only suitable for specialist applications (e.g. spacecraft) (Hawkins et al, 2006: p4).

The potential fuel cell application that is most strongly linked to hydrogen as its fuel is that of vehicles. The low-temperature, fast start-up time and load-following capabilities of PEMFCs are important for vehicle applications, and as has been discussed, these fuel cells require pure hydrogen. However, even in vehicles, the use of a similar low-temperature proton-exchange membrane fuel cell running on methanol, the direct-methanol fuel cell (DMFC), shows that pure hydrogen is not the inevitable fuel of choice. DMFCs have been used in a number of niche transport applications (Butler, 2008a).

Auxiliary power units (APUs)

APUs are devices for providing additional on-board power for vehicles, aside from the primary requirement for motive power. A number of fuel cell types could potentially be used for APU applications, Agnolucci (2007b) identifying PEMFCs and SOFCs, with discussions in Hughes (2006) and the review by Butler (2008b) additionally emphasizing a growing market share for DMFCs. Agnolucci (2007b) has carried out a detailed assessment of the economic prospects for fuel cell APUs across eight kinds of civil vehicle – transits, pick-ups, recreational, specialized utility, refrigeration, luxury passenger and law enforcement vehicles, and heavy-duty trucks. Because vehicles in normal operation can provide significant power from the alternator, and because APUs seem to offer few additional benefits (and at present entail substantial extra cost) compared to this power source, the opportunity for APUs would seem to be restricted to those vehicles which require significant power when idling or stationary, or which have exceptional power demands during use. APUs are also known to be of interest in military applications (particularly because they are silent and evade infra-red detection), but information about these is restricted. It should be borne in mind that widespread military deployment may lead to cost reductions and applications that spill over into the civil market, but these possibilities are not further discussed here.

The services provided by fuel cell (FC) APUs may be provided by diesel APUs (the only difference being that the latter are not silent) or, for trucks, by electrified truck-stops (which provide less flexibility for stopping, but a range of additional services which may be highly valued by drivers). Technologically, FC APUs will need to decrease in size if they are substantially to penetrate the market for smaller vehicles, and in cost if they are to compete with diesel APUs and electrified stops. However, a number of scenarios suggest that, with mass production, the cost of FC APUs could become competitive with these rivals. Certainly, there is substantial private investment going into these devices, and at least one existing application in a luxury passenger vehicle, which suggests that some manufacturers at least believe them to have a commercial future.

Portable fuel cells

Portable fuel cell (FC) systems may be defined as those with a power of up to 5kW and a weight of less than 10kg. Some portable FC systems (up to 50W) are intended to replace batteries in portable electronic devices such as computers and mobile phones (DMFCs are currently receiving most interest for such uses). In the range of 1–5kW are portable generators (in which PEMFCs, SOFCs and DMFCs are competing), which provide power for camping and other recreational activities, in remote locations or for military purposes. Demand for portable FCs will therefore depend on the demand for the products containing them and on the competing technologies which can also provide the desired energy services. The desired energy services will be increased by the desire for increased functionality, but reduced by energy-saving innovations that allow this extra functionality to be delivered with lower energy use. FC portable generators have the advantage that they are silent, clean and more efficient than diesel generators (the incumbent technology); the only advantage of portable FCs over batteries in electrical appliances is the potential to supply energy for longer continuous use between recharging.

Undoubtedly there are likely to be some suitable applications for portable FCs, where longer life or increased power are very much valued (e.g. surveillance systems or military applications). However, these are very small markets. For mass commodities, in particular electronic appliances, it is not clear that there is strong demand for power characteristics that batteries cannot, or will not be able to, satisfy. Certainly, to penetrate these markets significantly, portable FCs will need to reduce their size and cost significantly – the latter by around 10 per cent pa over a five-year period, according to one projection (Darnell, 2003).

There are currently few portable FCs on the market. Agnolucci (2007c: pp4323, 4326) reports some delays in bringing new products to market, and Nokia has decided against an early introduction of FCs in its mobile phones. However, a number of other major manufacturers (e.g. Casio, Sanyo, Toshiba, NEC, Hitachi) remain active in developments in this area (although they are also developing competing technologies). Agnolucci's (2007c: p4326) conclusion is that portable FCs are never likely completely to replace batteries, but may capture market-share for those users who value extra power or longevity between charges highly and are prepared to experience some extra cost, size and inconvenience to achieve it. The size of this market share will depend on the extent to which FC technology development is able to reduce the gaps in these characteristics between FCs and batteries.

For portable applications as a whole, the major competition is currently between PEMFCs and DMFCs. According to Jollie (2004: p5), 'the latter is winning, particularly in the high profile consumer electronics market'.

Stationary power

Fuel cells (FCs) generate power, and some of them also generate heat, which opens up the possibility of them being used as sources of stationary power on a relatively small scale and, perhaps, of combined heat and power (CHP), which would increase their energetic efficiency. However, FCs which run on hydrogen require the hydrogen to be produced from other energy sources, as described above, and normally it will be preferable (in terms of both energy efficiency and cost) to use these other sources to generate electricity directly, rather than via hydrogen production. It is for these reasons that a report by E4 Tech et al (2004) largely rules out the use of hydrogen-fuelled FCs for stationary power production as a cost-effective means of reducing CO_2. The report nonetheless acknowledges the possibility of cost-effective CO_2 reductions from stationary fuel cells operating on conventional fuels. A well-known UK example is the 200kW PAFC unit, which operates on reformed natural gas to provide heat and power services to Woking Council-owned buildings and local electricity networks (Woking Borough Council, 2007). In such cases, CO_2 savings are due to the increased efficiency of the fuel use, rather than a switch to a low-carbon fuel.

However, on the basis of their review of the literature, Hawkins et al (2006) consider that hydrogen FCs could find niche applications for stationary power, for example, for back-up power for essential services, in remote off-grid situations or where there is surplus renewable energy to produce the hydrogen. The latter application may become increasingly important as policies aimed at decarbonizing electricity generation increase the penetration of inflexible low-carbon generation technologies on the grid. A cycle of producing hydrogen from electrolysis and then reversing the process to produce electricity in a stationary fuel cell could act as an 'electricity store' to manage supply-demand imbalances on a heavily decarbonized grid.

A range of different FCs could be used for stationary power. High-temperature fuel cells such as SOFCs could potentially generate additional power from their waste heat; low-temperature fuel cells such as PEMFCs, and mid-temperature fuel cells such as PAFCs could produce heat at a suitable temperature for domestic space and water heating. The costs and challenges of supplying pure hydrogen to low-temperature stationary fuel cells could be a significant obstacle, meaning that early applications are likely to prefer either high-temperature fuel cells operating on available fuels such as natural gas, and reforming internally, or low- to mid-temperature fuel cells with separate on-site reforming units. Lower temperature fuel cells such as PEMFCs have the benefit of fast start-up time and flexible load-following capabilities, which could be beneficial for domestic CHP applications.

Fuel cells are currently three to five times as expensive as diesel and petrol engines and gas turbines, indicating the kind of cost reductions that will be required for them to compete effectively with these other small-scale sources of power. However, they are the subject of substantial R&D expenditure from both private and public sources, so that some cost reduction may confidently be expected. How much is, of course, uncertain.

Fuel cell vehicles (FCVs)

FCVs are estimated to be two to three times more efficient than conventional petrol vehicles, and one-and-a-half to two times more efficient than diesel-electric hybrids. If hydrogen is produced by SMR (without CCS) and transported by pipeline, this increased efficiency is estimated to yield a 'well-to-wheels' reduction in carbon dioxide emissions of 30–60 per cent compared with conventional petrol-engined vehicles (although diesel-electric hybrids have been estimated as able to deliver comparable savings) (Hawkins and

Hughes, 2006: p20). Most futures that involve the widespread use of hydrogen as an energy carrier envisage the mass diffusion of FCVs (see Table 4.1, Chapter 4). The prospects for FCVs have therefore tended to be considered as critical to the question of whether or not hydrogen will come to be widely used.

The cost of FCs is the most important element in the overall cost of FCVs. HyWays (2006; cited in Hawkins and Hughes, 2006: p5) give the current cost of the fuel cell system (comprising fuel cell stack and balance of plant) for a passenger car to be over €4,000/kW, while IEA (2005; cited in Hawkins and Hughes, 2006: p8) puts the cost much lower, at US$1,826/kW. The US Department of Energy (DoE) perceives that, to be competitive with the internal combustion engine (ICE), the fuel cell system cost would have to be in the range $30–45/kW, so an enormous cost reduction is required. Most of this cost reduction is envisaged to be achieved through the economies of scale associated with mass production (of the order of 500,000 vehicles per year), and the DoE has a target to achieve the $30/kW cost by 2015. The review of studies by Hawkins and Hughes (2006: Table 1, p7) suggests that the mass production of even current technology could achieve a cost of $28–181/kW. The IEA (2005) estimate production of only 4,000 vehicles per year, but technical advances in respect of materials, power density and other technology is $103/kW, possibly falling to $50/kW with even more technical progress. There is, therefore, still some uncertainty as to how the required cost reduction for competitiveness with ICEs is to be achieved. However, key objectives are considered to be reduction of platinum loading, and greater integration of cell stacks, possibly with the use of injection moulding techniques, reducing the number of component parts and facilitating mass-production (Heinzel et al, 2004; TIAX, 2005; Hughes, 2006).

Of course, the FC is only part of the costs of the FCV, which also requires an electrical drivetrain, control electronics and hydrogen storage, with, perhaps, a complete redesign of the vehicle itself. Each of these elements introduces new uncertainties into the cost projections. In the review of studies of vehicle costs (Hawkins and Hughes, 2006: Table 4, p13), one study from 2002 suggests that the cost of a hydrogen FCV in 2007 would be $36,500. The range of costs for 2015–30 is $18–34,000. In some cases these are projected to be competitive, in others to cost 15–20 per cent more than comparable ICE vehicles. These estimates are based on FC costs of $35–75/kW, and so clearly assume either mass production or substantial technical progress, or both.

Perhaps the area in which technical progress is most required is hydrogen storage. Hawkins and Hughes (2006: p14) write: 'No current technologies are capable of meeting the storage requirements set by US DoE targets for satisfactory performance of hydrogen vehicles.' Without such performance it is unlikely that any kind of mass penetration of vehicle markets by FCVs will be perceived possible, and without such perception no mass production of FCVs, required to bring down their cost, will take place. As Hawkins and Hughes

(2006: p15) report:

> *The reviewing committee of the FreedomCar programme reported hydrogen storage to be one of the 'greater risks for reaching the programme goals in 2015', stressing that the area needs a 'breakthrough discovery as the forerunner of development and innovation.'* (NRC, 2005: p68)

There is also the whole chicken-and-egg issue in respect of mass production and infrastructure, referred to above, the full dimensions of which are now apparent. It is clear that FCVs will never even approach cost-competitiveness with ICE vehicles without mass production (at least 500,000 vehicles per year). However, it is not clear how they will achieve this level of sales until the cost (and therefore price) reductions of FCVs have taken place. Nor is it clear either that such sales will take place until the requisite infrastructure to service the vehicles is in place, or who will provide the finance for the huge investment in infrastructure that would be required. Possible policies and strategies that may resolve these difficult transition problems are discussed in a number of chapters later in this book, with Chapter 12 drawing conclusions and making some recommendations.

The issue of transitions in respect of FCVs is made even more difficult because, unlike some other applications in which FCs offer extra performance qualities, which may command a premium price, as noted by Agnolucci (2006), even the most optimistic advocates of FCVs do not suggest that they will do more than match ICE vehicles in mechanical performance (though FCVs may produce less vibrations and noise, and require less maintenance). As will be discussed further in Chapter 4, their prospective benefits nearly all involve public goods (fewer local emissions, potentially lower carbon emissions, reduced dependency on oil). One possible exception to this (perhaps of most interest to fleet owners with predictable travel demands) is that FCVs could be 'plugged into' the grid at times of peak power demand and premium-rate electricity costs, and earn thereby an income stream.

Other driver concerns explored by Agnolucci (2006) and in Chapter 4 are infrastructure requirements (affecting the convenience and required time for refuelling), costs, image and safety. If infrastructure is to be provided incrementally, as seems likely (see above), then FCVs are likely to start in fleets (e.g. buses, delivery vehicles) which return to depots each night, and which can be refuelled there, or with company cars and urban vehicles, which have a known route or operate in a certain area where filling stations are available. Leaving aside the cost of the FCV itself, and potentially lower maintenance costs, cost benefits from their use, especially when oil-based motor fuels but not hydrogen are subject to taxation, may derive from their greater fuel efficiency. However, fuel efficiency in itself does not seem to be a primary concern for drivers of ICE vehicles (Anable et al, 2006), and it is not clear why FCVs should be any different. It is possible that the image of a well-designed

FCV in an environmentally aware, technologically conscious society could be attractive. Safety, however, is more a risk factor for FCVs to be managed by the industry than a perceived benefit.

Other possible applications for fuel cells in vehicles are in boats, trains and aeroplanes (Hawkins and Hughes, 2006: pp22–23), and they may spur the development of fuel cells, but they have received much less attention than FCVs for road transport. However, recent reports indicate growing interest in the potential for fuel cells being used in boats and trains, due to less stringent constraints on space available for fuel storage than in road transport vehicles, as well as the anticipation of the possibility of tightening pollution regulations (Butler, 2008a and 2008b).

Conclusions on applications

A variety of different kinds of fuel cells are already commercially available in portable micro-electronic applications, as APUs and for stationary power. Whether they will become the dominant technology in any of these fields, and whether the FC concerned will use hydrogen or some other fuel, is still unclear. What is clear is that these applications in themselves offer few benefits beyond those to their private producers and users. It is possible that they may stimulate technological developments that have public benefits, such as FCVs, but this is far from certain, due to the different fuel cell designs employed in the various applications. They are not likely to get significant support from public policy, and will need to succeed in market terms.

FCVs are different, and have significant potential public benefits, in terms of reduced local emissions, potentially reduced carbon emissions (depending on the mode of hydrogen production) and reduced dependence on oil for transportation. They are therefore the hydrogen application that generates easily the most public interest and support. However, the discussion above makes clear that the private consumer advantages of FCVs compared to ICE vehicles seem thin, while the technical and economic challenges to be overcome for them to come anywhere near ICE vehicles in terms of cost and basic performance are very great. It is hard to avoid the implication that, if their development and deployment are to be as rapid and widespread as has been envisaged in some of the 'roadmaps' that have been produced (see Table 4.1, Chapter 4), then public policy will need to play a decisive and determined role over the long term. Some of the possible aspects of that policy support are discussed in Chapter 12.

Conclusions

There are many technologies which can produce hydrogen, many that can store and transport it, and many applications in which it can be used. Moreover, these technologies can be combined in many different ways to bring about a range of different hydrogen futures, as shown in detail in Chapter 5. It is not yet at all clear what combination of what technologies, if any, will deliver the private and public benefits that will be required for the mass diffusion of these technologies into society. Fundamental improvements in both cost and performance across the whole range of hydrogen technologies are still required for them to compete effectively in end-use mass markets, and to deliver the low emissions and energy security for which they are widely advocated. Achieving these improvements will require a greater commitment of public and private investment than has yet been forthcoming, and, in due course, long-term and credible strategies of market incentivization and enablement through determined public policy interventions. Different aspects of these topics form the subject matter of much of the rest of this book.

References

Agnolucci, P. (2006) 'Market Prospects of Fuel Cell Vehicles – A driver-based approach', UKSHEC Social Science Working Paper no 26, Policy Studies Institute, London

Agnolucci, P. (2007a) 'Hydrogen Infrastructure for the Transport Sector', *International Journal of Hydrogen Energy*, vol 32, pp3526–3544

Agnolucci, P. (2007b) 'Prospects of Fuel Cell Auxiliary Power Units in the Civil Markets', *International Journal of Hydrogen Energy*, vol 32, pp4306–4318

Agnolucci, P. (2007c) 'Economics and Market Prospects of Portable Fuel Cells', *International Journal of Hydrogen Energy*, vol 32, pp4319–4328

Amos, W. A. (1998) 'Costs of Storing and Transporting Hydrogen', National Renewable Energy Laboratory, Golden, Colorado. Available at http://www.nrel.gov/docs/fy99osti/25106.pdf

Anable, J., Lane, B. and Kelay, T. (2006) *An Evidence Based Review of Attitudes to Climate Change and Transport*. Report for the Department of Transport, Department for Transport, London

Arnason, B. and Sigfusson, T. (2000) 'Iceland – a future hydrogen economy', *International Journal of Hydrogen Energy*, vol 25, pp389–394

Balta-Ozkan, N., Kannan, R. and Strachan, N. (2007) 'Analysis of UKSHEC Hydrogen Visions in the UK MARKAL Energy System Model', UKSHEC Social Science Working Paper no 32, PSI, London. Available at http://www.psi.org.uk/ukshec/ publications.htm

Bossel, U., Eliasson, B. and Taylor, G. (2005) 'The Future of the Hydrogen Economy: Bright or Bleak?'. Available at: http://www.efcf.com/reports/E08.pdf

Butler, J. (2008a) 2008 Niche Transport Survey, Volume 1. Fuel Cell Today. http://www.fuelcelltoday.com/media/pdf/surveys/2008-Niche-Vol1-Free.pdf

Butler, J. (2008b) 2008 Niche Transport Survey, Volume 2. Fuel Cell Today. http://www.fuelcelltoday.com/media/pdf/surveys/2008-Niche-Vol2-Free.pdf

Cheng, S. and Logan, B. (2007) 'Sustainable and efficient biohydrogen production via electrohydrogenesis', *Proceedings of the National Academy of Sciences*, vol 104, no 47, pp18871–18873

Cherryman, S. J., Maddy, J., Hawkes, F. R., Hawkes, D. L., Dinsdale, R., Guwy, A. J. and Premier, G. C. (2004) 'Hydrogen and Wales', Hydrogen Research Unit, University of Glamorgan, Pontypridd, Wales

Cooney, M., Maynard, N., Cannizzaro, C. and Benemann, J. (2007) 'Two-phase anaerobic digestion for production of hydrogen-methane mixtures', *Bioresource Technology*, vol 98, pp2641–2651

Darnell Group Inc. (2003) 'Fuel Cells for Portable Power: Markets, Manufacture and Cost', Revised Final Report (4) for Breakthrough Technologies and US Fuel Cell Council, submitted 13 January 2003, Corona, California

Department for Transport (DfT) (2005) Transport Statistics Bulletin. National Travel Survey: 2005. Department for Transport, London

DoE (US Department of Energy) (2002) 'National Hydrogen Energy Roadmap'. Available at http://www.hydrogen.energy.gov/pdfs/national_h2_roadmap.pdf

DoE (US Department of Energy) (2004) 'On Board Fuel Processing Go/No Go Decision', DOE Decision Team Committee Report. Available at http://www1.eere.energy.gov/hydrogenandfuelcells/pdfs/committee_report.pdf

E4 Tech, Element Energy, Eoin Lees Energy (2004) 'A Strategic Framework for Hydrogen Energy in the UK: Final Report', E4 Tech, London. Available at http://www.dti.gov.uk/energy/sources/sustainable/hydrogen/strategic-framework/page26734.html

Eames, M. and McDowall, W. (2005) 'UK-SHEC Hydrogen Visions', UKSHEC Social Science Working Paper no 10, PSI, London. Available at http://www.psi.org.uk/ukshec/publications.htm

Eames, M. and McDowall, W. (2006) 'Transitions to a UK Hydrogen Economy', UKSHEC Social Science Working Paper no 19, Policy Studies Institute, London.

FutureGen (2009) FutureGen Alliance [Official Website]. Available at http://www.futuregenalliance.org/alliance.stm

Galindo Cifre, P. and Badr, O. (2007) 'Renewable hydrogen utilisation for the production of methanol', *Energy Conversion and Management*, vol 48, pp519–527

Guo, Z., Shang, C. and Aguey-Zinsou, K. (2008) 'Materials challenges for hydrogen storage', *Journal of the European Ceramic Society*, vol 28, pp1467–1473

Hawkins, S. (2006) 'Technological Characterisation of Hydrogen Storage and Distribution Technologies', UKSHEC Social Science Working Paper no 21, Policy Studies Institute, London

Hawkins, S. and Hughes, N. (2006) 'Technological Characterisation of Hydrogen Fuel Cell Vehicles', UKSHEC Social Science Working Paper no 22, Policy Studies Institute, London

Hawkins, S. and Joffe, D. (2006) 'Technological Characterisation of Hydrogen Production Technologies', UKSHEC Social Science Working Paper no 25, Policy Studies Institute, London

Hawkins, S., Joffe, D. and Hughes, N. (2006) 'Hydrogen Fuel Cells for Stationary Power: Technology Characterisation and Market Assessment', UKSHEC Social Science Working Paper no 24, Policy Studies Institute, London

Heinzel, A., Mahlendorf, F., Niemzig, O. and Kreuz, C. (2004) 'Injection moulded low cost bipolar plates for PEM fuel cells', *Journal of Power Sources*, vol 131, pp35–40

Hughes, N. (2006) 'Summary of discussions from expert stakeholder workshops on the economics of hydrogen technologies', UKSHEC Social Science Working Paper no 27, Policy Studies Institute, London.

HyWays (2006) 'HyWays – A European roadmap – assumptions and robust conclusions from Phase I'. Available at http://www.hyways.de/

IEA (International Energy Agency) (2005) *Prospects for Hydrogen and Fuel Cells*, IEA, Paris

IHS (2007) 'Honda Debuts FCX Clarity Advanced Fuel Cell Vehicle'. Available at http://auto.ihs.com/news/honda-fuel-cell.htm, accessed November 2008

ITM Power (2009) Company Website. http://www.itm-power.com/

Joffe, D. (2006) 'The potential for hydrogen production from waste in London'. Report to London Hydrogen Partnership. Available at http://www.london.gov.uk/lhp/documents/LHPReportFinal3LR.pdf, accessed November 2008

Joffe, D. and Strachan, N. (2007) 'Review of Modelling Approaches to the Development of a "Hydrogen Economy"', UKSHEC Social Science Working Paper no 30, PSI, London. Available at http://www.psi.org.uk/ukshec/publications.htm

Joffe, D., Strachan, N. and Balta-Ozkan, N. (2007) 'Representation of Hydrogen in the UK, US and Netherlands MARKAL Energy Systems Models', UKSHEC Social Science Working Paper no 29, PSI, London. Available at http://www.psi.org.uk/ukshec/publications.htm

Jollie, D. (2004) 'Fuel Cell Market Survey: Portable Applications', *Fuel Cell Today*, September. Available at http://www.fuelcelltoday.com/FuelCellToday/FCTFiles/FCTArticleFiles/Article_857_Portable0904.pdf

Logan, B., Call, D., Cheng, S., Hamelers, H., Sleutels, T., Jeremiase, A. and Rozendal, R. (2008) 'Microbial electrolysis cells for high yield hydrogen gas production from organic matter', *Environmental Science and Technology*, September 2008

McDowall, W. (2004) 'Promising Niches: a Survey of Early Markets for Hydrogen Technologies', October, mimeo, Policy Studies Institute, London

McDowall, W. and Eames, M. (2004) 'Report of the September 2004 UK-SHEC Hydrogen Visions Workshop', UKSHEC Social Science Working Paper no 9, PSI, London. Available at http://www.psi.org.uk/ukshec/publications.htm

McDowall, W. and Eames, M. (2006) 'Forecasts, scenarios, visions, backcasts and roadmaps to the hydrogen economy: A review of the hydrogen futures literature', *Energy Policy*, vol 34, no 11, July, pp1236–1250

Melaina, M. (2003) 'Initiating hydrogen infrastructures: preliminary analysis of a sufficient number of initial hydrogen stations in the US', *International Journal of Hydrogen Energy*, vol 28, pp743–755

Miliband, E. (2009) 'Carbon Capture and Storage', statement by Ed Miliband to the House of Commons, 23 April 2009. Available at http://www.decc.gov.uk/en/content/cms/news/090423_ccs_sta/090423_ccs_sta.aspx

Mori, D. and Hirose, K. (2009) 'Recent challenges of hydrogen storage technologies for fuel cell vehicles', *International Journal of Hydrogen Energy*, vol 34, no 10, May, pp4569–4574

NRC (National Research Council) (2005) *Review of the Research Program of the FreedomCar and Fuel Partnership*, National Academies Press, Washington, DC

NRC and NAE (National Research Council and National Academy of Engineering) (2004) *The Hydrogen Economy: Opportunities, Costs, Barriers, and R&D Needs*, The National Academies Press, Washington DC

Ogden, J. M. (1999) 'Prospects for building a hydrogen energy infrastructure', *Annual Review of Energy and the Environment*, vol 24, no 1, pp227–279

Padró, C. and Putsche, V. (1999) 'Survey of the Economics of Hydrogen Technologies', National Renewable Energy Laboratory, Colorado. Available at http://www.nrel.gov/docs/fy99osti/27079.pdf

Rozendal, R. A., Jeremiasse, A. W., Hamelers, H. V. M. and Buisman, C. J. N. (2008) 'Hydrogen production with a microbial biocathode', *Environ. Sci. Technol.*, vol 42, pp629–634

Satyapal, S. (2008) 'Hydrogen Storage Sub-Program Overview', US DoE Hydrogen Program (2008) Progress Report, Section IV. Available at http://www.hydrogen.energy.gov/annual_progress08_storage.html#f

Satyapal, S., Petrovic, J., Read, C., Thomas, G. and Ordaz, G. (2007) 'The US Department of Energy's national hydrogen storage project: progress towards meeting hydrogen powered vehicle requirements', *Catalysis Today*, vol 120, pp246–256

Sigfusson, T. I. (2007) 'Hydrogen Island: the story and motivations behind the Icelandic hydrogen society experiment', *Mitigation and Adaptation Strategies for Global Change*, vol 12, pp407–418

Smith, A. F. G. and Newborough, M. (2004) *Low-Cost Polymer Electrolysers and Electrolyser Implementation Scenarios for Carbon Abatement*. Report to the Carbon Trust and ITM-Power PLC

Strachan, N., Kannan, R., Balta-Ozkan, N. and Pye, S. (2006) 'First and Second Interim Reports on the Updated UK MARKAL Energy Systems Model', UKERC (UK Energy Research Centre) Working Paper. Available at www.ukerc.ac.uk/content/view/142/112

TIAX (2005) 'Cost analysis of PEM fuel cell systems for transportation'. Available at http://www.tiax.biz/aboutus/pdfs/nrel_fnlrpt_093005.pdf

Woking Borough Council (2007) 'Woking Park Fuel Cell CHP'. Available at http://www.woking.gov.uk/environment/climate/Greeninitiatives/sustainablewoking/fuelcell.pdf

4
Hydrogen Markets: An Assessment of the Competitiveness of Fuel Cells

Paolo Agnolucci and Nick Hughes

Introduction

Several contributions (e.g. NRC and NAE, 2004; Ogden et al, 2004; Hisschemöller et al, 2006; Solomon and Banerjee, 2006) have assessed the possibility and desirability of a 'hydrogen economy' and the costs that might be involved. For the transition to hydrogen and fuel cells to occur in a largely market-based economy, these technologies must compete effectively with the fossil-fuel alternatives (NRC and NAE, 2004).

The prospects for hydrogen technologies to achieve comparable performance with incumbent technologies have been discussed in Chapter 3. This chapter starts from a different perspective, with the assumption that if market drivers were strong enough, the technical barriers to deployment would be overcome by private technology developers. It therefore focuses on the potential barriers to the market apart from those specifically associated with hydrogen technology development, as well as assessing what additional features hydrogen technologies could offer to consumers, if successfully developed, and the extent to which such features may (or may not) distinguish them from other, potentially competing, technologies.

As is noted in Chapter 3 and throughout this book, a hydrogen economy might take many forms and involve many different kinds of technologies. However, one of the most important enabling end-use technologies for the diffusion of hydrogen as an energy vector is the fuel cell. This is because although hydrogen can deliver energy in internal combustion engines, the greater efficiency of the fuel cell is likely to be a vital benefit to partially offset the efficiency losses involved in hydrogen production and distribution (as discussed in Chapter 3). Hence, as a means to understand more clearly the market potential of hydrogen energy, this chapter focuses on several market applications of fuel cells. It must of course be recognized that, depending on their design, fuel cells can also operate using other fuels than hydrogen – notably natural gas and methanol. Hence a demand for fuel cells does not necessarily correspond to a demand for hydrogen. However, for the reasons of efficiency mentioned above, the link between fuel cells and hydrogen is usually considered reasonably strong, and it could be argued that even fuel cells which initially run on fossil fuels could become a transitional stage to the use of hydrogen in fuel cells. The strength of this assertion will be considered in this chapter.

This chapter discusses three markets for fuel cells. The first and second, microfuel cells and auxiliary power units (APUs), are likely to be two of the earliest applications for these technologies. The third, for vehicle transportation, is the one which has achieved far more attention within government policy documents and roadmaps, due to its considered potential to meet high-level 'public good' objectives such as emissions reduction and security of supply.

From an economic point of view (see Figure 4.1), the demand for fuel cells can be considered a 'derived demand'.[1] Because fuel cells will be embedded in other products (e.g. mobile phones, laptops, vehicles), the demand for fuel cells will partially depend on the demand for those products. The fuel cells themselves provide the energy source for these products, which delivers the energy services (radio waves, electric power, mobility) that enable the product to function and deliver the desired services to consumers. The demand for fuel cells therefore depends on two demands: the demand for an energy source; and the demand for the product which it powers. Fuel cells will need to compete with other energy sources, and the products they power will need to compete with other products that deliver similar or substitute services. The competition will be won by the energy sources and associated products which perform best in meeting consumer preferences.

This chapter analyses the potential for fuel cells to satisfy consumer demands in each of the three markets, and evaluates the potential for fuel cells to penetrate in each of the markets, considering what other factors might influence this penetration, and what the overall benefits of fuel cell penetration in the different markets would be. A caution is in order here. Market prospects in an area like hydrogen applications can change quickly, and existing data are both difficult to access comprehensively (because of understandable commercial considerations) and open to different interpretations (perhaps based on privately held data that are not widely accessible). The fact that there is considerable private research and development in hydrogen applications means that some investors consider it a reasonable commercial prospect, and those at the cutting edge of commercialization obviously have an interest in

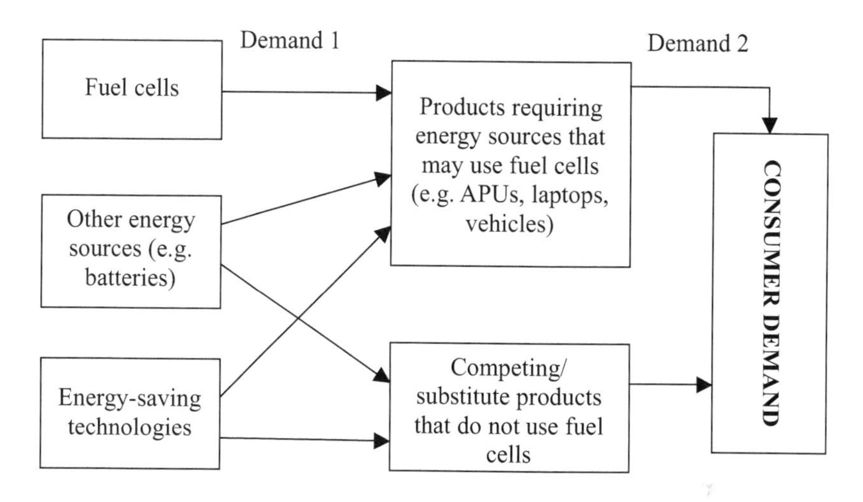

Figure 4.1 *Schematic representation of the derived demand for fuel cells*

talking up this prospect. What follows is our considered independent judgement of market potential, but it is a snapshot of a fast-moving field and should be read as such, rather than as a cast-iron prognosis.

Portable fuel cells

As outlined in Chapter 3, a major potential market for portable fuel cells would be to replace batteries in portable electronic devices such as laptops and mobile phones, with the attraction of offering greater amounts of energy storage. The competitiveness of portable fuel cells is therefore normally championed on the basis of the growing power needs of such portable electronic devices. Portable fuel cells are considered by some (e.g. Neah (2005)) as the technology capable of filling the 'power gap', that is, the difference between the power demanded by customers and that provided by current portable energy storage technologies. The power gap is allegedly due to: (i) the increasing average power demand of electronic devices; (ii) the increasing dependency of users on these devices; (iii) the increased amount of time spent by users without having access to electricity sources and (iv) the diffusion of wireless connectivity.

However, despite the optimism of some in the portable fuel cell industry, at the moment there is no evidence that the limited battery lives of some consumer products is hindering their adoption. For example, according to the technical details published by the manufacturer, the batteries of the new 3G iPhone can provide up to five hours' talk time or internet use when on 3G, and about ten and 30 hours of video and audio playback, respectively. Similar battery life can be seen in the BlackBerry Storm, while the Nokia E71 clocks about ten hours' talk time. While the limited battery life does not seem to have prevented customers from embracing these new handsets, it is also interesting to notice that the battery lives above are much shorter than those in some of the most advanced handsets available on the market only a couple of years ago.[2] This suggests that while the power gap is probably important, consumers are ready to trade-off extended power in their handsets with slicker and less bulky design.

At the same time, it is also unclear whether there will be a strong user-demand for all the sophisticated high energy-consuming applications that are becoming available. Demand for video-calling seems to have been rather modest so far, at least in Europe and the US, probably due to its costs. The demand for energy services must also be analysed in conjunction with the amount of time spent by users without access to an electric plug. While users might tend to spend more time out of their homes, this does not imply being far from electric plugs, as AC sources are available in offices, and increasingly in a range of other potential 'mobile office' locations, including in coffee shops and on board trains. As hours at night can be used to charge the batteries of electronic devices, users have no urgent need to replace batteries, if the daily consumption of power by electronic devices does not exceed the amount of power which can stored by batteries and if they remember to plug in their handsets at night.

In the case of laptops, it is often pointed out that batteries cannot power these devices for an ordinary eight-hour working day, although some devices are approaching this threshold (e.g. Toshiba's Tecra M1 and Samsung's P30 MVC 1500). IBM's Centrino technology has contributed to a remarkable extension of battery life. On the other hand, wi-fi shortens the time a laptop can run on its batteries, as the technology requires a considerable amount of power (Darnell, 2003; Anon, 2004a). However, although wi-fi was supposed to provide internet access at cafés or airports, the so-called hot-spot market is just a small share of all wi-fi applications: in the US there are millions of private wi-fi access points, in homes and offices, and a mere 3,400 public ones (Anon, 2003a). Once again, in homes and offices, portable fuel cells face competition from electric plugs. Overall, consumers do not yet seem to have bought into the potential of wi-fi technology for providing casual, on-the-run access to the internet. A much more promising avenue for portable fuel cells seems to be the broadband mobile services recently introduced in most European markets (Anon, 2007). A rapid uptake of this service could result in increasing portable power storage needs of the kind which could see significant demand for portable fuel cells.

It should be acknowledged that apart from the development of novel portable energy storage technologies such as fuel cells, an alternative way of bridging the 'power gap' is to reduce the energy demand of portable devices through incorporating energy-saving technologies in their designs. For example, Intel has announced that they intend to deliver a factor 10 breakthrough, that is, reduce energy consumption ten-fold or increase by ten times the performance of today's products (Anon, 2005a). Intel has also presented a polysilicon screen that consumes one-fifth of the current displays (Anon,

2003b). The strategy adopted by Intel clearly shows that fuel cells are not perceived as a panacea for the energy needs experienced by the laptop industry, as sometimes stated by fuel cells' advocates. While investing in some fuel cell start-up companies (PolyFuel and Neah Power Systems), Intel has also invested in firms pursuing other technologies which supply energy services (Zinc Matrix Power Inc. and cap-XX) (Anon, 2004b, 2005b), in addition to the power-saving technologies mentioned above.

On the positive side, some customers could be attracted by the fact that when using portable fuel cells, they will not need to charge their devices as often as experienced today. The longer time allowed between recharging could induce them to adopt fuel cells (Hughes, 2006). While the introduction of the latest additions to mobile technologies has been met with somewhat lukewarm enthusiasm in Europe and the US, a different perspective seems to be predominant in Asian markets, such as Japan and Korea. In these countries there is a significant demand for mobile technologies requiring a considerable amount of energy, such as videocalling, mobile TV etc. Fuel cells might substitute for the external chargers reported to be sold in those markets. In most OECD countries, microfuel cells are likely to supersede batteries only when they become user-friendly, small, reliable and cost as much as batteries, and *not* only when they provide a higher quantity of energy services. However, prospects for fuel cells might be better in Asian countries, where the so-called power gap seems to be more urgently felt by consumers (Hughes, 2006). If proved successful in that market, it is conceivable that portable fuel cells could be adopted in countries which currently feel the power gap less urgently.

Costs and market forecasts

Cost and market analysis for portable fuel cells is very difficult to locate in the literature, most likely due to the commercial interests surrounding the technology. Although the cost of batteries is high, fuel cells are currently much more expensive than rechargeable batteries (Anon, 2003a) and will likely continue to be so in the near future. Earlier figures on the cost of fuel cells, like those in Darnell (2003), tended to be rather optimistic (Hughes, 2006). More recent figures have tended to be higher, arguably a sign of increased realism in the industry. Similarly, earlier market forecasts on the introduction of fuel cells have been generally very optimistic. Allied Business Intelligence projected 200 million units sold by 2007 (quoted in Chang, 2001), although the number of laptops projected to be sold with integrated fuel cells was later scaled down to 2,000 by 2004 (quoted in Abreu, 2003). In 2005, Allied Business Intelligence announced that another 18–24 months would be needed (mid-2006/early 2007) to bring early, limited units to specified customers. In fact, Butler (2009) reports that around 9,000 units were shipped in the portable fuel cell sector in 2008 and forecast a similar amount for 2009. Unfortunately, while shipments trebled between 2006 and 2007, they have been fairly stable since then. It is also interesting to notice that the majority of these shipments were fuel cell toys and demonstration kits; only a handful of units were developed in the consumer electronics space, and these are largely still pre-commercial beta units. No laptops with integrated fuel cell systems have been sold. Butler (2009) concludes that 2008 did not live up to be quite the breakthrough year that had been widely expected, although he expected 2009 to be a key year, in particular predicting the commercial roll-out of DMFC battery chargers by one or more companies.

Commercialization strategies

Portable fuel cells can be commercialized either as external chargers for conventional batteries, therefore creating hybrid (batteries/fuel cells) systems, or as part of the electronic products. Introducing hybrid systems has some appeal, as they provide revenues for the R&D needed to further squeeze the size of the cells. In addition, they do not expose fuel cells to a premature competition with the battery industry. It is interesting to notice that small start-ups, like Medis Technologies, are focusing exclusively on external chargers. However, as external chargers imply carrying small devices additional to batteries, they are more likely to become a niche product sold to consumers experiencing a compelling demand for energy services. A relatively bulky product or a higher retail price will not put these users off, although Baker et al (2005) and Jollie (2004) are sceptical about the future sales of external chargers and their ability to bring about the economies of scale needed to reduce costs, or the revenues needed to fund further R&D. The 24/7 Xtreme Portable Power Solution and related products commercialized by Medis Technology are an example of this strategy. This product is being marketed at around $40 for the starter kit, followed by $20 for replacement packs. Replacement and recycling of spent fuel cartridges is undertaken by mail between the company and its customers (LaMonica, 2008). As the company has secured a wide commercialization network, although on-line only (Anon, 2009), the response of the customers will probably be an important indicator to gauge the interest in portable FCs as a whole.

Unlike small start-ups, big manufacturers, funding their R&D activities from their balance sheets, have tended to focus on fuel cells incorporated into consumer products. As in the case of small start-ups, a number of big manufacturers (e.g. Toshiba and NEC), have postponed market introductions of fuel cell products. These postponements, although perhaps disappointing, should be seen from the perspective of large companies which, like those mentioned above, have very wide product ranges and do not need revenues from sales for further fuel cell R&D (Hughes, 2006). More recently, a number of big manufacturers including Toshiba and Sony have been reported to be now focused on employing fuel cells as an external charging device (Butler, 2009). This move away from ambitious plans for integrated fuel cells has been noticed in the laptop, as well as the headset market. Further delays in the launch of these devices have also occurred. For example, Toshiba announced that its external charger would be launched in March 2009, although it later said that it would delay sales of the charger due to issues in supply chains.

Considering the impact that marketing a faulty product can have on the brand, it seems reasonable for big manufacturers to introduce the new technology only after acquiring full confidence in its reliability. On the other hand, the numerous delays and false dawns in the commercialization process, and the fact that a number of small start-ups have either gone bust (Millennium Cell), or have been de-listed from stock exchanges or are preparing to take this step (CMR Fuel Cells, Medis Technologies and MTI Micro), due to considerable falls in their share prices,[3] makes us wonder if the issues which have to be overcome to launch a successful portable fuel cell on the market turned out to be much more challenging than those anticipated by many industrial players and commentators.

Currently, it appears that external chargers are closer to commercial roll-out than fuel cells directly integrated within appliances themselves. It might be argued that external chargers would not be convenient enough for average users of appliances, and thus would be restricted to niches of particularly power-hungry professional users such as news teams on outside broadcasts (Ross, 2008). The prospect of portable fuel cells integrated into electronic devices to directly replace lithium ion batteries would seem to offer a more likely route to mass markets, but the challenges of 'miniaturization, system integration, fluid management and cost' have so far prevented any commercial roll-out of portable fuel cells integrated within electronic devices (Butler, 2009).

Fuels

Though Butler (2009) reports that approximately two-thirds of portable FCs shipped in 2008 were PEMFCs, thus running on hydrogen, it seems that most of these were for fuel cell toys or demonstration kits, such as the Horizon fuel cell toy car (Horizon, 2009). The potentially more long-term and substantial market of consumer electronics units is dominated by DMFC technology – the reduced balance of plant requirements of this kind of fuel cell are an advantage at small scale. Medis Technology's 24/7 Power Pack range operate on a sodium borohydride solution, which the company provides directly to the customer through mail order (LaMonica, 2008). Lilliputian Systems is intending to release an SOFC external charger that will run on butane, a widely available fuel used in cigarette lighters, cooking and camping devices (Butler, 2009).

Auxiliary power units

Auxiliary power units (APUs) are considered an interesting early application for FCs. Rather than replacing the main internal combustion engine (ICE) as a source of propulsion for a vehicle, in this market FCs would provide power and heat for on-board services, such as entertainment, heating, air conditioning, and so on. APUs can improve generation efficiency, reduce emissions, extend the engine life and eliminate noise if power is needed when vehicles are parked. Lutsey et al (2003) identify a number of applications for FC APUs on board civil vehicles.

Less promising markets

Public transport vehicles such as buses and coaches do not seem to be a good potential market for FC APUs. On one hand, they have plenty of space and a plethora of entertainment devices to make long journeys more comfortable. Weight is also not a big concern. However, Stratanova et al (2003) concluded that APUs increase the use of fuel because engine idling during normal stop-and-go operations is nonetheless required when using FC APUs. Overall fuel consumption when idling an ICE and operating an APU is, in fact, higher than when idling the engine to supply accessory power in the conventional manner. Nor are contractor trucks and pick-ups likely to be a promising market for FC APUs. Pick-up manufacturers (e.g. Daimler, GM and Dodge Ram) intend to produce vehicles able to supply a considerable amount of power (Lutsey et al, 2003). As the load is normally needed when the engine would otherwise be switched off, an FC APU would have the same functionality and higher efficiency. However, considering the other options available (diesel generators integrated in the vehicles, portable generators and vehicles such as the Dodge Ram Contractor Special), and the fact that the silent mode of FC APUs is not likely to be much appreciated by contractors, the market prospects in this application do not seem that promising.

Specialized utility trucks are also unlikely to be a promising market. On the positive side, many of these vehicles use engines for power take-off devices which are normally used when the vehicle is stationary. However, FC APUs are likely to imply a high price per kW delivered, because the large range of power requirements means that manufacturers will be constrained in the use of mass-production techniques if they try to manufacture FCs for all specialized purposes. On the other hand, if they concentrate on large power applications only, users requiring smaller systems will need to buy over-rated devices. Even if FC APUs with different power rates are produced, it is not clear whether APUs are suited for specialized utility vehicles, as some of these devices are used sporadically. Finally, refrigeration vehicles are not likely to be a promising market. Medium and heavy-duty units use separate engine compressors with highly efficient operation ranges (Lutsey et al, 2003). Therefore, potential emissions and fuel savings from FC APUs are going to be limited.

More promising markets

Navigation information systems, heated seats, entertainment devices and the substitution of mechanical and hydraulic subsystems by electric systems have contributed to the increased demand for on-board power, especially in luxury cars. FC APUs are an appropriate power source only for those devices, requiring more-or-less constant power for a considerable amount of time. According to Lutsey et al (2003), this corresponds to a load of about 5–6kW. Some scepticism about the need for new power sources can, however, be found in the literature (Meissner and Richter, 2003). In fact, several of the new functions, especially those providing improved reliability and comfort, can be satisfied by existing 14V electrical systems (Meissner and Richter, 2001). Although higher electrical loads are being demanded when the engine is off or idling, the authors are confident that modifications will be introduced in a stepwise fashion. It also seems likely that the case for FC APUs would be weakened by the diffusion of diesel or gasoline hybrids, as these vehicles have larger batteries. The market for FC APUs is likely to be limited, unless the price of FC APUs is comparable to that from competing technologies. At the early stages, only specialized vehicles, such as limousines, are likely to adopt FC APUs due to their driving pattern, that is, stop-and-go in city traffic, and the presence of several electricity-thirsty gizmos needed to provide entertainment for well-heeled passengers. The average owner of a luxury car might not feel an imperative need to buy an extra power source, especially if FC APUs take a considerable amount of space in the boot. On the other hand, as suggested by Kurani et al (2004), a growing number of car owners might be attracted by the optional entertainment devices that could be accommodated in cars. Intensive marketing of FC APUs by car retailers, or even better by car manufacturers, could make their sale prospects much more encouraging.

Law enforcement vehicles seem to be an attractive market for FC APUs. Firstly, power is required for specialized appliances, such as sirens, radios and computers. Secondly, they are likely to idle longer than conventional cars. Thirdly, the introduction of alternative fuels is much easier because these vehicles can be centrally refuelled. While policemen might not be very concerned about the loss of boot space to accommodate FC APUs, the use of APUs or the introduction of alternative fuels will be accepted only if the car's performance, in particular speed and acceleration, is not impaired. Law enforcement bodies could also be particularly sensitive to energy saving and emission reductions delivered by FC APUs.

Long-haul trucks in which drivers sleep overnight are probably the best market for FC APUs, because of the power needed for climate control devices and cab compartment accessories (Stodolsky et al, 2000; Little AD, 2001; Brodrick et al, 2002;). In most cases these needs are currently supplied by idling the engine. According to government statistics quoted in Stodolsky et al (2000), in the US drivers sleep in 450,000 trucks. On board long-haul heavy-duty trucks, FC APUs will compete with a number of partially established alternatives, namely direct-fired heaters (for heating only), thermal storage systems, ICE APUs and electrification of truck stops. Direct-fired heaters, which can be used to heat the cab and the engine, are lightweight and widely commercialized, although their diffusion is somewhat impaired by retrofitting costs and unknown reliability. Diesel APUs (a small diesel ICE with heat recovery), normally mounted externally on the truck cab, are available as an option on some trucks (Anon, 2005c). Thermal storage systems (TSSs) can provide heating and cooling, but not electrical power. Some truck manufacturers have recently started offering these devices as options (Anon, 2005c, 2005d). Finally, in the case of electrified truck stops, the trucker would simply plug in electrical devices into electric hook-ups.

An idea of the market for FC APUs can be obtained by comparing the payback period of an FC APU (i.e. the amount of time needed to recover the cost of the product), with the payback from the technologies mentioned above. The payback period of a certain technology is obtained by comparing its costs with those of delivering the same services with a conventional engine idling. Brodrick et al (2002) discovered that the average payback for an FC APU is 3.2 years, although they present a range of values, owing to the uncertainty about a number of parameters. Considering that the American Trucking Association desires a two-year payback on equipment purchases, the results are quite encouraging. If FC APUs are retailed on the basis of the technical and cost specifications used in the study, a $1,500 government incentive 'could reduce the payback period to the desirable 2-year timeframe' (Brodrick et al, 2002). While there are some reasons to think that Brodrick et al (2002) might understate the actual payback of FC APUs, the high retail price of diesel in 2008 (about twice the mid-range price used in Brodrick et al, 2002) could fully compensate for apparently favourable assumptions. On the other hand, the payback of direct-fired heaters, thermal storage, direct heat with storage cooling, ICE APUs and electrification of truck stops is much shorter (Stodolsky et al, 2000), although only the last two provide a range of services comparable to those from FC APUs.

Truck stop electrification not only matches the services offered by FC APUs – silent delivery of power included – but also offers additional services, such as wireless internet, movies on demand and interactive driver training programmes (FleetOwner, 2003), the demand for which is particularly strong, according to the US EPA (2005). Compared to APUs, electrified trucks have the disadvantage of forcing drivers to stop at determined locations. However, drivers are likely to stop at truck stops anyway because of the availability of services such as showers, laundry facilities and restaurants (Truck Research Institute, 1996; US EPA, 2005), and because of concerns about the safety of the carried load. One can conclude that there are serious reasons to think that sales for FC APUs in this market could be quite limited, if electrification of truck stops proceeds at a high pace. Increased interest in the electrification of truck stops is reported in DEQ (2004), FleetOwner (2003) and US DoE (2005). In addition, if the figures presented in Perrot et al (2004) are reliable, stop electrification is likely to become widespread, as the payback to the owner of the stops is about three years, based only on the supply of power. Revenues from other services, such as cable TV, telephone and internet, will reduce the payback period even further (FleetOwner, 2003). Currently, there are 108 electrified stops in the US Highway system using the services of IdleAire, the leading provider of truck stop electrification (Anon, 2007b). While it seems that European countries are not following the US lead in the deployment of this technology, no technological impediments can be foreseen in exporting electrified truck stops to other countries, provided that an opportune regulation limiting idling is passed by local policy-makers.

Perhaps the strongest market for FC APUs appears to be in providing ancillary energy services in large vehicles used for camping and leisure activities. Most caravan parks do not allow the use of diesel generators due to the noise from operation, but in these parks there are normally plenty of electricity plugs, therefore decreasing the benefits arising from FC APUs. Motor homes rather than conventional caravans could be a much stronger market for FC APUs, because these vehicles are often used outside camp sites (Hughes, 2006). As FC APUs on board recreational vehicles would rarely be used – due to the sporadic use of the vehicles themselves – one would expect owners to be very price-sensitive. On the other hand, holidaying consumers might be willing to pay a premium price for power in order to enhance their leisure experience. This might be particularly the case for users interested in remaining off-grid for longer periods. Butler (2008b) reports that whereas a standard battery in a campervan would typically have to be recharged at least every two days, a DMFC accompanied by a 10-litre tank of methanol could provide power for up to four weeks. An APU from Smart Fuel Cell (SFC) has been integrated as standard equipment in the S-class, that is, the premium line of Hymer vehicles, although it is only an option in all other classes (Adamson, 2005). SFC's cumulative sales of APUs for camping and leisure vehicles are reportedly now over 10,000 units (Butler, 2009).

Portable FCs and APUs: 'niches' contributing to a sustainable hydrogen transition?

As discussed in Chapter 2, the role of niches has been observed within past socio-technical transitions, as providing 'protected spaces' for technologies before they become widespread within the socio-technical regime. In the context of a prospective hydrogen transition, it is interesting to consider whether, if fuel cells were successful in the applications of portable fuel cells and APUs discussed above, they could grow from these niches towards a broader transition of sustainable use of hydrogen energy. An important factor to consider is the type of fuel cell, and the fuel of choice, being used in these various niche applications. APU markets are currently dominated by DMFCs running on methanol. Portable fuel cells are also increasingly using DMFCs, in particular in applications as chargers for electronic devices. In both markets, SOFC-based designs are still present, and have the potential advantage of being able to operate on a range of readily available fuels such as butane, propane and kerosene. PEM FCs using hydrogen account for a tiny proportion of APU devices. Though their share in portable applications is greater, they seem mainly to be applied to toys and demonstrations (Hughes, 2006; Butler, 2008b, 2009).

The hydrogen application which is often understood to be most synonymous with sustainable hydrogen energy use is that of vehicular transportation. The majority of designs for hydrogen fuel cell vehicles are based on PEM FCs (though there are some exceptions in niche transport markets (Butler, 2008a)). If fuel cells were successfully deployed in the niche markets reviewed, the technology choices summarized above make it seem unlikely that they would stimulate developments in and production of PEM FCs, or of the development of supply chains for the production of low carbon hydrogen. Moreover, as their market prospects are in general predicated on large increases in energy use, it is hard to see how they could in themselves constitute the first step towards a wider sustainable hydrogen energy transition.

There is significant technological separation between the various markets, in particular of portable fuel cell and APU markets, from the current predominant designs of fuel cell vehicles (FCVs). This means that apart from the possibility of some shared benefits in membrane and catalyst technologies, there would probably be limited scope for technological transfer from a successful uptake of portable FCs or APUs, which would benefit the potentially more significant market in terms of carbon reduction possibilities of hydrogen fuel cell vehicles (Hughes, 2006).

Fuel cell vehicles

A transition towards the large-scale use of hydrogen fuel cell vehicles for transportation appears to be a prospect that is valued by public policymakers across the world. Visions, policy plans and roadmaps for the rolling-out of a hydrogen economy have been drawn up by regional governments, national administrations and supra-national institutions. Selected activities at a variety of levels are summarized in Table 4.1. More detailed reviews and discussions can be found in Solomon and Banerjee (2006) and Hodson et al (2008).

As is clear from Table 4.1, in most considerations of hydrogen futures, a widespread penetration of hydrogen FCVs is considered central to realizing the social benefits of the energy carrier. The precise motivations for encouraging such a transition are numerous, and are emphasized to different extents in the different programmes. They include decarbonization of the transport sector, local air-quality improvements, economic growth and regeneration, and improving security of fuel supply. Quite clearly, the major perceived benefits of hydrogen transportation are 'public goods'. Correspondingly, the importance in the early stages of development of public funding for basic R&D, and a supportive policy environment, are usually stressed. However, ultimately, the roadmaps expect the majority of the innovation and development to be delivered by the private sector. Most of the activities described in Table 4.1 involve some form of public–private partnership, and assume that finite levels of public support will ultimately allow the private sector to deliver hydrogen and fuel cell technologies which are able to compete in the market place against other technologies. This expectation is perhaps most clearly embodied in the US DoE's series of performance targets, designed to deliver hydrogen technologies with equivalent performance to incumbent technologies

Table 4.1 *Summary of hydrogen policy plans and roadmap objectives in selected regions*

Region/country	*Key objectives or visions*	*Notes*	*References*
Iceland	All road vehicles and fishing fleet running on hydrogen by 2030.	Hydrogen produced from renewable energy (geothermal).	Sigfusson (2007); Arnason and Sigfusson (2000)
United States	Hydrogen to be cost-competitive in transport and stationary applications. Envisages FCVs breaking into markets in 2015 and accounting for 40% of annual sales of light-duty road vehicles by 2030.	Hydrogen produced from wide range of domestic energy sources.	US DoE (2002); NRC and NAE (2004)
European Union	Envisages a coordinated roll-out of infrastructure across the EU starting from 'early user centres'. Envisages 40–75% penetration of FCVs in vehicle fleets by 2050.	Production methods differ across member states, though sustainable (low CO_2) hydrogen a major objective.	HyWays (2008)
California	Provision of infrastructure ('hydrogen highway') for refuelling of hydrogen vehicles. Aiming for 50–100 refuelling stations, servicing 2,000 hydrogen vehicles by 2010.	Local air quality, public health and security of energy supply provide primary interests.	CEPA (2005)
Canada	To establish Canada as a world-leading provider of hydrogen energy technologies.	Focused on identifying strengths of Canada's H_2 and fuel cell industry and how to consolidate these, through demonstration projects and building supply chains.	Government of Canada (2005); CHFCC (2008)

Additional sources: Solomon and Bannerjee (2006); Hodson et al (2008)

by the year 2015 (DoE, 2006). However, if hydrogen FCVs are genuinely to compete in the market place, it is not sufficient for them to achieve equal performance to incumbent technologies – they would also have to offer significant additional attractions to consumers. This is particularly the case as existing transportation technologies and user practices are well established, and therefore extremely hard to uproot and replace.

Technological transitions and socio-technical regimes in transport

In the transport sector, current ICE technologies fuelled by petrol and diesel are both supported and 'locked in' by chains of technological infrastructure (manufacturing supply chains, oil extraction and export infrastructure, distribution and refuelling infrastructure) and by social conventions (expectations of vehicle performance such as range and speed, expectations of cost, and refuelling and servicing practices). These well-established networks of technologies and social practices have co-evolved over time, with the result that they now appear to provide the perfect 'fit' for each other. This reinforces the perception that a particular technology is the ideal solution to a set of incontrovertibly fundamental needs, making it extremely hard for any new technology with different performance characteristics and different associated behaviours to break in and substitute the existing technology. Frank Geels has called this mutually reinforcing set of technological and social practices a 'socio-technical regime' (Geels, 2002). As discussed in Chapter 2, Geels situates this socio-technical regime within a multi-level framework, of which the other component parts are the 'niche' level, where technologies may be used and valued by particular groups of users for particular reasons, which would not be held as strongly by the wider regime; and the 'landscape' level, which describes higher-level priorities and attitudes of society at large, as well as broader policy frameworks.

Major technological change can occur when technologies found in niches 'break through' into the wider regime. The Geels framework indicates that such a breakthrough can be stimulated in different ways. It may occur in a spontaneous, endogenous fashion, where the regime becomes aware of the value of a technology and the practices associated with it, which had previously been evident only to a small number of specialist users within a 'niche'. Hence what had previously been a niche technology becomes a mainstream one, 'disrupting' the regime and bringing changes to associated infrastructure and user practices, and ultimately feeding through to more fundamental 'landscape' changes. This process is broadly recognizable as the classic 'S-curve' model of technological change (see Figure 2.1), a notable recent example of which was the uptake of the mobile phone. Alternatively, a major shift in the landscape of broader social and policy priorities can cause a reorganization of regime values and needs. This creates new technological spaces in response to new social needs, allowing technologies which had previously been stranded within niches to 'rise up' into the regime level.

These two processes – disruption from the niche level or from the landscape level – have in common that they are both associated with a social value shift, though the order of causation is different. When a technology breaks into the regime from a niche, it usually contributes to bringing about a value shift through the new social practices it stimulates. When the landscape changes, a value shift occurs which itself brings about a demand for new technologies to meet new social needs.

Agnolucci and Ekins' (2007) location of the concept of 'values' within the multi-level framework is helpful in clarifying this. A technology can be successful in a niche if it satisfies well the values of that niche. However, the fact that it is successful in a niche and not in the wider regime indicates that the particular values of that niche are not held by the wider regime. It will therefore remain in that niche unless the values of the regime shift. This could happen either because the regime notices the values of the niche and spontaneously decides to adopt them, or because landscape pressures reconfigure the regime and effectively force it to accept those values. In either case a major value shift has occurred, emphasizing Freeman and Louça's conclusion that political and cultural dynamics are as important to technological change as science, technology and economics (Freeman and Louça, 2001).

Values, niches, regimes and landscapes in the context of fuel cell vehicles

The values associated with private car travel within the current regime may be said to include:

- speed and acceleration;
- minimum of 300-mile range per tank;
- safety;
- space for four passengers;
- attractive exterior design;
- affordability;
- on-board comforts (air conditioning, heating, music systems).

It may be that FCVs will one day achieve comparable performance to petrol and diesel ICEs on all of these parameters. However, as has been discussed, even this would not be sufficient to stimulate a major substitution by hydrogen FCVs of incumbent transport technologies, particularly when one considers the pre-existing social and technical infrastructure which supports and 'locks in' the latter. Hydrogen FCVs would have to offer 'new' characteristics which would satisfy values *not* currently held by the existing socio-technical regime, but which the regime *could be persuaded to adopt.* Such values might be:

- need for zero emissions;
- low noise levels;
- technological novelty.

As shall be seen in the ensuing discussion, there are some applications where for particular reasons some of the above values are already held, and where consequently hydrogen vehicles already appear to have good prospects. There are also particular applications where it is easier to see how policy interventions could create those kind of values.[4]

Understanding if and how such values could transfer from such 'niches' (though they may be very large, in terms of vehicle sales) to the wider regime is an important question – whether it could take place with the regime somewhat spontaneously developing the kind of values which FCVs are well placed to satisfy, or whether such values could only be engineered within the regime through landscape-level intervention.

It must also be acknowledged, in line with the 'twice-derived demand' for hydrogen discussed earlier, that even if such values were adopted by the regime, hydrogen and fuel cells need not necessarily be the only or best-placed technology to fulfil them. In particular, electric and battery-based technologies are ever-present competitors to meet more effectively the needs of the values on which the success of hydrogen depends.

The next section explores in some more detail the particular kinds of values which hydrogen FCVs may be well placed to satisfy, and analyses in each case whether there is any good case for expecting that such values may be more widely adopted in the future. The prospects are first considered from the perspective of the mainstream family private car, after which some other market segments and niches are considered.

Mainstream private FCVs

Potential advantages of mainstream FCVs

Efficiency

Fuel cells operate at a significantly higher level of efficiency than internal combustion engines – tank-to-wheel efficiencies for internal combustion engines are typically around 30 per cent, with hydrogen fuel cells achieving 50–60 per cent (Hawkins and Hughes, 2006). Evidently, in terms of expenditure, the efficiency of the vehicle is of no significance without considering the cost of the fuel. It might be argued though that the higher efficiencies of FCVs would improve their prospects for cost-conscious consumers even if the price of hydrogen fuel was higher than that of petrol. However, there is evidence that the actual cost of fuel at the pump makes the biggest impact in cost considerations of consumers, and that the factoring in of different engine efficiencies is rarely followed through in practice – the price difference between diesel-engined and petrol-engined vehicles has been considered one of the reasons hindering the penetration of diesels in the market (Greene, 1996; Cowan et al, 2003; Oertel and Fleischer, 2003).

There is not conclusive evidence as to the extent to which fuel economy influences purchasing decisions. According to the US DoE (2002), consumers rank fuel economy relatively low on the list of desired attributes for automobiles. Considering that for the average 1999 American car, fuel costs amounted to only 10 per cent of the annualized costs (Azkarate and Pelkmans, 2003), drivers' lack of interest is quite understandable.

With higher average fuel costs than the US, it might be expected that fuel economy would be a higher priority in the UK and Europe. Recently, there has been some evidence that fuel economy is influencing car-purchasing behaviour in the UK (Angle et al, 2007). On the other hand, a review of the evidence base on attitudes to transport and climate change suggested that while efficiency is sometimes expressed by consumers as a priority, often as a 'proxy' for environmental performance, its importance is ceded at the point of purchasing in favour of higher order preferences such as 'costs, performance, image, reliability, and safety' (Anable et al, 2006). While fuel economy may come to play an increasing role in car purchasing decisions, particularly with the roll-out of information campaigns such as vehicle efficiency labelling, it is currently unclear to what extent it alone can influence consumer behaviour.

However, it is quite interesting to evaluate which drivers might find cost savings arising from higher tank-to-wheel fuel efficiency of FCVs more attractive. Considering that 17 per cent of the energy in a tank goes wasted in idling (Azkarate and Pelkmans, 2003), urban drivers might be more interested in the adoption of FCVs. In particular, the owners of fleet vehicles could also see immediate benefits to the bottom line from reduced operating costs (Hughes, 2006).

In a context of generally rising fuel prices, a more efficient use of fuel can be an important consumer benefit. However, this is clearly highly dependent on how the cost of hydrogen would compare to that of conventional fuels, and only becomes relevant if, when efficiency is combined with the cost of the hydrogen fuel, it results in competitive operational costs in pence per mile.

While increased simplicity of FCVs when compared to internal combustion-engined vehicles (ICEVs) might not be very appealing, the reduced levels of vibration and noise could be of interest to customers. If the increased mechanical simplicity of FCVs translates into lower maintenance costs, cost-conscious customers and those driving a high mileage per year could be attracted by FCVs. This could also be perceived as a benefit for operators of fleet vehicles, for whom maximizing time 'on the road' is a major cost consideration (Hughes, 2006).

One potential benefit of FCVs could be the efficient on-board supply of energy and voltage for comfort load. However, it is not clear whether ICEVs or other technologies will be unable to accommodate higher demands for on-board power, as discussed above. The introduction of FC APUs could even hinder the diffusion of FCVs, as it would increase the potential power supply in ICEVs. The introduction in a limited number of European markets (e.g. in Italy) of the Smart ForFour DVD – an ordinary model with DVD reader and two seven-inch screens – shows that ICEVs may compete with FCVs even when the on-board load for entertainment and comfort increase.

Technological novelty

An attribute that might feature heavily in the advertising campaigns for FCVs is innovative design. Fuel cell technology allows developers and designers a great deal of flexibility because of the removal of the front engine transmission block typical of ICEVs. The components of the fuel cell system can be installed horizontally on the vehicle floor, while four electric motors can be placed in the hubs of the wheels (Oertel and Fleischer, 2003). General Motors has already presented a concept vehicle, AUTOnomy, implementing this approach (Burns et al, 2002).

The possible benefits, from a design point of view, of the flexibility of the arrangement of the power train system would be to offer quite different arrangements of the body of vehicle, opening up largely unconsidered opportunities for possible user advantages, such as the ability to switch between right- and left-hand drive, or fully opening sides for easier access for users with lower mobility (Hughes, 2006). However, it is not yet clear whether such potential advantages are likely to become important values for car users. Most recent fuel cell vehicle prototypes have returned to attempting to replicate standard vehicle types, some even situating the fuel cell system within the body of an existing model. Indeed, following their experiment with AUTOnomy, GM's latest fuel cell vehicle is housed within a body highly familiar to their customers, based on their Chevrolet SUV range (Hydrogen Cars Now, 2009).

Grid interactions

Another possible attraction of hydrogen FCVs could be their use as 'mobile power stations', using their fuel cell to generate electricity from 'spare' hydrogen and sell it back on to the grid at times of low supply. This possibility would be particularly relevant in the context of the likelihood of an increasing proportion of 'intermittent' or inflexible electricity generation capacity feeding into the grid, as the electricity sector is pushed to achieve stringent decarbonization targets. Vehicle owners would enter into agreements with electricity suppliers to make their vehicle available at certain times of day or night, to provide an agreed proportion of its full fuel tank for electricity generation and feed into the grid, if required. A large number of such vehicles would offer a highly distributed alternative to spinning reserve. Kempton and Tomic (2005a) discovered that plug-in vehicles are competitive for spinning reserves and highly competitive for regulation.[5] The benefits of plug-in vehicles to grid operators consist in substituting expensive generating capacity, which is currently used for spinning reserve and generation that sits unused most of the time. Owners of fleet vehicles are the most likely beneficiaries of the vehicles-to-grid (V2G) market, as their vehicles are used on fixed schedules that is, it would be relatively easy for fleet owners to guarantee the availability of their vehicles to grid operators (Kempton and Tomic, 2005b). This is particularly convenient for the introduction of FCVs, as fleet operators are also one of the actors which might easily circumvent the lack of an extensive infrastructure in the first years after the introduction of FCVs. As the spinning reserve and regulation market is much bigger than the capacity provided by fleet vehicles, owners of ordinary vehicles could obtain an interesting income stream from the V2G market.

This is perhaps the least certain of the potential consumer advantages of hydrogen vehicles. It would depend for one thing on a genuine consumer interest in being involved in such energy system interactions, which would be quite a shift from the current tendency of consumers to expect energy services to be delivered without their active involvement. It would also require significant regulatory interventions to provide sufficient financial rewards to be a truly attractive prospect, either to individuals or fleet owners. It would also be dependent on investment in infrastructure, such as the technologies to receive and monitor the feed-in of electricity from FCVs onto the grid, and on the future development of a more flexible distribution network with a greater ability to deal with highly distributed power flows. The need for grid management due to intermittency is itself dependent on very large penetrations of renewable energies actually coming on stream in the future, and a lack of reliance on other options such as spinning reserve or other kinds of storage. Finally, it must of course be acknowledged that in many ways a more obvious candidate for V2G services would be battery electric vehicles; hence, this cannot be seen as an advantage applying solely to hydrogen vehicles.

Barriers to mainstream FCVs

User practices

It is likely that the most significant market barriers for FCVs would be any changes in users' practices which would be implied by their diffusion. Clearly, technology performance targets such as those laid out by the US Department of Energy are aimed at delivering technologies which imply no change in user practices; that is, technologies which can entirely imitate, and thus directly replace, incumbents. However, it is clearly a possibility that hydrogen technologies could attain some of these performance targets, but not others. In such a case, the likelihood of hydrogen vehicle diffusion would be dependent on the extent to which consumers are flexible enough to accept reduced or different levels of performance in some areas, in exchange for any attractions or improved benefits in other areas (such as those discussed above). In particular, the penetration of FCVs is likely to be influenced by the time needed to fill up the tank (Oertel and Fleischer, 2003). The question of vehicle range is also crucial, and the prospects of hydrogen vehicles in mass markets are currently considered to be dependent on them being able to achieve a range between refuellings of at least 300 miles, with the reviewing committee of the US DoE's FreedomCar programme reporting hydrogen storage to be one of the 'greater risks for reaching the programme goals in 2015' (NRC, 2005). However, it is worth bearing in mind also whether for certain applications a lower vehicle range would be acceptable – this will be explored further in the next section.

Infrastructure

The availability of infrastructure is another major challenge to the diffusion of hydrogen vehicles. Particularly when competing against petrol and diesel ICEs for which refuelling infrastructure is so widely and readily available, the attractiveness of investing in a novel vehicle technology, when the possibilities for refuelling it are so uncertain, is significantly diminished.

The features of the infrastructure that are most likely to affect consumers' choice among competing powertrains are the cost and the density of filling stations. The former is important insofar as it influences the price of the fuel, and because the cost of converting filling stations to new fuels is likely to affect the speed of their diffusion. It is interesting to note that the density of filling stations in the early years after the introduction of FCVs could vary for different types of FCV. In the case of methanol, although current petrol stations would need to undergo some refurbishment due to the corrosive properties of methanol, conversion would be relatively inexpensive – Hart et al (2000) suggested a cost of about £30,000. It is likely that the number of methanol stations could increase relatively rapidly, if demand arises. As the conversion of a petrol station to dispense hydrogen is reportedly much more expensive (Wang, 1998), hydrogen fuel infrastructure 'is likely to be deployed gradually and be severely limited in the early years' (US DoE, 2002).

Such a gradual deployment of hydrogen filling stations could be perceived as a major barrier to some potential early users of hydrogen vehicles. Early adopters of FCVs would have to drive out of their way to reach the nearest fuel station. This could be particularly problematic for vehicles with low driving ranges, as it is not unlikely that fuel cell vehicles would be, due to the storage challenges described in Chapter 3. However, even assuming high vehicle ranges which would not limit drivers' mobility in absolute terms, drivers will nevertheless have to change the current casual approach to refuelling vehicles, that is, stopping when they see a station. While driving to the closest filling station may not be so inconvenient in one's own neighbourhood, driving in areas where the location of a hydrogen station is not known will be more challenging. However, as pointed out by Bevilacqua and Knight (2001) and E4Tech (2005), the diffusion of on-board GIS-based station-locating systems could easily tackle this issue.

It is interesting to analyse which users might be less sensitive to the lack of an extensive hydrogen infrastructure. The most obvious candidates are fleet (delivery firms, ambulances, police cars etc.) and bus vehicles which return to the depot every night. If a tank full of hydrogen is enough for the mileage driven daily, hydrogen infrastructure is relatively superfluous to these types of vehicles, provided that hydrogen can be produced at the depot. Other potential early adopters might be taxi drivers. As in this profession it is not uncommon to have social facilities visited by drivers once a day or more to enjoy a break, one could conveniently locate a hydrogen station near these premises. Company cars, which are normally driven within a certain area, are another potential early adopter because they can easily plan the refuelling and know the location of hydrogen stations. A vehicle which is used as a city car in a family would be in a similar position, although it might be subject to more flexible use. The vehicles mentioned above are important for the diffusion of a hydrogen infrastructure as their geographical concentration can guarantee an acceptable utilization rate of refuelling stations, therefore avoiding lengthy loss-making periods with under-utilized capacity. On the other hand, owners of the main family car may be particularly reluctant to buy FCVs as long as the infrastructure is not reasonably diffused, as they would not wish to be limited in where they were able to drive their vehicle.

It should also be noted that a possible technological breakthrough of a small-scale hydrogen production technology, such as small-scale electrolysis, could dramatically reduce the need for transmission and distribution infrastructure, potentially removing the question of infrastructure as a barrier altogether. As discussed in Chapter 3, such a breakthrough has been reported by ITM Power, though the market readiness of the application remains unclear (ITM Power, 2009).

Concerns about safety might also be a barrier to the take-up of FCVs. Although hydrogen can be considered a safe product in the chemical industry, completely different kinds of users will come into contact with hydrogen when it is used as an energy carrier. The extent of the problem is unclear. Thomas (1997: vii–viii) concludes that 'in normal operation FCVs should have less potential hazard than either a natural gas vehicle or a gasoline vehicle', while in a tunnel collision, 'FCV should be nearly as safe as a natural gas vehicle, and both should be potentially less hazardous than a gasoline or propane vehicle'. The greatest potential risk to the public could occur in the event of a slow leak in an enclosed home garage. However, Swain (1998: v) concludes that 'the use of passive ventilation is sufficient to prevent the accumulation of a flammable mixture of hydrogen'. Ricci (2005) considered that although past and current industrial experience with hydrogen cannot fully inform a comprehensive assessment of risks to safety associated with substantially different uses of hydrogen as an energy vector, it is very likely that any safety concerns will be tackled by either hydrogen producers or car manufacturers. In the case of methanol, safety and toxicity are still under discussion, although it seems that adequate measures and devices can tackle the major problems (Oertel and Fleischer, 2003). If the safety of the new powertrains is not comparable to that of existing ICEVs, FCV owners would face higher premiums for insurance. However, drivers are unlikely to buy a powertrain if they do not perceive it to be safe. Indeed, public focus groups on the issue indicate that consumers will tend to assume that if a product is on the market, it must *ipso facto* have been adequately tested for its safety to have been proven (see Chapter 11 for further discussion of public attitudes to hydrogen).

There are other institutional factors that are sometimes considered as having a potential effect on consumers' choice between ICEVs and alternative powertrains such as FCVs. It might be that availability of finance for novel technologies could be limited in the early stages. However, in the case of retail lenders, if the price of different types of powertrains is similar, it is not clear why financial institutions should be more inclined to lend money to buy one rather than another. There might also be some concern regarding limitations on parking of hydrogen vehicles, given that currently some underground parking facilities do not allow cars running on LPG to park, due to safety fears of escaping gas in enclosed spaces. It is possible that the same constraint might be applied to hydrogen vehicles, which could reduce their attractiveness to consumers due to the reduced flexibility. Discussions with expert stakeholders identified this as a potential problem, but by no means an insurmountable one;

the perception was that the early involvement of bodies such as the Health and Safety Executive in understanding and verifying the safety of hydrogen vehicles would be a necessary step prior to commercialization, rather than a stumbling block (Hughes, 2006). However, as shown by the experience of the ENV Bike, discussed below, regulatory procedures for new technologies can cause delays in bringing them to market which, depending on simultaneous progress in competing technologies, may have significant effects.

Competing technologies

Another important barrier to the diffusion of hydrogen vehicles which should not be underestimated is the potential for competing technologies to fulfil many of the key values which, if they became more prominent at the regime level, would provide important market pulls on which hydrogen commercialization depends. Perhaps the most important of these competitors is provided by battery electric vehicle drive trains, which have very similar attractions in many respects, including their zero emissions at point of use and the potential for grid interactions. Moreover, battery electric vehicles are already finding genuine commercial markets in certain key niche applications such as urban commuting vehicles – for example, it is claimed that there are currently 1,000 G-Wiz electric vehicles on the road in the UK (GoinGreen, 2009). Further, recent UK government proposals to offer purchase grants of up to £5,000 specifically for electric vehicles, as well as to invest £20m in building recharging infrastructure and undertaking pilot projects, seems to indicate a policy trajectory which would present additional challenges to the successful diffusion of hydrogen vehicles (Financial Times, 2009). In the US, the development of a policy trajectory away from hydrogen vehicles and towards electric vehicles is clearly discernible in the new Obama administration's decision in 2009 to cut $100m from the hydrogen and fuel cell research budget, and refocus the programme away from hydrogen vehicles and towards stationary fuel cells (Biello, 2009). At a similar time, the American Recovery and Reinvestment Act found $2.4 billion in funding for electric vehicles (DoE, 2009a), significantly overshadowing the $41.9m devoted to hydrogen and fuel applications (DoE, 2009b) – which did not include mainstream hydrogen FCVs.

The large auto-manufacturing companies continue to exhibit an interest in moving zero-emission vehicles beyond the niche application and into the mainstream family car markets; some companies favour the fully electric vehicle, while some opt for a hydrogen fuel cell drive train (though this is now increasingly supplemented by some form of battery storage, often making use of regenerative braking, to increase range). Recent developments indicate that, although these mainstream vehicles have yet to progress far beyond the prototype stage, there is evidence of genuine ongoing competition to fill a market space which it is anticipated will appear. In 2007, Honda launched its FCX Clarity. This employs a single tank of hydrogen compressed at 350 bar, but due to its regenerative battery system, its manufacturers are claiming it could reach a range of 270 miles (IHS, 2007). At the same time, strong claims continue to be made for the ranges of prototype electric vehicles – the Tesla Roadster is purported to be able to achieve 240 miles range, simply by being packed up with lithium ion batteries (Tesla, 2008).

In other words, both kinds of vehicles are nearing the kind of range which would make them viable direct alternatives to the mainstream family vehicle. From the perspective of hydrogen vehicles though, it is by no means clear that they will be able to decisively outcompete electric vehicles on the issue of range.

One way in which hydrogen vehicles may have a clearer advantage over electric vehicles is in refuelling time; there is some concern that the time taken to refuel hydrogen vehicles could be somewhat more than that of conventional ICEs. However, for gaseous storage, this is unlikely to be much more than ten minutes – less convenient, but a not inconceivable time lag for drivers to get used to. Battery electric vehicles, on the other hand, may take up to eight hours to fully recharge, potentially offering a clear advantage for hydrogen. Nonetheless, it is possible that developments in battery technology could erase this advantage as well: a Nevada-based company, Altairnano, have recently announced new nanotitanate technology which could allow very rapid recharging of electric vehicles (The Register, 2007).

Conclusions on mainstream FCVs

In summary, the prospects for hydrogen vehicles to penetrate within mainstream markets for 'family' cars are extremely challenging. It is hard to identify distinct values which could plausibly emerge to encourage the average consumer to favour hydrogen vehicles above conventional ICEs. The advantages of hydrogen vehicles in the context of such values seem particularly uncertain when the potential market barriers are considered, such as lack of infrastructure and potential behavioural changes required in their operation.

The value in view of which hydrogen vehicles would be seen to have major advantages over conventional ICE, would be the need for zero-emission vehicles: this would be a value under which conventional ICEs could not compete, but under which hydrogen vehicles could be well suited. Currently, if this value does exist, it is entirely as a public good, and thus cannot strictly be interpreted as a market driver for consumers.

It is not inconceivable that such a value could become a dominant one within the regime of mainstream car markets. Whether this could be achieved by an external, landscape pressure on the regime, through strong government-led policies on the markets, or through a more endogenous shift in values which creates a new demand for low-carbon vehicles in the regime, is an important question. However, it should also be acknowledged that should such a value shift come about, electric vehicles could be equally well-placed to fill such a space. Indeed, given that such vehicles are already commercially available in many zero-emission vehicle niches, and are now beginning to receive significant and directed policy support, it might be argued that they, not hydrogen vehicles, are in 'pole position'.

Niche applications

According to the characterization developed in Chapter 2, technologies can be developed and 'incubated' within certain 'niches', which have 'values' that are somewhat different or more demanding than those of the wider 'socio-technical regime'. If the values of the socio-technical regime shift to the extent that they resemble more the values of a particular niche, then the technologies that have been incubated in that niche have a good opportunity to break through into the wider socio-technical regime.

The market analysis of the prospects for hydrogen vehicles in main–stream 'family car' applications showed that the most important value the socio-technical regime would have to adopt, in order to create a real demand for hydrogen vehicles, would be that of a need for zero-emission vehicles. There currently exist some niches which already have a well-established value attached to zero-emission vehicles, because of the particular requirements of that niche. There also exist certain niches where, due to the public service nature of what is delivered, as well as the reduced numbers of actors involved in delivering them, it may be somewhat easier to 'prise in' a zero-emission value.

Forklift trucks

Forklift trucks (or pallet trucks), vehicles designed to perform heavy lifting of goods inside warehouses, have for some years been seen as a niche market of great potential for automotive fuel cells. Moreover, though it may be considered a niche market, it is one of some considerable size – approximately 350,000 forklift trucks are currently in use in the UK alone (Fork Lift Truck Association, 2008).

The incumbent technology for providing the powertrain for these vehicles is a lead-acid battery. This has been favoured because of the importance of having a zero-emission, low-noise vehicle for operation within an enclosed warehouse environment. As well as being well suited to equal performance in these two areas, it is claimed that fuel cells can offer the following additional attractive characteristics compared to lead-acid batteries (Butler, 2008a):

- longer running time;
- more sustained power (batteries lose power towards the end of their charge time);
- shorter refuelling time, reducing downtime;
- less space required for storing batteries;
- avoidance of disposal/handling issues.

Almost all of the companies developing fuel cell vehicles for this application are using PEMFCs (Butler, 2008a); hence, the success of this application would be likely to directly stimulate hydrogen production as well. The year 2007 saw significant progress in terms of commercial orders, with the Wal-Mart chain making purchase orders for forklift fuel cell power units from Plug-Power, following successful trials at two of the company's distribution centres (Fuel Cell Today, 2007). However, it is unclear so far whether such activity represents the beginning of a take-off for the sector, as Plug-Power's annual deliveries currently remain in the relatively small region of 'tens of units' (Butler, 2008a).

Nonetheless, the forklift truck application appears to offer evidence of a genuinely promising 'niche', where specific characteristics of the new technology can offer significant benefits over the incumbent technology – in this case, all the listed benefits are concerned with an increase in productivity for warehouse operators. The example also serves as a useful demonstration of the principle of the twice-derived demand for hydrogen. The first demand is that for a lifting vehicle, and was already present by nature of the application; the second is for an energy source to provide the power for lifting and mobility; the third is for a fuel source with zero emissions, because of use of the vehicle in confined spaces. It is the zero-emission feature of hydrogen energy, plus perceived advantages over purely electric drive trains, that has allowed hydrogen vehicles to become established in the market for forklift trucks.

Public transport – buses

The zero-emission characteristic of hydrogen buses, as in the case of the vehicle fleet as a whole, is a public good. However, in contrast to the mainstream private vehicle market, particular bus fleets are concentrated in particular and easily definable service areas, and if, not owned, are at least commissioned and regulated by public administrative bodies. This means that the potential prize of reducing local air pollution becomes much more tangible, and the means of 'prising in' the value of zero emissions through regulation becomes much more achievable, as it is potentially within the remit of a recognized public body.

This means that though 'zero emissions' is not currently a value of highest priority within the niche of public buses, it is much easier to see how it could be made so, and with what tangible benefits, than in the wider market of private vehicles.

The penetration of fuel cell buses within urban centres has so far been shown to be very closely linked to the extent of charismatic political leadership within the local administration in charge of public transport procurement. Motivations can include local air quality, but also relate to contributions to reducing carbon emissions, as well as a desire for self-styled 'world cities' to be at the forefront of new technological developments.[6] There is a clear public policy driver for local authorities to specify high environmental standards for public transport technologies, in order to improve the air quality of their local urban spaces. Buses are therefore thought to be important potential niche applications, as public policy objectives may justify investment even when more costly than alternatives. Moreover, predictable drive cycles and refuelling arrangements allow for a greatly simplified provision of refuelling infrastructure.

However, there is potentially a problem with stimulating mass production of units by manufacturers, while penetration goals set by local authorities remain somewhat low – London's goal for ten buses by 2012 seems unlikely to tempt manufacturers into setting up production lines. Nevertheless, joint procurement arrangements can help to address this. In this respect, the EU's Clean Urban Transport for Europe (CUTE) project can be seen as highly significant, as it brought together nine European cities to commission a total of 33 Citaro fuel cell buses. In an attempt to maintain the momentum of this project and to continue to generate confidence on the part of suppliers in the future existence of demand, a memorandum of understanding was signed in 2006 by representatives of Amsterdam, Barcelona, Berlin, British Columbia, Hamburg and London (HyFleet/CUTE, 2009), undertaking to share experience and engage in joint procurement. It remains to be seen whether such activities will generate sufficient confidence in potential suppliers of fuel cell buses, who have so far been reluctant to scale up production lines for uncertain demands (Hughes, 2006).

Light-duty vehicles

The use of fuel cell vehicles within light-duty urban delivery fleets would be dependent in the first instance on policy initiatives to create a demand for low- or zero-emission vehicles. The key driver for such policy action is likely to be air-quality concerns, and key instruments could be congestion or road-charging schemes, perhaps graded according to the environmental performance of the vehicle. It may be that in such a scenario FCVs would face fierce competition from other low-emission vehicles, such as electric vehicles. However, it is worth considering in this context the productivity benefits which apparently are being demonstrated by fuel cells over batteries in forklift applications. Given the comparable functions of materials handling and transportation, albeit over longer distances, it is not inconceivable that fuel cell vehicles would hold attractions to fleet owners over battery electric vehicles due to their potentially swifter recharging times and more consistent power output.

Boats

Discussions in Hughes (2006) observed that boats, particularly tourist recreational boats in capital cities, might be a suitable application, as their predictable drive cycles and tendency to return to a single point would simplify provision of infrastructure, in addition to the fact that their large size would make storage of hydrogen less problematic. In his review of fuel cell niche transport applications, Butler (2008b) argues that tightening legislation controlling emissions on inland lakes and waterways could provide an additional driver for this market, and for many applications the low noise levels would be additionally attractive. Further, the largely unregulated marine environment is now also coming under scrutiny through national and EU level measures, with the International Maritime Organization (IMO) also considering legislation to reduce emissions from shipping. All of this, Butler argues, could add up to a 'significant opportunity for fuel cells'. Currently, applications remain at the demonstration stage, such as the University of Birmingham's canal boat, the

Ross Barlow (University of Birmingham, 2009). On a slightly larger scale, though still essentially at the demonstration stage, is the Zero Emission Ship, or ZEMShip, produced by Proton Motor. This pleasure cruiser, which plies the waters of Lake Alster in Hamburg, is powered by two 50kW PEM systems and carries up to 100 passengers. It first sailed in 2008 and was scheduled to run for two years (Proton Motor, 2008).

Urban run-arounds

Another key market niche is felt to be that of urban dwellers who would be happy to own vehicles which are designed only to manage short distances, usually because they also own a second vehicle which is more suitable for long-range travel. Again, policy instruments such as exemption from congestion, road and parking charges could assist in making such niche vehicles more attractive. This is also the application where it is felt that aesthetic considerations may play most strongly, and where well-targeted, well-branded vehicles, particularly two-wheelers, which defy comparison with any incumbent model, could be successful in tapping into a 'style conscious' market segment (Hughes, 2006). Perhaps the hydrogen vehicle which most explicitly encapsulates this approach is Intelligent Energy's ENV Bike, a PEMFC powered motorbike whose slick design values are a real contrast to the almost defiantly 'dinky' look of the G-Wiz electric vehicles previously mentioned. In fact, Intelligent commissioned design agency Seymour Powell to produce the exterior design of the bike. The company has announced its intention to have the vehicles available for purchase in 2009, though the process of achieving EU regulatory approval is still to be negotiated. A retail price is not yet available, though the company hopes that they will be available 'at a competitive price' (Intelligent Energy, 2009). A new UK-based company, Riversimple, intends to launch a two-seater vehicle through a leasing rather than purchasing model, at costs to the consumer of around £200 per month plus fuel costs (Fuel Cell Power, 2009).

Conclusions on niche opportunities

All of these applications are dependent on some kind of 'landscape' pressure to re-orient the values of the transport regime, such that zero emissions becomes a priority value. Once this has happened, there will be competition to meet those low-emission transport needs between fuel cell vehicles and other options – in particular, battery electric vehicles. It seems clear that for more mainstream applications, battery electric vehicles are ahead in terms of cost, supporting policy processes and market positioning. However, there are arguments that fuel cells could outcompete battery electric vehicles on particular aspects such as recharging/refuelling time and evenness of power output, as shown by the interest in fuel cell drive trains in the well-established forklift truck market. It remains to be seen whether these attractions will stimulate a take-off in the market for fuel cell forklift trucks, and if so whether these attractions will be transferable to other applications. For boats, the problems of space taken up by hydrogen storage become less acute than on board smaller vehicles, which may open up opportunities for hydrogen fuel cells. In other niche markets, it may still be that the right image and a well-directed marketing approach could be enough to create a critical point of break-in for fuel cell technologies.

Conclusions on FCVs

The comparison of the prospects of fuel cell vehicles with those of electric vehicles assumes a primary demand for zero-emission vehicles. In order to bring about that crucial primary demand, a major shift in the values associated with car purchasing decisions would be required. Research into public attitudes to transport and climate change shows that despite the public concerns regarding the environment, these issues play little part in the car-purchasing process. While fuel economy is used by some car buyers as a 'proxy' for environmental performance, 'the importance attached to it drops off nearer to the purchasing decision ... in order to legitimise higher order preferences such as costs, performance, image, reliability, and safety' (Anable et al, 2006). Hence it seems that public environmental preferences alone are unlikely to create mainstream demand for more expensive vehicles. If such vehicles are to diffuse widely, policy incentives to improve their economic performance will be required.

A number of policies might be considered. Assuming FCVs run on hydrogen, a competitive hydrogen fuel price would increase the attractiveness of hydrogen vehicles – perhaps particularly for fleet owners, for whom running costs are a major consideration, but who may be more able to spread capital costs than the average private consumer (Hughes, 2006). Given the high efficiencies of fuel cells, a competitive fuel price may encourage users to calculate savings in running costs. Lower fuel taxes or reduced sales duties on hydrogen could facilitate this – however, if there was a major uptake of hydrogen it is unlikely that taxes would remain unapplied. On the other hand, for private consumers who are more sensitive to capital costs, purchase grants or reduced purchase taxes on the vehicles themselves could be more effective.

Incentives for FCVs might also be given by exemption from congestion or parking charges. It is important to note, however, that such policies would not necessarily incentivize only hydrogen vehicles. Indeed, in London, the only UK city to have successfully introduced a congestion charge, the exemption from it is a significant selling point for the electric and hybrid vehicles already on the market.

Conclusions

Portable FCs and APUs have the potential to make more spontaneous market breakthroughs in a socio-technical system similar to the current one, and thus are likely to be less dependent on policy support. The extent of their breakthrough is largely dependent on how exponential the continuation in increases in consumer demand for mobile energy proves to be. However, given this significant dependence on energy consumption growth, although in some cases these devices are likely to offer more efficient and less polluting ways of producing energy, they are unlikely to represent any major overall reduction in carbon emissions.

FCVs could have major environmental benefits. However, their benefits are entirely public and thus not sufficiently valued in the current socio-technical system to make a spontaneous market-driven mass penetration likely. A market breakthrough would almost certainly have to be driven by strong policy, in particular by the significant tightening of air quality and carbon reduction legislation to create a genuine demand for zero-emission vehicles. However, as has been argued, even if such legislation was enacted, hydrogen vehicles would then be competing against other zero-emission options, in particular battery electric vehicles. Although the emergent market interest in fuel cell powered forklift trucks, an application currently dominated by batteries, suggests that there may be characteristics of fuel cells which could allow them to be more valued than battery electric vehicles, the currently small levels of sales do not yet confirm this. Neither is it entirely clear whether the characteristics of fuel cells apparently valued in forklift trucks would transfer to other applications in similar competition with batteries. Meanwhile, as Anable et al (2006) report that 'image' is one of the higher order preferences of vehicle buyers, it may be that the high design values of applications such as the ENV Bike could be enough to influence a purchase decision being made between two zero-carbon transport options. The role of such cultural factors in technological change is sometimes significant. In this case they may yet spark – perhaps against the odds – a market breakthrough for hydrogen fuel cell vehicles.

Notes

1 Wikipedia gives the following definition of derived demand: 'Derived demand is a term in economics, where demand for one good or service occurs as a result of demand for another. This may occur as the former is a part of production of the second. For example, demand for coal leads to derived demand for mining, as coal must be mined for coal to be consumed' (Wikipedia, 2009.)

2 One of the most advanced handsets available on the market around 2006, the Sony Ericsson p910i came with a battery supplying up to 13 hours' talk-time and up to 400 hours' standby time.

3 On 21 June 2009, Medis Technology was trading at about $0.42, a quote which does not compare favourably to the $15 which two years earlier were needed to buy a share.

4 While it is acknowledged that in combination such applications may represent a very large potential market, such observations may blur somewhat the neatness of the distinction between niche and regime applications – nonetheless, the term 'regime' is maintained to signify the majority of transport applications, which must include personal transportation.

5 Spinning reserves are supplied by generators set-up and ready to respond quickly in case of failures. They would typically be called, say, 20 times per year for about

ten minutes, although they must be able to last up to one hour. Regulation is used to keep the frequency and voltage steady, as they might be called 400 times per day for a few minutes at a time. Spinning reserves and regulation are paid in part for just being available (Kempton and Tomic, 2005b: 282).

6 See, for example, the London Hydrogen Project: http://www.london.gov.uk/lhp/

References

Abreu, E. M. (2003) 'PluggedIn: laptop fuel cells – ready for takeoff', published on-line at www.reuters.com

Adamson, K. (2005) 'Fuel cell today market survey: niche transport (Part 1)', *Fuel Cell Today*

Agnolucci, P. and Ekins, P. (2007) 'Technological Transitions and Strategic Niche Management: The Case of the Hydrogen Economy', *International Journal of Environmental Technology and Management*, vol 7, nos 5/6, pp644–671

Anable, J., Lane, B. and Kelay, T. (2006) *Evidence based review of public attitudes to climate change and travel behaviour*. Report to Department for Transport

Angle, H., Brunwin, T., Gosling, R. and Buckley, K. (2007) 'Climate Change campaign benchmark stage: Driving behaviour and car purchasing'. Report by British Market Research Bureau (BMRB) to the Department for Transport

Anon (2003a) 'Hotspots and fries', *The Economist*, 27 March 2003

Anon (2003b) 'The shunning of 3G', *The Economist*, 18 September 2003

Anon (2004a) 'Untangling Ultrawideband', *The Economist*, 16 September 2004

Anon (2004b) 'New battery technology in development to potentially double laptop run times'. Available at www.zmp.com

Anon (2005a) 'Intel CEO outlines new platform directions'. Available at www.intel.com/pressroom/archive/releases/20050823corp.htm

Anon (2005b) 'Intel capital case studies – truly mobile power requires new approaches'. Available at www.intel.com

Anon (2005c) 'Western star'. Available at _tsi.expeditersonline.com/products.html

Anon (2005d) 'Western star improves interior details'. Available at www.roadking.com/inside/story273.php

Anon (2007a) 'Products and Services. Mobile Broadband'. Available at www.three.co.uk/personal/products_services_/mobile_broadband_/index.omp

Anon (2007b) 'IdleAire locations: ATE service locations'. Available at http://www.idleaire.com/locations/IA_ATE_active

Anon (2009) 'Where To Buy'. Available at http://www.medistechnologies.com/Default.aspx?SecId=53

Arnason, B. and Sigfusson, T. (2000) 'Iceland – a future hydrogen economy', *International Journal of Hydrogen Energy*, vol 25, pp389–394

Azkarate, G. and Pelkmans, L. (2003) 'New Passenger Cars: Economic Rates Evolution and Trends in Fuel Consumption and Emissions', in Pelkmans, L. and Christidis, P. (eds) *Trends in Vehicle and Fuel Technologies: Review of Past Trends* pp93–151 IPTS Technical Report Series EUR 20746 Seville, European Commission Joint Research Centre IPTS – Institute For Prospective Technological Studies

Baker, A., Jollie, D. and Adamson, K. (2005) 'Fuel cell today market survey: portable applications', *Fuel Cell Today*

Baratto, F., Diwekar, U. M. and Manca, D. (2005) 'Impacts assessment and trade-offs of fuel cell-based auxiliary power units. Part I system performance and cost modelling', *J Power Sources*, vol 139, pp205–213

Bevilacqua and Knight Inc. (2001) 'Bringing Fuel Cell Vehicles to Market – Scenarios and Challenges with Fuel Alternatives West Sacramento, October, CA: California Fuel Cell Partnership'. Available at http://ntl.bts.gov/lib/24000/24000/24071/ScenarioStudy_v1–1.pdf, 14 April 2009

Biello, D. (2009) 'R.I.P. hydrogen economy? Obama cuts hydrogen car funding', *Scientific American*, 8 May 2009. Available at www.scientificamerican.com/blog/60-second-science/post.cfm?id=rip-hydrogen-economy-obama-cuts-hyd-2009–05–08. Accessed 26 June 2009

Brodrick, C., Brodrick Lipman, T. E., Farshchi, M., Lutsey, N. P., Dwyer, H. A., Sperling, D. et al (2002) 'Evaluation of fuel cell auxiliary power units for heavyduty diesel trucks', *Transp Res* Part D, vol 2002, no 7, pp303–315

Burns, L. D., McCormick, J. B. and Borroni-Bird, C. E. (2002) 'Vehicle of change', *Scientific American,* vol 287, no 4 pp64–73

Butler, J. (2008a) '2008 Niche Transport Survey, Volume 1', *Fuel Cell Today.* Available at http://www.fuelcelltoday.com/media/pdf/surveys/2008-Niche-Vol1-Free.pdf

Butler, J. (2008b) '2008 Niche Transport Survey, Volume 2', *Fuel Cell Today.* Available at http://www.fuelcelltoday.com/media/pdf/surveys/2008-Niche-Vol2-Free.pdf

Butler, J. (2009) 'Portable Fuel Cell Survey 2009', *Fuel Cell Today.* Available at http://www.fuelcelltoday.com/online/survey?survey=2009–04/2009-Portable-Survey

California Environmental Protection Agency (CEPA) (2005) 'California Hydrogen Blueprint Plan', vol. 1. Available at http://www.hydrogenhighway.ca.gov/plan/reports/volume1_050505.pdf. Accessed April 2009

Canadian Hydrogen and Fuel Cell Committee (CHFCC) (2008) 'Hydrogen Portal: Moving Canada Towards a Hydrogen and Fuel Cell Future'. Available at http://www.hydrogeneconomy.gc.ca/home_e.html

Chang, H. (2001) 'Materials and design for small fuel cells; 600mW DMFRC cell pack and 200W PEMFC stack', in *Knowledge foundation. Small fuel cells and battery technologies for portable power applications.* Proceedings of the 3rd annual international symposium, 22–24 April 2001, Washington, DC

Cowan, R., Hultén, S. and Hmimda, N. (2003) 'The Introduction of Diesel Engines in Cars', in Pelkmans, L. and Christidis, P. (eds) *Trends in Vehicle and Fuel Technologies: Review of Past Trends*, pp186–197. IPTS Technical Report Series EUR 20746, Seville, European Commission Joint Research Centre IPTS – Institute For Prospective Technological Studies

Darnell Group Inc. (2003) 'Fuel cells for portable power: markets, manufacture and cost'. Revised Final Report (4) for Breakthrough Technologies & US Fuel Cell Council, submitted 13 January 2003, Corona, California

Defra (2007) 'e-Digest Statistics about Climate Change'. Available at http://www.defra.gov.uk/environment/statistics/globatmos/gagccukem.htm

DEQ (2004) 'Reduced idling at truck stops'. Portland, OR: Oregon Department of Environmental Quality; 2004. Available at www.deq.state.or.us/aq/factsheets/04-AQ-009_DieselTSE.pdf

E4Tech (2005) 'The Economics of a European Hydrogen Automotive Infrastructure', study for Linde AG, 14 February, London. Available at www.linde.com/hydrogen_flashsite_final/pdf/E4tech_hydrogen_study.pdf

Financial Times (2009) 'Electric car buyers to get £5,000 grant', *Financial Times*, 17 April 2009. Available at http://www.ft.com/cms/s/0/fb1643a6–2ae5–11de-8415–00144feabdc0.html

FleetOwner (2003) 'Turn idle time into cash. A how-to handbook on trading engine idle time for profit', Special Industry Report produced by the FleetOwner Magazine. Available at www.eere.energy.gov/cleancities/idle/trade_journal.html

Fork Lift Truck Association (2008) 'Saving Life and Limb (Literally)', 1 September 2008. Available at http://www.fork-truck.org.uk/safetyfinaldoc?p=1

Freeman, C. and Louça, F. (2001) *As Time Goes By,* Oxford, Oxford University Press

Fuel Cell Power (2009) 'Riversimple's strategy for hydrogen powered vehicles around the world'. Available at www.fuelcellmarkets.com/3,1,6250,1,28385.html

Fuel Cell Today (2007) 'Plug Power receives order from Wal-Mart', *Fuel Cell Today*, 23 October 2007. Available at http://www.fuelcelltoday.com/online/news/articles/2007–10/Plug-Power-receives-Wal-Mart-order

Geels, F. W. (2002b) 'Technological transitions as evolutionary reconfiguration processes: a multi-level perspective and a case-study', *Research Policy*, vol 31, pp1257–1274

GoinGreen (2009) 'Press Release: 75 miles with the G-Wiz L-Ion'. Available at http://www.autobloggreen.com/2009/03/24/new-lithium-ion-g-wiz-has-75-mile-range-15–795-price-tag/

Government of Canada (2005) *Charting the course: a program roadmap for Canada's transition to a hydrogen economy*, Ottowa, Government of Canada Hydrogen and Fuel Cell Committee

Greene, D. L. (1996) *Transportation and Energy,* Washington, DC, Eno Transportation Foundation, Inc.

Hart, D., Leach, M. A., Fouquet, R., Pearson, P. J. and Bauen, A. (2000) 'Methanol infrastructure – will it affect the introduction of SPFC vehicles', *Journal of Power Sources*, vol 86, pp542–547

Hawkins, S. and Hughes, N. (2006) 'Technological Characterisation of Hydrogen Fuel Cell Vehicles', UKSHEC Social Science Working Paper no 22, Policy Studies Institute, London.

Hisschemöller, M., Bode, R. and van de Kerkhof, M. (2006) 'What governs the transition to a sustainable hydrogen economy? Articulating the relationship between technologies and political institutions', *Energy Policy*, vol 34, pp1227–1235

Hodson, M., Marvin, S. and Hewitson, A. (2008) 'Constructing a typology of H2 in cities and regions. An international review', *International Journal of Hydrogen Energy*, vol 33, pp1619–1629

Horizon (2009) 'Horizon Fuel Cell Technologies – Toy Products'. Available at http://www.horizonfuelcell.com/toy_products.htm. Accessed 26 June 2009

Hughes, N. (2006) Report on the workshop 'Market and technologies for portable and APU fuel cells', London: Policy Studies Institute

Hydrogen Cars Now (2009) 'GM Chevy Equinox Fuel Cell SUV'. Available at http://www.hydrogencarsnow.com/chevy-equinox-fuel-cell-suv.htm

Hyfleet/CUTE (2009) Information Centre Public Downloads. Available at http://www.global-hydrogen-bus-platform.com/InformationCentre/Downloads

Hyways (2008) 'The European Hydrogen Roadmap'. Available at http://www.hyways.de/docs/Brochures_and_Flyers/HyWays_Roadmap_FINAL_22FEB2008.pdf

IHS (2007) 'Honda Debuts FCX Clarity Advanced Fuel Cell Vehicle'. Available at http://auto.ihs.com/news/honda-fuel-cell.htm. Accessed November 2008

Intelligent Energy (2009) 'ENV- Frequently asked questions'. Available at http://www.intelligent-energy.com/index_article.asp?SecID=104&secondlevel=106

ITM Power (2009) Company website, http://www.itm-power.com/

James, B. D., Baum, G. N., Lomax Jr., F. D., Thomas, C. E. and Kuhn Jr., I. F. (1996) 'Comparison of Onboard Hydrogen Storage for Fuel Cell Vehicles', Study prepared for the Ford Motor Company, Arlington, VA: Directed Technologies, Inc.

Jollie, D. (2004) 'Fuel cell market survey: portable applications', *Fuel Cell Today*

Kempton, W. and Tomic, J. (2005a) 'Vehicle-to-Grid Power Fundamentals: Calculating Capacity and Net Revenue', *Journal of Power Sources*, vol 144, pp268–279

Kempton, W. and Tomic, J. (2005b) 'Vehicle-to-Grid Power Implementation: From Stabilizing the Grid to Supporting Large-Scale Renewable Energy', *Journal of Power Sources*, vol 144, pp 280–294

Kurani, K. S., Turrentine, T. S., Heffner, R. R. and Congleton, C. (2004) 'Prospecting the future for hydrogen fuel cell vehicle markets' in Sperling, D. and Cannon, J. S. (eds) *The Hydrogen Energy Transition,* Burlington, MA, Elsevier Academic Press

LaMonica, M. (2008) 'Medis Power Pack: A fuel cell gadget charger', *CNet News*, 12 September 2008. Available at http://news.cnet.com/8301–11128_3–10039102–54.html. Accessed 26 June 2009

Little, A. D. (ADL) (2001) 'Conceptual design of POX SOFC 5 kW net system. Final Report to the Department of Energy', National Energy Technology Laboratory

Lutsey, N., Brodrick, C., Sperling, D. and Dwyer, H. A. (2003) 'Markets for Fuel Cell Auxiliary Power Units in Vehicles – A Preliminary Assessment', *Transportation Research Record 1842*, Paper 03-3443, pp118–126

Meissner, E. and Richter, G. (2001) 'Vehicle electric power systems are under change! Implications for design, monitoring and management of automotive batteries', *J Power Sources,* vol 95, pp13–23

Meissner, E. and Richter, G. (2003) 'Battery monitoring and electrical energy management – precondition for future vehicle electric power systems', *J Power Sources*, vol 116, pp79–98

National Research Council and National Academy of Engineering (NRC and NAE) (2004) *The Hydrogen Economy: Opportunities, Costs, Barriers, and R&D Needs*, Washington, DC, The National Academies Press, www.nap.edu

Neah (2005) 'The power gap'. Available at www.neahpower.com/powergap

NRC (2005) *Review of the Research Program of the FreedomCar and Fuel Partnership*, Washington, DC, National Academies Press

Oertel, D. and Fleischer, T. (2003) *Fuel Cells Impact and consequences of Fuel Cells technology on sustainable development*, *IPTS* Technical Report Series EUR 20681, Seville, European Commission Joint Research Centre IPTS – Institute for Prospective Technological Studies

Ogden, J., Williams, R. and Larson, E. (2004) 'Societal lifecycle costs of cars with alternative fuels/engines', *Energy Policy*, vol 32, pp7–27

Perrot, T. L., Constantino, M. S., Kim, J. C., Tario, J. D., Hutton, D. B. and Hagan, C. (2004) 'Truck stop electrification as a long-haul tractor idling alternative', Paper presented at the 84th transportation research board annual meeting of national academies, 11–15 January 2004. Available at www.epa.gov/otaq/smartway/documents/dewitt-study.pdf

Proton Motor (2008) 'First fuel cell ship goes into service'. Available at http://www.proton-motor.de/zem-ship-zero-emission-ship.html

The Register (2007) 'Quick charging electric cars could be round the corner'. Available at http://www.theregister.co.uk/2007/06/20/quick_charge_electric_cars/. Accessed November 2008

Ricci, M. (2005) *Experts' assessments and representations of risks associated with hydrogen*, UKSHEC Social Science Working Paper 12, ISCPR, University of Salford. Available at http://www.psi.org.uk/ukshec/publications.htm#workingpapers

Ross, P. (2008) 'Loser: Another Fuel-Cell Charger Flunks', IEEE Spectrum, January 2008. Available at http://www.spectrum.ieee.org/green-tech/fuel-cells/loser-another-fuelcell-charger-flunks. Accessed 26 June 2009

Sigfusson, T. I. (2007) 'Hydrogen Island: the story and motivations behind the Icelandic hydrogen society experiment', *Mitigation and Adaptation Strategies for Global Change,* vol 12, pp407–418

Solomon, B. and Banerjee, A. (2006) 'A global survey of hydrogen energy research, development and policy', *Energy Policy*, vol 34, pp781–792

Stodolsky, F., Gaines, L. and Vyas, A. (2000) 'Analysis of technology options to reduce the fuel consumption of idling trucks', Report ANL/ESD-43, Argonne IL, Argonne National Laboratory

Strategy Analytics (2004) 'Fuel cell disappoint a portable devices battery market surges to $9 billion by 2010', Boston, Strategy Analytics

Stratonova, M., Lasher, S. and Carlson, E. (2003) 'Assessment of fuel cell auxiliary power systems for on-road transportation applications', in US DoE, Hydrogen, Fuel Cells, and Infrastructure Technologies FY 2003 Progress Report, Washington, DC, US DoE

Swain, M. R. (1998) 'Addendum to Hydrogen Vehicle Safety Report: Residential Garage Safety Assessment', study prepared for the Ford Motor Company, Coral Gables, Florida, University of Miami

Tesla (2008) 'Tesla Motors'. Available at http://www.teslamotors.com/. Accessed November 2008

Thomas, E. (1997) 'Direct-Hydrogen-Fueled Proton-Exchange-Membrane Fuel CellSystem for Transportation Application – Hydrogen Vehicle Safety Report', study prepared by Ford Motor Company for US Department of Energy Office of TransportationTechnologies, Arlington, VA, Directed Technologies, Inc.

Truck Research Institute (TRI) (1996) *Commercial driver rest area requirements: no room at the inn*, Alexandria, VA, Truck Research Institute

University of Birmingham (2009) *Hydrogen hybrid canal boat: clean and silent propulsion for the Inland Waterways*. Available at http://www.original.bham.ac.uk/energy/news/hydrogen-canal-boat.shtml

US Department of Energy (DoE) (2002) *National Hydrogen Energy Roadmap*, based on the results of the National Hydrogen Energy Roadmap Workshop, Washington, DC, US DoE. Available at www1.eere.energy.gov/hydrogenandfuelcells/pdfs/national_h2_roadmap.pdf

US Department of Energy (DoE) (2005) 'Clean cities program – idle reduction'. Available at www.eere.energy.gov/cleancities/idle

US Department of Energy (DoE) (2006) 'Hydrogen Posture Plan. An integrated Research, Development and Demonstration Plan'. Available at http://www.hydrogen.energy.gov/pdfs/hydrogen_posture_plan_dec06.pdf

US Department of Energy (DoE) (2009a) 'President Obama Announces $2.4 Billion in Funding to Support Next Generation Electric Vehicles'. Available at http://www.energy.gov/news2009/7066.htm. Accessed 26 June 2009

US Department of Energy (DoE) (2009b) 'Secretary Chu Announces $41.9 Million to Spur Growth of Fuel Cell Markets'. Available at http://www.energy.gov/news2009/7262.htm. Accessed 26 June 2009

US EPA (2005) 'Truck stop electrification codes and electrical standards; notice of data availability [FRL-7783-3] – summary of comments'. Washington DC, US EPA

Wang, M., Mintz, M., Singh, M., Stork, K., Vyas, V. and Johnson, L. (1998) *Assessment of PNGV fuels infrastructure, phase 2 – final report: additional capital needs and fuel cycle energy and emissions impacts*, Argonne, IL: Argonne National Laboratory, Center for Transportation Research and Decision and Information Sciences Division

Wikipedia (2009) 'Derived Demand'. Available at http://en.wikipedia.org/wiki/Derived_demand. Accessed 11 June 2009

5
Hydrogen Transitions: A Socio-technical Scenarios Approach

Malcolm Eames and William McDowall

Introduction

Despite its promise to deliver sustainable, secure, low-carbon energy, hydrogen is today still largely only a potential energy carrier of the future. While there are plenty of demonstration projects, prototypes and even some niche products, hydrogen plays a negligible role in the present-day energy system. Instead, it is expectations about, and visions of, the future of hydrogen that are currently driving investment and research.

This chapter explores these expectations, in particular examining two important questions: what might a sustainable hydrogen future look like, and how could such a future come about? There are a multitude of proposed answers to these questions, revealing a widely divergent array of opinions and beliefs about: what would constitute a sustainable energy system; why society should pursue hydrogen energy; what sorts of technology a hydrogen future should actually involve; and how society might manage any large-scale transition to a hydrogen energy system.

This chapter explores these divergent expectations and visions by developing four scenarios, which each describe one way in which a hydrogen energy system might emerge. The four scenarios are:

- Structural Shift → *Electricity Store.*
- Corporate Race → *Ubiquitous Hydrogen.*
- Government Mission → *Centralized Hydrogen for Transport.*
- Disruptive Innovation → *Synthetic Liquid Fuel.*

Each scenario articulates a distinctive socio-technical pathway to a different possible sustainable hydrogen future. The scenarios are not intended to be predictive. Rather, they seek to illustrate different ways in which the large-scale socio-technological changes required for the establishment of a hydrogen economy might come about, and so highlight the choices and policy options facing the research community, business, policy-makers and civil society alike.

The future of hydrogen is contested

In recent years the idea of a hydrogen economy has been promoted vigorously by scientists, politicians, business interests and environmental NGOs alike as a potential solution to the twin challenges of energy security and climate change. Hydrogen research initiatives have been established by leading industrialized and emerging economies (US, Japan, Germany, UK, Norway, EU, Korea, China, India), by energy companies (most notably Shell and BP) and almost all of the world's major motor vehicle companies (Solomon and Banerjee, 2006).

In his 2003 State of the Union address, US President George Bush famously committed some $1.7 billion in funding (from 2002 to 2007) for the FreedomCAR (Cooperative Automotive Research) and Fuel Initiative, to develop hydrogen-powered fuel cells, hydrogen infrastructure and advanced automotive technologies. A Whitehouse factsheet published at the time described hydrogen as:

> *...the simplest element and most plentiful gas in the universe. Yet hydrogen never occurs by itself in nature, it always combines with other elements such as oxygen and carbon. Once it has been separated, hydrogen is the ultimate clean energy carrier. (Whitehouse Press Office, 2003)*

This description can be seen as part of a 'common script' deployed by hydrogen advocates across the political spectrum. Hydrogen is 'abundant'[1]; it is a 'pure' fuel; it is the 'fuel of the future'. Indeed, a number of authors have even argued that hydrogen is the logical conclusion of a steady transition in fuels, moving from hydrocarbons with higher proportions of carbon to those with higher proportions of hydrogen (from wood, to coal, then oil, then gas and, finally, 'inevitably' to hydrogen). Or as Seth Dunn puts it: 'the reality of an eventual transition to hydrogen becomes more evident when one takes an atomic view of energy history' (Dunn, 2001).

However, when we look past this overarching narrative about hydrogen energy, a much more complex and indeed deeply contested picture emerges. In our work exploring expectations of the future of hydrogen (through literature reviews, scenario workshops and expert interviews), we have found radically different ideas of what a hydrogen future would actually entail (McDowall and Eames, 2006). For example:

- Hydrogen futures differ in the degree to which they are centralized or decentralized. In some hydrogen visions, hydrogen is produced entirely in large-scale centralized installations, such as nuclear power plants or even vast solar thermal arrays in the Sahara. In others, hydrogen is produced and consumed in small installations in people's basements and kitchens.
- Hydrogen futures differ in the way in which they see hydrogen being used. For some, it is a transportation fuel, replacing petrol, but otherwise leaving the dominance of the personal automobile intact. For others, it plays a much broader role, competing with electricity and natural gas in the provision of energy services such as heating and lighting.

These different technological visions are informed by divergent understandings of what hydrogen may mean for society. On the one hand, hydrogen (and hydrogen fuel cell vehicles in particular) are conceived as a 'technical fix' for challenges such as energy security and climate change. In this view, hydrogen can substitute for existing energy and transport technologies with minimal disruption. On the other hand, we find a radical view that sees hydrogen as the catalyst for fundamental shifts in both social and technological systems. This radical view often couples hydrogen with a shift towards localization and decentralized energy systems, and a social trend towards the growth of community-oriented and environmental values (Eames et al, 2006).

Visions and expectations in technological change

Studying technological visions and expectations provides a 'window' on the way in which particular social and economic interests promote different types of technology: automotive firms see hydrogen as a replacement for dependence on oil; environmental groups envisage hydrogen futures that involve a reorientation of society towards lower consumption and stronger environmental values, and so on. But technological visions are not just a reflection of existing positions. Expectations and visions play an active role in shaping research agendas and investment, and ultimately play a role in determining which technologies are developed. Technological expectations can be self-fulfilling: when scientists, innovators and investors believe that a particular technology is likely to succeed, they put greater effort, money and resources behind it (Van Lente, 1993). As a result, technological expectations and visions are a contested space in which different interests compete to promote their agendas. Indeed, technological visions and expectations can be actively deployed in an effort to shape the direction of innovative activity.

Using scenarios to think about the future

The fact that visions and expectations help to shape the direction of innovative activities suggests a need to critically examine the futures and visions that are promoted. Participatory scenario studies are one way of doing this, and our work has used scenarios to explore the values and assumptions that lie behind different visions of a hydrogen future (McDowall and Eames, 2007). Such debate is important: the direction of technological change is not the inevitable result of scientific discovery, but is rather shaped and directed by social interests in ways that matter for society as a whole (Stirling, 2007).

Scenarios provide a way of opening up social dialogue and debate around what a hydrogen future might or should mean. But they also have a second role: by exploring a range of plausible and possible futures, scenarios enable us to explore uncertainties and make more robust decisions. Planning for the future requires us to think creatively and flexibly about the many possibilities that exist, and to identify strategies that will be robust against a range of different possible futures. Exploratory scenario approaches have been developed in order to help decision-makers think through the implications of different possible futures, and to explore different possible patterns of change. Their purpose is not to predict the future, but to illuminate the range of possibilities, in order to help policy-makers make more robust decisions (Schwartz, 1996).

Backcasting is a form of scenario analysis designed to help decision-makers understand how a future goal might be achieved (Robinson, 2003). We have used a backcasting approach to explore different possible ways in which a hydrogen future might arise.

Developing socio-technical scenarios

Scenario approaches have become common in the prospective analysis of long-term technological change (Greeuw et al, 2000). However, many scenario studies are remarkably poor at taking into account what is known about the dynamics of innovation and socio-technical change (McDowall and Eames, 2006). This shortcoming has led to the development of 'socio-technical scenarios' approaches, which are explicitly informed by theoretical insights from innovation studies (Geels, 2002a). We use the term 'socio-technical' to recognize that social and technological changes co-evolve, and that technological systems are embedded in a set of social norms and networks and comprise more than the technological artefacts and techniques themselves. If this concept of 'socio-technical' sounds complicated, consider all the rules (traffic laws, driving tests), infrastructure (roads, petrol stations, suburbs), business networks (suppliers, manufacturers, retailers, repairers) and habits (the school run) that have co-evolved with the automobile to make its use convenient and straightforward.

The development of a hydrogen energy system requires a broad and integrated set of changes: in infrastructure and technology; in rules, regulations and codes; in behaviours and habits; and in patterns of investment. Such broad change can be characterized as a 'technological transition', from one socio-technical system – or regime – to another. Historical examples include the emergence of commercial aviation, the transition from sail to steam in shipping, and the spread of electric lighting. Scenarios which seek to illuminate such transitions must reflect our knowledge of the dynamics of socio-technological change.

In recent years, researchers working in evolutionary economics, sociology, history of technology and other fields have developed a framework for thinking about the way in which technological transitions occur. The 'multi-level perspective', which was introduced in Chapter 3 but will be discussed further here, provides a structured way of thinking about the dynamics of socio-technical change (Geels 2002b, 2005), and provides a useful heuristic for informing the development of socio-technical scenarios.

During a transition, developments take place on three levels: here termed niches, system and landscape. New technologies first enter use in 'niches': demonstration projects, niche markets and among enthusiasts. Technologies are further developed in niches, as their use enables learning and refinement. For the technology to enter the mainstream, the conditions must be right at higher levels – both within the industries, mainstream markets and regulatory systems that make up the middle 'systems' level, and at the 'landscape level' of long-term social and economic context. Most of the time, the conditions are not right, and existing systems resist the entry of newcomers. But there are times when windows of opportunity emerge for new technological systems to develop: particularly when innovations at the niche level combine with pressures of shifting landscape conditions, such as concerns about energy supplies; or when firms look to radical new technologies to provide competitive edge.

Figure 5.1 represents the path of a new technology as it first develops in niches, and later diffuses into mainstream markets. By simultaneously focusing on how technologies develop in niches, on the dynamics of the incumbent systems, and on the wider changes for society, we can get a better insight into the possible future for hydrogen.

While this multi-level perspective is useful for structuring scenarios of how transitions might unfold, it does not, on its own, provide a systematic way to

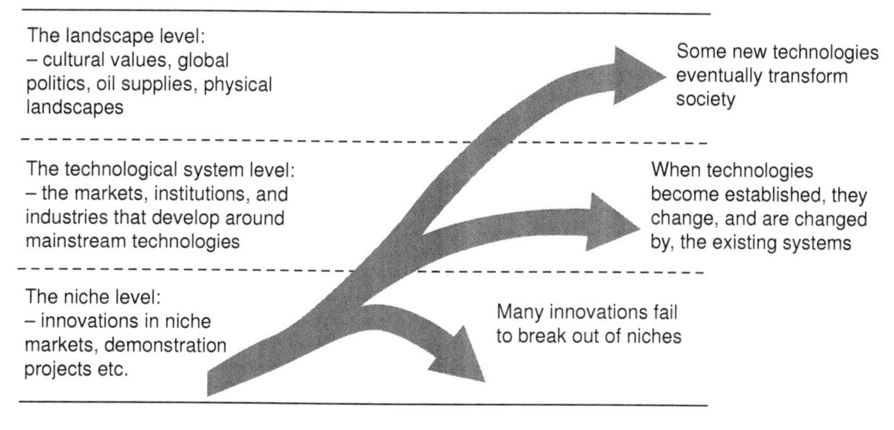

Adapted from Geels (2002b)

Figure 5.1 *A multi-level perspective on socio-technical transitions*

explore different types of transition. Berkhout et al (2004) have developed an evolutionary model that generates four distinct 'transition contexts'. These differentiate types of transitions, based on two core dimensions:

1. Whether change is envisaged and actively coordinated.
2. Whether change is based on resources internal to the existing system (or regime).

Other attempts to describe the contexts in which different types of technological transitions might occur have focused on the importance of governance. Elzen and Wieczorek (2005), and Hisschemoller et al (2006), both argue that different types of transitions might be understood in terms of the type of governance structure. Hisschemoller et al explore the relationships between political institutions and processes and transition trajectories to a hydrogen economy. In doing so, they outline four archetypal 'governance paradigms' that are applied to technological change: governance by government; governance by policy networking; governance by corporate business; and governance by challenge.

Building transition scenarios

As part of the work of the UK Sustainable Hydrogen Energy Consortium (UKSHEC), we developed four 'transition' scenarios that describe how four different kinds of sustainable hydrogen economy could emerge. These transition scenarios are intended to illustrate different ways in which the future of hydrogen might unfold, by highlighting key drivers, and exploring different possible innovation patterns. Each transition scenario leads to a distinct hydrogen future vision, created as part of a previous scenario-building exercise (McDowall and Eames, 2004).

Both the transition scenarios, and the visions to which they lead, were developed through a participatory stakeholder process involving an extensive series of interviews, workshops and expert review (Eames and McDowall, 2006; McDowall and Eames, 2007).[2]

The transition scenarios were informed by the theoretical perspectives on technological transitions discussed above. Specifically, the UKSHEC Transition Scenarios are framed by two key dimensions of change, adapted from the work of Berkhout et al (2004). These dimensions are:

- The degree to which innovation is shaped by a shared normative *guiding vision*. In the past, large-scale transitions of energy and transport infrastructures have usually occurred as an emergent result of interacting drivers and activities, rather than as the outcome of a managed transition. This axis allows us to explore how hydrogen might emerge without a coherent action plan, as well as through concerted efforts to bring about a hydrogen future.

- The extent to which innovation is driven by existing *actors and institutions*, or by new actors and institutions (or existing actors taking on new roles in driving innovation). This axis invites us to think through the various possible roles of the different actors and institutions that will be involved in any possible transition: local, regional and national governments; major industries; new entrants and entrepreneurs, and so on. The axis helps us to consider the interplay of different interests and agendas, and avoid assuming that any particular actor alone holds the key to the development of hydrogen energy.

In order to enrich the institutional and policy dimensions of the scenarios, each of the resulting quadrants (or transition contexts) was also associated with one of Hisschemoller et al's (2006) four governance paradigms (Figure 5.2; for full details, see Eames and McDowall, 2006).

The particular mapping of the transition pathways to the end visions in Figure 5.2 is only one possibility. There will be many other ways in which a transition to any particular hydrogen future could play out. Our purpose was not prediction, but to stimulate imaginative and critically informed thinking about how the future might unfold.

The four quadrants provide a useful way to distinguish different types of transition pathway. Each scenario is also described in terms of a second, multi-level, structure, adapted from the multi-level perspective on socio-technical transitions described above.

The major drivers for hydrogen at a landscape level – climate change and security of primary energy supplies – are well established. To a lesser extent, local air quality and regional or national competitiveness also provide drivers

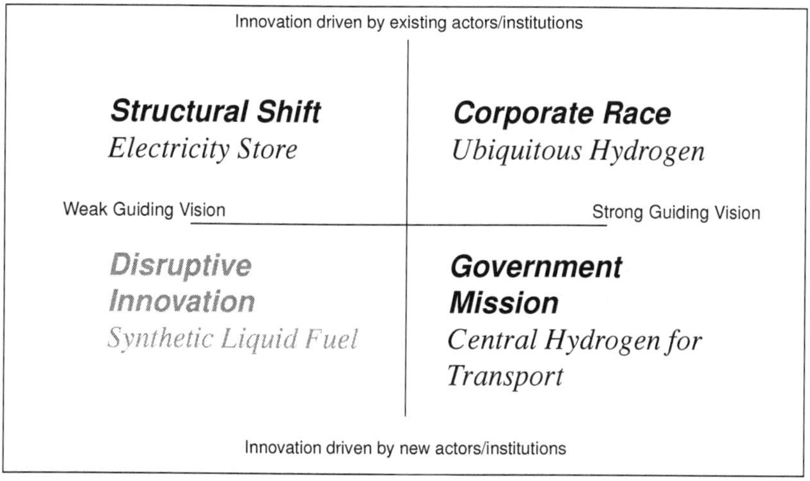

Note: Disruptive innovation / synthetic liquid fuel is shown in the diagram in lighter text, to highlight its status as an alternative or 'wild card' scenario.

Figure 5.2 *The UKSHEC transition scenarios*

for policy-makers to consider support for the development and diffusion of hydrogen technologies. In addition, landscape-level drivers for the energy system more broadly include rates of economic growth (and hence of energy demand), and the social values that prevail.

In addition to these landscape-level policy drivers, it is important to consider drivers at the systems and niche levels that influence the dynamics of change by either articulating, or responding to, changes at the landscape level, such as the strategic activities of firms and industries; national and regional energy and transport policies (e.g. carbon trading, 'zero emissions mandates' etc.); lobbying by hydrogen and fuel cell associations, activists, NGOs and others; the activities of scientists and engineers in advancing the state of hydrogen and fuel cell technologies; the growth in portable and on-vehicle power demands, leading to funding, support and the creation of niche markets for fuel cell products; and so on. These drivers interact in different ways in the four transition scenarios.

Each scenario comprises: i) a short description of a distinctive hydrogen future (or end vision); ii) a summary of the 'storyline' of the transition scenario, illustrating how the end vision is reached; iii) a detailed 'multi-level' narrative describing the transition pathway in terms of landscape, niche and systems changes; and iv) a 'transition diagram' providing a visual representation of the innovation dynamics and key developments along the individual pathway.

The UKSHEC transition scenarios

The UKSHEC transition scenarios are not predictions. They are intended to shed light on possible innovation processes and transition pathways by which a future hydrogen economy might be achieved. They seek to illustrate different ways in which the large-scale socio-technological changes required for the establishment of a hydrogen economy might come about, and so highlight the choices and policy options facing the research community, business, policy-makers and civil society alike on the road to a sustainable hydrogen economy. Whilst the scenarios have a UK focus, they seek to place the prospective developments they describe in a broader European and global context.

Scenario 1: Structural Shift → Electricity Store (see Figure 5.3)

In this scenario the transition to *Electricity Store* emerges from a restructuring of the energy market, triggering rapid changes in the behaviour of existing firms, new entrants and their customers.

In the face of mounting concerns about climate change and energy security, the UK government restructures the market to provide much stronger economic incentives for renewable electricity and microgeneration. While developments in hydrogen transport are initially limited to a few high-profile demonstration projects, hydrogen enters commercial use as a distributed storage medium to buffer intermittent renewable electricity supplies in the

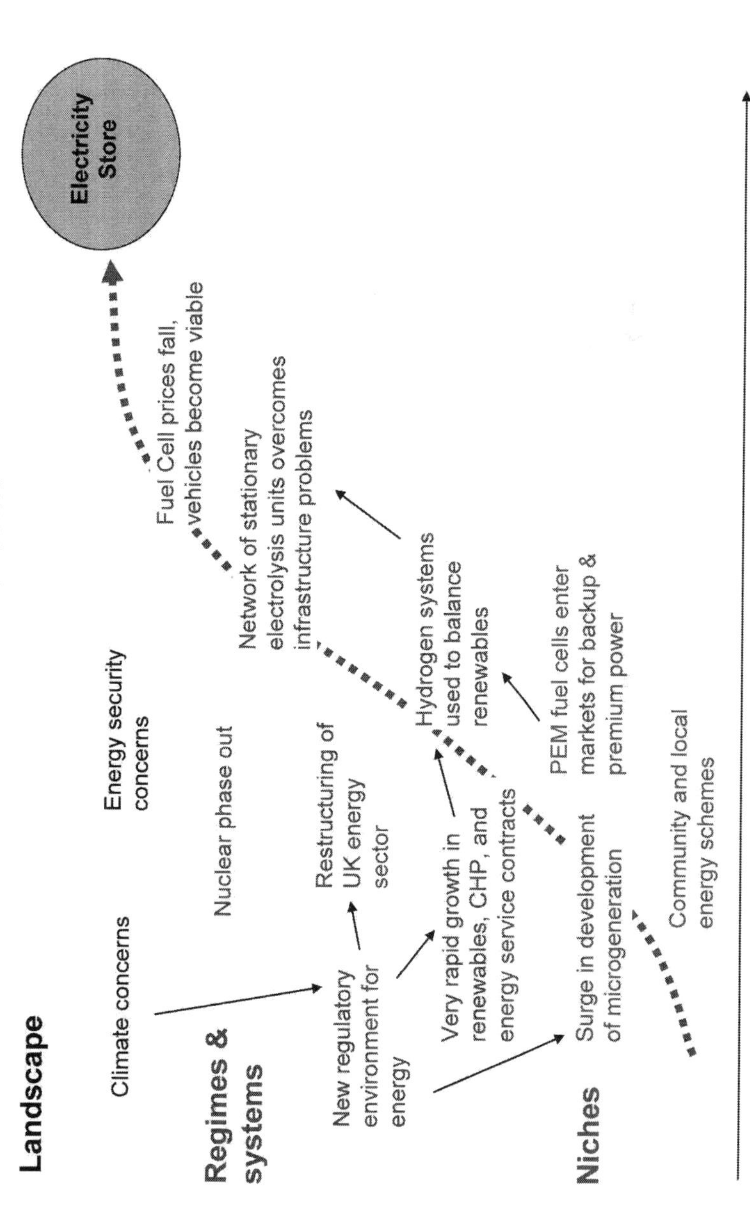

Figure 5.3 *Graphical representation of the Structural Shift → Electricity Store scenario*

Table 5.1 *Summary of the qualitative indicators for the UKSHEC transition scenarios*

	Structural Shift → *Electricity Store*	***Corporate Race*** → *Ubiquitous Hydrogen*	***Government Mission*** → *Centralized Hydrogen for Transport*	***Disruptive Innovation*** → *Synthetic Liquid Fuel*
Dimensions	Innovation driven by existing actors/institutions Weak guiding vision	Innovation driven by existing actors/institutions Strong guiding vision	Innovation driven by new actors/institutions Strong guiding vision	Innovation driven by new actors/institutions Weak guiding vision
Drivers	Strong UK government and social concern for climate change and energy security Greater social awareness of need for demand reductions Societal rejection of nuclear and carbon capture and storage	Strategic positioning by big auto and big oil in the face of climate change and energy security concerns High demand and volatile supplies for oil and gas lead to increasing prices	Strong UK/EU government concerns over climate and energy security Societal acceptance of nuclear and carbon capture and storage, and greater social trust in science and technology	Emerging climate and energy concerns Emphasis on building competitive markets and high innovation Social preference for liberalized markets and consumer economy
Key technologies	Fuel cells Storage and handling Electricity grid updates Smart metering Renewables	Gas separation Fuel cells Onboard storage Gasification Pipelines and metering Carbon capture and storage Waste, biomass gasification Renewables	Storage and handling Fuel cells High-temperature nuclear Pipelines and liquefaction Gasification technologies Carbon capture and storage (CCS) New nuclear power	Direct methanol fuel cells (DMFC) Synthetic liquid fuel synthesis Fuel reformers or scale-up of DMFC Renewables Carbon capture
Decision points and milestones	Renewables reach a high enough proportion of grid electricity to require buffering of supply and demand	Nuclear and CCS go/no-go decisions Commercialization decisions of big auto Hydrogen injected into natural gas grids	'Go' decision on major hydrogen programme, and on nuclear	'No-go' decision on major government hydrogen programme

Source: Eames and McDowall (2006)

Box 5.1 A description of the hydrogen future 'Electricity Store'

Electricity Store: In this hydrogen future, hydrogen is not only the dominant road transport fuel, it also plays a vital role providing distributed energy storage to overcome the intermittency problems of renewable electricity generation. Hydrogen is produced locally in small-scale electrolysis units for forecourt refuelling and on-site storage, for use in domestic and commercial CHP units at times of peak electricity demand/limited supply.

energy sector. As the use of hydrogen for distributed energy storage becomes widespread, eventually it provides an alternative refuelling infrastructure, allowing the rapid expansion of hydrogen transport.

This pathway results largely from a 'reorientation of trajectories', where radical innovation within the energy sector, and later transport, emerges as a result of an 'external' shock in the form of restructuring of the electricity supply market to promote low-carbon generation and energy efficiency.

The scenario 'storyline'

Driven by concerns about climate change and energy security, government acts to tackle energy-sector emissions, while maintaining emphasis on liberalized markets. In the face of stalling growth of renewables, and with new nuclear build struggling in the face of economic difficulties and societal opposition, the UK government restructures the wholesale and domestic electricity markets to provide stronger economic incentives for renewables. This includes guaranteed feed-in tariffs for a portfolio of renewables and measures at the regional and local level to facilitate distributed generation.

Renewables grow rapidly, with two sectors showing particularly strong growth: offshore wind, and small-scale and micro-generation (including CHP). Local authorities increasingly adopt local energy planning guidelines that involve on-site energy generation, following the examples of Merton and Croydon. The growth in distributed energy helps drive public engagement with efficiency and renewables support, with consumers increasingly aware of their energy choices, and less likely to oppose renewable energy developments. NGOs work to promote this trend, and some form joint initiatives with energy companies to provide energy service contracts and innovative financing for the installation of renewables, in the same way that NGOs and utilities provided 100 per cent renewable contracts over the last few years.

Hydrogen shows slow progress in transport in the medium term, partly because of difficulties related to refuelling infrastructure. However, fuel cells find markets in some niche stationary applications, for back-up and premium power, and in off-grid applications. However, in the long term, as intermittent renewables become an increasingly important part of the electricity supply mix, niches in demand-side management and load-balancing emerge. This opportunity allows the rapid development of a hydrogen fuelling infrastructure, as hydrogen energy stations provide fuel, are demand-side flexible and can provide back-up power services. Policies support the diffusion of hydrogen into transport, with high taxes on carbon fuels. In the long term, this allows the development of a system much like that described in *Electricity Store*, in which renewable electricity is used to generate hydrogen where it is needed, at times when electricity supply exceeds demand.

Multi-level perspective

Landscape

In this scenario, liberalized, competitive markets remain an important policy goal, and political ends are achieved through a policy-networking approach, rather than through unilateral government action. There are strong concerns about both climate change and energy security, and increasingly high fossil-fuel prices. This is also a society that is increasingly environmentally conscious, and wary of nuclear power and carbon sequestration.

Technologies, niches and early markets

Early markets for hydrogen in this scenario arise as a result of growing demands for premium, uninterruptible and back-up power. A niche market for hydrogen fuel cell systems also develops for off-grid applications, and community energy cooperatives or local authority-run energy schemes make use of fuel cells in CHP systems. However, more significant opportunities are created by increasing levels of intermittent renewables in electricity generation, as markets develop for demand-side management and peak generation.

Key actors involved in the establishment of early markets and opportunities include the legislative and regulatory bodies that enable the shift in energy markets; the local authorities involved in developing community energy schemes; the activities of existing energy companies, many of whom move towards renewables and energy service company (ESCO) models of service provision; fuel cell developers; and NGOs.

This scenario relies on advances in stationary applications for fuel cells, on smart metering and grid technologies, and on substantial expansion of renewables.

Market growth and systems change

As a result of changes to regulatory frameworks around energy, there is a major restructuring of the UK energy sector, with new models of generation, distribution and supply becoming important. In particular, distributed generation, energy service contracts and community energy schemes emerge as important. However, in the short to medium term, there is little impact on the transport sector, where hydrogen makes slow progress. The success of hybrids, and for a time the increased use of biofuels, mean that policy pressures for hydrogen in transport are insufficient to overcome the challenges of infrastructure development. It is only later, once fuel cell prices have fallen and a nascent infrastructure has become established, that hydrogen vehicles start to make progress.

The important policies in this transition are those that restructure the energy market, which later creates a window of opportunity for the transition to hydrogen use in vehicles. These include the establishment of strong renewables and emissions targets; re-establishment of the fuel tax escalator; and a wholesale restructuring of the energy regulatory system to enable renewables, distributed generation and efficiency, combined with changes to planning guidelines to enable renewables.

Infrastructure for hydrogen in transport develops from a network of fuel cells and hydrogen back-up systems that provide buffering for intermittent renewables, and co-produce heat, power and fuel for transport. It is the development of a high-efficiency, renewables-based energy system that creates a window of opportunity for the introduction of hydrogen, and as a result, almost all hydrogen in this scenario is generated from renewable electricity.

Scenario 2: Corporate Race → Ubiquitous Hydrogen (see Figure 5.4)

In this scenario, the transition to *Ubiquitous Hydrogen* is driven by the actions of corporate business, initially by strategic competition between global companies within the auto-oil sectors.

Despite the continued failure of inter-governmental action on climate change, global automotive and energy companies increasingly see the shift to a low-carbon energy system, as in their long-term interests. A strategic race develops to achieve leadership in hydrogen technologies. Regional and local governments play an important role facilitating demonstration projects and early 'flagship' initiatives in partnerships with corporate players. Rapid improvements in on-board storage and fuel cell technologies promote the rapid penetration of hydrogen in the transport sector. Later, as natural gas prices rise, fuel providers use the natural gas grid to supply hydrogen, ultimately moving to an integrated hydrogen grid, with decentralized as well as centralized hydrogen production.

Box 5.2 A description of the hydrogen future 'Ubiquitous Hydrogen'

Ubiquitous Hydrogen: In this hydrogen future, gaseous hydrogen is not only the dominant road transport fuel. Many buildings also use fuel cell CHP systems running on hydrogen. Distributed renewable generation predominates, reducing the need for long-distance transmission and distribution, and allowing hydrogen to compete directly with electricity as the main energy vector for the provision of domestic and commercial heat and power. Regional grids of hydrogen pipelines connect (predominantly local) hydrogen supplies with local needs.

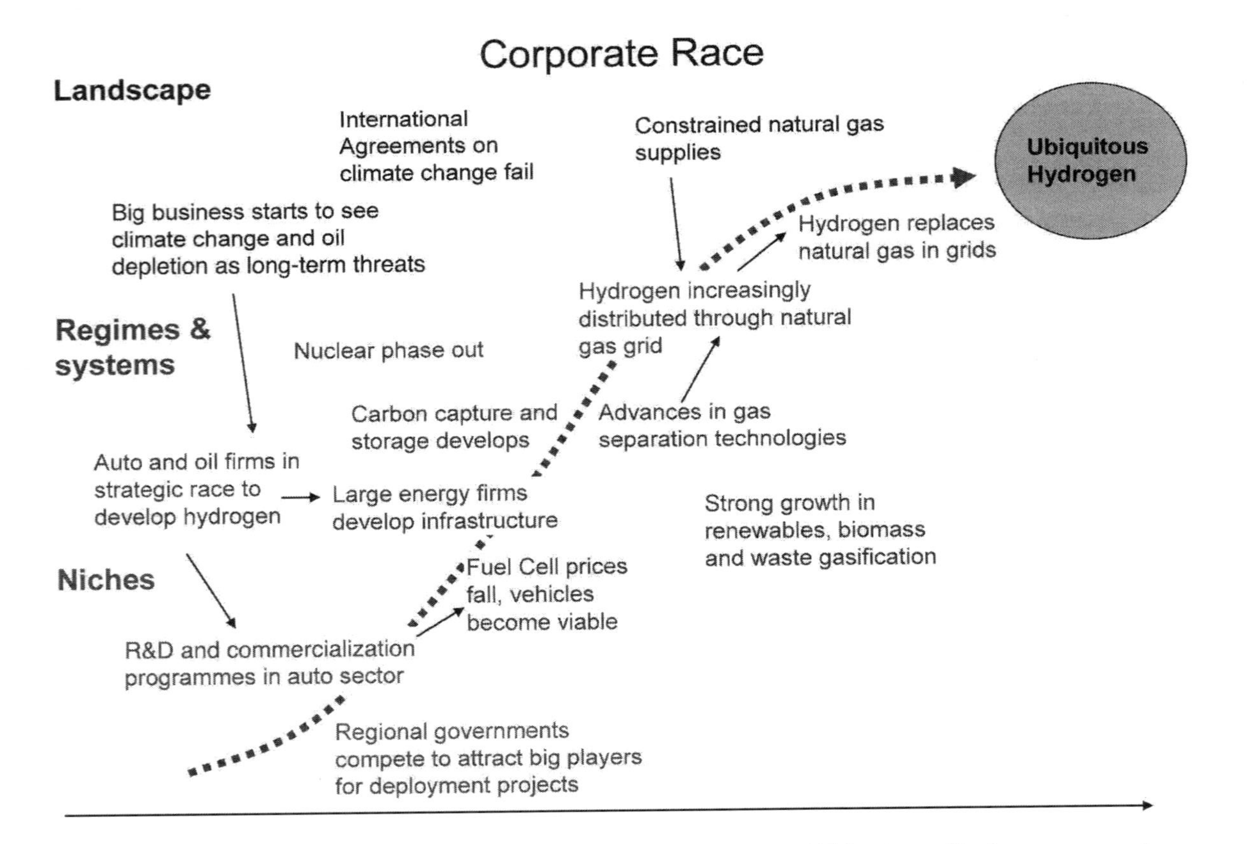

Figure 5.4 *Graphical representation of the Corporate Race → Ubiquitous Hydrogen scenario*

This pathway is one of 'endogenous renewal', where innovation arises largely out of the R&D activities and investment decisions of companies within the existing transport system, more specifically the major global companies within the automobile and oil industries.

The scenario 'storyline'

In this transition, the large automotive and oil companies start to see oil depletion and climate change as major strategic challenges to their core business. As a result, a strategic race develops to gain market leadership in the hydrogen technologies that increasingly look like being part of the solution. Large automotive firms plough resources into R&D and commercialization programmes, setting up new joint ventures and strategic partnerships to develop fuel cell vehicles (FCVs), while the major energy companies start to invest in hydrogen production and infrastructure. The existing players in both industries take action to drive hydrogen into transport.

Inter-governmental frameworks to take action on climate change fail. However, regional governments interested in both environmental concerns and in regional competitiveness form partnerships with large global corporations to create early centres of hydrogen development and deployment. These regional attempts to attract the big players are important niches in the development of hydrogen systems, as are low-emission zones in big cities, providing policies to enable hydrogen in the absence of national level policy action.

The investments in R&D drive down costs in both hydrogen production and in fuel cell vehicles. At first, sales are restricted to high-end markets, but as prices fall, fuel cell vehicles become increasingly adopted in the mainstream. Those companies with successful hydrogen vehicle programmes seek to exploit their first-mover advantage by lobbying for tougher vehicle emissions and other regulatory measures to support the introduction of FCVs. Major energy companies develop infrastructure, at first through distributed natural gas reforming and through trucked liquid hydrogen, and hydrogen becomes the dominant transport fuel.

The success of hydrogen fuel in transport opens up possibilities for change in the wider energy system. As natural gas prices rise, gas companies, which have been increasingly profiting from the growing market in hydrogen vehicles, start to look for alternatives to dependence on finite natural gas reserves. Biogas and hydrogen from gasified waste and coal start to be injected into the natural gas network, after health and safety regulations are changed to allow the use of alternative gas sources in the network. Advances in gas separation technologies allow hydrogen and natural gas to be efficiently separated, and for a while the natural gas network carries a mix of hydrogen and methane. As natural gas prices continue to rise, and shortages emerge, the proportion of hydrogen increases, and policy-makers concerned about emissions and energy security introduce a non-fossil gas obligation to encourage the use of biogas and hydrogen in gas grids. Ultimately, a system much like that described in *Ubiquitous Hydrogen* emerges.

Multi-level perspective

Landscape

The backdrop for this transition is provided by the failure of intergovernmental action on climate change, and by mounting concerns about climate change and oil depletion within the oil and auto sectors, where they are seen as long-term strategic challenges. It is also a scenario that occurs in the context of high demands for natural gas, and increasingly volatile and insecure gas supplies over time, with real constraints on affordable gas supplies by mid-century. Regardless of government decisions concerning nuclear power, there is resistance to new nuclear, and eventually little, if any, is built. In this scenario, there is a continued emphasis on the importance of liberalized markets, and society accepts that major corporations alone have the competence and power to enact large-scale technological change.

Technologies, niches and early markets

In this scenario, big corporate players create and expand strategic R&D units developing hydrogen vehicle and infrastructure technologies. These 'skunk works' are to some extent protected from immediate market priorities by long-term strategic concerns. Early markets are established through projects linking major global energy and auto companies, and local and regional authorities, to create large-scale demonstration and deployment projects. These innovation and deployment activities are developed and protected by the dominant players, rather than through the emergence of new players and new systems on the periphery of the mainstream.

At the centre of this scenario are a number of key technologies and technological developments. Rapid progress in automotive fuel cell systems, including the fuel cell itself and on-board storage, are achieved through the substantial investments of the auto industry. Pipeline and metering technology is important for the build-up of infrastructure. As natural gas becomes increasingly expensive, gasification and gas separation technologies become important, allowing hydrogen to be used in the natural gas grid. Waste, biomass and renewable technologies, and carbon capture and storage, are all increasingly important as the hydrogen supply is decarbonized.

The key actors in the establishment of early markets and protected niche developments are the major oil and auto firms, local governments competing to attract global companies to set up demonstration projects, and the industrial gas companies with expertise in hydrogen handling and supply.

Market growth and systems change

As R&D and the learning and development experience within deployment projects lead to decreased costs, hydrogen vehicles enter commercial markets, at first in high status and luxury car sectors. Those companies with successful hydrogen vehicle programmes seek to exploit their first-mover advantage and increasingly lobby government for the introduction of tougher vehicle emissions standards, zero-emission mandates, zoning and market transformation programmes. Infrastructure is developed by large energy firms, principally from the existing oil sector, in collaboration with the large automotive companies, and as hydrogen fuel becomes more widely available, hydrogen vehicles diffuse into more markets. The infrastructure is developed heterogeneously, with both centralized and decentralized hydrogen production, to suit local circumstances. Hydrogen is initially supplied from natural gas, much of it reformed at the refuelling station. As gas prices rise, gas distribution companies seek to maintain and grow their new transport-oriented market, injecting pure hydrogen directly into the grid in increasing concentrations. As concerns about climate grow, hydrogen is increasingly produced from gasified biomass and waste, and from coal with carbon sequestration. A non-fossil gas obligation is introduced, increasing the percentage of biogas and hydrogen in gas grids. Renewables, particularly distributed renewables, also contribute.

The role of governments in this scenario is relatively weak, although there is some strengthening of regional innovation policies, and strengthening of green policies, as leading firms lobby for high environmental standards. Health and safety standards play an important role, in particular in enabling the use of hydrogen in natural gas grids.

The major industries involved in transport and energy adapt in the face of the substantial pressures of oil depletion, climate change and the emergence of new technologies, managing to fight off newcomers and maintain their dominant positions.

Scenario 3: Government Mission → Centralized Hydrogen for Transport (see Figure 5.5)

In this scenario, the transition to *Central Hydrogen for Transport* is driven by strong government at both a national and regional/international (EU) level. The public sector and 'national champion' industries work in partnership to build a hydrogen transport infrastructure.

Problems of climate change and energy security are increasingly seen as too pressing to be left to the market and as warranting more direct government intervention. National governments in the leading advanced and rapidly industrializing economies (US, Japan, China, India) and EU take strategic decisions to prioritize the rapid development of hydrogen transport. Partnerships are established with national industry champions. Regulation, subsidies and public procurement are all used to push hydrogen, making extensive use of near-term technologies and large centralized supply routes.

This pathway is one of 'purposive transition', where innovation is driven by the goals and expectations of national political elites, and scientific, policy and business interests become enrolled in a shared mission to transform the existing system.

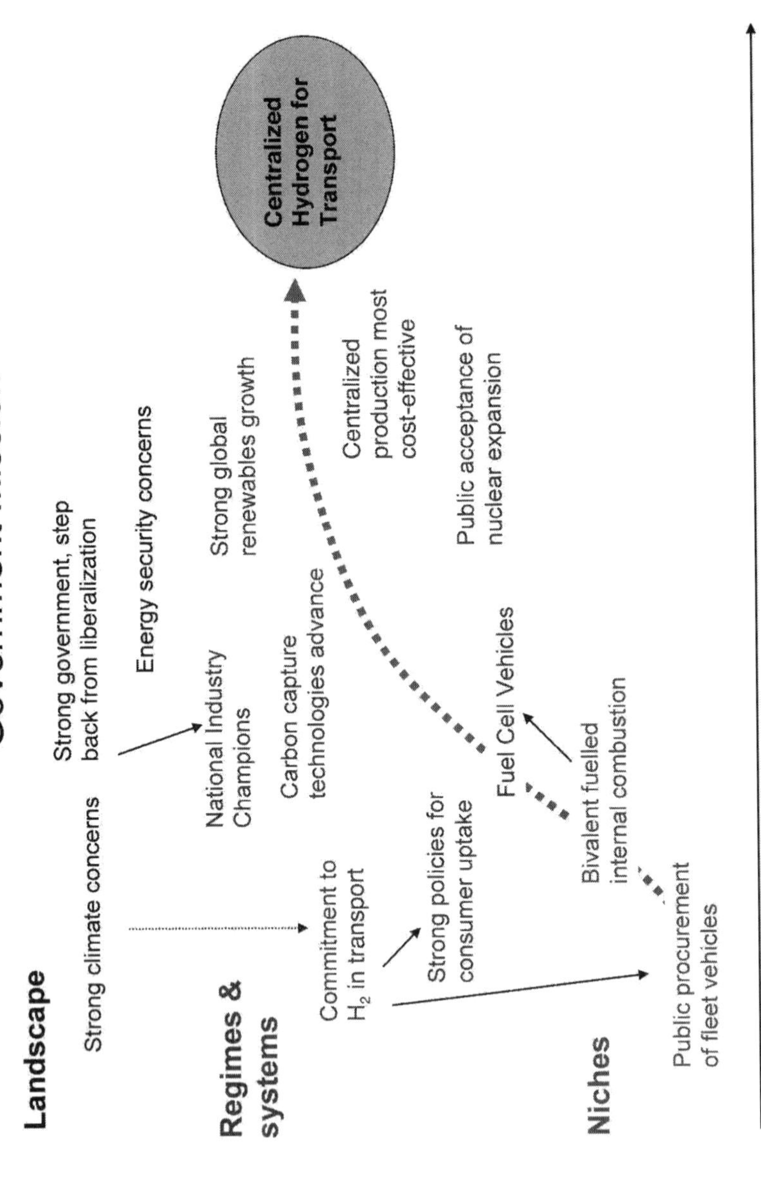

Figure 5.5 *Graphical representation of the Government Mission → Centralized Hydrogen for Transport scenario*

Box 5.3 A description of the hydrogen future 'Centralized Hydrogen for Transport'

Centralized Hydrogen for Transport: In this hydrogen future, hydrogen has become the dominant transport fuel, and is produced centrally from a mixture of sources. Hydrogen is distributed as a gas by dedicated pipeline and as a liquid. In some applications, liquid hydrogen is the on-board storage mechanism, while in others, compressed gaseous hydrogen is used.

The scenario 'storyline'

This scenario sees governments putting their full weight into steering a transition towards a hydrogen transport system, driven by concerns about climate change and energy security. The approach has a clear vision of the kind of hydrogen future that must be delivered, and there is a strong sense of 'mission' driving developments. With market mechanisms alone increasingly seen as unable to deliver a transition, emphasis turns to the development of national or EU level industry champions to work with government. Publics accept the need for firm government action, and accept that technologies such as nuclear and carbon sequestration are necessary to avoid dangerous climate change.

Governments promote the development of a market for hydrogen through public procurement of fleet vehicles, and encourage private fleet vehicles to move to hydrogen fuel. Many of these early vehicles have internal combustion engines and are bivalent fuelled, able to run on both petrol and hydrogen, allowing consumers to avoid concerns about limited hydrogen refuelling opportunities. European and national governments review state aid rules, to enable governments to underwrite national nuclear industries and new industries for carbon capture and storage. Changes in competition regulation encourage mergers and partnerships among major European energy and engineering firms, creating national and European champions to develop a hydrogen production and distribution infrastructure. European government also forces European automotive and energy firms to agree on common industry standards, preventing costly 'standard wars', and enabling more rapid diffusion of hydrogen vehicles into markets. Strong policies for consumer uptake are introduced, with hypothecated taxes on carbon used to subsidize hydrogen fuel. Governments consider very stringent approaches, such as eventually banning sales of non-hydrogen vehicles, or placing limits on petrol and diesel sales.

At first, hydrogen is provided mainly through natural gas reforming. However, as a pipeline infrastructure is built where transport demand is high, and liquid hydrogen facilities provided for remoter sites, centralized hydrogen production becomes more important. Nuclear, coal with carbon capture and storage, and centralized renewable installations, are all important supply sources. These new players enter transport fuel markets, helping to transform the system to look similar to *Centralized Hydrogen for Transport*.

Multi-level perspective

Landscape

This scenario occurs in the context of a shift in governance style. It becomes widely recognized that only the state has the power to effect large-scale change for the public interest, and current models of governance emphasizing liberalized markets are increasingly seen as only a partial solution. Strong government is needed, because the challenges of climate change and energy security are too important to leave to the market. There is a clear strategic vision of replacing the oil-based transportation system with hydrogen, and an acceptance on behalf of the wider public that this is necessary and that nuclear power is part of the solution. This scenario sees an increase in levels of public trust in science and technology, as publics increasingly recognize the challenges of climate change, and support government measures to tackle it.

Technologies, niches and early markets

In this scenario, governments create early opportunities for hydrogen vehicles through public procurement of fleet vehicles. These early deployments help reduce costs and establish the first hydrogen refuelling stations. The early markets are created and protected through the activities of government, in partnership with UK and European engineering and energy companies, and with large automotive firms.

The technological emphasis in the early stages of this transition is on incremental, low-cost steps, including bivalent fuelled hydrogen internal combustion engine vehicles. Hydrogen storage and handling technologies are important, as is small-scale steam methane reforming. As hydrogen develops, hydrogen production shifts increasingly to new, high-temperature nuclear power and gasification technologies. Pipeline and liquefaction technologies also are central for distribution and storage.

Market growth and systems change

Public procurement for captive fleets (such as buses) expands from the early government-sponsored deployments, and this, combined with strong policies to encourage consumer uptake and supply-side investment in infrastructure, pushes hydrogen into wider markets. The emphasis remains on incremental changes and hybrid systems, with infrastructure developing off the natural gas grid with small-scale reforming where appropriate, and with bivalent fuelled internal combustion vehicles much more common than fuel cells in the near term.

The scenario sees a restructuring of the EU energy and transport sectors, driven by government interventions. New actors and new institutions are created, though government stops short of nationalizing major industries. Major shifts in policy include changes to EU state aid rules, to allow governments to underwrite the financial risks of nuclear power and carbon capture and storage, and changes in competition regulation, encouraging mergers between large firms to re-establish national or supranational (European) champions. Changes to planning systems enable the development of a hydrogen infrastructure, and EU government works with the champion industries to set technology standards, in a bid to promote rapid adoption (avoiding costly 'standard wars') and to help provide European industry with an advantage internationally. As the transition proceeds, governments may consider strong command-and-control policies such as capping sales of non-hydrogen vehicles, or of petrol and diesel.

Government underwrites the development of infrastructure, using private finance initiatives and granting captive markets to champion industries. Early infrastructure is based on local steam methane reforming, but increasingly pipelines are built from centralized production facilities, and liquid hydrogen tankers are used where pipelines are not feasible or economic. Hydrogen is produced in new nuclear power plants, a range of centralized renewable plant (including some substantial offshore developments) and from gasified coal, with the carbon captured and stored in depleted North Sea oil and gas reservoirs.

Scenario 4: Disruptive Innovation → Synthetic Liquid Fuel – an alternative scenario (see Figure 5.6)

In this alternative scenario, the transition to *Synthetic Liquid Fuel* is driven by the market forces, with the role of government largely restricted to fostering competitive markets and the knowledge economy.

Despite ongoing concerns about climate change and energy security, hydrogen in its pure form fails to take off. In particular, failure to develop more efficient on-board storage remains a significant barrier to the widespread adoption of hydrogen as a transport fuel. However, innovation in the electronics sector and niches outside of the mainstream transport and energy systems opens up novel technological opportunities, changing consumer behaviour and expectations, and resulting in the growth of new markets for portable power and synthetic liquid fuels.

This pathway is largely one of 'emergent transformation'. Innovation outside of the mainstream transport and energy systems opens up novel technological and market opportunities, resulting in the growth of new industries and consumer services, as well as unexpected solutions to existing problems.

Box 5.4 A description of the hydrogen future 'Synthetic Liquid Fuel'

Synthetic Liquid Fuel: In this hydrogen future, renewably produced hydrogen again provides the dominant transport fuel. In this case, however, it is 'packaged' in the form of a synthetic liquid hydrocarbon, such as methanol, to overcome the difficulties of hydrogen storage and distribution. The carbon for fuel synthesis comes from biomass and from the flue gases of carbon-intensive industries.

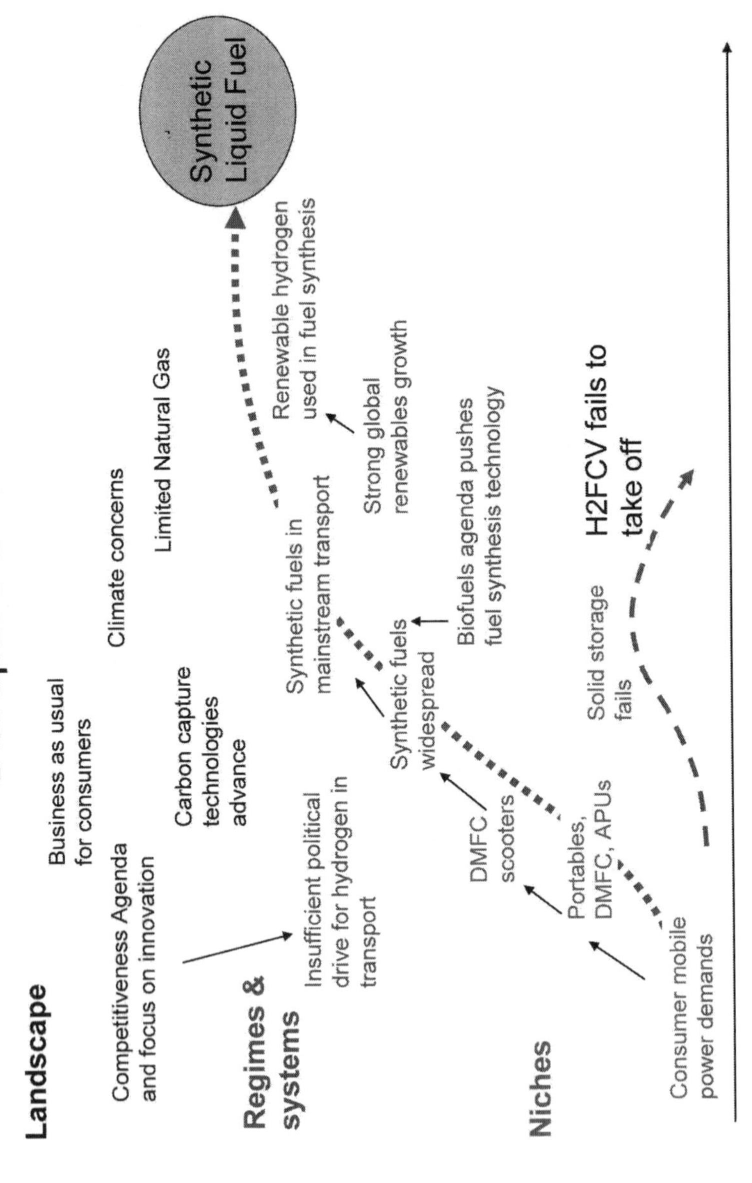

Figure 5.6 *Graphical representation of the Disruptive Innovation → Synthetic Liquid Fuel scenario*

The scenario 'storyline'

In this alternative scenario, hydrogen in its pure form fails to take off as a major fuel. Governments focus their attention on competitiveness and innovation, and there is antipathy towards supporting any one technology. The focus of carbon reductions is on the energy sector, and after the stalling of nuclear power, renewables and carbon capture and storage become the major growth areas.

Fuel cells, running directly on liquid hydrocarbons such as methanol, find large and expanding markets in the portable power sector, including laptops, mobile phones, military power packs, and a range of consumer electronics and portable electrical equipment. Fuel cell prices fall through this deployment, and a dominant design emerges around the direct hydrocarbon fuel cell. As users become increasingly accustomed to mobile power, their needs adapt and change, with higher mobile power demands becoming the norm. The infrastructure of fuel cartridges that this industry creates also serves a growing market for fuel cell scooters, again fuelled with a synthetic hydrocarbon. As technological developments continue, and consumers increasingly expect mobile power from their vehicles, fuel cell companies enter automotive supply chains, providing fuel cells for auxiliary power or for propulsion. Developments in fuel cell technology then ultimately lead to dominance of the synthetic hydrocarbon in transport markets, both in fuel cells and in internal combustion engines.

At first, fuel is supplied from natural gas, but as gas prices rise, and as governments increasingly enforce emissions reductions, fuel suppliers look for alternatives. Governments change regulations, such as the Biofuels Directive, to enable the use of synthetic renewable fuels. A variety of routes emerge, but by the middle of the century, electrolytic hydrogen from renewables has become a primary feedstock, along with carbon from biomass and from the flue gases of carbon intensive industries, and the transport fuel system looks much like that described in *Synthetic Liquid Fuel.*

Multi-level perspective

Landscape

This alternative scenario takes place in a world with increasing climate and energy concerns, but with an antipathy to attempts at 'picking technological winners', and an emphasis on innovation and competitiveness. It is believed that government should not aspire to direct change, but to create the conditions for competitive, innovative markets. Efforts are made to remove barriers to the entry of new technologies and entrepreneurs into markets, and an antitrust approach aims to keep competition and innovation at the forefront of change. There is an emphasis on liberalized markets, and a consumer economy, but governments do create incentive structures to reduce carbon emissions. This scenario also occurs against a background of steadily rising gas prices.

Technologies, niches and early markets

This scenario is driven by market demands, and the important early developments are in niche markets for portable power, auxiliary power on-board vehicles, and on niche vehicles (such as forklifts). Fuel cells enter use in laptops and portable electronic appliances, mostly running on methanol or a similar liquid hydrocarbon fuel. The military is an important 'protected space' for the development of portable fuel cell technologies, as portable power, and 'engine-off' power on vehicles, is highly valuable in military operations. This sees the military put significant investment into portable applications, and leads to developments with spill-over benefits to the civilian sector. Fuel cell scooters are also an important early market, particularly in East Asia, where electric scooters and bicycles are already common.

The early markets and niches are created and developed by companies largely outside the automotive and energy sectors, with electronics and battery firms playing an important role. This scenario is driven by the mobile power demands of end users – consumers who want mobile power to enjoy the full benefits of mobile communications and IT.

Unlike the other scenarios, direct methanol fuel cell or fuel reformer technologies are at the heart of this transition. Synthetic fuel synthesis, renewables and carbon capture technology are also key.

Market growth and systems change

The early markets in portable electronics, the military, niche vehicles and scooters allow high-volume fuel cell production, and subsequent cost reductions. A distribution infrastructure of liquid fuel cartridges becomes established, enabling greater expansion of fuel cells into portable applications and on-board auxiliary power. As consumers become accustomed to on-demand mobile power, there is a growing market of complementary products, providing mobile entertainment, communications and IT. Cost reductions, and changes in user preferences towards maximizing the on-board power potential of vehicles, leads to the entry of synthetic fuel vehicles into transportation. Carbon reduction policies steadily decarbonize fuel synthesis.

The scenario sees rapid growth and restructuring in the electronics and battery industries, as new players emerge and disrupt supply chains in the automotive industry. The fuel supply industry undergoes radical change, with battery firms dominating early markets, and with fuel synthesis becoming a major business. The infrastructure for fuel is initially based on the distribution of cartridges, but as markets expand in transport applications, refuelling stations increasingly provide synthetic fuel, in a pattern similar to today.

Two areas of policy enable this transition to take place. The first area concerns removing barriers to innovation, strengthening anti-trust legislation and encouraging entrepreneurs. A second key area of policy is focused on decarbonization, leading ultimately to the use of recycled or biomass-derived carbon in the synthetic liquid fuel. This enables a transition from the initially natural gas or coal-derived synthetic fuel to a low-carbon alternative.

Discussion and conclusions

The UKSHEC transition scenarios suggest a number of insights for any future large-scale transition to hydrogen. These relate both to messages from the individual scenarios, and lessons which can be drawn from looking across the scenario set as a whole.

Messages from the individual UKSHEC scenarios

Scenario 1: Structural Shift → *Electricity Store*
Much of the literature and policy discussions around the future of hydrogen in the UK emphasizes the role of hydrogen as a transport fuel, and assumes that breakthroughs will come about as a result of developments with respect to fuel cell vehicles. By contrast, this scenario illustrates a transition driven by moves towards a low-carbon energy system. Here the emergence of hydrogen is not driven by a particular guiding vision, but rather is an emergent response to a restructuring of energy markets and the broader technological changes this creates. This scenario therefore focuses attention on the importance of market structure and regulation as a driver of innovation. It challenges the assumption that a major programme of investment in infrastructure will be required for the development of a hydrogen transport system.

Scenario 2: Corporate Race → *Ubiquitous Hydrogen*
Often it is assumed that government holds the key to the development of a hydrogen economy. This scenario emphasizes the role and power of global companies, and the potentially positive outcomes of strategic competition as a driver for radical innovation. It draws attention to the relationship between global companies, niche experimentation and regional systems of innovation with respect to hydrogen, and the importance of environmental regulation in fostering new markets for clean technologies.

Scenario 3: Government Mission → *Centralized Hydrogen for Transport*
Despite the scale of the challenge posed by the climate and energy security drivers of a hydrogen economy, much of the current policy discussion about hydrogen is constrained by prevalent assumptions about the dominance of the market, the limits of government and antipathy to attempts at 'picking winners'. This scenario reminds us that stronger government intervention may be required for a rapid transition to hydrogen, and challenges us to critically reconsider the ability of liberalized markets to deliver the purposive, large-scale socio-technological and infrastructural developments that may be required in an increasingly unstable and hostile world.

Scenario 4: Disruptive Innovation → *Synthetic Liquid Fuel*
This is an alternative or 'wild card' scenario. Conventional wisdom suggests that the market alone will not deliver a transition to a hydrogen economy, and

that the automotive industry in particular has moved away from research into the use of synthetic liquid fuels such as methanol as a possible source of power for future fuel cell vehicles. The Disruptive Innovation → *Synthetic Liquid Fuel* transition scenario challenges us to rethink these assumptions and re-examine the sorts of technological developments, firms and industrial sectors which might drive the transition to hydrogen, and indeed what a hydrogen economy might actually look like.

Lessons across the UKSHEC scenarios

Despite very different governance structures and policies across the scenarios, all contain at least some attempts by policy-makers to reduce carbon emissions and enhance primary energy security. This reminds us of the importance of the policies and regulatory processes that embody society's desire to maintain a secure and sustainable energy system for the future.

Although the scenarios envisage the use and deployment of a range of technologies, there is a portfolio of technologies that is common across the scenarios. This includes:

- a range of fuel cell technologies (principally low-temperature fuel cells for vehicles, but also fuel cells for stationary use, or running on fuels other than pure hydrogen);
- hydrogen production technologies;
- hydrogen storage and handling technologies;
- hydrogen purification and clean-up technologies.

However, some of the technologies envisaged do not fit across all the scenarios. The development and widespread use of stationary hydrogen 'energy stations', nuclear power, gasification, methanol fuel cells, carbon capture and storage, and pipeline technologies, would fit into some pathways but lead others elsewhere. Decisions to support some but not others of these would clearly influence the direction of technological change, and create a different set of choices in the future. Picking a 'winning' set of technologies with any degree of assurance is currently impossible, given the uncertainties inherent in their development, and yet the market alone or 'business as usual' may not deliver the technologies that make a transition possible. Instead, support for portfolios of promising technologies may be the most robust approach.

The scenarios also highlight a number of broader strategic decision points, for government, business and wider society, which are likely to prove influential in shaping the direction of future technological developments with respect to hydrogen. These include decisions over:

- Primary energy production and options for the replacement of the UK's ageing nuclear and coal plant (e.g. whether new nuclear build occurs, decisions regarding new coal-fired power plants, carbon capture and storage, and large-scale renewables policies).

- Whether it is viable to distribute hydrogen through natural gas pipelines.
- The commercialization decisions of major automotive firms and a UK decision point similar to the US Department of Energy's 2015 'go/no-go' commercialization decision on support for FCVs.[3]

One of the potential shortcomings of a backcasting approach is that it can neglect the competing and alternative developments that would close off the vision or transition pathway described. It is therefore important to also consider competing technologies, and potential barriers that could lead away from hydrogen and fuel cells. Several of these are common across all the transitions.

In technological terms, there are competitors in all potential hydrogen applications (e.g. transport, stationary power, grid buffering and portables). These include, for example: battery electric vehicles (including vehicles with super or 'ultra' capacitors); plug-in hybrids; biofuels; alternative energy storage and demand side management technologies to deal with intermittent electricity generation; advances in battery technologies for portable power. Major developments in these technologies could forestall the transition pathways described, although some of the engineering developments involved in the production of battery electric and plug-in hybrid vehicles (in transmission, power electronics, regenerative braking etc.) may also contribute to the eventual commercialization of fuel cell vehicles.

In addition to these direct technological competitors, it is also possible that hydrogen technologies will themselves simply fail to be developed as rapidly as expected, or that they will never overcome some of the current problems and constraints preventing them entering widespread use. Such 'showstoppers' might include: failure to develop adequate onboard storage technologies; difficulties with fuel cells (cost, fuel purity questions, durability); or, limitations in the supply or costs of raw materials (such as platinum).

Finally, of course, as with many new technologies, public and consumer acceptance will be critical: an early disaster with hydrogen could have a major impact on perceptions and serve to set back developments for many years,

Conclusions

The proponents and developers of technologies are driven by expectations about what the future is likely to hold. These expectations, often informed by normative visions of what the future should be, play a role in shaping the direction of innovative activities. Investments in renewable energy, fuel cells and hydrogen infrastructure are all dependent on beliefs about the way in which the future will unfold. The scenarios in this chapter help to explore the normative frameworks and framing assumptions (such as belief in the role of markets versus the state) that underpin expectations and thus guide innovative activity; they also help to explore the uncertainties and risks facing the development of a hydrogen energy system. As such, scenarios can remind us to think flexibly about the future, and challenge us to recognize our role as a society in shaping technology.

Notes

1 Hydrogen is often referred to as the most abundant element in the universe; it is rarely acknowledged that it is not, however, the most abundant element on Earth, a rather more relevant fact.
2 The four end-visions were adapted from a set of six hydrogen visions, which had previously been taken through an extensive expert-stakeholder multi-criteria sustainability appraisal. *Centralized Hydrogen for Transport* is an amalgamation of two of the six original UKSHEC Hydrogen Visions: *Central Pipeline* and *Liquid Hydrogen*.
3 The US Department of Energy Hydrogen Program was structured to support a 2015 private sector decision on whether to commercialize fuel cell vehicles. This 'go/no-go' decision point enables the targeting of DOE resources to a specific, time-based objective. The DOE has also set out a timetable of incremental 'go/no-go' decision points for specific technological elements, such as onboard reforming of hydrocarbon fuels, on which a 'no-go' decision was made in 2004.

References

Berkhout, F., Smith, A. and Stirling, A. (2004) 'Socio-technical regimes and transition contexts', in Elzen, Geels and Green (eds) *System innovation and the transition to sustainability: Theory, evidence and policy*, Camberley, Edward Elgar
Dunn, S. (2001) 'Hydrogen Futures: Toward a Sustainable Energy System', Worldwatch Paper 157, Washington, DC, Worldwatch Institute
Eames, M. and McDowall, W. (2005) 'UKSHEC Hydrogen Visions', UKSHEC Social Science Working Paper no 10, London, Policy Studies Institute
Eames, M. and McDowall, W. (2006) 'Transitions to a UK Hydrogen Economy', UKSHEC Social Science Working Paper no 19, London, Policy Studies Institute
Eames, M., McDowall, W., Hodson, M. and Marvin, S. (2006) 'Negotiating generic and place-specific expectations of a hydrogen economy', *Technology Analysis and Strategic Management*, vol 18, pp361–374
Elzen, B. and Wieczorek, A. (2005) 'Transitions towards sustainability through system innovation', *Technological Forecasting and Social Change*, vol 72, pp651–661
Geels, F. W. (2002a) 'Towards sociotechnical scenarios and reflexive anticipation: Using patterns and regularities in technology dynamics', in Sorensen, K. H. and Williams, R. (eds) *Shaping technology, guiding policy: concepts, spaces and tools*, Cheltenham, Edward Elgar
Geels, F. W. (2002b) 'Technological transitions as evolutionary reconfiguration processes: a multi-level perspective and a case-study', *Research Policy*, vol 31, pp1257–1274
Geels, F. W. (2005) 'Processes and patterns in transitions and system innovations: Refining the co-evolutionary multi-level perspective', *Technological Forecasting and Social Change*, vol 72, pp681–696
Geels, F. W. and Schot, J. (2007) 'Typology of socio-technical transition pathways', *Research Policy*, vol 36, pp399–417
Greeuw, S. C. H., van Asselt, M. B. A., Grosskurth, J., Storms, C. A. M. H., Rijkens-Klomp, N., Rothman, D. and Rotmans, J. (2000) 'Cloudy crystal balls: an assessment of recent European and global scenario studies and methods, Environmental Issues Series no 17, Copenhagen, European Environment Agency
Hisschemoller, M., Bode, R. and Van der Kerkhof, M. (2006) 'What governs the transition to a sustainable hydrogen economy? Articulating the relationship

between technologies and political institutions', *Energy Policy*, vol 34, no 11, pp1227–1235

McDowall, W. and Eames, M. (2004) 'Report of the September 2004 UKSHEC hydrogen visions workshop', UKSHEC Social Science Working Paper no 9, London, Policy Studies Institute

McDowall, W. and Eames, M. (2006) 'Forecasts, scenarios, visions, backcasts and roadmaps to the hydrogen economy', *Energy Policy*, vol 34, pp1236–1250

McDowall, W. and Eames, M. (2007) 'Towards a sustainable hydrogen economy: a multi-criteria sustainability appraisal of competing hydrogen futures', *International Journal of Hydrogen Energy*, vol 32, pp4611–4626

Robinson, J. (2003) 'Future subjunctive: backcasting as social learning', *Futures*, vol 35(8), pp839–856

Schwartz, P. (1996) *The Art of the Long View*, New York, Currency Doubleday

Solomon, B. D. and Banerjee, A. (2006) 'A global survey of hydrogen energy research, development and policy', *Energy Policy*, vol 34, pp781–792

Stirling, A. (2007) 'Deliberate futures: precaution and progress in social choice of sustainable technology', *Sustainable Development*, vol 15, pp286–295

Van Lente, H. (1993) Promising Technology: the dynamics of expectations in technological development. Enschede, Department of Philosophy of Science & Technology, University of Twente

Whitehouse Press Office (2003) 'Hydrogen economy fact sheet'. Available at www.whitehouse.gov/news/releases/2003/06/20030625-6.html. Accessed 2 January 2009

6
Hydrogen System Modelling

Nazmiye Balta-Ozkan and Neil Strachan

Introduction

This chapter builds upon a series of UKSHEC working papers that review the literature on hydrogen energy modelling (Joffe and Strachan, 2007), compare and contrast the hydrogen modelling approach in three international MARKAL energy systems models (Joffe et al, 2007), and undertake an enhanced representation of hydrogen modelling in the UK MARKAL model (Balta-Ozkan et al, 2007). A summary of an extension to spatial hydrogen modelling is based on Strachan et al (2008a). Further detail on the methodology and policy insights of UK hydrogen modelling is given in a recent journal paper (Strachan et al, 2009).

Challenges in hydrogen systems modelling

The possible future development of a 'hydrogen (H_2) economy' has been subject to much speculation, discussion and analysis. As such energy systems do not yet exist, much of the analysis on the ways in which H_2 may develop as an energy vector has been through quantitative modelling.

Different modelling approaches to new economy-wide hydrogen (H_2) networks and infrastructure systems are all subject to a number of challenges[1] (Joffe and Strachan, 2007):

- interactions within the rest of the energy system, notably competition for primary energy resources;
- the level of (future) technical detail required to appropriately represent the various H_2 pathways; and
- the inherently spatial nature of H_2 infrastructure development.

Alternative pathways for H_2 or other energy vectors will depend on competition for primary and secondary energy resources which could be used elsewhere in the energy system. Prime examples of this are the use of renewable electricity for H_2 production via electrolysis versus its direct use in the electricity system and the reforming of natural gas or bio-methane into H_2 versus using that methane direct for residential heating. In addition, the price of energy in competitive energy markets is the result of demand and supply for that resource.

H_2 technologies, for production, infrastructures and demand applications (in both the transport and the power sectors (e.g. micro-generation)), are at an immature stage of technical development, when compared with current incumbent technologies. Future technical developments would have a major impact on efficiencies, availabilities, lifetime, range (for transport), power output, weight and size, with resulting implications for the fixed and variable costs of operating these technologies. The evolution of these cost parameters is partly related to engineering improvements, but also to economies of scale, economies of learning in production and the development of niche markets (Agnolucci and Ekins, 2007; Chapters 2, 3, 4 of this volume). Models can account for future economic costs through technological vintages (i.e. new generations of technologies) or learning curves (cost reductions through increasing deployment, which may be modelled exogenously or endogenously). Furthermore, some technical parameters denote engineering requirements for successful operation (e.g., linked to intermittent use or part-loading). Hence an overly simple representation of H_2 technologies can potentially assume infrastructures that are suboptimal or even technically unviable.

Due to the difficulties and expense of distributing hydrogen, the development of new H_2 infrastructure is, by necessity, likely to be highly geographically dependent. Variation in available resources and carbon sinks, as well as the density and requirements of demand in different locations (notably, urban versus rural or liquid versus gaseous form), are likely to lead to infrastructures that differ in capacity, length, sectoral coverage and the degree of centralization. A non-geographical model is limited in representing these issues, although approximations can be achieved via discrete investments and costs of infrastructures by scale and distance, as well as by other constraints/assumptions. The optimal solution to how centralized H_2 infrastructure should be is a trade-off between the economies of scale available in H_2 production and the costs of H_2 distribution, which are strongly dependent on the distribution distance and flow rate (Yang and Ogden, 2007).

Approaches to hydrogen systems modelling

The scope of modelling or economic analyses, as well as the policy questions to be answered, has inevitably led to modelling trade-offs in the depiction of these key challenges.

Energy systems optimization models (e.g. MARKAL, POLES, TIMES) have been used to generate least-cost pathways for the development of economy-wide uses of H_2 (Tseng et al, 2005; European Commission, 2006; Endo,

2007; Contaldi et al, 2008; IEA, 2008; van Ruijven et al, 2008). A key strength of energy systems models is their representation of entire energy chains, from primary energy resource to energy service demands. This allows the model to identify synergies between measures on the demand and supply sides, as well as the infrastructure that connects them. In addition, they contain an extensive depiction of technology costs and characteristics, and can be used to examine the impact of different taxation and subsidy approaches. Further detail on energy system (MARKAL) approaches to H_2 modelling is given below.

An alternative approach is to focus on optimizing technological and socio-economic detail of future H_2 systems within a consistent energy scenario (Oi and Wada, 2004; Hugo et al, 2005; Prince-Richard et al, 2005). The bpIC-H_2 model by Hugo et al (2005) uses the mixed-integer linear programming (MILP) technique, with technological detail, consideration of H_2 demand sites and evolving demands to dynamically optimize H_2 infrastructure development, including the trade-offs between centralized versus decentralized infrastructures. In these approaches, high levels of technological and socio-economic detail can be built into the analysis, although with the loss of resource, demand and sectoral interactions.

A set of sectoral and energy system models utilize geographical information systems (GIS) tools to characterize the spatial aspects and costs of energy resources, infrastructures and demands (Stamatina-Parissis et al, 2005; Lin et al, 2006; Ball et al, 2007; Johnson et al, 2008). The Hydrogen Infrastructure Transition (HIT) model (Lin et al, 2006) is a spatial optimization dynamic programming model. It is one of few models that consider the optimal build-up of refuelling facilities over time, for an exogenously determined build-up of H_2 demand and penetration in the transport sector. This trades off the refuelling network versus driving time in the coverage of fuelling stations. The model is purely focused on H_2 infrastructure and therefore does not include any explicit aspect of resource competition, energy prices etc.

Scenario-based models depart from a focus on optimality, and instead attempt to quantify the consequences and implications of multiple plausible storylines, or scenarios. This enables these scenarios to include 'soft' drivers and constraints that are difficult to model in an optimization framework. The Tyndall Hydrogen Energy Scenario Investigation Suite (THESIS) (Dutton et al, 2005) assesses the evolution of electricity generation and/or H_2 production capacity, according to technology profiles specific to each scenario and a range of other drivers. Impacts on greenhouse gas and local air-quality emissions are then calculated. The Hydrogen Infrastructure Techno-Economic Spatial (HITES) model (Joffe, 2008) is a scenario model that combines assumptions about demand growth, geographical areas of demand, infrastructure development, choice of technologies, availability of feedstock and energy prices. The model incorporates a detailed characterization of the technologies and simulates the operation of specified infrastructures, analysing their performance and identifying potential areas for refinement. All economic parameters are supplied exogenously, and the model focuses only on one part of the energy system – the development of H_2 infrastructure.

A further alternative is to utilize other economic tools including options analysis (van Benthem et al, 2006). In this analytical category, the impact of alternative taxation and subsidy approaches can be examined, as well as some depiction of behavioural and institutional drivers in the movement from niche to mainstream markets. Last, top-down macro-economic models have traditionally not focused on H_2 scenarios, due to their lack of sufficient technological detail. However, any transition to an H_2 economy would have significant macro-economic implications, including possible changes in government revenue from fuel taxes (Babiker et al, 2003).

Importance of hydrogen modelling for UK energy policy

Hydrogen technologies and infrastructures may offer significant contributions in meeting the UK's primary energy goals,[2] which are stringent long-term reductions in carbon dioxide (CO_2) emissions and security of energy supplies. At the time of doing the modelling, the results of which are reported in this chapter, the UK government had adopted a target of a 60 per cent reduction in greenhouse gas (GHG) emissions, from 1990 levels, by 2050, and this is therefore the target that is modelled.[3] Moreover, the target was applied to emissions of CO_2 only, because other GHGs are not represented in the model. All results in this paper are relative to a base year 2000, and the target is applied to that, rather than the 1990 level of CO_2 emissions. Unlike many countries, UK CO_2 emissions fell from 1990 to 2000 (592MtCO_2 to 545MtCO_2), so that the same percentage targets are associated with lower outcome emission levels.

In this context, various studies have been carried out in the UK to analyse what roles H_2 can play in a future UK energy system. Notably, H_2 has the potential to achieve CO_2 reductions in sectors such as transport, which have been shown to be the hardest to decarbonize (IEA, 2008). Using socio-techno-economic scenarios of H_2 deployment, these focus on technical feasibility (E4Tech, 2004), the economic and social impacts (Dutton et al, 2005), and the links with renewable energy deployment (Hart et al, 2003). Under the UK Sustainable Hydrogen Energy Consortium (UKSHEC), four H_2 visions and pathways have been developed, based on an extensive literature review, stakeholder workshops and scoping interviews (see McDowall and Eames, 2006; and Chapter 5). These four visions are: use of H_2 only in the transport sector through central production (*Centralized Hydrogen for Transport*); use of H_2 in both stationary applications and transport (*Ubiquitous Hydrogen*); a *Synthetic Liquid Fuel* scenario; and use of H_2 as a medium to buffer intermittent energy supplies (*Electricity Store*). This chapter undertakes formal energy-economic modelling to investigate the long-term energy system pathways and impacts implied by these scenarios.

The chapter is structured as follows. The next section introduces the modelling approach using the UK MARKAL energy system model, including discussion of hydrogen energy pathways and characterization of H_2 infrastructures. Extensions on hydrogen taxation and H_2 spatial modelling are summarized. The section after this details the quantification of the UKSHEC H_2 visions and analysis of system-wide impacts under a long-term 60 per cent CO_2 reduction target. Further insights are provided on how taxation of H_2 would affect such transitions, and on exploratory scenarios utilizing a methodological development in the use of GIS in characterizing a UK H_2 network within a full energy system model. The final section gives conclusions and insights from a UK energy policy perspective.

Hydrogen and energy systems modelling

Overview of the UK MARKAL energy systems model

MARKAL is a widely applied bottom-up, dynamic, linear programming (LP) optimization model (Loulou et al, 2004). MARKAL models have a long track record of policy and academic research (e.g. Smekens, 2004; IEA, 2008).

As one of its major strengths, MARKAL portrays the entire energy system from imports and domestic production of fuel resources, through fuel processing and supply, explicit representation of infrastructures, conversion to secondary energy carriers (including electricity, heat and H_2), end-use technologies and energy service demands of the entire economy. As a perfect foresight partial equilibrium optimization model, MARKAL minimizes discounted total system cost by choosing the investment and operation levels of all the interconnected system elements. The imposition of a range of policy and physical constraints, implementation of all taxes and subsidies, and inclusion of base-year capital stocks and flows of energy, facilitates realistic evolution of the energy system under different scenarios.

The UK MARKAL model hence provides a systematic exploration of least-cost configurations to meet exogenous demands for energy services – derived from standard UK forecasts for residential buildings (Shorrock and Uttley, 2003), transport[4] (DfT, 2005), the service sector (Pout and Mackenzie, 2006), and industrial sub-sectors (Fletcher and Marshall, 1995). Generally, these sources entail a low-energy growth projection, with saturation effects in key sectors.

One set of key input data is resource supply curves (BERR, 2006a). Multipliers are used to translate these baseline costs into both higher cost supply steps, as well as imported refined fuel costs. A second key input is description of future technology choices, which are characterized through data covering capital and operating costs, efficiency, availability, operating lifetime, and diurnal or seasonal characteristics. Future costs are estimated through expert assessment of technology vintages, or for less mature electricity and H_2 technologies, via exogenous learning curves derived from an assessment of learning rates (McDonald and Schrattenholzer, 2002), combined with global forecasts of technology uptake (European Commission, 2006). Endogenous progress ratios for less mature technologies are not employed, as the relatively small UK market is assumed to be a price taker for globally developed technologies. A third key input is an explicit depiction of infrastructures, physical and policy constraints. All UK legislated environmental and economic policies as of 2006 are included (BERR, 2007).[5]

UK MARKAL is calibrated in its base year (2000) to data within 1 per cent of actual resource supplies, energy consumption, electricity output, installed technology capacity and CO_2 emissions (all from DUKES, 2006). The model then solves from year 2000 to 2070 in five-year increments. A complete description of all input parameters is given in the model documentation (Kannan et al, 2007). All prices are in £ (2000). Full details of the UK MARKAL energy systems model are given in Strachan et al (2007), with additional insights on model variants focusing on macro implications (Strachan and Kannan, 2008) and international drivers (Strachan et al, 2008b).

Hydrogen energy pathways and infrastructures in MARKAL modelling

It is illustrative first to compare the approaches to H_2 infrastructure representation taken by other MARKAL models.

Rather than allowing a choice of distribution options, the US MARKAL model (Shay et al, 2005)[6] assigns a distribution infrastructure, corresponding to different scales of H_2 production: Central Station, Midsize and Distributed. Only transport-related generic H_2 applications are considered. The options in the model have hence been constructed to form complete 'production plus delivery' infrastructures, each of which would supply H_2 all the way to the end user. For large-scale production facilities, pipeline distribution is assumed, while mid-size production is combined with H_2 liquefaction and distribution by road. The distributed-scale H_2 production requires no specific infrastructure. As such, each of the options is equivalent from the end users perspective and the option selected by the model is therefore simply a function of the size and growth rate of demand. The model uses a mixed integer investment option to ensure that only whole numbers of each option can be selected. This use of only a limited subset of 'aggregated' representations of H_2 infrastructure ensures that options for 'delivered' H_2 compete on a level playing field, and that only plausible solutions for H_2 infrastructure development are considered.

The Netherlands MARKAL model (developed by ECN: Martinus et al, 2005) has very considerable detail on H_2 production (both centralized and decentralized), using electrolysis, steam methane reforming and gasification of coal or biomass. Major storage and transportation options include:

- distribution by road in compressed or liquid form;
- development of a dedicated H_2 pipeline distribution network; or
- mixing H_2 with natural gas in the existing pipeline system.

Finally, a full set of end-use technologies is depicted in the transport, buildings and industrial sectors. The issue of optimizing scale and distance in H_2 infrastructures is handled by drawing a distinction between the local H_2 'distribution' pipeline systems and longer distance 'transmission' pipelines, in a similar way to the treatment of natural gas pipeline infrastructure, and by using the integer investment feature for different capacities of pipeline to be specified. The ECN MARKAL model allows the flexibility to choose from a large number of appropriate combinations of H_2 production and distribution technologies. However, this flexibility may allow some implausible solutions for H_2 infrastructure development.

The UK MARKAL model has a detailed representation of H_2 pathways (Figure 6.1) that covers a range of technologies and resources in production, distribution and end-use (see Balta-Ozkan et al, 2007). In addition to imported H_2, two scales of production technologies are represented:

- Large-scale H_2 production from steam methane reforming (SMR) of natural gas, electrolysis and gasification of coal, biomass or municipal waste. Carbon capture and sequestration (CCS) is included as an option for large-scale SMR and coal/gas gasification technologies.
- Small-scale H_2 production from SMR of natural gas and electrolysis.

Imported and large-scale H_2 are delivered to central H_2 distribution terminals and then distributed to potential end-users. Two main gaseous hydrogen (GH_2) transmission options via pipeline and road trailer, together with liquefied hydrogen (LH_2) distribution by road, are included. Small-scale generation makes use of existing natural gas and electricity networks, avoiding H_2 infrastructure costs.

All end-use H_2 technologies (transport and stationary) are represented with dynamically evolving costs and efficiencies to reflect global learning rates (see Kannan et al, 2007 for full details). Detailed specification of transport modes include air transport, rail and several modes of road transport, namely buses, cars, light goods vehicles (LGVs), heavy goods vehicles (HGVs) and two-wheelers. Dynamically evolving transport end-use technologies meet energy service demands, and are defined based on their input fuel, efficiencies, capital and operating costs, lifetime, available year and applicable hurdle rates to reflect non-cost barriers to adoption. Similarly, in the service, residential and industrial sectors, a range of H_2 fuel cell technologies are included for stationary power generation and/or micro-generation (both CHP and electricity-only).

A major enhancement to this non-spatial energy systems model was to disaggregate H_2 networks by distribution distances and flow rates, according to different transport and stationary applications. Alternative H_2 networks (liquid and gaseous) are determined by demand requirements; for example, air and rail transport would require few large fuelling hubs – which might be close to resource or import sites – due to their large scales, but cars would need filling stations throughout the country with lower flow demands to each station.

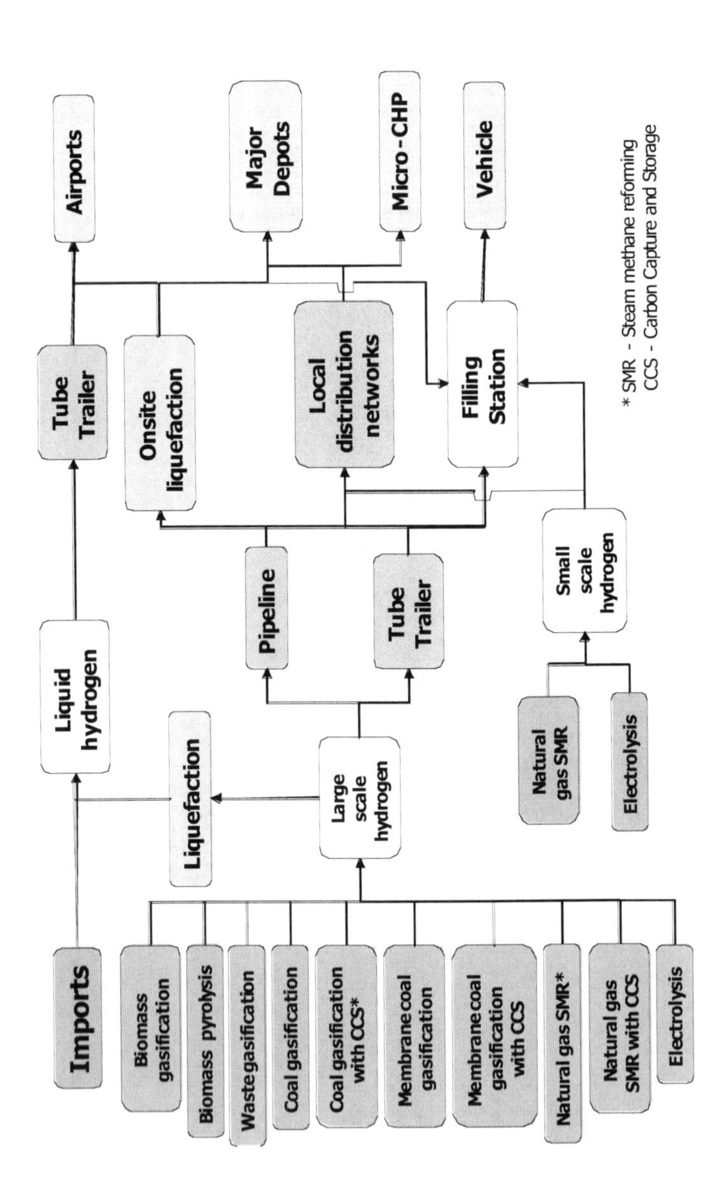

Figure 6.1 *Structure of the hydrogen module in the UK MARKAL model*

H_2 distribution characterization thus needs to take into account the distance and flow-rate relationship for individual end-use options. Following Yang and Ogden (2007), four H_2 distribution classifications are assumed to take place based on a distribution distance of 50km versus 300km, and a flow rate of 15 tonnes per day (t/day) versus 100t/day. Hence, in UK MARKAL, each transport mode (together with H_2 distribution for stationary micro-generation technologies) is assigned to a quadrant in a 2 x 2 matrix, formed by these two axes for all the distribution networks (see Table 6.1). Liquid H_2 (via road tanker) is impacted only by the distance of transfer, while gaseous H_2 (via pipelines or tube trailer) is impacted by both distance and scale of transfer.

However, different types of transport also require hydrogen in liquid (LH_2) versus gaseous (GH_2) form. While air transport requires only the former, the other transport types may take H_2 in liquid or compressed gas form, with the exception of two-wheelers and rail transport. Hence, for several types of road transport – namely buses, cars, HGVs, LGVs and air transport – on-site H_2 liquefaction technologies are introduced, in addition to the centrally produced and distributed liquid H_2 chain. These on-site liquefaction technologies can take GH_2 – either centrally produced and distributed via pipelines or tube trailers, or locally produced GH_2. An end-use conversion from LH_2 to GH_2 is allowed, as this reflects a simple expansion process.

As small-scale H_2 production is assumed to take place at a site close to demand points, there are no H_2 distribution or transmission costs associated with them. Instead, the distribution is via the electricity or natural gas infrastructures, and implicitly incurs the efficiency losses and costs associated with those infrastructures.

Hence the UK model represents detailed H_2 infrastructures, corresponding to the locations of different options, and the distribution options appropriate to differing scales of H_2 production. This detailed approach to H_2 energy pathways builds on the approach in the ECN model, while an extension in a subsequent section to connect UK MARKAL to a GIS spatial model of infrastructure development builds on the US EPA approach of specifying plausible distribution infrastructures.

Model extension: taxation of hydrogen

In the UK, depending on the variation in global oil prices, current road duties make up between 65 per cent and 75 per cent of petrol and diesel prices. Hence, not applying road duties to some competing fuels might result in an uneven

Table 6.1 *UK hydrogen distribution network by mode*

	Distribution Distance	
Flow rate	*Short (50km)*	*Long (300km)*
High (100t/day)	Air, rail, ship	Heavy goods vehicles (HGV)
Low (15t/day)	Bus, two-wheeler	Car, light goods vehicles (LGV), micro-generation (stationary sectors)

playing field for a technology comparison. From a government perspective, road duties (combined with an additional sales taxation (VAT) component) contribute approximately £30.2 billion or 5.2 per cent of current UK government general revenues (HMT, 2008). Although in the last 20 years the relative share of fuel duties has varied in real terms, due to the imposition and cancellation of the fuel duty escalator,[7] the inelastic demand for road transport has made this revenue source a mainstay of the UK Budget (Adam and Browne, 2006). Although a transport niche market may be appropriate to apply tax incentives (Bomb et al, 2007), any mainstream switch to non-taxed alternative fuels would require significant adjustments in the UK central government budget.

In the UK MARKAL model, it is assumed that all alternative transport fuels (H_2, bio-diesels, CNG, electricity, ethanol, LPG and methanol) are taxed similarly to fossil fuels and set at the year 2000 rate of 13.6–14.1 £/GJ. Sensitivity analysis is undertaken on reduced or delayed H_2 taxation levels. Previous studies have found that H_2 taxation is either the main driver of H_2 penetration levels (van Ruijven et al, 2008), or much less important than other technological uncertainties (van Benthem et al, 2006). All studies on H_2 taxation and long-term deployment suggest that the wider economic impacts need to be further investigated (Tseng et al, 2005).

Model extension: spatial modelling of UK hydrogen infrastructures

A methodological extension (Strachan et al, 2008a) was to soft-link a geographical information systems (GIS) -based spatial model of plausible gaseous and liquid H_2 infrastructures and delivery systems with the UK MARKAL model.[8]

The first step was identification and characterization of demand centres in the GIS model. The UK's nine urban H_2 demand centres were initially identified by population and fully assessed using GIS data. These centres represent nine urban aggregations, including London and other key city groups (Liverpool, Manchester and Salford, in the urban centre of 'Lancashire'). Remaining areas in the UK were divided in the GIS model into one of three settlement types: 'other urban', with populations over 10,000; 'rural – less sparse', having over 50 per cent in small communities; and 'rural – sparse' having over 80 per cent in small communities. The geographical location of these nine urban demand centres is presented in Figure 6.2.

Then, transport energy service demands (in billion vehicle kilometres) for LGVs (TL), HGVs (TH), passenger rail (TR) and freight (TH) were disaggregated,[9] based on population share of each region (Table 6.2). For buses (TB), and cars (TC), demand is weighted by London's disparate share relative to population (DfT, 2006). Domestic (TA) and international aviation (TI) energy service demands[10] are disaggregated based on airport passenger flows (DfT, 2003).

The location of potential UK H_2 supply points (Table 6.3) was based upon the anticipated use of UK resources in a CO_2 constrained economy, as well as

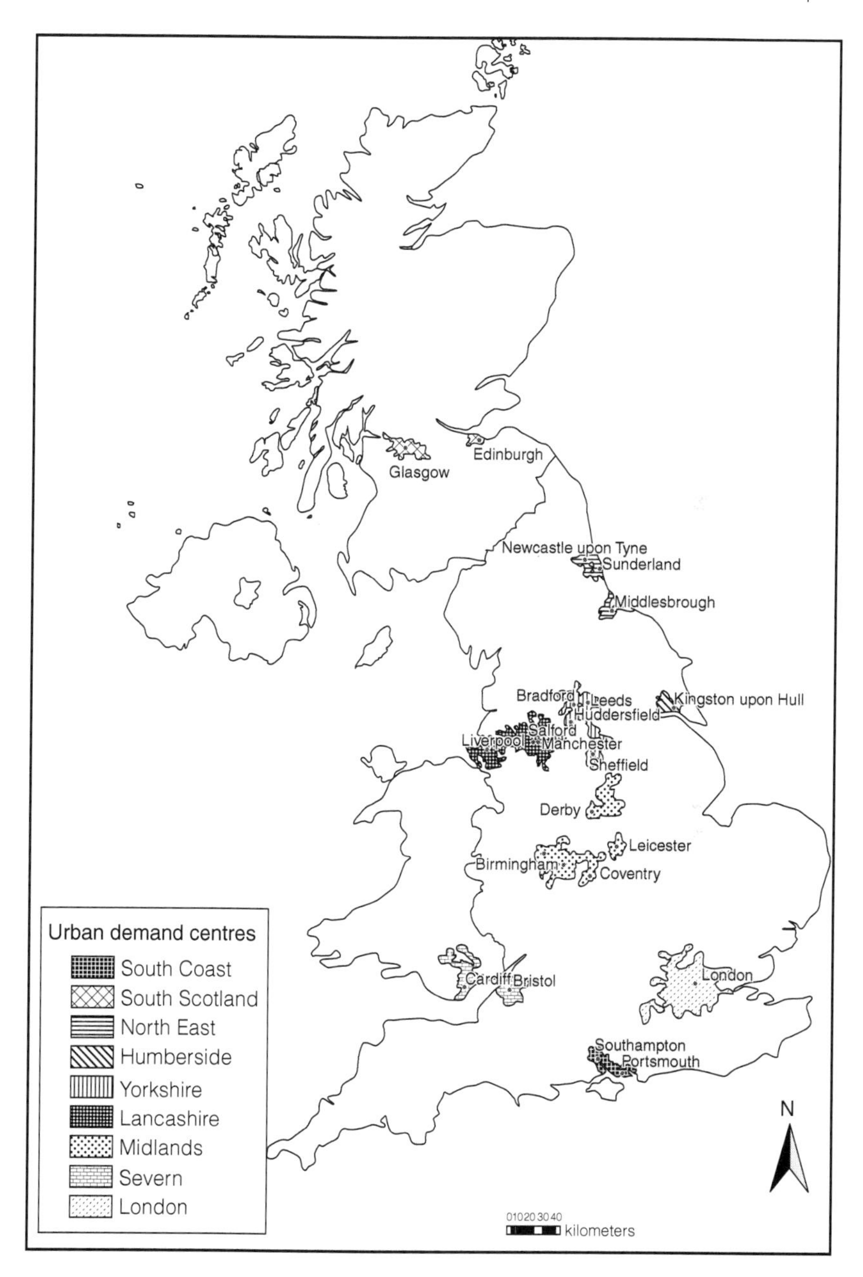

Figure 6.2 *UK urban demand centres*

current and expected location of liquid H_2 and liquefied natural gas (LNG) terminals. This included remote renewables (offshore wind, onshore wind, wave, tidal) (BERR, 2006b), and carbon capture and sequestration (CCS) sites (Holloway, 2007).

The topological focus of the model was in linking these disaggregated 12 major demand[11] and six supply options. Three H_2 infrastructure options are

Table 6.2 *Disaggregation of transport energy service demands by regions*

Region	Area	Pop. share (%)	Adjusted ratios by each transport mode TA	TB	TC	TF	TH	TI	TL	TR
A	South Scotland	3.07	22.5	2.1	3.3	3.1	3.1	3.7	3.1	3.1
B	North East	2.88	3.3	1.9	3.1	2.9	2.0	1.8	2.9	2.9
C	Humberside	0.65	0.1	0.4	0.7	0.7	0.7	0.3	0.7	0.7
D	Yorkshire	4.90	1.3	3.3	5.3	4.9	4.9	0.8	4.9	4.9
E	Lancashire	7.15	10.1	4.8	7.8	7.2	7.2	11.8	7.2	7.2
F	Midlands	8.19	4.4	5.5	8.9	8.2	8.2	5.7	8.2	8.2
G	Severn	2.86	1.4	1.9	3.1	2.9	2.9	2.2	2.9	2.9
H	London	16.20	38.6	44.0	9.1	16.2	16.2	71.7	16.2	16.2
I	South Coast	1.62	1.8	1.1	1.8	1.6	1.6	0.4	1.6	1.6
J	Other Urban	28.73	16.5	19.2	31.2	28.7	28.7	1.6	28.7	28.7
K	Rural – less sparse	20.07	0.0	13.4	21.8	20.1	20.1	0.0	20.1	20.1
L	Rural – sparse	3.68	0.0	2.5	4.0	3.7	3.7	0.0	3.7	3.7
	TOTAL	100	100	100	100	100	100	100	100	100

Table 6.3 *Potential UK hydrogen supply points*

Supply point	Area	H_2 production	Carbon constrained H_2 production
1	Peterhead	Coal, natural gas, large-scale electrolysis	CCS
2	Teesside	Coal, natural gas, large-scale electrolysis, LH_2, LNG terminals	CCS, LH_2, LNG terminals
3	Humberside	Coal, natural gas, large-scale electrolysis	CCS
4	Isle of Grain, Thames	LH_2, LNG terminals, natural gas, large-scale electrolysis	LH_2, LNG terminals
5	Milford Haven, Wales	LH_2, LNG terminals, coal, large-scale electrolysis	LH_2, LNG terminals
6	North West Scotland	Renewables	Renewables

considered: liquid delivery by tankers, large-scale gaseous pipeline networks, and small-scale on-site production.

A core assumption is that liquid hydrogen (LH_2) delivery costs are dependent only on distance rather than scale, as the latter would affect the frequency rather than the volume of regular tanker delivery to a given transport fuelling facility. The GIS model was used to identify the most likely routes for LH_2 transportation using a cost-weighted shortest path function, weighted in favour of travel via motorways, which was then translated into costs and efficiencies in the UK MARKAL model. Additionally, all liquefaction facilities have discrete investment sizes to account for minimum-scale economies in production.

Based on the six supply points, the GIS approach was utilized to construct feasible large-scale H_2 pipeline infrastructures to the nine urban demand regions.[12] Using input cost data (Yang and Ogden, 2007), together with H_2 vehicle conversion efficiency per mode (Kannan et al, 2007), and expected pipeline losses, the distance and then costs of the pipeline infrastructure are built up in predetermined deployment networks to meet regional demands.

The H_2 pipelines must adhere to least-cost and topologically feasible paths. In addition the pipeline networks must be built up sequentially from supply points to nearer demand regions, before being extended to more remote regions and other modes. For computational reasons the model has access to only 100 feasible pipeline 'meta' infrastructures (listed in Strachan et al, 2008a).

An alternative is small-scale gaseous H_2 production (utilizing either the existing electricity or natural gas networks for small-scale electrolysis and steam methane reforming respectively). This option avoids additional H_2 distribution and transmission costs and is assumed to be possible in all the demand regions, given the current coverage of these infrastructures to UK households.

UK hydrogen scenarios and modelling results

Scenarios

The focus of this energy system model analysis is on UK hydrogen (H_2) scenarios under economy-wide long-term CO_2 constraints (minus 60 per cent by year 2050 from 2000 levels). Under such scenarios, H_2 vectors must compete for low-carbon resources with other zero carbon energy carriers, with conversion and demand technologies that utilize alternate fuels, and with demand-side conservation options. The four core scenarios discussed here,[13] including two of the H_2 scenarios (TH and UH below, corresponding respectively to *Centralized Hydrogen for Transport* and *Ubiquitous Hydrogen* in Chapter 5) from the UKSHEC visions exercise (McDowall and Eames, 2006), are:

- Base case (**BAU**): A business-as-usual case, that is, without any CO_2 constraint, where UK fiscal and regulatory energy and environmental policies as of 2006 are included.
- Reference case (**REF**): A run with an economy-wide CO_2 constraint applied at 30 per cent below 2000 levels in 2030 and declining linearly to 60 per cent below 2000 levels in 2050.
- Transport from hydrogen (**TH**): CO_2 constraint as in the reference case, with an additional constraint to deliver 16 per cent of final energy from H_2 by 2050. This scenario portrays an H_2-dominated UK transport sector. In the CO_2-constrained (REF) case modelling horizon (2000–50), fuel use in the transport sector accounts for at least 21 per cent of the final energy demand. However, for technical and socio-economical reasons,[14] it may not be possible to move the entire transport fleet to H_2.
- Ubiquitous hydrogen (**UH**): CO_2 constraint as in the reference case, with an additional constraint to deliver 50 per cent of final energy from H_2 by 2050. This ubiquitous H_2 scenario assumes a dual role for H_2, a fuel for road transport, as well as an energy carrier for domestic and commercial heat and power generation.

A further set of scenarios with different taxation of H_2 is compared to the REF case (which assumes H_2 road technologies incur conventional road fuel taxation levels), involving scenarios with:

- no taxes (NTAX);
- lower taxes (LTAX): 25 per cent of current fuel duty from 2030 onwards;
- progressive taxes (PTAX): 25 per cent of current fuel duty between 2015 and 2030, 50 per cent between 2030 and 2050 and 100 per cent from 2050.

A final set of modelling runs is based on the spatial disaggregation of infrastructure through the GIS soft-link, and these runs are compared with the non-spatial model results.

Core modelling results

Energy system evolution

Even in the BAU case, considerable technological change throughout the whole energy system, combined with fuel switching and increased efficiency and conservation uptake in end-use sectors, results in low growth of energy demand. BAU primary energy demand is reduced by 15 per cent from 2000 levels by 2050 (from 8,583PJ to 7,323PJ).[15] In the BAU case, electricity from coal, and natural gas use in buildings, are the dominant energy sources. More efficient vehicles (including H_2 – primarily from coal) lowers transport demand for oil, whilst modest renewable and biomass growth rates are driven by existing government policy on electricity and minimum share obligations for renewable transport fuels.

The REF scenario imposition of a 60 per cent CO_2 reduction by 2050 (starting in 2030) further reduces primary energy to 5,855PJ (–32 per cent from 2000 levels), due to switching to more efficient and less carbon-intensive upstream technologies (e.g. hydrogen (H_2) from coal CCS, nuclear electricity and large-scale renewables).

In order to meet high H_2 targets by 2050, in both TH and UH scenarios, overall primary energy demand increases. This reflects thermodynamic losses in the large- and small-scale electrolysis routes, the large- and small-scale-natural gas SMR routes, and the use of imported liquid H_2, as the model meets an additional constraint for H_2 production in a low-carbon economy.

There are multiple interactions between the electricity and H_2 sectors, most notably zero-carbon resource limitations (including CCS), the use of the existing network for electrolysis, and alternate hydrogen versus electric vehicles and heating boilers. Hence further H_2 constraints can either decrease the demand for electricity (by 2050: 1,440PJ in the TH scenario versus 1,621PJ in the REF scenario) as H_2 is imported rather than being produced domestically from electrolysis, or dramatically increase overall electricity production (by 2050: 2,362PJ in the UH scenario) as stationary applications require on-site electrolysis.

This new emphasis on H_2 production also alters the sectoral contribution to decarbonization efforts. The power sector remains a key source of zero-carbon energy provision. However, in terms of end-use sectors, transport's share of residual 2050 UK CO_2 emissions falls from 30 per cent in the REF scenario to 22 per cent, and 17 per cent in the TH and UH scenarios, respectively.

Hydrogen consumption, production and infrastructure

In the four core scenarios, H_2 demand is focused on the transport sector. H_2 demand in the BAU and REF scenarios is 490PJ and 425PJ respectively by 2050 (making up around 40 per cent of total transport fuel demand). This reduction in the REF case illustrates the zero-carbon resource competition in the overall energy system and that CO_2 constraints are not necessarily a driver for H_2 deployment. Demand for H_2 is nearly doubled in the TH scenario, reaching up to 827PJ (accounting for 67 per cent of transport fuel demand), and then increases substantially in the UH scenario to 2,525PJ by 2050. In the UH scenario, 58 per cent of H_2 demand is used in stationary applications, and the remaining H_2 accounts for 82 per cent of transport fuel demand.

Figure 6.3 shows H_2 production over time. It can be seen that H_2 only plays a significant role in later time periods. This is due to the timing of the CO_2 and H_2 constraints, and also as the model prefers to wait until the costs of H_2 energy chains have reduced through global economies of learning and scale. In the BAU scenario, H_2 is sourced from coal and small-scale electrolysis. However, the REF case gives not only a lower production of H_2, but a switch to coal with CCS and higher utilization of small-scale electrolysis technologies for H_2 generation (which is produced from zero-carbon sources such as nuclear and renewables). Coal CCS is preferred to SMR so that low carbon natural gas can be used for direct applications in the other end-use sectors (i.e. industrial, residential and (to some extent) service sectors).

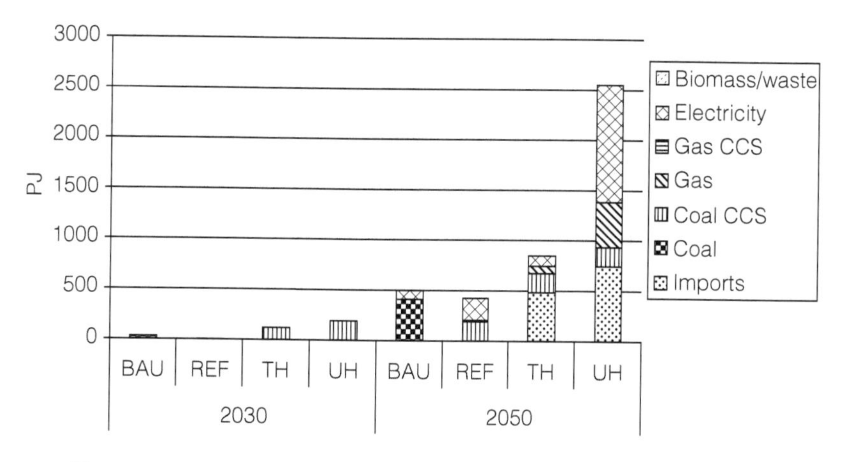

Figure 6.3 *Core scenarios: hydrogen production (2030, 2050)*

In both the TH and UH scenarios, in order to utilize ever higher levels of H_2, imports of liquid H_2 (478PJ to 741PJ) become a viable option, due to the competitive combined production and shipping costs taken from benchmark data. As H_2 requirements increase dramatically in the UH scenario, small-scale SMR (307PJ), large-scale SMR (145PJ) and small-scale electrolysis are employed based on trade-offs in economies of scale from large-scale production against transmission and distribution costs. Biomass H_2 production is not employed, due to the limited domestic and imported biomass resources being diverted to transport bio-fuels.

Figure 6.4 illustrates H_2 demand by mode and illustrates a logical uptake sequence based on infrastructure requirements, and also the importance of evolving vehicle technology costs and efficiency characteristics. In all the scenarios, demand for H_2 starts with two-wheelers (2WH), which do not require a major distribution network as they are assumed to be in urban areas (with short driving distances) by 2015. From 2030, H_2 finds applications in rail and buses (in the BAU and REF cases) due to lower infrastructure costs (with few depots at central locations), with limited penetration in LGV and car applications by 2050.

In the TH and UH scenarios, increasing H_2 target levels by 2050 drive H_2 penetration into buses, HGVs, and crucially increase the H_2 share of the large demand and more diffuse sectors of LGVs and cars. The extreme requirements of the UH scenario drive car H_2 uptake to its maximum (non-rural) penetration, into stationary applications and even into domestic aviation (where the capital costs and energy density requirements of aircraft place H_2 at a distinct disadvantage).

The choice of H_2 distribution options is driven by differentiated infrastructure costs across transport modes, technological requirements for liquid versus gaseous H_2, and competition for low-carbon production and for

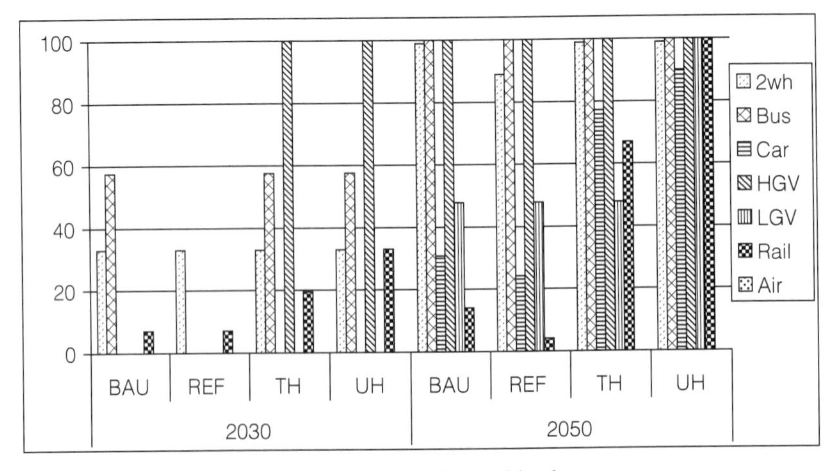

Figure 6.4 *Core scenarios: share (%) of hydrogen per transport mode (2030, 2050)*

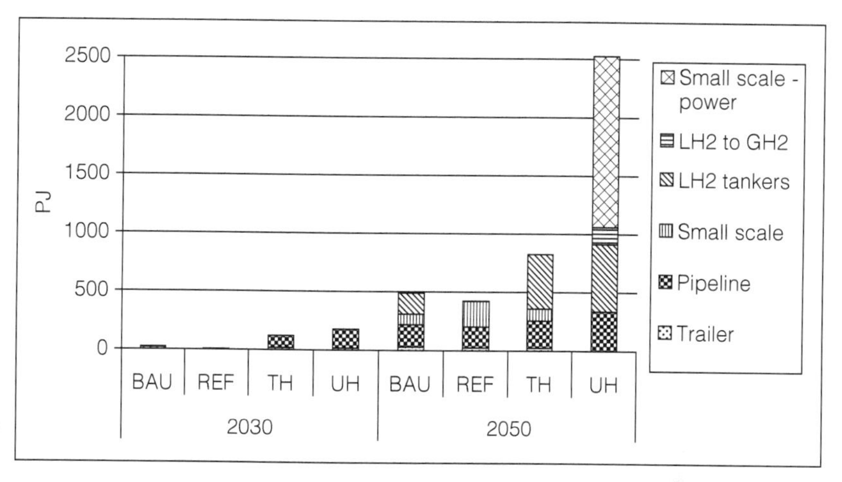

Figure 6.5 *Core scenarios: hydrogen transmission and distribution (2030, 2050)*

existing electricity and natural gas infrastructures. Figure 6.5 details H_2 transmission and distribution (and can be compared to H_2 production sources in Figure 6.3). Economies of scale of coal CCS and large-scale SMR utilize H_2 pipelines, and hence compete with small-scale H_2 generation via the current electricity and natural gas networks. All imports are liquid H_2, which is then distributed by road tankers. Liquid H_2 has a higher energy density, although gaseous H_2 use in fuel cell vehicles is more efficient. Again, as H_2 requirements increase dramatically in the UH scenario, increases in small-scale SMR and electrolysis are seen in transport and stationary applications.

A final implication of the H_2 pathway trade-offs is the type of H_2 vehicle selection. While only fuel cell vehicles (FCVs) utilizing gaseous H_2 appear in the REF scenario, liquid H_2 internal combustion engine (ICE) vehicles find applications in the remaining scenarios, and indeed have a larger overall transport fuel demand in the TH and UH scenarios by 2050. In order to utilize high levels of H_2 imposed in the TH and UH scenarios, less efficient but cheaper ICE technologies are selected, highlighting the significance of capital versus operational cost trade-off in the H_2 energy chains. In the UH scenario, the large requirement for stationary application hydrogen remains gaseous H_2.

Economic cost impacts

The combination of thermodynamic inefficiencies, reallocation and expansion of both low-carbon resources and existing infrastructures, and selection of higher capital cost end-use technologies, increases total energy system costs (Table 6.4). Cost increases are weighted towards later periods, reflecting the penetration of both low-carbon and H_2 energy pathways. The CO_2 constraint alone (REF case) raises undiscounted energy systems costs by £4.8 billion in 2050, with the additional H_2 constraints resulting in significantly higher system cost increases in 2050 of £8.0 billion in TH and particularly of £41.1 billion in UH, illustrating the difficulty in utilizing H_2 in those transport modes

Table 6.4 *Core scenarios: (undiscounted) energy system costs*

Scenario		*2000*	*2030*	*2050*
BAU				
	Total energy system costs (£m_{2000})	92,911	291,219	325,173
	% change from BAU	-	-	-
REF				
	Total energy system costs (£m_{2000})	-	291,269	329,971
	% change from BAU	-	0.02%	1.48%
TH				
	Total energy system costs (£m_{2000})	-	291,444	333,219
	% change from BAU	-	0.08%	2.47%
UH				
	Total energy system costs (£m_{2000})	-	291,574	366,255
	% change from BAU	-	0.12%	12.63%

and stationary applications with relatively higher-cost hydrogen infrastructure and technologies.

Hydrogen taxation sensitivity runs

Sensitivity analysis on the cost of H_2 technologies and the relative cost of other fuels is presented in an earlier version of the model (Balta-Ozkan et al, 2007). Here the focus is on fuel taxes, as UK road fuel duties make up 65–75 per cent of current fuel prices, and provide around 5 per cent of total UK government general revenues. Although it may be appropriate to apply tax incentives to support a transport niche market, any mainstream switch to non-taxed alternative fuels would require significant adjustments in the UK central government budget. The BAU, REF, TH and UH scenarios apply current road duty rates to all new transport fuels in the model (CNG, LPG, transport electricity, ethanol, methanol, biodiesel, second-generation biodiesel and H_2), through to 2050.

Compared to the REF case, removing all H_2 road duties (NTAX) or setting them at 25 per cent of current duties from 2030 (LTAX) more than doubles H_2 demand (see Table 6.5). In these lower excise duty scenarios, imports of liquid H_2 become the main production source, as less efficient end-use H_2 applications (ICE vehicles) are now favoured. The electricity sector and limited CCS capacity is now able to decouple from H_2 production through lowered electrolysis requirements. In NTAX and LTAX, a change in H_2 production has a corresponding switch in H_2 infrastructure to LH_2 distribution by road tanker. The progressive tax scenario (PTAX) shows only a very limited final expansion in H_2 use compared to the REF case.

However, the progressive imposition of H_2 taxes (PTAX) does alter the timing of H_2 uptake. In the REF case, H_2 starts penetrating into 2WH by 2015 (which have limited infrastructure costs), and only by 2040 are significant amounts of HGV (60 per cent) and bus (38 per cent) fuel demand met from H_2. By 2050, REF case growth in H_2 use ensures 24 per cent of car, 48 per cent of LGV, and all HGV demands are met from H_2. PTAX accelerates the

Table 6.5 *Alternate taxation: hydrogen supply and distribution (2050)*

	Hydrogen production sources (%)					Hydrogen distribution network (%)				
	Imports	Coal CCS	Gas	Electricity	Total (PJ)	Trailer	Pipeline	Small scale	LH_2 tankers	LH_2 to GH_2
REF	0.76	43.42	4.79	51.03	429.9	5.91	41.64	51.70	0.75	0.75
NTAX	60.55	19.32	4.88	15.25	970.0	2.98	21.03	15.53	60.45	-
LTAX	63.73	21.35	5.98	8.93	877.7	3.30	23.87	9.12	63.72	-
PTAX	-	40.98	9.00	50.02	443.9	4.59	44.82	50.60	-	-

diffusion of H_2, for example, with the HGV fleet completely switching to H_2 by 2030. The LTAX and NTAX scenario show a similar early increase in H_2 demand, and an overall doubling of H_2 demand by 2050. In the NTAX and LTAX scenario, in addition to increases in 2WH and rail H_2 demand, the large car market (except very rural locations) and the LGV fleet[16] both switch to H_2.

In terms of tax revenues, increasing vehicle efficiencies in the BAU case already lowers tax revenues from road fuels, from around £23.0 billion in year 2000 to £13.2 billion in 2050. Altering H_2 taxation further erodes government revenues from 2050 (Table 6.6), from a REF CO_2 constrained case by an additional £2.8 billion (PTAX), £6.9 billion (LTAX) and £11.1 billion (NTAX). Especially when factoring in the revenue losses going from BAU to REF, this would require a substantial shift in the tax base for government revenue raising. Macro-economic modelling would be required to analyse the broader economic impacts of such a shift.

Table 6.6 also shows that (non-tax) energy systems costs rise if H_2 is not taxed at a similar rate to other transport fuels. Thus this non-optimal mix of technologies and infrastructures combines higher energy system costs with lower tax receipts in a double effect, which should be taken into account when considering whether to use long-term tax incentives to support H_2 deployment as a contributor to a low-carbon (and potentially more secure) future energy system.

Spatial modelling sensitivity runs

A final set of scenarios compares a methodological extension (Strachan et al, 2008a), which soft-link UK MARKAL to a geographical information systems (GIS)- based spatial model of H_2 supply, demand and plausible gaseous and

Table 6.6 *Alternate taxation: (undiscounted) energy system costs and tax revenues, 2050*

Scenario	Energy system costs (£m_{2000})		Tax revenue (£m_{2000})	
	2050	Change from REF	2050	Change from REF
BAU	311,897	–5,822	13,276	1,024
REF	317,719	0	12,252	0
NTAX	321,258	3,539	1,149	-11,103
LTAX	320,050	2,331	5,397	-6,855
PTAX	317,946	227	9,443	-2,809

liquid H_2 infrastructures, with the earlier updated non-spatial version of the UK MARKAL model (Balta-Ozkan et al, 2007). The spatial model is used to generate alternative reference and CO_2-constrained runs (GIS-C60, involving a 60 per cent CO_2 reduction by 2050, now implemented from 2010; in these runs, international air transport is included).

At an aggregate level, introducing a spatial treatment lowers cumulative discounted energy system costs. This is primarily a function of optimized distances (and hence costs) for H_2 and other transport fuel distribution compared to an averaged UK approach. The spatial model's 50-year cumulative cost (at a 10 per cent market discount rate) for the reference and –60 per cent CO_2 target cases is –0.61 per cent (£–13.9 billion) and –0.57 per cent (£–13.2 billion) lower respectively than the corresponding runs in the non-spatial model. Assigning the annual (e.g. 2050) energy system costs reduction to the relevant transport mode selected for H_2 under these scenario runs amounts to approximately a 15 per cent cost reduction in these modes.

Introducing a spatial treatment for H_2 gives a far more nuanced depiction of H_2 share across transport modes. Under a CO_2 reduction target, H_2 deployment in the spatial model is relatively higher (at 36 per cent of transport energy and 12 per cent of total final energy) due to improved (economic) matching of supply and demand points.

This logical geographical pattern of supply and demand is seen in the GIS-C60 case (see Figure 6.6). A major H_2 expansion occurs by additionally servicing the car fleet. The supply-demand structure also changes. With competition for the UK CCS capacity from the power sector combined with competition for LNG resources, the model switches overwhelmingly to liquid H_2 imports[17] into terminals at Teesside, Thames and Wales, and distributed via LH_2 road tanker. Teesside then supplies demand regions Scotland, North East, Humberside, Lancashire, Yorkshire and rural areas. Thames supplies demand regions London, Midlands, South Coast and other urban areas, while the much smaller Wales provision is for the Severn demand region only.

Analysis of the liquid H_2 infrastructure chosen by the spatial model shows a preference for large-scale production with increased distribution distances with clustered demand points, rather than smaller-scale production closer to demand centres. The model prefers the supply economies of scale achieved from clustering demand.

Pipelines are restricted to <10 per cent of the H_2 flows in the UK. Contributing factors to why the model is slow to invest in H_2 pipeline infrastructures include that each 'meta'-pipeline option is characteri*ze*d as having fixed demand and supply centres, for fixed volumes of demand, as well as a 20-year planning horizon. This lack of flexibility means that H_2 flows can only be approximately adjusted within the model's iterations as it seeks to find the cost-optimal configuration. However, such model simplifications are not dissimilar to the kind of drawbacks with pipeline infrastructures in reality, which being inherently inflexible infrastructures are highly problematic for long-term investment decisions in situations of uncertainty.

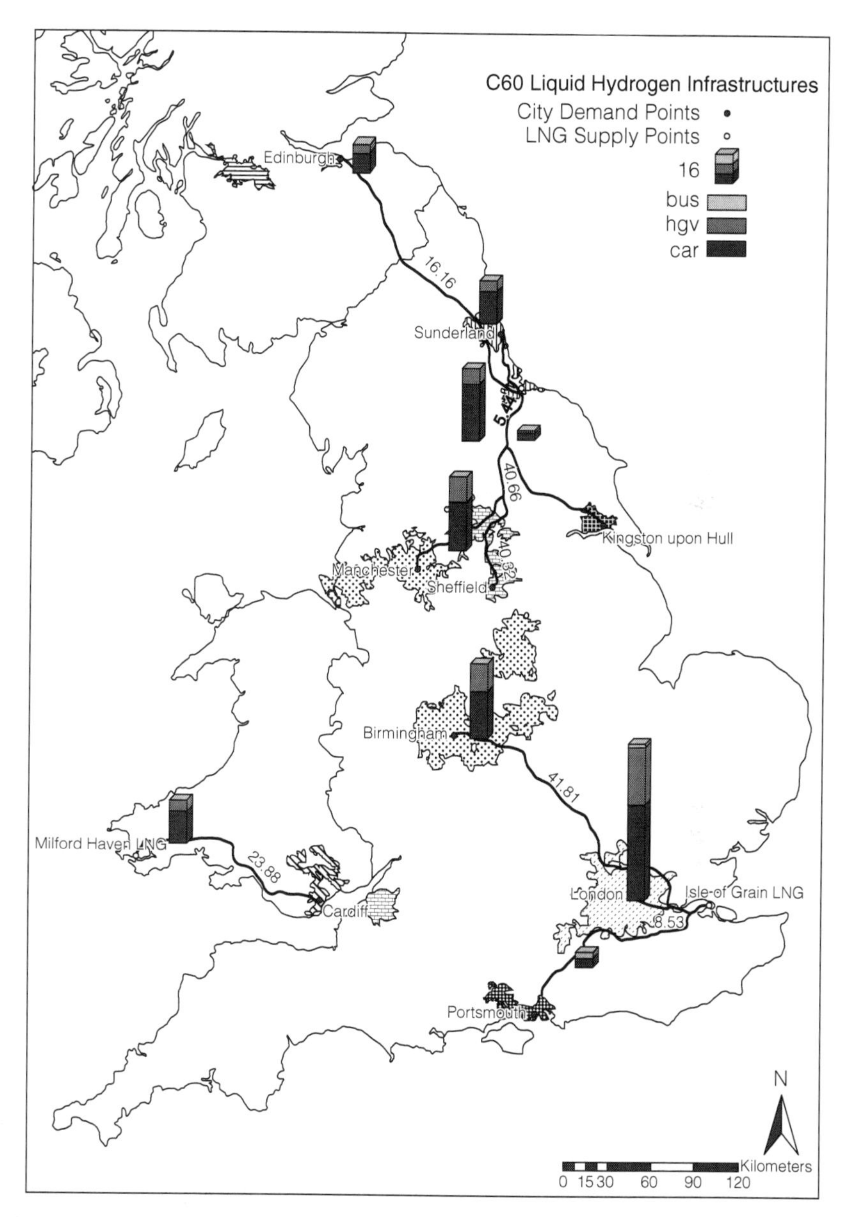

Figure 6.6 *Alternate GIS scenarios: GIS-C60 (–60% CO_2) liquid hydrogen infrastructures, 2050*

Conclusions and insights

This chapter has summarized energy system modelling of UK scenarios of hydrogen (H_2) pathways. Further information on the methodology and policy insights of UK H_2 modelling is given in Balta-Ozkan et al (2008) and Strachan et al (2009). This work sits within a detailed and extensive literature on H_2

modelling, which includes optimization and scenario-based approaches, characterized at either the energy system or more detailed socio-technical level. These different modelling approaches to new H_2 network and infrastructure systems all face the generic challenges of how to treat:

- interactions within the rest of the energy system, notably competition for primary energy resources;
- the level of (future) technical detail required to appropriately represent the various H_2 pathways; and
- the inherently spatial nature of H_2 infrastructure development.

However, given that large-scale H_2 energy systems do not yet exist, policy-makers rely on quantitative modelling to generate analytical insights into how H_2 may develop as a major energy vector.

Energy system modelling has the advantages of a detailed representation of both technology detail and of resource competition. The work described in the UK MARKAL core scenarios discusses model efforts to characterize the scale and distance drivers of H_2 infrastructures in a non-spatial model. Further extensions are outlined, which focus on the role of H_2 transport taxation and some spatial H_2 scenarios with a soft-link to a GIS model.

Insights from the core scenarios begin with H_2 being most appropriate for deployment in the transport sector. Only in later periods are economy-wide H_2 systems preferred due to sunk investments in existing infrastructures and the time required to drive down the costs of H_2 networks and technologies. It is noted that due to competition for low-carbon resources (including CCS), H_2 does not necessarily see greater diffusion from a CO_2 price signal alone. In addition, a lower-carbon H_2 vector can be more energy intensive than conventional options, owing to thermodynamic losses.

Under constraints to boost H_2 deployment, a major interaction is with the electricity sector, both through the use of electrolysis to generate H_2 and the competition of H_2 technologies with electric (plug-in) vehicles and electric heating boilers. Small-scale electrolysis would require an expansion of the electricity network (as opposed to the construction of a bigger H_2 network). Wider energy systems interactions include the use of the existing gas network for building heating requirements, as opposed to SMR H_2 production, and the use of bio-fuels over H_2 for transport modes.

The deployment of H_2 follows a logical progression based on transport infrastructure requirements and the cost comparison of vehicle technologies. This progression is from two-wheeled vehicles, rail and buses, heavy then light goods vehicles, to the large personal car market, and finally to aviation and stationary applications. The use of gaseous or liquid H_2 is determined by a wells-to-wheel cost and carbon comparison. As low-carbon H_2 penetration increases, a substantial energy system cost penalty is seen due to higher resource and infrastructure requirements and the penetration into less attractive H_2 end uses. Compared to a BAU case, by 2050 a low-carbon REF case entails a 1.5 per cent increase in energy system costs. Raising H_2 deployment to 16 per cent of final energy (TH) increases the cost differential from BAU to 2.5 per cent, while a 50 per cent final energy share (UH) of H_2 results in a 12.6 per cent cost increase.

No- or low-tax H_2 sensitivity scenarios lead to a doubling of H_2 demand by 2050, and an emphasis on liquid H_2 import and distribution, as less emphasis is placed by the model on highly efficient gaseous H_2 fuel cell vehicles. Even a progressive tax implementation advances the timing of H_2 penetration. However, these H_2 taxation sensitivities result in both further reductions in the tax revenues from road fuel duties and increased energy system costs from a sub-optimal technology mix.

Scenarios using a spatial model result in lower costs (15 per cent reduction in transport sector costs) and higher low-carbon H_2 penetration, due to better matching of supply and demand. Importantly, the spatial model finds clustering of demands to take advantage of supply economies of scale. A logical ordering of supply-demand locations is served primarily by liquid H_2 imports and tanker delivery, in part due to the inflexible nature of investments in H_2 pipelines.

Notes

1. It is noted that a range of additional factors are important in any transition to a hydrogen economy, including technological change and innovation, behavioural change and attitudes to risk, clustering of new infrastructures, and institutional drivers. Other chapters in this book cover these issues.
2. Additional UK energy policy goals are the competitiveness of the economy and fuel affordability.
3. Following advice from the newly established Committee on Climate Change (www.theccc.org.uk), the target was increased to 80 per cent, and this higher target was incorporated in the Climate Change Act of 2008, but, as noted, was not the subject of the modelling reported here.
4. In accordance with UNFCCC emissions accounting, international aviation and shipping are not included in the UK energy and emissions budget.
5. Climate Change Levy (CCL), hydrocarbon duty, transport fuel duty, Large Combustion Plant Directive (LCP), renewables electricity obligation (at least 15 per cent renewable generation by 2015), renewable transport fuel obligation, Energy Efficiency Commitment (EEC), buildings standards, but not the EU-ETS, due to profound uncertainty in future carbon permit prices.
6. Developed by the Office of Research and Development, US Environmental Protection Agency (EPA).
7. The UK fuel duty escalator operated from 1994 to 1999 and raised road fuel duties in real terms by a certain percentage each year.
8. In a follow-up study, some progress has been reported where decisions on when, where and what type of hydrogen infrastructure to build is determined endogenously within the UK MARKAL model (Balta-Ozkan and Baldwin, 2008).
9. Two-wheelers (2WH) and domestic shipping (TS) are proportionally very small in final energy terms and were treated in aggregate.
10. Including saturation effects in airport infrastructure to limit energy use.

11 Intermediate demand centres along H_2 infrastructure routes are not served by these major infrastructure routes – a modelling extension to address this is discussed in Strachan et al (2008a).
12 Due to low demand densities, other demand regions (J–K) do not have the option of gaseous H_2 pipelines.
13 Note that additional H_2 scenarios are presented in Balta-Ozkan et al (2007).
14 For example, road transport in rural or islands communities, and the incomplete electrification of the UK rail network.
15 Note that 1PJ (petajoule) = 0.024MTOE = 0.278TWhrs.
16 LTAX has slower switching to LGV hydrogen vehicles.
17 Note that the price and availability of low-carbon imported H_2 is highly uncertain. Insensitivity runs the model switches to domestic sources, including remote Scottish renewables (Strachan et al, 2008a).

References

Adam, S. and Browne, J. (2006) 'A survey of the UK tax system', IFS briefing paper no 9, London, Institute of Fiscal Studies

Agnolucci, P. and Ekins, P. (2007) 'Technological transitions and strategic niche management: the case of the hydrogen economy', *International Journal of Environmental Technology and Management*, vol 7, nos 5–6, pp644–671

Babiker, M., Metcalf, G. and Reilly, J. (2003) 'Tax distortions and global climate policy', *Journal of Environmental Economics and Management*, vol 46, no 2, pp269–287

Ball, M., Wietschel, M. and Rentz, O. (2007) 'Integration of a hydrogen economy into the German energy system: an optimising modelling approach', *International Journal of Hydrogen Energy*, vol 32, nos 10–11, pp1355–1368

Balta-Ozkan, N. and Baldwin, E. (2008) 'Analysis of hydrogen infrastructure development in the UK: How does the scale vary across different infrastructure options?', British Institute of Energy Economics Conference, 24–25 September 2008, St John's College, Oxford

Balta-Ozkan, N., Kannan, R. and Strachan, N. (2007) 'Analysis of UKSHEC hydrogen visions in the UK MARKAL energy system model', UKSHEC Social Science Working Paper no 32. Available at www.psi.org.uk/ukshec

BERR (2006a) 'Updated energy projections', London, Department of Business Enterprise and Regulatory Reform, July 2006

BERR (2006b) 'UK atlas of marine renewable energy resources', Department of Business Enterprise and Regulatory Reform. Available at www.berr.gov.uk/energy/sources/renewables/explained/wind/page27403.html

BERR (2007) 'Energy White Paper: Meeting the energy challenge', Department of Business Enterprise and Regulatory Reform. Available at www.berr.gov.uk/energy/whitepaper/page39534.html

Bomb, C., McCormick, K., Deurwaarder, E. and Kaberger, T. (2007) 'Biofuels for transport in Europe: Lessons from Germany and the UK', *Energy Policy*, vol 35, no 4, pp2256–2267

Contaldi, M., Gracceva, F. and Mattucci, A. (2008) 'Hydrogen perspectives in Italy: analysis of possible deployment scenarios', *International Journal of Hydrogen Energy*, vol 33, pp1630–1642

DEFRA (2007) Draft Climate Change Bill, Department of Environment, Food and Rural Affairs. Available at www.official-documents.gov.uk/document/cm70/7040/7040.pdf

DfT (2003) 'Passenger forecasts: Additional analysis', London, Department for Transport. Available at www.dft.gov.uk/about/strategy/whitepapers/air/docs

DfT (2005) National Transport Model (NTM), London, Department for Transport

DfT (2006) 'Transport statistics for Great Britain', London, Department for Transport

DUKES (2006) Digest of United Kingdom Energy Statistics, including internet-only foreign trade (Annex G), London, Department of Business Enterprise and Regulatory Reform

Dutton, G., Bristow, A., Page, M., Kelly, C., Watson, J. and Tetteh, A. (2005) 'The hydrogen energy economy: its long-term role in greenhouse gas reduction', Tyndall Centre for Climate Change Research. Available at http://www.tyndall.ac.uk/research/theme2/final_reports/it1_26.pdf

E4Tech (2004) 'A strategic framework for hydrogen energy', a report to DTI by Element Energy and Eoin Lees Energy. Available at www.berr.gov.uk/files/file26737.pdf

Endo, E. (2007) 'Market penetration analysis of fuel cell vehicles in Japan by using the energy system model MARKAL', *International Journal of Hydrogen Energy*, vol 32, nos 10–11, pp1347–1354

European Commission (2006) 'World energy technology outlook 2050 – WETO H_2'. Available at http://ec.europa.eu/research/energy/pdf/weto-h2_en.pdf

Fletcher, K. and Marshall, M. (1995) 'Forecasting regional industrial energy demand: The ENUSIM end-use model', *Regional Studies*, vol 29, no 8, pp801–811

Hart, D., Bauen, A., Chase, A. and Howes, J. (2003) 'Liquid bio-fuels and hydrogen from renewable resources in the UK to 2050: a technical analysis', A report to the DfT, London

HMT (2008) Budget 2008, Table C6, p.187, London, HM Treasury. Available at http://budget2008.treasury.gov.uk

Holloway, S. (2007) 'CO_2 capture and geological storage potential in the UK', British Geological Survey, presented H2Net summer meeting

Hugo, A., Rutter, P., Pistikopoulos, S., Amorelli, A. and Zoia, G. (2005) 'Hydrogen infrastructure strategic planning using multi-objective optimization', *International Journal of Hydrogen Energy*, vol 30, no 15, pp1523–1534

IEA (2008) 'Energy technology perspectives 2008: Scenarios and strategies to 2050', Paris, International Energy Agency

Joffe, D. (2008) 'Modelling technical, spatial, economic and environmental aspects of hydrogen infrastructure development for London's buses', PhD thesis, Imperial College London

Joffe, D. and Strachan, N. (2007) 'Review of modelling approaches to the development of a hydrogen economy', UKSHEC Social Science Working Paper no 30. Available at www.psi.org.uk/ukshec

Joffe, D., Strachan, N. and Balta-Ozkan, N. (2007) 'Representation of hydrogen in the UK, US and Netherlands MARKAL energy systems models', UKSHEC Social Science Working Paper no 29. Available at www.psi.org.uk/ukshec

Johnson, N., Yang, C. and Ogden, J. (2008) 'A GIS-based assessment of coal-based hydrogen infrastructure deployment in the state of Ohio', *International Journal of Hydrogen Energy*, vol 33, no 20, pp5287–5303

Kannan, R., Strachan, N., Balta-Ozkan, N. and Pye, S. (2007) UK MARKAL model documentation, UKERC working paper. Available at http://www.ukerc.ac.uk

Lin, Z., Ogden, J., Fan, Y. and Sperling, D. (2006) 'The hydrogen infrastructure transition model (HIT) & its application in optimizing a 50-year hydrogen infrastructure for urban Beijing', University of California, Davis, UCD-ITS-RR-06–05. Available at http://repositories.cdlib.org/itsdavis/UCD-ITS-RR-06–05

Loulou, R., Goldstein, G. and Noble, K. (2004) MARKAL reference manual. Available at http://www.etsap.org
Martinus, G., Smekens, K. and Rösler, H. (2005) 'Modelling the transition towards a hydrogen economy', British Institute of Energy Economics Conference, 22–23 September 2005, St John's College, Oxford
McDonald, A. and Schrattenholzer, L. (2002) 'Learning curves and technology assessment', *International Journal of Technology Management*, vol 23, nos 7/8, pp718–745
McDowall, W. and Eames, M. (2006) 'Forecasts, scenarios, visions, back-casts and roadmaps to the hydrogen economy: A review of the hydrogen futures literature', *Energy Policy*, vol 34, no 11, pp1236–1250
Oi, T. and Wada, K. (2004) 'Feasibility study on hydrogen refuelling infrastructure for fuel cell vehicles using the off-peak power in Japan', *International Journal of Hydrogen Energy*, vol 29, no 4, pp347–354
Pout, C. and MacKenzie, F. (2006) 'Reducing carbon emissions from commercial and public sector buildings in the UK', BRE Client Report for Global Atmosphere Division, Department for Food and Rural Affairs, London
Prince-Richard, S., Whale, M. and Djilali, N. (2005) 'A techno-economic analysis of decentralized electrolytic hydrogen production for fuel cell vehicles', *International Journal of Hydrogen Energy*, vol 30, no 11, pp1159–1179
Shay, C., Loughlin, D., Johnson, T., Decarolis, J., Wilson, E. and Vijay, S. (2005) USEPA MARKAL documentation, United States Environmental Protection Agency, Office of Research and Development
Shorrock, L. and Utley, J. (2003) 'Domestic energy fact file', Buildings Research Establishment, UK
Smekens, K. (2004) 'Response from a MARKAL technology model to the EMF scenario assumptions', *Energy Economics*, vol 26, pp655–674
Stamatina-Parissis, O., Joffe, D., Hart, D. and Bauen, A. (2005) 'Renewable Hydrogen Supply Options for London', Imperial College London, 2005 European Hydrogen Energy Conference, Zaragoza, Spain
Strachan, N. and Kannan, R. (2008) 'Hybrid modelling of long-term carbon reduction scenarios for the UK', *Energy Economics*, vol 30, no 6, pp2947–2963
Strachan, N., Kannan, R. and Pye, S. (2007) Final report for DTI-DEFRA on scenarios and sensitivities using the UK MARKAL and MARKAL-Macro energy system models. Available at http://www.ukerc.ac.uk
Strachan, N., Balta-Ozkan, N., Kannan, R., Hughes, N., McGeevor, K. and Joffe, D. (2008a) 'State-of-the-art modelling of hydrogen infrastructure development for the UK: Geographical, temporal and technological optimisation modelling', Final report to the DfT, London. Available at www.psi.org.uk
Strachan, N., Pye, S. and Hughes, N. (2008b) 'International drivers of a UK evolution to a low carbon society', *Climate Policy*, vol 8, ppS125–S139
Strachan, N., Balta-Ozkan, N., Joffe, D., McGeevor, K. and Hughes, N. (2009) 'Soft-Linking Energy Systems and GIS Models to Investigate Spatial Hydrogen Infrastructure Development in a Low Carbon UK Energy System', *International Journal of Hydrogen Energy*, vol 34, no 2, pp642–657
Tseng, P., Lee, J. and Friley, P. (2005) 'A hydrogen economy: opportunities and challenges', *Energy*, 30, pp2703–2720
van Benthem, A., Kramer, G. and Ramer, R. (2006) 'An options approach to investment in a hydrogen infrastructure', *Energy Policy*, vol 34, no 17, pp2949–2963

van Ruijven, B., Hari, L., van Vuuren, D. and Bert de Vries, B. (2008) 'The potential role of hydrogen energy in India and Western Europe', *Energy Policy*, vol 36, no 5, pp1649–1665

Yang, C. and Ogden, J. (2007) 'Determining the lowest cost hydrogen mode', *International Journal of Hydrogen Energy*, vol 32, pp268–286

7
Hydrogen in Cities and Regions: An International Review

Mike Hodson, Simon Marvin and Andrew Hewitson

Introduction

This chapter[1] is primarily focused on developing a conceptual typology of place-based hydrogen initiatives. Our international review of place-based hydrogen initiatives revealed a plethora of projects, demonstrations, test-beds, ambitions and expectations at a wide range of spatial scales. These include islands, cities, regions, transportation corridors, national plans, cross-border collaboration and supranational initiatives. This exposed a wide range of activity at a range of different spatial scales, seeking to reorient places around the hydrogen economy to establish some sort of competitive advantage in economic, technological or ecological terms (see Chapter 9 of this volume).

Consequently, we were primarily interested in understanding whether there is anything distinctive about these different spatial scales. At a particular scale, the city or island, are there always particular sets of social interests, technologies, levels of ambitions and particular sets of orientations to the hydrogen economy? For example, do islands always seek to develop hydrogen to build autonomy? We argue that the typology we construct allows us to start identifying the distinctiveness of the different scales of activity that then leads to significant new research questions about the coordination and interconnections between hydrogen initiatives across a range of scales.

Why does the question of distinctiveness and scale require further analysis? We believe it does to further critical understanding of the following three problematic assumptions that tend to underpin existing research and policy analysis of scale and hydrogen.

What is distinctive about urban and regional hydrogen initiatives?

First, there is a significant public and private sector investment in hydrogen initiatives at a number of different scales, but we currently have no way of conceptualizing what is distinctive about these different scales (Hodson and Marvin, 2009). Where questions of scale have been addressed in scenario and pathways exercises, these tend to be focused on the international and national scale, with an absence of focus on cities and regions. Consequently it is often not clear 'where' the hydrogen economy is actually located within national states or supranational initiatives.

Instead, we argue that places do appear to be important in the development of new socio-technologies in a whole variety of ways, not just as sites for experiments. The hydrogen economy has to be developed in particular contexts that are not just passive. Whether they comprise active experimentation with fuel cells or wider regional economic strategy, place-based issues become important in resisting or embracing innovations, and particular stakeholders form place-based coalitions to facilitate new relations between users and producers around systemic initiatives designed to facilitate a hydrogen economy. But we should never ignore the fact that national and international scales of activity have to touch down somewhere, whether in the laboratory, experiment or application.

Are cities and regions sites for passive 'test-beds' or active 'construction' of the hydrogen economy?

Second, when cities and regions are addressed, they are usually seen simply as 'test-beds' (see Vandenborre and Sierens, 1996; Kai et al, 2007; Weinert et al, 2007). In this sense, cities and regions tend to be seen as the recipients of demonstrations and experiments that are part of wider initiatives developed nationally or internationally. Consequently, where locales are undertaking hydrogen-related activities, these are usually regarded as passive sites for experimentation.

But our previous work has shown that, increasingly, responsibility for key aspects of technology and infrastructure policy is being devolved to cities and regions, so that they are much more active in shaping hydrogen initiatives in context and collaboratively with selected scales, and other cities and regions. Rather than place being an accident or simply a recipient of experiments, we see that places are actively generating discourses and debates about the hydrogen economy, and trying to reposition the locality to gain some sort of competitive advantage around economy, technology, security and/or ecology. Accordingly, we should see places as actively reinterpreting and seeking to reposition the local context (energy infrastructure, local industrial specialism, local research capacity etc.) in response to expectations of what local benefits a hydrogen economy can bring.

How are the relations between different scales of activity around hydrogen understood?

Finally, there tends to be an assumed implication that there is a hierarchy that privileges the national and international scales, and that the local scale is simply a site for implementation. Such a position tends to assume that there is a simple hierarchy of linkages between high-level initiatives at the 'top' – meaning the national/international scale – and their implementation at the 'bottom' – meaning the local. Consequently, there is an assumed hierarchy that prioritizes a particular scale and is based on an assumption of simple top-down relations in the implementation or testing of the hydrogen economy.

Previous empirical and theoretical work on innovation and socio-technical change has required a multi-level perspective which recognizes that interaction and coordination between different levels and scales of activity can be significant in reshaping socio-technical systems and developing new infrastructures. Critical questions emerge here about the extent to which a particular scale can shape a socio-technical transition to a hydrogen economy within a particular place, or the extent to which it needs to reshape national and international regulations and policy to make such a transition possible. Accordingly, we need to understand how the linkages between different scales of activity may be constructed and developed; not as a simple hierarchy, but through different coalitions between scales or across scales. Here there may be particular forms of by-pass – for example, missing out central government, as cities collaborate. A key issue is how coordination is forged across different scales, through what mechanisms and with what types of consequence.

The rest of this chapter is structured in three sections. The next section develops a 'typology' of the role of cities and regions in nascent hydrogen economy transitions. The third section outlines seven ways of seeing cities and regions. The final section summarizes the key findings of the chapter and details the key research and policy conclusions.

A typology of hydrogen cities and regions

This section outlines a 'typology' of different ways of seeing cities and regions and their roles in transition to a hydrogen economy. We developed this typology by undertaking a comprehensive web-based review of hydrogen experiments, demonstrations and projects in three stages.

First, a large sample of over 50 initiatives was identified through web-based and documentary reviews. These initiatives were then reviewed, focusing on two dimensions of their characteristics: the first being the scale of the initiative such as national, urban or regional; and the second focusing on their view of the urban such as whether it was test-bed or building more self-reliance. This then produced an initial seven-fold typology (see column one of Table 7.1).

Second, a smaller sample of 15 initiatives was selected, based upon the initial seven-fold typology for more detailed analysis. These schemes were

Table 7.1 *A typology of hydrogen cities and regions*

'Type'	*View of the Urban*	*Motivations and Drivers*	*Prevalent Social Interests*	*Exemplars*
Hydrogen Nations – Creating a welcoming environment	Responding to national leadership	'Hands off & Light touch' 'Creating the conditions' Energy security Economic competitiveness Early adopters	National government Multinational automobile and energy interests	US Canada Iceland
Hydrogen Islands – Exporting the microcosm	Relatively bounded experi-mental context for replication	First mover 'Self-sufficiency' Security of energy supply Export power	National and state energy authorities Universities and research institutes Multinational automobile and energy interests	Iceland Hawaii Prince Edward Island
Hydrogen Cities – Securing energy and economic independence	Reconceptualizing autarkic cities	Economic and resource security 'Self-sufficiency' and re-scaling infra-structures – withdrawal from national and regional infrastructures of provision Attracting nation-state and inward investment	Municipalities Nation-state Multinational automobile and energy interests	San Francisco London
Hydrogen Regions – Promoting regional economic development through innovation clusters	Regions as context for economic regeneration	Economy and innovation through clusters of regional strengths Linking hydrogen to economic development, innovation and research strategies at regional scale	Regional/state energy/transport authorities and development agencies Regional government Multinational automobile and energy corporations	New York California Teesside
Hydrogen City Networks – Show-casing test-beds	Global agglomerations of new mobility systems	Developing technology experiments in cities. Extracting and comparing data on performance	Major 'world' cities Multinational automobile and energy interests Supranational political institutions	CUTE initiative
Hydrogen Lighthouses and Mini-Networks – Upscaling the hydrogen economy	Cities and regions as contexts within which infrastructures can become increasingly connected	Highly visible demonstration of the up-scaling of demonstrations projects in particularly high-profile and visible places	Multinational automobile and energy interests 'Go ahead' mayors and governors Research base	Shell Lighthouse Projects
Hydrogen Corridors – Linking up and rolling-out the hydrogen economy	Making infrastructure con-nections between cities and regions	Connecting the mini-networks and clusters together to roll-out the hydrogen economy though corridors and highways	Multinational automobile and energy interests 'Go ahead' mayors and governors Research base	California Hydrogen Highway Network BC Hydrogen Highway

selected because they were characteristic of a particular scale of development, as evidenced by the number of times these schemes were referred to in the web review; the apparently more 'advanced' stage of their development; and the extent to which they provided a range of differing place-based contexts in an international comparative review. Then a more detailed documentary analysis of reports and websites associated with these initiatives was undertaken using a proforma, which focused on a series of key questions that allowed us to organize the data in a comparative format. In a number of cases, interviews with key stakeholders were undertaken to fill any missing data that was not available from secondary sources for the proforma.

Finally, these two phases were brought together in the construction of a typology of the key scales of activity and the synthesizing of the key features of each scale of activity illustrating these through 'emblematic' cases. Table 7.1 identifies the seven different scales of initiative by outlining five key sets of characteristics. First, the type of initiative organized by the main scale of the activity, ranging between the national, islands, cities, regions and new scales such as lighthouses, mini-networks and corridors. Second, the way each type views and encapsulates the concept of the urban – ranging from a site of response, experimentation, autarchy, regeneration, and context for infrastructure development and extension. Third, a summary of the key motivations and drivers for the development of an initiative at the particular scales – ranging from creating the conditions for hydrogen innovation, to first mover status, addressing environmental scarcity, developing the economy etc. Fourth, a review of the main social interests – both commercial and public-sector institutions – behind the development of the particular initiative. Finally, we identify the key exemplar initiatives that most usefully provide an illustration of the type of initiative being developed at that particular scale.

Overall, the method provides a useful way of developing an understanding of the distinctiveness of different scales of activity in relation to the hydrogen economy. But it also needs to be recognized that there are clearly overlaps between the different scales of activity – and a particular context may also be host to a range of initiatives that coincide. The relationships between initiatives in a particular place and the relations between different scales of activity requires further research using more intensive research methods – as discussed in the conclusion.

Seven ways of seeing cities and regions

This section identifies the key features of each of the seven 'types' by outlining the ways in which they encapsulate particular views of the urban, identifying their key characteristics and the key social interests involved, and illustrating each type through key exemplar initiatives. Overall, the objective is to illustrate the distinctive features of hydrogen initiatives at different scales of activity.

Hydrogen nations: creating a 'welcoming environment'

National views of the role of cities and regions primarily see them as sites of 'application' of hydrogen demonstrations or for 'validation'. Cities and regions are often characterized as being sites of 'end-use' application at the end of a linear chain of innovation. Such approaches are often 'technology-led', in that attempts are made for technological 'solutions' to address broader strategic national political aspirations.

National political aspirations to develop a hydrogen economy are predicated around attaining greater energy and economic security by reducing dependence on foreign sources of energy. In this respect, the key aspect of national motivations in transitions to a hydrogen economy are based on developing energy and economic security through a greater degree of self-sufficiency, whilst at the same time seeking to position a given country as a first mover, an exemplar and thus an exporter of both hydrogen-based expertise and energy.

Characterizing national views of the transition to a hydrogen-based future is about securing national competitiveness through being a 'first mover' and not 'falling behind' in the competitive 'race'. In this respect, Iceland seeks to be the world's first hydrogen economy by 2050 (Sigfússon, 2003), the US aspires to secure national competitiveness through using hydrogen to 'make our air significantly cleaner, and our country much less dependent on foreign sources of energy' (Bush, 2003), and Canada has a 'long-term objective to maintain its position as a world-leader in the evolution of a hydrogen economy'.[2] In the UK context, according to a civil servant with a close knowledge of policy related to hydrogen: 'from a government perspective…they were very much exercised by the fact [other] governments seemed to be spending a lot more and doing a lot more and making a lot more noise, and I think that's probably…the single biggest thing that was exercising [their interest in the hydrogen economy]'.[3]

These aspirations to remain in the competitive race frequently meet national governing arrangements which are about providing 'light touch' governing frameworks for 'steering' action, rather than a tighter managing of sub-national activities. 'Light touch' governing arrangements provide 'visions', 'roadmaps' and other 'aspirational' forms of documentation. This can be seen, for example, in the US Hydrogen Posture Plan (DoE, 2006) or the Canadian Government's 'roadmap', Charting the Course (H2FCC, 2004). In doing this, the materialization of the hydrogen economy is largely for 'others', particularly different levels of government, and the automotive and energy industries. The role of public policy is seen to be as a 'catalyst' in creating a 'welcoming environment' for 'others' to translate 'visions' and 'roadmaps' into material manifestations. Hydrogen initiatives in a national context are presented within loose policy contexts that intend to position the country as a welcoming environment for different hydrogen initiatives to take place. Rather than a centralized and collective directive, national hydrogen initiatives are often a collection of projects taking place at different – but primarily urban – scales.

Although these are fundamentally government-led initiatives, actual policy dictates delivered on a national scale are not prescriptive, rather they emphasize the potential benefits of hydrogen calling for a series of 'public–private partnerships' to deliver national hydrogen infrastructures. This is seen as a two-way process with a strong government role supporting R&D, providing a basis for 'technology readiness'; once this has been achieved, the intention is for the private sector, in the form of energy providers and automotive companies, to take the mantle and lead the commercialization and application of hydrogen.

Hydrogen islands: exporting microcosms of the hydrogen economy

Hydrogen islands can be characterized as encompassing a particular set of responses to 'light touch' approaches of hydrogen nation-states. Island hydrogen initiatives are currently underway in a wide variety of locations across the globe – including Iceland, Hawaii and Prince Edward Island. Although these may differ enormously in terms of their ambition and scale, there is an apparent uniformity to them in how the urban is viewed.

Hydrogen islands view the city as a context where attempts to develop a microcosm of a transition to the hydrogen economy are taking place. The physical boundedness of islands is mobilized to develop a view which claims that island urban contexts offer a view in microcosm of the hydrogen economy, a model, which can be transferred to other contexts (see Figure 7.1).

Again, the mix of being 'leaders' or 'first mover' is mobilized, taking advantage of the natural resources (wind, waves etc.) often available to islands. The availability of these resources provides justification for withdrawing from dependence on imported fossil fuels (Hawaii, for example, sources 90 per cent of its energy needs from petroleum) and improving energy and economic security. Narratives of 'self-sufficiency' are common (e.g. see the Norwegian island of Utsira), as are similar narratives of the economic regeneration of island communities through transitions to hydrogen. In this respect, hydrogen transitions can be seen as a strategic response to large-scale job losses, as, for example, with the Scottish Shetland Isle of Unst, and for economic growth opportunities for local communities (see, for example, Canada's Prince Edward Island and Hawaii). Additionally, despite the embedded nature of many of these initiatives, there is a view that not only can energy and technologies be exported from these island contexts, but so also can the models of transition to hydrogen which are being developed.

Efforts to build island hydrogen economies are often underpinned by the development of 'public–private partnerships' of intermediary organizations which provide the locus, and capacity building context for the development of island hydrogen economies. One can see this in examples such as the Hawaii Natural Energy Institute (HNEI) and Icelandic New Energy. Icelandic New Energy is constituted by the majority shareholder, VistOrka (EcoEnergy) – a company which includes and seeks to coordinate business venture funds, key energy companies, academic institutes and the Icelandic government – but also

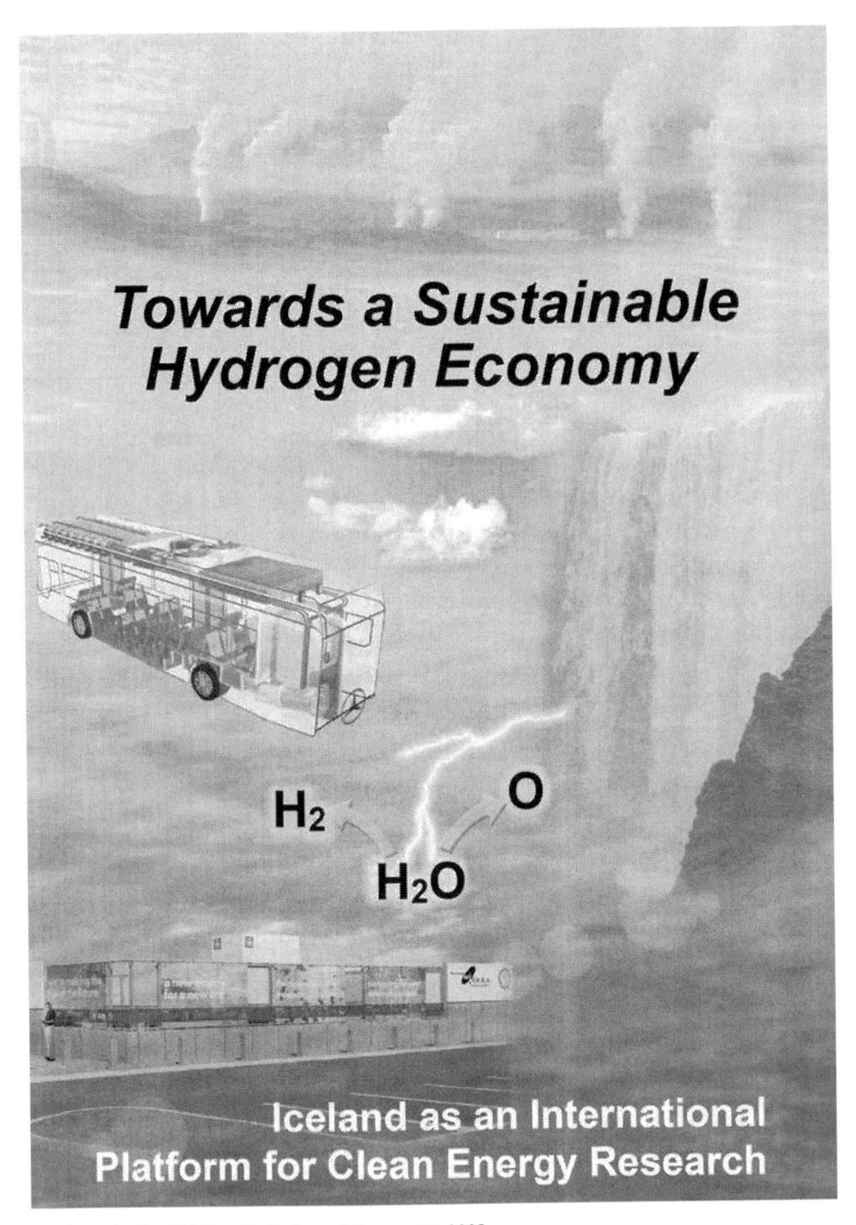

Source: The Icelandic Ministry of Industry and Commerce, 2003

Figure 7.1 *Islands as international platforms*

by large corporate interests in hydrogen, including DaimlerChrysler (demerged in 2007), Norsk Hydro and Shell Hydrogen. Similarly, HNEI is active in trying to develop 'partnerships'. In doing this, these partnerships become part of the process of producing 'roadmaps' and also plans of action for island hydrogen economies.

In the Hawaiian context, the roadmap provides a timeframe with a concerted plan of action to enable the shift towards a Hawaiian hydrogen economy. This ten-year approach is a plan to develop an island hydrogen economy – see Figure 7.2. This process begins with a feasibility study, workshops for 'partnership' building, before developing a variety of demonstration projects, upscaling these to a hydrogen fuel cell transportation infrastructure, before purchasing fleet vehicles, or the commercialization of fuel cell power, and ends with the ambitious plan of exporting hydrogen and fuel cell technology to emerging markets.

Hydrogen cities: securing energy and economic independence

Hydrogen cities can primarily, though not exclusively, be viewed as 'endogenous' city-level strategic responses to the challenges for cities posed by peak oil and climate change. Hydrogen cities often, either explicitly or implicitly, acknowledge the extent to which urban economic and everyday life is predicated on oil, coal and gas. In responding to the challenges of a peak in both the sources and production of oil and the threats and possibilities of climate change, hydrogen cities are underpinned by a large-scale reconfiguration of cities' infrastructures to produce more 'self-sufficient' and 'autarkic' cities.

The hydrogen city as a concept, in its more 'utopian' reading, encompasses aspirations that see hydrogen, produced from renewable sources of energy such as solar and wind, inform the development of community grids and

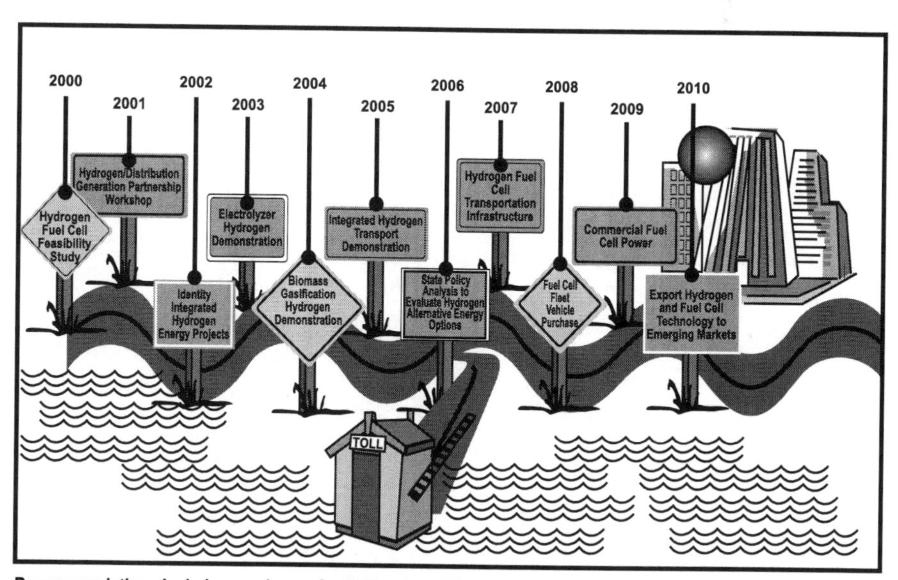

Recommendations include a roadmap of activities to validate hydrogen energy

Source: Hawaii Natural Energy Institute and Sentech Inc (2004: vii)

Figure 7.2 *Representing the roadmap to an island hydrogen economy*

city-level mobility systems. This move towards becoming more 'self-sufficient' is part of a strategy of prioritizing the preparation of cities to address the challenges of peak oil and climate change. It is a strategy of ensuring that cities, with their dependence on fossil fuels, can protect their economic positions. It is also a strategy which allows cities to address – and in many ways set more ambitious targets than national government – targets for greenhouse gas emissions reduction and for air quality. San Francisco, for example, has a greenhouse gas emissions reduction goal of 20 per cent by 2012, whilst London, under its former Mayor Ken Livingstone, adopted a target to reduce its carbon dioxide emissions by 60 per cent from 1990's level by 2025 (the national UK target at the time the London target was introduced was 60 per cent by 2050).

One consequence of increasing 'self-sufficiency' and the development of city-level infrastructures is a degree of withdrawal, and a decoupling of cities' metabolisms from national and regional infrastructures. In this re-scaling of systems of infrastructure provision, hydrogen cities position themselves as demonstrators of renewable energy and environmentally benign systems of infrastructure provision that are achievable at a city scale, both in terms of transportation and stationary applications.

Attempts to translate a concept of hydrogen cities are being made in a number of cities, including 'world cities' such as San Francisco and London, and also cities such as Columbia, South Carolina. These cities have 'committed' to becoming hydrogen cities, with the symbolic consequence of declaring aspirations for energy independence. They are currently working on a small number of demonstration projects and positioning themselves through a series of activities. These activities not only include demonstration projects, but also promote the adoption of hydrogen technology more widely and support economic development initiatives, including support for hydrogen and fuel cell companies, both large and start-up, a commitment to examine the use of hydrogen in public buildings and fleet vehicles, and through attracting hydrogen-related conferences.

The issue of attracting inward investment and hydrogen and fuel cell companies indicates the tensions inherent in strategies of 'self-sufficiency'. Similarly, hydrogen cities are often also positioning themselves for national and supranational funding related to demonstration projects and attracting inward investment, including corporate automobile and energy interests.

Hydrogen regions: promoting regional economic development through innovation clusters

Hydrogen regions provide a context to promote regional economic development through energy innovation. They provide the possibility for a strategic response to the challenges of climate change, energy security, but also, importantly, to economic globalization. Hydrogen regions are primarily about revitalizing regional economies with the secondary potential to address carbon emissions reductions.

Revitalizing regional economies is done through building and adapting existing regional strengths to align with the possibilities of a transition to a hydrogen economy. Hydrogen regions, such as New York State, California and Teesside, position themselves as contexts for hydrogen research, development and demonstration, which inform the construction of different pathways to a hydrogen economy. The concept of industry clusters is important as regions seek to develop hydrogen and fuel cell specializations. This can relate to adapting or utilizing a range of regional assets, including local natural and geographical resources, the skills of the regional workforce, existing regional investments in research and development, existing infrastructure, and various support programmes and services. Developing specialist clusters underpins attempts to retain existing companies and economic activities but also to attract new companies and investment, and also underpin growth and attract wealth to a region more generally.

In different regional economies this can encompass a wide variety of different interests which, in trying to come to a regional position, requires 'stitching together' the agendas of various local and regional agencies and organizations (Hodson, 2008). This frequently involves a key role in bringing together the regional knowledge base and universities, the energy and fuel cell industry, and a role for national government and regional agencies in providing business support, skills and infrastructure more generally.

This 'stitching together' is a means of aligning different actors – frequently with different motivations and aspirations – research and development, demonstrations and, ultimately, commercial activities. Attempts to achieve this are often through a number of phases. Usually in an initial phase this is through 'formal' processes, frequently 'visioning' workshops, such as those undertaken by the Welsh Hydrogen Valley initiative, and also more informal discussions and negotiations between different interests. This usually leads to a 'roadmap' or a strategy such as the New York State Hydrogen Energy Roadmap (Energetics Incorporated et al, 2005), which encapsulates strategic planning and implementation.

In translating the strategic plan into action, there may or may not be a dedicated intermediary organization specifically set up as a regional locus for building networks of different industrial, business, education and public policy interests, funding and knowledge, such as, for example, the Tees Valley Hydrogen Project. Because of their emphasis upon regional investment and their incipient nature at this stage, hydrogen regions are dominated and led by regional public authorities; indeed, the New York State Roadmap was initiated purely on a public basis, as it was 'drafted as part of a coordinated effort among government departments to develop hydrogen as a means of reducing our dependence on imported fuels, improving the environment and driving economic growth'.[4]

In an urban context, hydrogen regions are indicative of a regionalized process of innovation driving regional economies. In a regional context this is not about breaking connections; indeed, it is seen to be an intrinsic part of a wider process of connectivity regarding hydrogen infrastructures. Hydrogen regions are deeply embedded within wider processes of regional development which emphasize utilizing, building upon and adapting established networks, institutions and infrastructures within a regional context, as a means of connectivity both internal and external to the region.

Hydrogen city networks: global agglomerations of new mobility systems

Increasingly, transnational networks of 'world' cities, national and supranational government and the private sector, are coming together in global agglomerations to develop new mobility systems. In these agglomerations, cities themselves are only one of a myriad of actors. These networks primarily encompass multinational automobile and energy corporations, supranational political funding and 'world' or large cities. These moves towards new mobility systems are embryonic and at a stage where networks of transport demonstrations are taking place (Hodson and Marvin, 2007).

The Clean Urban Transport for Europe (CUTE) initiative, for example, established at the end of 2001, and which finished at the end of 2005, was primarily a coalition of supranational political interests (the European Commission) and multinational automobile (DaimlerChrysler) and energy (BP) organizations. CUTE involved the demonstration of 27 fuel cell powered buses in nine European cities (Amsterdam, Barcelona, Hamburg, London, Luxembourg, Madrid, Porto, Stockholm and Stuttgart), alongside associated projects in Reykjavik and Perth.

For BP and DaimlerChrysler the initiative was primarily part of an unfolding process of developing, testing in context and redeveloping demonstrator technologies, based on learning from the demonstrations about the performance and costs of different 'pathways' or technological configurations of hydrogen production, distribution, storage and end-use technologies. The cities provided the highly visible 'operating contexts' – often also as cities where national parliaments and media organizations were located – in which these different pathways were to be tested and from which lessons could be learned.

Although there were different forms of negotiation with 'local' actors, cities were represented as places within which combinations of technologies could be demonstrated under 'different operating conditions' to be found in Europe, where the role of these cities was as a network of urban laboratories where the technologies could be 'dropped-in', be tested out, and performance data extracted (see Figure 7.3).

To this 'top-down' view of the role of cities in these emerging global agglomerations can be added an increasingly strategic – if differential – 'bottom-up' response of 'world' cities. The economic success of these cities is largely predicated on their infrastructures supporting the flows of economic activity, people, labour and finance within and between them. In the context of trying to secure their pre-eminent position and continued economic growth in an era

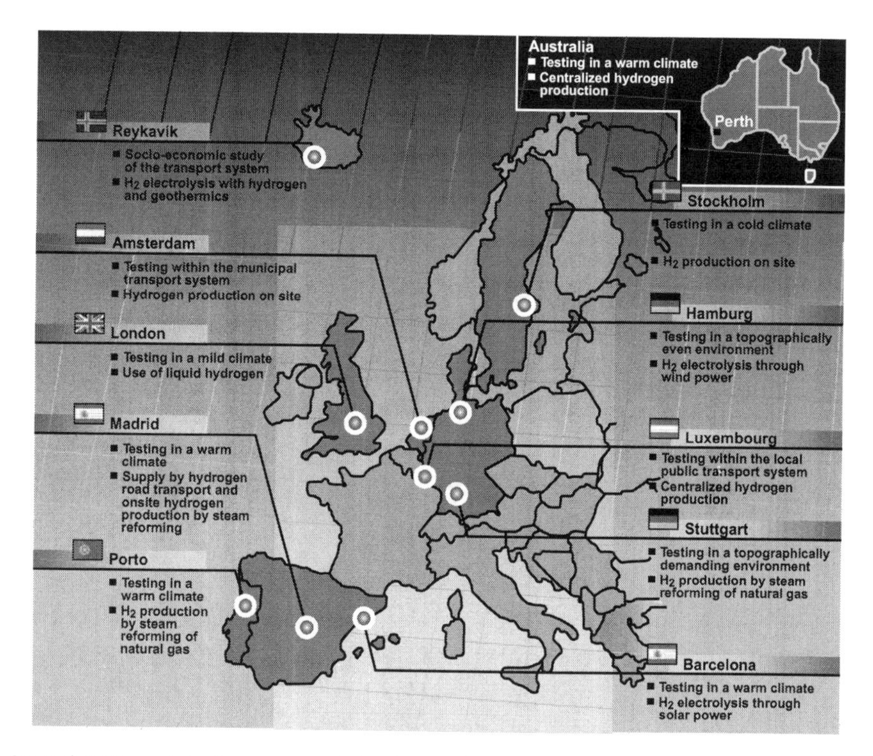

Source: http://www.fuel-cell-bus-club.com/index.php?module=pagesetter&func=viewpub&tid=1&pid=11. Accessed 16 August 2007

Figure 7.3 *Testing-out on cities*

of climate change, there is an acknowledgement that there is a need to significantly improve the effectiveness and quality of intra-city-regional transport systems. There is also an understanding that cities cannot do this on their own – they require the technical expertise and financial weight of multinationals, the financial support of supranational organizations, and relationships with each other to start to develop the economies of scale and visibility and awareness that are required to underpin a radical shift in systems of transport mobility.

Hydrogen lighthouses and mini networks: upscaling the hydrogen economy

In moving from individual or small-scale hydrogen fuel cell automotive demonstration projects to a network of demonstration projects, the 'chicken and egg' issue of whether the vehicles or the infrastructure comes first is frequently raised. Within the wider context of peak oil, energy producers are becoming interested in alternative fuels and energy. Addressing these twin issues, Shell's business strategy for hydrogen focuses on large-scale demonstration projects: what Shell calls 'Lighthouse Projects'.

In developing the concept of Lighthouse Projects, Shell aims to address the chicken and egg problem through creating 'mini-networks', or clusters of hydrogen fuelling stations in different cities and regions. A Lighthouse Project upscales the common notion of a demonstration project and, according to Shell Hydrogen, 'should include' fleets that 'build up to' 100 vehicles and beyond, which are fuelled from networks of between four and six dual hydrogen and gasoline filling stations, which aim to be semi-commercial but also partly publicly subsidized, and located in 'high visibility' urban areas (such as Tokyo, Los Angeles and New York and also Washington, DC, 'where key policymakers live and work').[5] This is because 'people must be able to see the miracle of hydrogen – technology with their own eyes'[6] (see, for example, Shell's Benning Road fuel station development, which is situated in close proximity to Congress in Washington, DC).

In building 'Lighthouse Projects', Shell Hydrogen outlines a requirement for 'partnership' which involves both public and private interests, including vehicle manufacturers, energy companies, technology developers, large fleet owners and national and international government authorities, including public subsidies (Shell Venster, 2004). Shell's projects have specifically addressed hydrogen in terms of a fuel for transportation. In this capacity there has been strong emphasis upon projects embedded in an urban context. As with the majority of large-scale hydrogen projects, the intention is to provide a high degree of visibility, whilst at the same time providing a foundation for ongoing partnerships with public partners in local and regional government. In this capacity, Shell's strategy is to build and link a variety of demonstration projects together.

Lighthouse Projects are part of a five-step approach Shell has developed. Step One was concerned with 'stand-alone' projects with restricted public access; for example, this would include depots for hydrogen-fuelled buses. Step Two focused on developing publicly accessible hydrogen fuel stations which were separate from existing gasoline stations, such as, for example, Shell's Reykjavik station, opened in 2003. Step Three sees the integration of hydrogen fuel stations with traditional fuel stations. The Lighthouse Projects, as Step Four, encompass mini-networks of hydrogen fuel stations which were planned to start before the end of 2009.

Hydrogen corridors: linking up and rolling-out the hydrogen economy

The logic of Shell Hydrogen's approach is to upscale and 'roll-out' hydrogen refuelling infrastructure even further over the period (2010–20) through a fifth step, which connects the mini-networks through developing 'corridors' and which fill in the 'white spaces' between mini-networks. The notion of Hydrogen Corridors is not specific to Shell, and more generally is one which aims to provide hydrogen fuelling stations along specific highways that transcend state and in some cases national boundaries – see Figures 7.4 and 7.5. The development of mini-networks of fuelling stations between mini-networks links together urban centres.

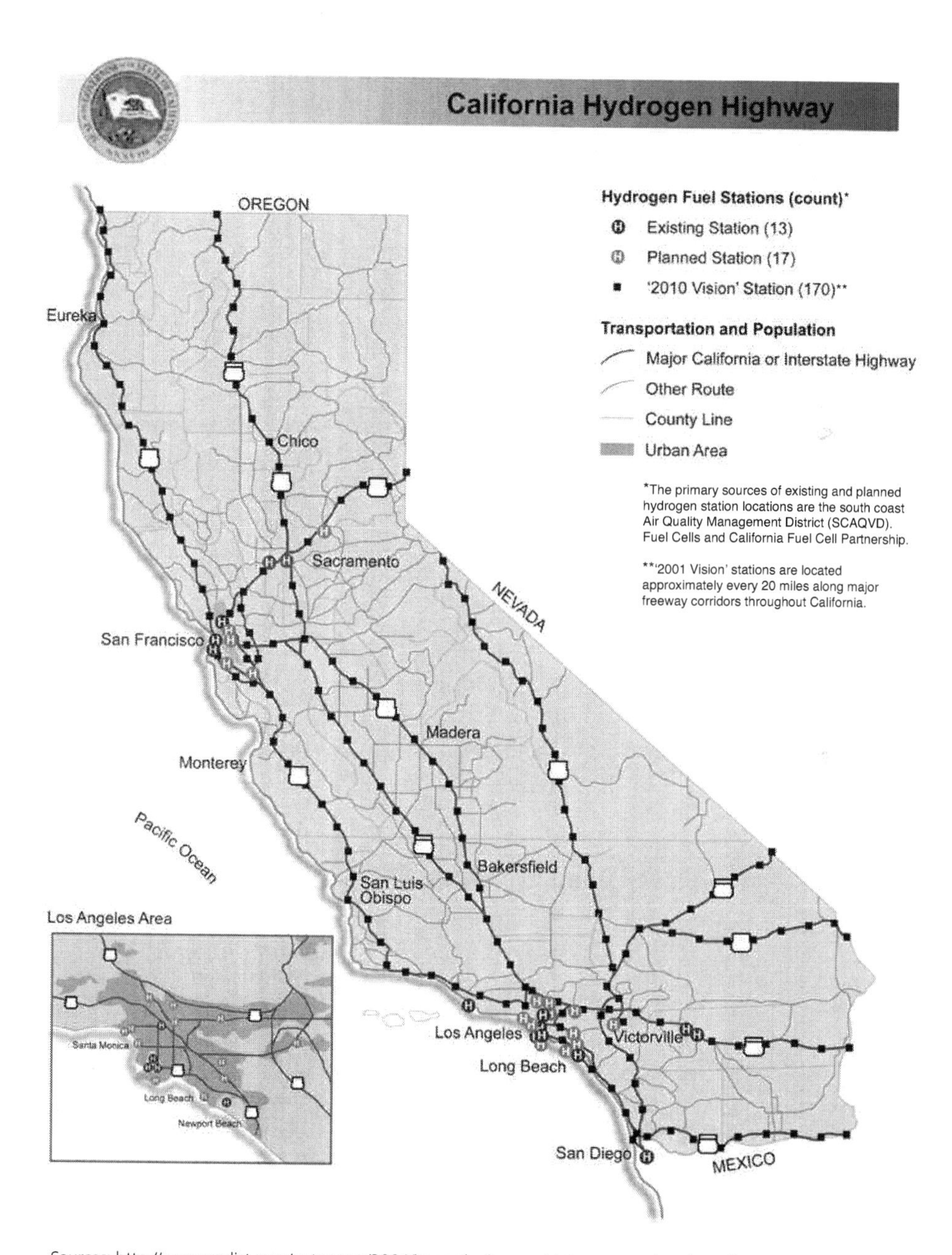

Sources: http://www.carlist.com/autonews/2004/image/hydrogen_highway_map.jpg; http://www.nrc-cnrc.gc.ca/highlights/2004/0405hydrogen_e.html. Accessed 16 August 2007

Figure 7.4 *The California Hydrogen Highways Network*

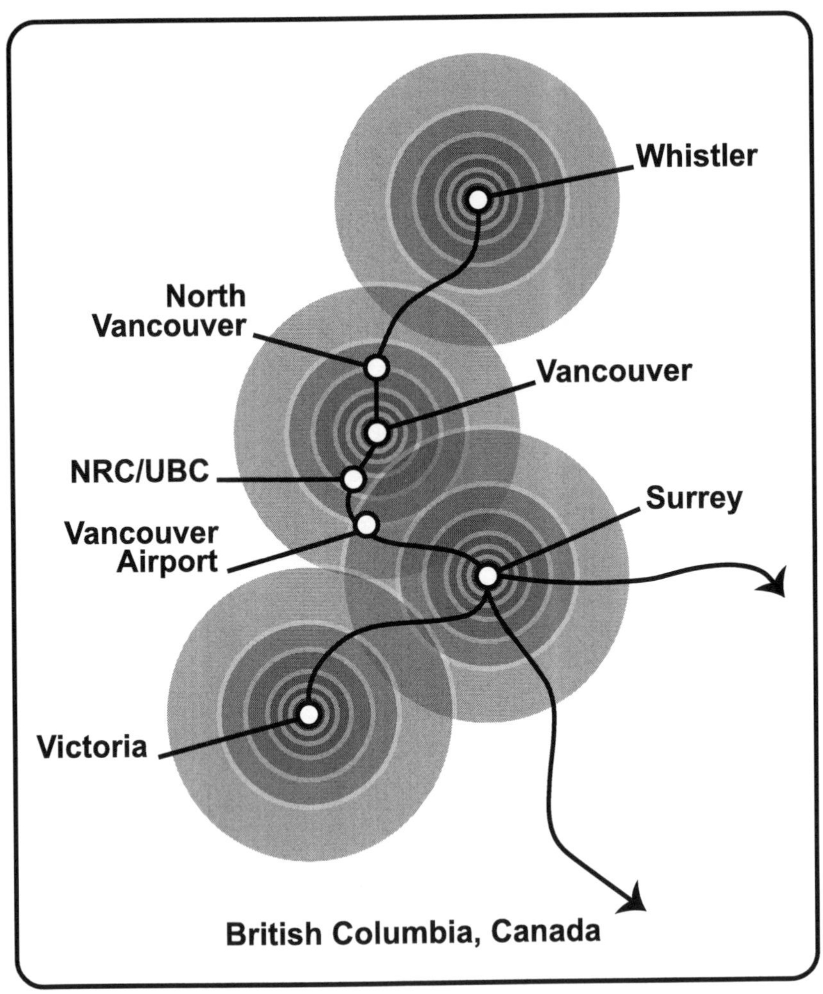

Figure 7.5 *The British Columbian Hydrogen Highway*

In 2004, Governor Arnold Schwarzenegger signalled the intention that California would build a Hydrogen Highway. Subsequently, California's 21 interstate freeways were designated as the underpinnings of the 'California Hydrogen Highway Network', which would see the development of a state Highway Network in six years. Schwarzenegger envisaged the Highway as positioning California as a leader or exemplar in addressing the issues of air quality, public health, energy security and diversity and national security at a state level. In particular, the aspiration was that the California Hydrogen Highway Network should achieve a 30 per cent reduction in greenhouse gas emissions 'relative to a comparable number of today's fuels and vehicles' (California Environmental Protection Agency, 2005: p3). He requested the California Environmental Protection Agency (Cal/EPA) to lead the production of a Hydrogen Highway Blueprint Plan, which was published in 2005.

The first phase of developing the Highway illustrates the process of developing clusters of mini-networks, in that it aspired to develop 50 to 100 refuelling stations, servicing 2,000 hydrogen vehicles by 2010, with the stations initially clustered in the San Francisco Bay area–Sacramento region and the Los Angeles–San Diego region. In linking together these urban centres, there is then an aspiration to develop this further to totals of 250 stations servicing 20,000, vehicles to facilitate travel between these areas along inter-state routes.

The Blueprint includes an Action Plan which involved the creation of a 'public–private partnership' charged with building the Highway, which required the automobile industry, industrial gas corporations, energy corporations, government and academic institutions to work together. The funding for the first phase of station developments would be on a 50/50 basis between the State of California and the private sector. There would additionally be both infrastructure incentives and vehicle incentives provided by the state. This is part of the state developing policies to try to establish a 'business and regulatory climate favourable for establishing a hydrogen infrastructure' (California Environmental Protection Agency, 2005: p3). Following from this would be 'partnerships' of public and private interests to undertake the process of translating the Blueprint into action. In addressing research, development and demonstration, there would be an important role for the research base within the state.

In short:

> *The goal of the California Hydrogen Highway Network initiative is to support and catalyze a rapid transition to a clean, hydrogen transportation economy in California, thereby reducing our dependence on foreign oil, and protecting our citizens from health harms related to vehicle emissions. We have an opportunity to deal with these problems by investing in California's ability to innovate our way to a clean hydrogen future, thus bringing jobs, investment, and continued economic prosperity to California. We have an opportunity to prove to the world that a thriving environment and economy can co-exist.*[7]

Similarly, in 2004, plans were announced to develop the BC Hydrogen Highway, along a corridor between Vancouver and Whistler, subsequently stretching to Victoria on Vancouver Island. Constructing the Highway was to be part of a process to 'design, build, operate, test and evaluate' a hydrogen fuelling infrastructure. The concept of the Highway was extended to include not only mobile hydrogen and fuel cell technologies, but also stationary and small-scale fuel cell applications in the corridor area of British Columbia. In doing this, around C$1.1m was made available in funding, the majority of it to cover the costs of a BC Hydrogen Highway project manager, with the Highway initiative being managed by a steering committee. The development of the Highway requires the building of a network of multiple social interests, which includes universities, Canadian research councils, fuel cells and industrial gas companies, but with a considerable representation from Ballard, the British Columbia-based fuel cells company. The primary objective of the initiative is to provide a focus to bring together a consortium of these different social interests, but also to learn about the 'operational, economic, environmental and social feasibility of a hydrogen fuelling infrastructure that utilizes different hydrogen production and delivery pathways'.[8]

The plan is for seven initial hydrogen fuelling demonstration sites at a variety of sites, including Vancouver airport and Whistler Village, with a target for implementation at the time of the 2010 Olympic Games in Vancouver and Whistler. In this respect the Highway will act as a 'showcase' of both sustainable transportation, but is also an attempt of British Columbia to position itself as a national and international leader and exemplar.

The logic of this development, in time, could be to link together the British Columbia and California Highways (see Figure 7.6).

Because of the geographical reach of hydrogen corridors, the promotion of these initiatives is again a complex affair, with actors from a variety of public and private institutions. As with previous urban contexts, involvement from national and regional government is strong. However, due to their scale and

Source: http://hydrogencommerce.com/images/BC-CalifHH.jpg. Accessed 16 August 2007

Figure 7.6 *Rolling-out of hydrogen?*

visibility, involvement from the corporate sector, ranging from energy providers to the automotive industry, is particularly strong. The reasons behind corporate engagement in 'hydrogen corridors' are three-fold. Firstly, in an urban context, corridor initiatives are centred upon wide-scale visibility. The utilization of corridors projects a specific image of an emerging infrastructure across a specific locality. Secondly, they provide an interface between hydrogen applications and end users. Finally, presenting applications to end users is an intrinsic part of the process of developing an emerging infrastructure that is seminal if hydrogen is to reach the point of commercialization. In this context, hydrogen corridors are indicative of a process of 'linking up' and 'rolling out' in terms of partnerships, applications and geographies.

From these seven types of hydrogen development, a key set of distinct scales emerges from the analysis, with particular features, characteristics and ways of understanding cities and regions. Taking an external view from a national or international scale, the city and region are seen in very particular ways – usually as relatively passive test beds. Yet as you move through the typology, alternative internal views of the city and region emerge, based on a more active role in the shaping of hydrogen economies for local benefit. These different views of cities and regions simultaneously co-exist. A city is conceptualized as both passive and active in the sense that a city may be a participant as a test-bed in a national demonstration programme, but it also has the internal objective of actively seeking to build greater energy autarky and competitive advantage. Consequently, there are multiple and co-existing views of cities and regions.

Conclusion

This conclusion summarizes the key argument of the chapter, outlines the significance of the findings and offers directions for future research around this agenda.

In summary, this chapter has developed a characterization of seven 'types' of city and regional hydrogen initiatives. The construction of these different hydrogen initiatives is a varied and complex affair. Viewed through an urban lens, different characterizations envisage different views of the active role of cities and regions in constructing nascent hydrogen economies. In the guise of hydrogen economy developments, cities and regions can at one level be seen as responding to national agendas. Yet they also develop bounded, autarkic strategies of 'self-sufficiency' and security, and seek to utilize hydrogen to re-position themselves as exporters of energy and energy expertise. Cities and regions are contexts of experimentation and learning at that scale, but they are also seeking to position themselves as exemplars and contexts for replication. They position themselves competitively vis-à-vis other cities and regions, but they also collaborate with other cities and regions through developing global agglomerations of cities, regions and multinational companies.

Overall, there are three significant aspects of the typology. First, there is much flexibility in the roles of cities and regions in developing hydrogen economies. Second, these characterizations are conceptual and frequently overlap with each other in practice. Third, across these characterizations, corporate involvement is central to any notion of an emerging hydrogen economy. All the city and regional contexts described in this chapter place a great deal of emphasis upon corporate partners. In all these different characterizations it is multinational companies that are the ubiquitous presence in this story of the elasticity and interpretative flexibility of the role of cities and regions in developing hydrogen economies. Multiple actors are involved in the development of a hydrogen economy, but it is multinational companies which appear often to have the clearest strategic view of its involvement in these different characterizations of the hydrogen economy and, crucially, how these can be linked together to 'roll-out' tangible manifestations of the hydrogen economy.

In terms of the importance of the argument, there are three sets of emerging themes that appear to be of key significance for further research. The first of these are the potential tensions between the construction of 'autarky' through the aspiration to develop more self-reliant energy systems at a particular scale and the aspiration for 'exporting' a mode,l and/or the technology of urban hydrogen initiatives to other contexts for economic development or other objectives. This tension raises interesting issues between context specific and more generic knowledge development and technological innovations through the hydrogen initiatives. The second tension is between competition and collaboration between cities developing hydrogen initiatives – the desire for first-mover status to build competitive advantage often co-exists with urban networks sharing knowledge and understanding. Further work could try to develop a more nuanced and sophisticated understanding of how competition and collaboration exist, over what issues and with what consequences for the cities involved. The final issue is how linkages are made across different scales of activity within cities and regions, inside national states and between them across international boundaries. The typology shows that corporate interests – rather than national governments – appear to be most active in developing linkages across scales within 'amenable' national contexts. Clearly, further work is required to understand how coordinated across scales is achieved in this context, through what processes and with what consequences.

In respect of subsequent research, the apparently central role for multinational companies requires further development in empirical contexts. A key question is: How do multinational companies view the role of cities and regions in developing hydrogen economies? There is a series of questions related to this. Who do multinational companies work with and engage with in doing so? Conversely, who is excluded and ignored? Which cities and regions are privileged in developing and becoming the dominant characterizations of hydrogen economies? How are they seen? Are they experimental contexts for multinational companies to work on, or do they genuinely work in collaboration with multinational companies to mutually achieve different objectives? What does this relationship practically look like in different city and regional contexts? How is coordination achieved across scales? What does this mean for those 'second wave' of cities and regions aspiring to be hydrogen economies? Do possibilities become constrained? Are these 'types' transferable to cities and regions of the developing world. These are difficult but necessary questions to be asked in addressing what has hitherto been an area of neglect in studies of the hydrogen economy – the role of cities and regions in developing hydrogen economies.

Notes

1 This chapter is an amended and revised version of an article that previously appeared as Hodson, M., Marvin, S. and Hewitson, A. (2008) 'Constructing a typology of H2 in cities and regions: An international review', *International Journal of Hydrogen Energy*, vol 33, issue 6, March 2008, pp1619–1629.
2 http://tpc-ptc.ic.gc.ca/h2/epic/internet/inh2ea-aph2.nsf/en/Home. Accessed 16 August 2007.
3 Interview with authors.
4 Available from http://www.nyserda.org/Press_Releases/PressRelease.asp?i=89&d=2005. Accessed 18 May 2007.
5 http://www.shell.com/home/content/us-en/news_and_library/press_releases/2004/hydrogen_station_launch_111004.html. Accessed 16 August 2007.
6 http://www.shell.com/home/content/media-en/news_and_library/press_releases/2004/hydrogas_station_10112004.html. Accessed 16 August 2007.
7 http://www.hydrogenhighway.ca.gov/vision/vision.pdf. Accessed 16 August 2007.
8 http://www.nrcan.gc.ca/media/newsreleases/2004/200413a_e.htm. Accessed 16 August 2007.

References

Bentham, J. (2005) European Hydrogen and Fuel Cell Technology Platform special event, 16 March

Bush, G. W. (2003) State of the Union address. Available at http://www.whitehouse.gov/news/releases/2003/01/20030128-19.html

California Environmental Protection Agency (2005) *California Hydrogen Blueprint Plan*, vol 1, May. Available at http://www.hydrogenhighway.ca.gov/plan/reports/volume1_050505.pdf

DoE (2006) *Hydrogen Posture Plan: An integrated research, development and demonstration plan*, US Department of Energy/Department of Transportation

E4 Tech, ElementEnergy, Eoin Lees (2004) *A Strategic Framework for Hydrogen Energy in the UK*. Available at http://www.dti.gov.uk/energy/sepn/hydrogen_framework_full.pdf

Energetics Incorporated, Albany Nanotech and The National Hydrogen Association (2005) *New York State Hydrogen Energy Roadmap*, Report prepared for the New York State Energy Research and Development Authority, New York Power Authority and Long Island Power Authority

H2FCC (2004) *Charting the Course: A program roadmap for Canada's transition to a hydrogen economy*, Ottawa, Government of Canada

Hawaii Natural Energy Institute and Sentech Inc (2004) *Nurturing a Clean Energy Future in Hawaii: Assessing the Feasibility of the Large-Scale Utilization of Hydrogen and Fuel Cells in Hawaii*, Final Report for State of Hawaii Department of Business, Economic Development in Tourism

Hodson, M. (2008) 'Old Industrial Regions, Technology and Innovation: Tensions of Obduracy and Transformation', *Environment and Planning A*, vol 40, no 5, pp1057–1075

Hodson, M. and Marvin, S. (2007) 'Transforming London/Testing London: Understanding the role of the national exemplar in constructing "strategic glurbanisation"', *International Journal of Urban and Regional Research*, vol 31, no 2, June

Hodson, M. and Marvin, S. (2009) 'Cities Mediating Technological Transitions: Understanding Visions, Intermediation and Consequences', *Technology Analysis and Strategic Management*, vol 21, no 4, pp515–534

Hoffmann, P. (2001) *Tomorrow's Energy: Hydrogen, Fuel Cells, and the Prospects for a Cleaner Planet*, Cambridge, Ma, MIT Press

Icelandic Ministry of Industry and Commerce (2003) 'Towards a Sustainable Hydrogen Economy: Iceland as an International Platform for Clean Energy Research'

Kai, T., Uemura, Y., Takanashi, H., Tsutsui, T., Takahashi, T., Matsumoto, Y., Fujie, K. and Suzuki, M. (2007) 'A demonstration project of the hydrogen station located on Yakushima Island – operation and analysis of the station', *International Journal of Hydrogen Energy*, vol 32, no 15, pp3519–3525

Leggett, J. (2005) *Half Gone: Oil, Gas Hot Air and the Global Energy Crisis*, London, Portobello Books

McDowall, W. and Eames, M. (2006) 'Forecasts, scenarios, visions, backcasts and roadmaps to the hydrogen economy: A review of the hydrogen futures literature', *Energy Policy*, vol 34, no 11, pp1236–1250

Pirages, D. and Cousins, K. (eds) (2005) *From Resource Scarcity to Ecological Security: Exploring New Limits to Growth*, Cambridge, Ma, MIT Press

Rifkin, J. (2002) *The Hydrogen Economy: The Creation of the World-Wide Energy Web and the Redistribution of Power on Earth*, New York, TarcherPutnam

Romm, J. (2006) *The Hype about Hydrogen; Fact and Fiction in the Race to Save the Climate*, Washington, Island Press

Shell Venster (2004) 'Lighthouses for Hydrogen', November/December

Siblerud, R. (2001) *Our Future is Hydrogen: Energy, environment and economy*, Wellington, Co., New Science Publications

Sigfússon, A. (2003) 'Iceland: Pioneering the Hydrogen Economy', *Foreign Service Journal*, December, pp62–65

Vandenborre, H. and Sierens, R. (1996) 'Greenbus: A hydrogen fuelled city bus', *International Journal of Hydrogen Energy*, vol 21, no 6, pp521–524

Weinert, J., Shaojun, L., Ogden, J. and Jianxin, M. (2007) 'Hydrogen refueling station costs in Shanghai', *International Journal of Hydrogen Energy*, vol 32, no 16, pp4089–4100

8
Hydrogen in Vancouver: A Cluster of Innovation

William McDowall

Introduction

British Columbia is home to what was once described as 'probably the most successful example of a fuel cell industry' (Hart, 2002: i). The cluster of hydrogen and fuel cell companies centred around Ballard Power Systems employs well over 1,000 people in over 40 companies, and has an annual R&D spend of over $165m[1] (Industry Canada et al, 2006). It has a global reach: a recent survey indicated that well over half of the cluster's revenues come from sales outside Canada.

As other chapters of this book have made clear, the emergence of a hydrogen energy system would represent a significant 'technological transition', including the wholesale establishment of new systems, infrastructures, hard and soft institutions, networks, behaviours and markets. All of these developments must happen in particular cities and regions – such as Vancouver – and all are shaped by local contexts and conditions.

This chapter explores the development of a regional cluster of firms and initiatives developing hydrogen and fuel cell technologies in the Vancouver area. In doing so, the chapter aims to provide insight into the way in which the dynamics of a spatially bounded yet globally networked innovation system affect the shape and direction of a putative long-term transition. Comparisons are drawn with the UK, and in particular with the areas studied by Hodson and Marvin (Chapter 9).

Unlike some other chapters in this volume, this chapter was not undertaken as part of the UK Sustainable Hydrogen Energy Consortium, but was funded by Brunel Research in Enterprise, Innovation, Sustainability and Ethics

(BRESE) at Brunel Business School. The chapter is based on a series of 14 interviews, with key figures active in hydrogen and fuel cells in and around Vancouver during July 2006, and a review of the key policy documents and literature surrounding the development of the cluster.

Mapping the innovation network: industry, government and academia

British Columbia is home to more than 40 companies involved in hydrogen and fuel cells. At the core of this cluster is Ballard Power Systems, a firm that has been developing fuel cell technologies since the 1980s. Without Ballard, there would have been no industry cluster in Vancouver. Ballard has acted as a centre for education and training; as the leader in terms of R&D, employment and revenue; and as a symbol of the region's success and leadership. Many of the other companies in the cluster are staffed with ex-Ballard employees, have strategic partnerships with Ballard, or have positioned themselves along a supply chain to integrate with Ballard products.

As the first on the scene, Ballard attracted much of the early government funding and venture capital. It also attracted the interest of the major automotive firms and was perhaps the first point of contact for the emerging cluster, with broader energy and transport interests, looking to invest in hydrogen technologies. Ballard now employs more than 600 people, and had annual revenues of $50–100m between 2003 and 2007.

However, Ballard did not create the cluster alone: several other individuals and companies were central to the early development of the innovation network, including BC Hydro, Methanex, and financiers such as Ventures West and Chrysalix. Importantly, there were other industries that had an interest in the development of hydrogen and related technologies all along the supply chain, and who had the capacity to develop these interests. It is thus not just a fuel cell industry, but an industry that has built on local strengths in gas handling to have competences across hydrogen and fuel cells. The industry has expanded greatly over the last 20 years, and British Columbia now boasts a wide range of hydrogen and fuel cell technology companies. Despite this, there is considerable debate within the cluster as to whether or not it has achieved 'critical mass' – the point at which the cluster would continue to be viable even without the presence of Ballard.

Many of the archetypal 'cluster' studies by scholars of innovation involve a central role for a university or public research organization. In the Vancouver fuel cell cluster, it is industry that accounts for the great majority of R&D activity and spending in the cluster – nearly $1 billion between 2001 and 2005, with 80 per cent of that spent by Ballard (NRC, 2006). This compares with a total of less than $500m of public money over the last 20 years. This is not to suggest that public research organizations have been absent: the University of Victoria and the Institute for Fuel Cell Innovation are also important, but the degree of dependence on private industry is noteworthy.

Finally, Crown corporations have played an important role in the cluster. Crown corporations are a commonly used mechanism for providing public services in Canada. Wholly owned by government (in this case, the provincial government of British Columbia), the corporations are run as commercial companies, but with an eye to their broader social and environmental responsibilities. As a result, they have a special role within the industry, with somewhat different priorities and constraints than private companies.

Three such corporations are important in the local hydrogen innovation system: BC Hydro, the electricity utility; and Translink and BC Transit, which operate public transport in the greater Vancouver area and the rest of BC respectively. The two transit corporations have been involved as users in bus demonstrations, and BC Transit has been closely involved in developing demonstration projects (including a current project to operate 20 fuel cell buses in time for the 2010 Winter Olympics in Vancouver). Both BC Transit and Translink either have, or will soon have, hydrogen refuelling stations at one of their depots. Both also have a history of involvement with alternative fuelled vehicles, primarily because of air-quality concerns.

BC Hydro has also had a central role, seeing hydrogen as a potential way to expand the market for its core product (electricity) and through the involvement of its daughter company, Powertech Labs, which develops natural gas (and now hydrogen) storage, handling and refuelling technologies. BC Hydro is constrained by statute to operate solely within BC, though it is able to export power to other jurisdictions. This constraint has meant that, when windfalls arise, they cannot be spent by moving into new markets or expanding business in new regions. Investments in emerging technologies such as hydrogen, that both meet the social and environmental considerations of a Crown corporation and have the potential to expand markets for the core product of electricity, become obvious targets for spending. It is also worth noting that, as a result of its large-scale hydroelectric resources, BC has among the lowest electricity prices in North America.

Supporting the innovation chain: the role of governments

Several federal government bodies have played an important role in the development of the cluster, either through funding hydrogen projects (typically to help support technologies during the demonstration and pre-commercialization phases) or through providing policy and research support. These include:

- Natural Resources Canada (NRCan). NRCan is a major source of government investment in hydrogen technologies, and has been throughout the development of the cluster in BC. NRCan has also been closely involved in supporting the development of codes and standards, such as the Canadian Hydrogen Installation Code that governs refuelling stations and other facilities.
- Industry Canada (IC). The Industry Canada role has principally been around policy development, rather than direct funding, and Industry

Canada has been involved in the development of Hydrogen & Fuel Cells Canada, the Fuel Cells Roadmap, and in efforts to develop a National Strategy.
- National Research Council (NRC). The NRC operates research centres across Canada, including the NRC Institute for Fuel Cell Innovation (IFCI) in Vancouver. NRC also provides advisors for small- and medium-sized technology firms.
- Sustainable Development Technology Canada (SDTC). Sustainable Development Technology Canada is an arm's-length, not-for-profit foundation, established as part of Canada's climate change programme. It provides funding for innovative technology projects, including hydrogen energy projects.
- Technology Early Action Measures (TEAM). TEAM was a partnership programme of Environment Canada, Industry Canada and Natural Resources Canada, which provided funding for demonstration and development projects that reduce greenhouse gas emissions.
- Western Economic Diversification (WD). WD is a regional development agency that has provided significant funding for hydrogen projects.

In addition to federal government activities, the provincial government has provided significant support to the sector over the years. The province has committed funding for numerous demonstration projects, and is encouraging its Crown corporations to support hydrogen developments.

History of the cluster's development

The following section provides an overview of the development of the hydrogen and fuel cell innovation system in Vancouver, exploring the development of industry, and the formalized associations and networks established to move the cluster forward.

Early days: Ballard's breakthrough with PEM and the technology bubble

Founded in 1979, Ballard originally worked on battery technologies. In 1983, they attracted interest from the Department of Defence, to work on batteries for submarine propulsion. Shortly after this, interest turned to Polymer Electrolyte Membrane (PEM) fuel cell technology that had been developed and then abandoned by GE. The Department of Defence and Industry Canada, through the Defence Industry Productivity Programme, funded this work as part of their defence-oriented technology development programme. Ballard, with additional funding from Natural Resources Canada, found that a several-fold increase in stack power density was possible, using Nafion membranes produced by DuPont. This was a major breakthrough, and meant that PEM fuel cells could be taken seriously as a future automotive power source. Further investments from government took Ballard forward throughout the 1980s.

At around the same time, the California Air Resources Board developed its Zero Emissions Mandate. This had a profound impact on R&D within the automotive sector, especially given the requirement for zero, rather than low, emissions. The automotive firms focused on battery electric vehicles in the short term, but there was significant interest in fuel cells as a long-term option. As the focus shifted towards the automotive sector, BC Transit became involved, and Western Economic Partnership Agreement (joint federal-provincial) funding created demonstration projects with buses during the 1990s, including the first-ever fuel cell bus in 1993: Ballard's P1.

Ballard continued to grow, and demonstrated further buses in 1995 and 1997, with three buses trialled in Chicago in 1998. Throughout this period, substantial technological progress occurred, particularly with respect to power density, thus heightening interest and generating expectations of quick market success for industry, and economic success for the Province. Ballard was a founding member of the California Fuel Cell Partnership in 1999, demonstrating an outward-looking perspective that would be important for Ballard's and the cluster's future.

At the same time, other technological strengths in BC were important, though these have been frequently overlooked in accounts of the cluster. There had been some work on natural gas vehicles in the area, with local firm Westport Innovations playing an important role, and BC Hydro's Powertech labs exploring technologies for natural gas refuelling. As a result of windfall profits from exporting electricity to California during the energy crunch there, BC Hydro had the financial capacity to look at hydrogen as a way of extending the reach of electricity markets, and Powertech started working on compressed hydrogen infrastructure and refuelling. Similarly, a major methanol company, Methanex, was involved in funding hydrogen, as fuel cells were again seen as a way of extending the reach of the core product (in this case, methanol). This linked up well with local firm QuestAir, which had developed small-scale gas purification technology, originally for oxygen. The opportunities in hydrogen and fuel reformation became obvious, and they started working in the area. It is interesting to note that at this stage, Methanex and QuestAir were two of the more active members of the emerging cluster of firms, though methanol is now clearly off the automotive agenda, and their roles are much less pronounced. The capabilities developed through natural gas expertise at Westport and Powertech have been applied to hydrogen, with both moving into pure hydrogen applications (Westport in direct injection technology for hydrogen internal combustion engines, Powertech in hydrogen refuelling technology).

Towards the end of the 1990s, the sector was attracting significant venture capital interest. Part of this was through local venture capital firms, such as Ventures West, and later through Chrysalix Ventures, a specialist venture capital firm interested in fuel cell technologies.

By now, several other hydrogen and fuel cell companies were active in BC. Some of these were building on existing strengths and interests, others were a result of spin-outs from the Institute for Energy Systems at the University of Victoria, while others were positioning themselves along Ballard's supply chain. Questair was involved in hydrogen purification, BC Hydro and Methanex were interested in long-term opportunities to extend the markets of their traditional products, and BC Transit, the public transport agency, was interested as a potential user and was involved in the early bus prototypes.

Ballard also reoriented itself during this period, and became much more aggressive at marketing itself. In 1999, an alliance was formed with the automotive giant DaimlerChrysler, greatly enhancing expectations about Ballard in particular, and fuel cells in general.

Expectations, already heightened by millennial exuberance in high technology sectors, were further stoked at the 1999 Detroit Motor Show, at which Bill Ford declared hydrogen the fuel of the future. Ford was unveiling its P2000, claimed to be the 'first full-performance, full-size passenger fuel cell vehicle in the world' (Osborne, 2001). The engine of the P2000, based on a Ballard fuel cell, had been developed with funding from Natural Resources Canada, Industry Canada, Transport Canada and Environment Canada, as well as the US Department of Energy. At around this time, battery electric models developed by GM, Ford, DaimlerChrysler and Toyota were failing to sell, and there was a shift to seeing fuel cell vehicles as the 'cars of the future'.

Ballard's share price shot up, and in a second public offering in 2000, Ballard raised over half a billion Canadian dollars (Wright, 2002). The future for the fuel cell industry had never looked brighter.

Rationalization and disillusionment: hard times for the fuel cell sector

In late 2000, the dot.com bubble burst. Combined with poorer than expected performance in the fuel cell sector, this led to a drying-up of capital. Ballard was spending large amounts of money on R&D, but had yet to focus on a particular market. The company now recognizes that its innovation strategy was too much driven by a 'technology push' mentality – it was about exploring what was possible, rather than listening to the needs and demands of potential buyers. For some time after difficulties in accessing capital set in, Ballard and others had reserves from the good times, which they were able to live off. However, the R&D spend rates were unsustainable, and in 2003–04 the sector contracted across Canada, with a loss of over 600 jobs (NRC, 2006).

The government also was starting to suffer from a phenomenon known in the industry as 'fuel cell fatigue' – the promises had been too great, the results too little, and governments were tired of requests for funding backed up with promises of future economic and market success. Although there were no actual cut-backs in funding, at a time at which the sector felt it needed support, significant new amounts did not appear forthcoming, particularly from the Province.

In addition, a change of technological direction occurred when, in 2002, DaimlerChrysler dropped its methanol reforming programme. This left companies involved in methanol, such as QuestAir and Methanex, with little incentive to continue their active support of the industry.

As a result of these challenges, the sector as a whole went through a period of rationalization, which hit Ballard hardest. This was the largest in a sequence of expansions and contractions at Ballard. In retrospect, many of those closely involved in the cluster see those contractions as important moments, that in many ways had benefits for the industry cluster in BC. Those laid-off took with them detailed knowledge and skills learned at Ballard, and founded their own companies or joined others. Many of the 40+ companies working in the sector in Vancouver have ex-Ballard employees on their payroll, leading some to describe it as 'the University of Ballard'. Ex-Ballard employees founded Tekion, Cellex and many other companies, and the fact that these people knew each other personally created a collegiate atmosphere of cooperation, despite the necessary levels of secrecy in a business focused on intellectual property.

The rationalization also meant a growing focus on near-term markets. Companies such as General Hydrogen and Cellex compete in the fuel cell fork-lift truck market, and are considered some of the very first 'commercial' ventures. Angstrom Power, in the micro-fuel cell sector, is also focusing on near-term markets. QuestAir has to some extent diversified away from hydrogen energy, but maintains a small business supplying demonstration hydrogen refuelling units with purifiers, and is working on a joint venture with Exxon-Mobil on gasoline reformation. As for Ballard, they have refocused their attention on the development of fuel cell stacks, rather than integrated products, and on residential co-generation as a near-term market and providing fuel cells for niche transport markets. In 2008, Ballard sold its automotive fuel cell development units to Daimler and Ford, in an effort to further focus on near-term markets. This refocusing of the sector has been accompanied by a greater reserve in public statements about the future of fuel cells, with many feeling that the sector is now over-cautious, having been embarrassed by unrealistic claims five years ago.

It was not all bad news for the sector during this period. It was a time of consolidation, network-building and strategic focus, as the next section explores.

Uniting the industry: strategies, associations and networks

The story so far has concentrated on the development of technology and markets. This section turns to efforts to support the industry as a whole, through the development of government programmes and industry associations. These activities have been a result of both industry and government initiatives, and have involved an overlapping set of interests, priorities and agendas. Key features of this have been:

- the close-knit and informal nature of the links and initiatives emerging from within the cluster, combined with a supportive federal infrastructure that has encouraged further development and strategy;

- the role of demonstration projects in bringing people together;
- the dominant position of 'cluster theory' in framing developments.

An important stage in this process was the formation of Hydrogen and Fuel Cells Canada, an industry association. In the late 1990s, several key actors became interested in fostering greater cooperation within the industry, and helping to define common priorities. In 1998, a 'task force' was established (Government of Canada, 2003) to discuss how the industry might be moved forward. This concluded that an industry association was necessary, and the provincial and federal governments provided funding through a Western Economic Partnership Agreement (a joint Provincial-Federal mechanism for fostering industrial development in Western Canada).

As a result of this process, Hydrogen & Fuel Cells Canada was founded in 2000. Although the impetus for the development of the association came from BC, it was founded as a national, rather than regional, body. Hydrogen & Fuel Cells Canada was based in Vancouver, which is unusual for a national industry association, most of which are in the economic centres of Ontario and Quebec. The association developed strong links with the federal government, and helped influence the establishment of further programmes and processes to support hydrogen energy.

In 2001, in an effort to provide a clear rationale for continued policy support for the fuel cell sector in Canada, Hydrogen & Fuel Cells Canada retained PricewaterhouseCoopers to produce a report laying out the strengths of the Canadian fuel cell industry, and the potential benefits for Canada. *Fuel Cells: The Opportunity for Canada* was published in 2002, and provided a call for increased public support. The document projected substantial (and, in hindsight, somewhat optimistic) market growth for the sector, and argued that Canada was well placed to succeed in the sector as long as funding was forthcoming.

As this was being developed, Industry Canada, along with Hydrogen & Fuel Cells Canada, again employed PricewaterhouseCoopers to produce a 'consensus document' for the industry: the *Canadian fuel cell commercialization roadmap* (Industry Canada et al, 2003). This was intended to bring the industry together, so that the Federal government departments such as Industry Canada could hear 'one voice'; and to identify the key priorities for the industry as a whole. The document, published in March 2003, highlighted priorities, including the need to develop a national strategy. This led to the beginnings of a national strategy process, taken forward by the newly established Hydrogen and Fuel Cells Co-ordination Committee (HFCCC), comprising 22 departments and co-chaired by NRCan and Industry Canada.

In 2002, as the two PricewaterhouseCoopers documents were being developed, the National Research Council founded the Institute for Fuel Cell Innovation (NRC-IFCI) in Vancouver. This built on the fuel cell programme at the NRC Innovation Centre in Vancouver. In addition to R&D, part of the IFCI remit is to incubate new companies, and facilitate network building at the local level. This meant that, as a national strategy was being taken forward at the federal level, NRC was also helping the cluster to develop its thinking in terms of provincial and local concerns. The Centre now hosts Hydrogen & Fuel Cells Canada, as well as nine small fuel cell companies, and is located on the campus of the University of British Columbia, facilitating links with researchers there. It is something of a hub for the local industry.

As well as these national efforts, the cluster has worked towards the development of strategy within BC. The BC hydrogen and fuel cells strategy was written by an industry committee, at the request of the Premier's Technology Council (a body made up largely of BC industry leaders that advises the Premier of BC's provincial government on science and technology issues). The provincial government provided $2m in February 2005 to 'kick-start' implementation of the strategy.

Demonstration projects and the Hydrogen Highway

Demonstration projects have played, and continue to play, a key role in the development of the cluster, helping to build informal links between companies. They have also been an explicit focus of government policy, as they achieve network building, technology showcasing and the all-important branding of the cluster. Several demonstration projects were developed through the 1990s on an ad hoc basis, often through WEPA funding, but as more coherent industry development strategies arose, several more targeted initiatives were developed. Key early demonstrations included the Ballard buses during the 1990s, and the Ballard/Ford P2000 engine, with support from NRC, Natural Resources Canada, Industry Canada and Environment Canada in around 1993. Again, it is notable that the projects span hydrogen production, infrastructure and end-use, and all involve significant contributions by local technology providers.

Key demonstration projects since 2000 have included:

- The Compressed Hydrogen Infrastructure Program (CHIP) was developed by BC Hydro. CHIP involved $13m in federal and provincial government money, and brought together a group of partners (including Shell Hydrogen, BP, Dynetek, Stuart Energy and others) to build a 700mpa hydrogen refuelling and storage system.
- Vancouver Fuel Cell Vehicle Program was launched in 2003, largely funded by Natural Resources Canada. The project involved the five-year deployment of five Ford Focus fuel cell vehicles in Vancouver.
- The Integrated Waste Hydrogen Utilization Project is an $18m project involving the recovery of waste hydrogen from an industrial plant. The hydrogen produced is being used in a number of other projects, including buses running on a blend of hydrogen and natural gas.

In addition to these large projects, there is a series of smaller initiatives including:

- field trials of Angstrom Power's micro-fuel cell systems in flashlights, PDAs, bike lights and two-way radios;
- hydrogen-powered forklifts and baggage-tuggers at Vancouver International Airport;
- solar-hydrogen production facilities at NRC-IFCI.

All of the above projects are now under the umbrella of the BC Hydrogen Highway, which has become a focus for hydrogen activities in BC. The Hydrogen Highway was formally announced on 1 April 2004 by then Prime Minister Paul Martin, along with funding for a full-time manager provided by NRCan's Canadian Transportation Fuel Cell Alliance. The idea is to link seven 'nodes', each of which having a refuelling facility. Nodes are planned between Greater Vancouver and nearby Whistler (ski-resort, and site for much of the 2010 Winter Olympic Games), with further facilities in Victoria on Vancouver Island. Those involved in the project envisage an eventual link-up with similar initiatives in California and east across Canada, as the first stages in the development of a North American hydrogen infrastructure. The largest single initiative within the Hydrogen Highway is the establishment of a fleet of 20 fuel cell buses, to be operated by BC Transit. The provincial and federal governments have provided $89m in funding for the project, and the fleet began operation in late 2009.

Forces shaping innovation

From the history of the development of hydrogen and fuel cell activity in the Vancouver area, it is possible to identify and describe the driving forces that have shaped the path of innovation. These drivers vary over time, vary across scales and differ in character. This section outlines the macro-level conditions, the way in which government policies and markets respond to these conditions, the local competences that are deployed to respond, and the way in which these responses interact with the dominant systems of energy and transport. Finally, the section briefly outlines the way in which the direction of innovative activities has changed over the years.

Contexts for change: landscape conditions and cracks in the existing socio-technical 'regimes'

In general, we can identify a range of landscape or macro-level conditions, which provide the context for the day-to-day activities of energy and transport innovation systems. These include:

- Global economic performance, and global financial markets. The high technology financial boom during the late 1990s provided significant opportunities for raising capital in the fuel cell sector.
- Increasing evidence of climate change.

- Knowledge of the finite nature of fossil fuel reserves, and volatility of supply and price.
- Globalized industrial competition and trade arrangements, and the consequent focus on international competitiveness and innovation within a nation's private enterprise.

Secondly, there are pressures and constraints emerging with the dominant energy and transport 'regimes'. These include:

- air pollution;
- increasing demands for both quantity and reliability of electricity (particularly for businesses with a reliance on information technology), and occasional difficulties in meeting these (e.g. the black-outs in 2003 in Eastern Canada and the US).

These factors set the stage for both government policy and business strategy, and, through the activities of industry and policy-makers, are translated into push and pull factors on energy and transport innovation systems.

Government policy

Government activities in hydrogen help to raise the profile of the industry as a whole, and expectations of future government responses to major policy drivers such as oil security and depletion, air quality and climate change, strengthen a market pull that might otherwise be lacking. A recent OECD study argued that government policies are increasingly shaping the path of innovation in the Canadian fuel cell sector (OECD, 2006).

Clearly, policy drivers and priorities vary across scales:

- Federal: climate change, industrial competitiveness and innovation policy, reliability of energy supplies (especially after the 2003 black-outs), and the need to keep benefits 'Canadian', not just in BC.
- Provincial: competitive industries are the primary driver, balanced with the need to support the traditional resource-based industries of forestry and mining. Climate change and air quality are both important environmental drivers.
- Local: the key drivers at the municipal level are climate change and air quality, along with Vancouver's green self-image and aspirations to be known for hosting a 'green Olympics'.

In addition, policy drivers vary over time. The early days for the industry were a result of military interest in advanced battery and fuel cell technology for submarines. Air quality then became the major policy driver with bearing on fuel cells, as a result of the California Air Resources Board. The last 15 years have seen greater focus on industrial development and climate change as drivers of policy.

As a result of these policy drivers, Canadian governments have turned to a variety of instruments to foster the development of hydrogen and fuel cell technologies, and have:

- funded and supported R&D;
- supported network building and 'alignment';
- sponsored demonstration projects;
- supported the development of codes and standards;
- in some jurisdictions, governments are considering funding public procurement through Crown corporations, such as fuel cell buses for BC Transit.

At the regional and local level, air-quality concerns influence the way that the two provincial transit Crown corporations choose their technologies, with significant interest in low-emission vehicles. Translink, governed by the Greater Vancouver Regional District, has a long history of experimentation with low-emission buses.

Of course, it is not only governments within Canada that affect the innovation system. The policies of California's Air Resources Board were the initial inspiration for the sector, and various projects in Canada have been part-funded by the US Department of Energy.

It is important to note the importance of public funding in the sector. Funding from government has been essential to the development of the cluster, and there is an expectation within the industry that some dependence on government funds will continue: in a 2005 industry survey, 29 per cent of 2006–11 domestic revenues were expected to come from government (Industry Canada et al, 2006). Access to government funds and support has been facilitated by the way in which hydrogen companies have been able to tap into a wide range of drivers and agendas. Hydrogen, perhaps more than many other technologies, meets a wide array of policy drivers. This enables hydrogen enthusiasts to play a chameleon game with government, turning hydrogen from an 'innovation issue' into a 'climate issue' or an 'energy security issue' (although it is notable how little energy security features in Canadian hydrogen policy debates compared with, for example, the US). It also means that policy-makers at different scales can find clear rationales for support. While this means that the 'story' about the cluster is retold differently across scales, it allows for an integrated support hierarchy. As one interviewee remarked: 'the nice thing about hydrogen is that there's something for everyone'.

Markets: present and future

While government funding and policies have been important, the primary motivation for the innovative activity in the sector is the promise of future markets. These expectations are formalized through documents such as the 2002 PricewaterhouseCoopers Report, *Fuel Cells: The Opportunity for Canada*, which included optimistic projections for fuel cell sales. Expectations of future commercial success are related to the perceived future performance of the technology itself, and its ability to compete with incumbents in markets such as portable and distributed power, and also to anticipated future policies such as vehicle or carbon emissions restrictions. Wider context conditions, such as the rise in oil prices since 2000 and the development of the Kyoto Protocol, have made projections of future markets for fuel cell vehicles ever more plausible.

The formalized expectations are important, and those embodied in the PricewaterhouseCoopers report are found repeatedly through the literature supporting the cluster (e.g. the BC Hydrogen and Fuel Cells Strategy). However, from interviews with stakeholders, it is clear that expectations are seen to have followed the classic 'cycle of expectations' made popular by the consulting firm Gartner, and explored by scholars of expectations in technological change (Van Lente, 1993). See Figure 8.1.

Many in the industry now feel that the 'slope of enlightenment' has been reached, after the hype around 2000, and the subsequent 'fuel cell fatigue'. Some appear to be actively deploying this as a 'meta-expectation' – since the hype is in the past, current predicted markets are more realistic and thus more deserving of support. Others in the industry feel that the industry is still suffering from the 'trough of disillusionment', and that many are overly cautious about making claims about the future potential of their products.

Certainly, the drying-up of capital for the fuel cell sector, after the high-tech crash in 2000, has led to an increasing focus on near-term niche markets such as forklifts. Here, market pull is a result of the existing benefits of the technologies in small markets, rather than the future promise of fuel cells to compete in mainstream markets.

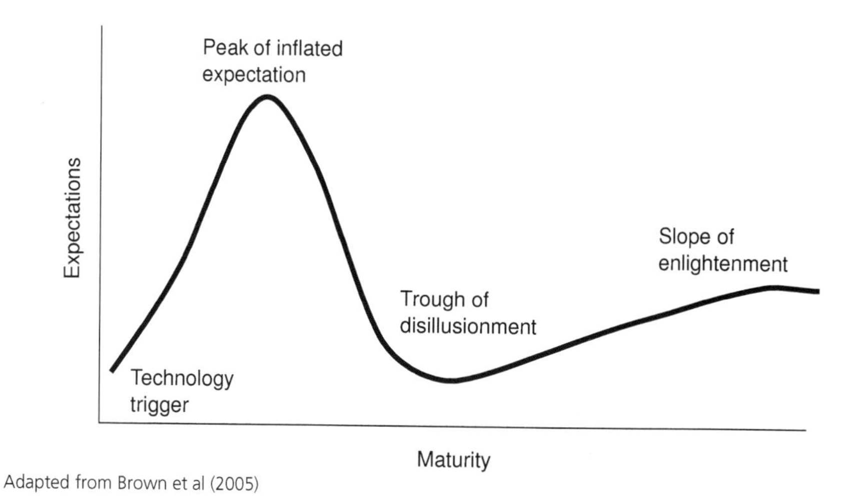

Figure 8.1 *The cycle of technological expectations*

Local factors: geography and local history

The shape of innovation in BC is a result of the over-arching conditions, policy drivers, and market push and pull factors, all being filtered through a series of contextual and local factors that are particular to the Vancouver area. Stakeholders and the documents reviewed suggested a range of local factors that help to explain the way in which those drivers set out above have led to the development of the cluster.

- Vancouver is a great place to live, topping the Economist Intelligence Unit's 2005 'Quality of Life' index. This results in a 'sticky' labour market, with skilled workers staying in the region even when times are tough and key companies like Ballard lay off staff.
- Physical geography: the proximity to California and the activities around the Air Resources Board's zero emissions mandate may have been important, as has access to engineering expertise in nearby Seattle's aerospace cluster. Vancouver's position as Canada's 'gateway to the Pacific' has seen attention shifting towards opportunities and markets in East Asia, with Ballard developing partnerships with EBARA in Japan and Shanghai Fuel Cell Vehicle Powertrain Co. in China, as well as supplying fuel cells to Hyundai in Korea. However, the position in Canada's far west has made tapping into the federal government more difficult than might perhaps be the case for Ontario- or Quebec-based industries.
- Locally powerful businesses and industries have been important in shaping the cluster, and the policies around it. The presence of companies in the area with interests in natural gas vehicles and refuelling (Westport Innovations, Powertech Labs) and methanol (Methanex) created opportunities for competences in hydrogen fuels, as well as fuel cells, and added to the momentum for the industry as a whole. The rules governing BC Hydro as a Crown corporation have also been important, preventing it from expanding into new jurisdictions, and thus channelling business development energy towards an alternative approach to market expansion for electricity – producing hydrogen fuel.

Alignment with incumbent regime – local interaction with global capital

While the local conditions within Vancouver and the hydrogen and fuel cell sector are important, these developments also link up with the interests and agendas of the global energy and automotive regimes. Clearly, the interest of the automotive sector in hydrogen, first spurred by the California Air Resources Board mandate, was vital for the development of the sector, most obviously with the investments made by DaimlerChrysler and Ford in Ballard. Support and capital from major oil and automotive firms have been important, and have ensured that the way in which hydrogen technologies develop are at least to some extent aligned with the interests of these actors.

In terms of the direction of innovative activities, many in the cluster agree that it was pressure from the oil industry, and from some automotive firms, that convinced Ballard and DaimlerChrysler to move away from on-board methanol reformation as a viable vehicle fuelling option. The example illustrates the way in which the local innovation system, and the direction of innovative activities, respond to the interests of global players.

Chance and contingency

Theories of technological change frequently provide accounts that can seem determinist, yet empirical studies serve as reminders that change is inevitably unpredictable and contingent on chance events and circumstances. The development of the hydrogen and fuel cell industry in Vancouver is no different.

First, many of the developments in the cluster are attributable to the personal energies and interests of key individuals. These include scientist-entrepreneurs such as Geoff Ballard and Paul Howard at Ballard; marketer Firoz Rasul, who raised Ballard's profile and facilitated the alliance with DaimlerChrysler; financier Mike Brown; network builders Denis Connor of QuestAir and Ron Britton of Methanex, who helped develop strategies and the industry association.

Second, the sector received a very large capital infusion in around 2000 as a result of the high-tech bubble. This timing worked greatly to the sector's favour, despite the hard times felt during the following crash. The chance confluence of the California Air Resources Board policies and the high-tech finance bubble created ideal conditions for the early development of the sector.

Other chance events (such as BC Hydro's windfall profits in the late 1990s, as a result of exports to California, which enabled BC Hydro to invest in hydrogen) have also played important roles. These, and other possible examples, suggest that more determinist accounts of the cluster would be incomplete.

The changing direction of innovative activities

The development trajectory of technologies is not predetermined – many non-technical factors influence the final shape of technologies. A detailed mapping of the course of innovative activities would clearly require a more comprehensive case study, complete with patent analysis. This is a brief overview of the way in which the factors outlined above have influenced the direction and focus of innovation and technology development within the cluster.

Early focus on military applications quickly shifted to automotive applications, where a strong focus remained throughout the 1990s. This emphasized problems of energy storage density, reliability in varying conditions, and power density, and clearly favoured low-temperature PEM fuel cells. The challenges of hydrogen storage meant that on-board methanol reformation was a major area of activity until 2002, when oil majors and other car companies convinced DaimlerChrysler to back away.

As technologies developed, many companies, and certainly Ballard, spent a period driven in part by 'technology push': markets were unclear, and a great deal of effort was devoted to probing technological possibilities. Indeed, Ballard's 2005 Annual Report notes that 'at times, Ballard "pushed" technology into new market applications without sufficient focus on the customer and the key commercial drivers' (Ballard Power Systems, 2005). Ballard decided to focus on near-term markets, such as their joint venture with EBARA in Japan, to provide fuel cells for residential co-generation.

From 2000 on, early markets started to become clearer, and many companies shifted focus from expected future markets to niches where hydrogen and fuel cell applications out-compete alternative technologies on performance and cost. BC Hydro has invested in the development of back-up power technologies, to support its distributed control systems and remote microwave repeater stations; Cellex and General Hydrogen compete in the market for forklift truck propulsion; and Angstrom focus on portable power packs. These developments have meant a diversification away from automotive propulsion as the principle focus of innovative activity. In 2008, Ballard sold its vehicle fuel cell business to DaimlerChrysler and Ford, signalling a further refocusing on near-term markets.

The role of 'cluster' thinking: policy frameworks and branding

Canada has a poor record in terms of innovativeness, when compared with other OECD countries (OECD, 2006), despite numerous attempts over the past few decades to move away from dependence on Canada's prodigious natural resources towards the vaunted 'knowledge economy'. In the late 1990s, many innovation researchers and academics from across Canada felt that a national-level approach to thinking about innovation policy (such as the increasingly dominant National Systems of Innovation approach) was inappropriate for a federation as large and diverse as Canada. Regional Innovation Systems (e.g. Braczyk et al, 1998), and Clusters (Porter, 1998; Cooke, 2001), seemed to be a more fruitful way of thinking about how innovation could be fostered. The Innovation Systems Research Network, a research programme involving innovation researchers across Canada, has been an important intellectual centre, driving thinking around innovation in the regions (www.utoronto.ca/isrn).

Canada's National Innovation Strategy, developed in 2002 by Industry Canada, is clearly influenced by Porter's approach to clusters: 'A paradox of the global, knowledge based economy is that sources of competitive advantage tend to be localized' (Industry Canada, 2002: p76). It includes the goal to 'by 2010, develop at least 10 internationally recognized clusters', with the BC fuel cell cluster highlighted as an example.

The National Research Council has been using its network of laboratories to support cluster development, by providing supporting infrastructure for R&D and conducting strategic R&D in support of industry. The Institute for

Fuel Cell Innovation (IFCI) in Vancouver is a good example of these activities: it provides basic R&D, testing and research facilities, and accommodation for Hydrogen & Fuel Cells Canada and nine small fuel cell companies, as well as managing its own fuel cell R&D programme. In 2008, the federal government announced $14m in funding for IFCI. The announcement was part of a larger programme of $118m, invested in six technology cluster initiatives across the country.

The extent to which the 'cluster model' of innovation support has been successful is perhaps still unclear, despite evaluation studies (Hickling Arthurs Low, 2006). Some observers from outside Canada have certainly been impressed: the 2002 UK Department for Trade and Industry fuel cell mission report lists the recommendation that 'consideration be given to an integrated approach (based on the Canadian "industry clusters" model)' (Hart, 2002: iv).

Branding: deploying the cluster story

The 'cluster' model does not only inform policy – it is also a common language through which participants in hydrogen and fuel cell innovation understand and communicate the development of the industry in and around Vancouver. The status of the Vancouver industry as a 'cluster' provides it with a brand image as a global centre for a growing industry.

Industry figures clearly recognize the value of the cluster brand, and actively work to maintain and enhance it. One interviewee from industry felt that Vancouver is one of a large number of jurisdictions competing in a global marketplace for demonstration projects and fuel cell vehicles, and that brand image is vital to the region's continued success. The Hydrogen Highway is seen as an important way of raising the profile of the region, and making sure that people know that 'this is where hydrogen happens'. Another interviewee felt that a fundamental part of demonstration projects is to maintain the image of the cluster as a centre for hydrogen activities, even if the direct local benefits are small. The language of industry clusters is thus actively deployed as a narrative about the dynamics of technological change, in order to mobilize support.

However, within any discussion of systems of innovation, industry clusters or industrial classifications, there are difficult boundary issues – what and where are the boundaries of the sector, the region, and the industry?

Is the cluster in Vancouver, BC, Western Canada, or is it simply Canadian? The geographical boundaries of the cluster are contested. A significant source of funding and support for the development of hydrogen and fuel cells in Vancouver is the Federal government. Industry Canada, for example, is charged with fostering industrial competitiveness across Canada, and while there is acceptance of the 'cluster model' as a useful way to pursue economic gains, there is also a perceived risk in emphasizing the growth of one region at the implicit cost of others. Hydrogen & Fuel Cells Canada have been careful to frame their efforts and publications in terms of a Canadian, rather than British Columbian, industry. However, many of those in the BC area appear to feel that it is the cluster's image as a regional cluster that is one of its core strengths.

It is not only the geographic boundaries of any cluster that are open to different perspectives. There are also debates about what exactly it is that is clustered: fuel cells, hydrogen fuels, or power technologies in general? Some within the cluster perceive a shift in the way in which the cluster is framed, as expectations have shifted around hydrogen. One interviewee suggested that, five years ago, other energy technologies attempted to attach themselves to hydrogen rhetoric. Now, power technologies in general are seen as the future, and hydrogen and fuel cells are attempting to maintain their profile within that broader firmament.

Competition and cooperation in clusters

In any industry cluster there is an inevitable tension between cooperation to further the development of the cluster as a whole, and competition between the companies in the cluster. This is pronounced in knowledge-intensive industries, where the core product can be intellectual property, leading to a culture of secrecy, rather than cooperation.

Those interviewed, and the documents reviewed, displayed a variety of views about the degree of cooperation or competition within the cluster. Interestingly, several stakeholders held the view that there is little competition within the cluster – and that there is a greater need for cooperation in the face of competitive threats from outside. This is in contrast to the way in which Porter, father of the 'cluster theory', emphasizes the role of rivalry and competition within clusters as essential to long-term viability (Porter, 1998).

In a globalized world, innovation is seen as key to maintaining competitiveness. With the 'cluster' model at the forefront of their minds, those charged with fostering the cluster and the industry appear to see the dynamics of innovation as concerned with competing regions, rather than competing firms. However, this view tends to obscure the way in which individual firms may have substantially greater collaborative links outside the cluster, with national and global partners.

Comparisons with the UK: Vancouver meets Wales, Teesside and London

In a similar effort to contribute to understanding of the way in which regional innovation dynamics relate to large-scale technological change, Hodson and Marvin conducted a series of case studies in the UK (Hodson and Marvin, 2005a 2005b 2005c). These explored attempts to develop hydrogen economies in three regions: London, Wales and Teesside, which are explored in more detail in the next chapter. This brief section explores some of the differences between hydrogen and fuel cell developments in those regions and in Vancouver.

Those promoting hydrogen in each of the regions, both in Canada and the UK, are competing in a global market to attract demonstration projects: the global automotive firms who develop fuel cell vehicles have little need to conduct real-world testing in more than a handful of locations. With only 250 fuel cell vehicles in existence, cities like London and Vancouver, and regions like Wales and Teesside, compete to make the case to be the location of choice. Each region tells a different story about itself to make that case.

In Vancouver, the story is about the fuel cell industry, and the potential opportunities that this might bring to the region. There is a widespread fear that, while Vancouver is currently a recognized leader in fuel cell technologies, other jurisdictions are 'buying their way in', and efforts must be dedicated to maintaining the region's profile and industry strengths.

In contrast, London's story makes little mention of the potential for the fuel cell industry to provide jobs and economic development. In London, the story is about hydrogen energy, not about the hydrogen industry. London sees itself as a 'world city', and as a place that has the profile to be a model for other cities to follow.

Teesside is an industrial region in the north of England, and a centre of Britain's chemical industry. There is a significant skills base in industrial chemistry, and an infrastructure of hydrogen production and distribution (including 30km of hydrogen pipelines). Hodson and Marvin's work describes how hydrogen promoters in Teesside tell a story about the region being a 'test-bed' for hydrogen systems and technologies (Hodson and Marvin, 2005). It is argued that the skills, infrastructure and a local population accustomed to large-scale chemical industry make Teesside the perfect place to try out different possible configurations of a hydrogen economy.

Finally, in Wales, the story about hydrogen ties together the promised sustainability benefits of hydrogen with the potential for regenerating Wales' automotive industry. With 'establishing Wales as a sustainable energy showcase' as one of the new Welsh Assembly's economic development goals, promoters of hydrogen in Wales argue that the principality has the political support, industry potential and resource base to make a hydrogen transition happen. However, as with London and Teesside, Wales has no real hydrogen energy industry.

Each of these regions have a different approach to thinking about, and supporting, the local development of hydrogen. While there are clear similarities, with regions competing to be seen as innovative and dynamics leaders, the differences are stark. Vancouver is at the centre of global innovation in fuel cells and hydrogen storage and handling technologies. Unlike Wales or Teesside, hydrogen promoters in Vancouver do not envisage a future manufacturing industry in Vancouver around fuel cells. Instead, Vancouver is a centre for research and development, and for generating intellectual property that can be sold around the world.

Note

1 This figure represents only public companies and respondents to the PricewaterhouseCoopers fuel cell sector survey, and is therefore an underestimate. All financial figures in this report are presented in Canadian dollars. While rates vary, the exchange rate with Sterling is approximately C$1 = £0.58.

References and further reading

Angstrom, Ballard, Chrysalix, Hydrogen & Fuel Cells Canada, Methanex, NRC, BC Hydro, PricewaterhouseCoopers, QuestAir and IESVic (2005) *British Columbia Hydrogen and Fuel Cells Strategy: an industry vision for our hydrogen future*, Victoria, Report for the Premier's Technology Council

Ballard Power Systems (2005) *Annual Report*, Burnaby, BC, Ballard Power Systems

Braczyk, Cooke and Heidenreich (eds) (1998) *Regional Innovation Systems*, London, UCL Press

Brown, N., Douglas, C., Eriksson, L., Rodrigues, E., Yearley, S. and Webster, A. (2005) *Researching expectations in medicine, technology and science: theory and method*. Position paper for the York workshop of the Expectations Network, University of York

Cooke, P. (2001) 'Regional innovation systems, clusters, and the knowledge economy', *Industrial and Corporate Change*, vol 10, no 4, pp945–973

Geels, F. W. (2002) 'Technological transitions as evolutionary reconfiguration processes: a multi-level perspective and a case-study', *Research Policy*, vol 31, nos 8–9, pp1257–1274

Government of Canada (2003) *From vision to reality: the making of Canada's Hydrogen and Fuel Cell Industry*, Ottawa

Hart, D. (2002) *Executive Summary – Fuel Cells: The Canadian Experience*. DTI International Technology Service Mission Report, London, Synnogy and DTI

Hickling Arthurs Low (2006) *Cluster studies for the NRC technology clusters initiative: Vancouver fuel cells cluster*, Report prepared for the National Research Council Strategy and Development Branch, Ottawa

Hodson, M. and Marvin, S. (2005a) *Re-Imagining Tees Valley in the Post-Industrial*, UKSHEC Social Science Working Paper no 4, SURF Centre, University of Salford

Hodson, M. and Marvin, S. (2005b) *The 'Journey' to Wales' Hydrogen Economy*, UKSHEC Social Science Working Paper no 5, SURF Centre, University of Salford

Hodson, M. and Marvin, S. (2005c) *London's Hydrogen Economy: Negotiating the 'Global', the 'Regional' and the 'Local'*, UKSHEC Social Science Working Paper no 6, SURF Centre, University of Salford

Hydrogen & Fuel Cells Canada and Government of Canada (2006) *Canada's Hydrogen and Fuel Cell Industry Capabilities Guide 2006*, Vancouver, Hydrogen & Fuel Cells Canada

Industry Canada (2002) *Achieving excellence: investing in people, knowledge, and opportunity*. Canada's Innovation Strategy, Ottawa, Industry Canada

Industry Canada, PricewaterhouseCoopers and Hydrogen & Fuel Cells Canada (2003) *Canadian fuel cell commercialization roadmap*, Ottawa, Industry Canada

Industry Canada, Hydrogen & Fuel Cells Canada and PricewaterhouseCoopers (2006) *Canadian hydrogen and fuel cell sector profile 2005*, Ottawa, Industry Canada

National Research Council (2006) *BC Hydrogen and Fuel Cell Cluster Roundtable*, Vancouver, NRC-IFCI

OECD (2006) *Innovation in energy technology: comparing national systems of innovation at the sectoral level*, Paris, OECD

Osborne, K. D. (2001) 'Ford's Zero Emission P2000 Fuel Cell Vehicle', *IEEE VTS News*, vol 48, issue 3

Porter, M. (1998) 'Clusters and the new economics of competition', *Harvard Business Review*, November–December, pp77–90

PricewaterhouseCoopers (2005) *Global 2005 Fuel Cell Industry Survey: a survey of 2004 financial results of public fuel cell companies*, Vancouver, PricewaterhouseCoopers

PricewaterhouseCoopers and Hydrogen & Fuel Cells Canada (2002) *Fuel cells: the opportunity for Canada*, Vancouver, PricewaterhouseCoopers

Van Lente, H. (1993) *Promising Technology: the dynamics of expectations in technological development*, Enschede, Department of Philosophy of Science & Technology, University of Twente

Wright, D. (2002) *Chapter 6: Financing and Venture Capital – Fuel Cells: The Canadian Experience*, DTI International Technology Service Mission Report, London, Synnogy and DTI

9
Hydrogen in the UK: Comparing Urban and Regional Drivers

Mike Hodson and Simon Marvin

Introduction

The promise of the hydrogen economy in addressing the issues of climate change, energy security and local air pollution has captured the imagination of politicians and policy-makers, not only internationally and nationally, but also at the city/regional level (see Bush, 2003; Prodi, 2003; Mayor of London, 2004). Much of this enthusiasm operates at a rhetorical level, making a multiplicity of claims about the possibilities of the hydrogen economy which, despite generating much political and policy excitement, has led to only a few highly selective and discretionary attempts to address the development of hydrogen economy initiatives in particular city/regional contexts (see Eames et al, 2006).

This chapter looks critically at the pressures and drivers underpinning the attempts of cities and regions in the UK to develop 'hydrogen economies'. It builds on a series of papers (Hodson and Marvin, 2005, 2007; Hodson, 2008) which reported on a wide range of interviews with stakeholders and policy-makers, both nationally and in places that were practically involved with hydrogen developments in the UK. The interviews, some of which are also reported here, revealed a clear gap in understanding, in both the policy and research communities, of the relationships between wider generic global and national drivers of the 'hydrogen economy', and more localized or context-sensitive motivations for developing place-specific hydrogen economies. Specifically we develop an understanding of urban and regional infrastructure drivers for the hydrogen economy not in isolation, but through carefully developing and populating a more socially and historically informed view of the significance of local context. By seeing urban and regional governance of the hydrogen economy not as bounded, but in relation to different scales of political activity that are manifest in particular places and initiatives, the key question is: what are the key drivers and pressures for UK urban and regional hydrogen economy development?

Our concern is that the dominant and conventional way of understanding energy systems – technology characterization – explicitly focuses on the generic issues associated with the development of hydrogen economies (Hodson and Marvin, 2006). This productionist perspective tends particularly to privilege knowledge and information about the technical features of alternative systems, and the economic costs associated with technological options. But it has relatively little to say about the specific contexts within which hydrogen might be used by particular sets of users or within specific urban and regional settings. Yet more widely, both policy-makers and researchers do recognize that hydrogen economies are not developed in an abstract context – on the head of a pin – and, in fact, different locations, stakeholders, technologies and users may be bundled together in quite different ways, so that the 'hydrogen economy' develops differently in different places. In fact, different contexts may have an important role in building an understanding of how the wider hydrogen economy may be practically configured. For example, a national level policy-maker told us:

> *I'm very struck by the fact that you're doing sort of a regional based thing because I think that's very much how the hydrogen economy is going to evolve. I don't think there'll be a sort of a one size fits all approach. Not in the early stages anyway.*

The rest of this chapter is structured in six sections. First, we briefly outline the critical policy drivers identified in debates around the hydrogen economy at European and national level, highlighting how these perspectives usually view urban and regional hydrogen economy developments as sites for technological demonstrations. Second, we develop a conceptual framework for comparing the 'gaps' between European and national understandings of the hydrogen economy and three case-study contexts in London, Wales and Teesside in the period 2004–05. In the three following sections of the chapter, we utilize our conceptual framework to examine why cities and regions develop their own discretionary view of the hydrogen economy, identify which different stakeholders are involved in the production of visions, and how, and then assess what are the key consequences of this activity in terms of material change and lessons learnt. Finally, the conclusion highlights the importance of developing a more contextual understanding of potential hydrogen economy developments.

European and national drivers for hydrogen economies: cities and regions as sites for demonstration

The development of future hydrogen economies is generally seen to be underpinned by a number of 'drivers', with varying emphases in different international, national and local and regional contexts. These 'drivers' often concentrate on concerns related to widespread reliance on fossil fuels, including reducing carbon dioxide emissions, confronting air pollution, increasing security of energy supply and addressing industrial competitiveness. In terms of thinking about UK regions it is useful to understand and 'unpick' these 'drivers' in terms of the European Union – operating in a 'global' context – the UK policy context, and the ways in which UK energy policy understands urban and regional contexts.

Europe in a 'global' context

European Union (EU) policy in respect of hydrogen, and energy more generally, has a particular emphasis on four issues: carbon dioxide emissions reduction; energy security; air quality and health improvements; and the promotion of industrial competitiveness. Underpinning the policy are relationships external to the European Union and, in particular, aspirations for Europe to be a 'leading world player'. Critically, however, 'the level of public support in Europe is still far below that in the United States. A substantial increase is therefore needed for Europe to compete with the US and Japan' (European Commission, 2003: p15). The EU sought to meet this 'global challenge' by aspiring to match levels of investment through individual states and the EU, and set up a High Level Group for Hydrogen and Fuel Cell Technologies in October 2002, to outline the actions that would be 'necessary to move from today's fossil based energy economy to a future sustainable hydrogen-oriented economy with fuel cell energy converters' (European Commission, 2003: p5).

An approach with five elements was developed to address the question: what can Europe do? (European Commission, 2003: pp16–23). The first of these was a 'political framework', with an emphasis on creating a 'consistent European policy framework with a sustainable energy policy at its heart' to take advantage of 'the substantial long-term public and private benefits arising from hydrogen and fuel cells' (p16). Second was a 'strategic research agenda', with the aim of 'bring[ing] together the best research groups in Europe today' and generating 'a critical mass in terms of resources, effort and competencies to analyse and address non-technical and socio-economic issues, and solve the remaining technical barriers to the introduction of hydrogen and fuel cells' (p17). The third element was a European roadmap for hydrogen and fuel cells – which acknowledges and addresses 'the complex range of options, [through offering] a framework for the introduction of hydrogen and fuel cells needs to be established' (p21). Fourth, a European Hydrogen and Fuel Cell Technology Partnership was created, supported by an Advisory

Council, to 'facilitate and accelerate the development and deployment of cost-competitive world-class energy systems and technologies for applications in transport, stationary and portable power'.[1] Finally, it was proposed that the Framework Programmes and national programmes should remain the main public-funding instruments for research, development and demonstration, while 'regional aid projects could provide opportunities for larger deployment initiatives' (European Commission, 2003: p21).

Cities and regions occupy a rather limited role in current European-level thinking about hydrogen, and are usually viewed as one type of stakeholder amongst many. Where local contexts are specifically identified, they are viewed as potential 'markets', 'niches' and 'demonstrations' for hydrogen technology. In terms of deployment, a particular emphasis has been put on the development of 'hydrogen communities' (HyCom) and also a 'demonstration and pilot programme to extend the technology validation exercises into the market development arena, through a number of "lighthouse" demonstration projects' (European Commission, 2003: p24). The idea behind HyCom was outlined by one key source, who said:

> *We've got larger demonstration activities that may combine transport and non-transport applications that may really lead us to a new type of project that would not be a market project or a commercial project but still a demonstration project. But in size and scale ... one could invent, kind of, hydrogen communities that, of course, they are not going to be 100 per cent hydrogen powered, but in which hydrogen ... will play a very important role and then, to establish such a hydrogen community as a demonstration project so that we could learn more about how to move towards such a hydrogen economy.*

The UK Energy White Paper

The UK Energy White Paper (DTI, 2003), *Our Energy Future*, provided an entry point to thinking about the hydrogen economy in the UK policy context. The White Paper set out a series of issues – environmental, in particular climate change; declining indigenous energy supplies; and ageing energy infrastructures – facing UK energy policy and posited a number of goals for addressing these issues. These included: cutting UK carbon dioxide emissions by 60 per cent 'by about' 2050 with 'real progress' by 2020; maintaining the reliability of energy supplies; the promotion of competitive markets both domestically and internationally in addressing 'sustainable' economic growth and improving productivity; and ensuring that every home is adequately and affordably heated.

The White Paper saw a role for hydrogen and fuel cells as part of a future fuel mix, stating: 'Hydrogen looks likely to play a key role in future low-carbon energy systems'; and in particular 'seems likely to play a key role in future transport technologies'. Measures in the White Paper to support the early development and take-up of hydrogen included, for example, the exemption of hydrogen from road fuel duty for a period; support for fuel cell research; part-funding of the trialling of fuel cell buses by Transport for London in 2003, and support for the hydrogen fuelling station being installed by BP; and working with London and other local and regional organizations on a wider network of demonstration trials, including linkages with existing local hydrogen distribution networks such as that on Teesside (DTI, 2003: p71).

The Energy White Paper explicitly recognized that local authorities and also Regional Development Agencies (RDAs) 'make decisions that are vital for energy policy – for example on planning, regeneration and development, procurement, housing, transport and sustainable development' (DTI, 2003: p116). The White Paper suggested building on these relationships to 'develop a new package of measures to promote national objectives through local and regional decision-making'. In many senses this reflects a view that the local and regional levels are sites for the implementation of national policy measures. These attempts to build relationships led one national level policy-maker to tell us that:

> *[On] energy policy generally, we're trying to work much more closely with the regions ... [we're] trying to develop a partnership framework with the RDAs on a number of fronts, energy is one of those ... It's trying to find ways of working with the RDAs and the regions and indeed the devolved administrations ... So, what they're trying to do is to find areas ... we give them £100,000 a year each as a, sort of, amount of money for energy promotion, and what we're looking for ... in my area we're trying to find regions that are interested in co-operating with us on [various] projects. We haven't got very far ... we haven't had that discussion yet.*

Yet at the same time, another closely involved policy-maker, when asked as to their understanding of energy developments in the regions, suggested that 'the information we have is pretty much based on those individuals who bother to come and see us'.

At the heart of these attempts to begin a process of working more closely with regions is a tension, according to another policy source:

> *In all areas to do with the regions we're trying to set central policy that will not constrain the regions, but equally we don't want to see regions competing with each other so it's, you know, that sort of balancing act.*

With this in mind, a key point to note is the regional variability in terms of the energy agenda in that: 'Regions have focused on different aspects of energy policy according to existing priorities' (DTI, 2004: p4). In many senses, although there was the aspiration in the White Paper to 'promote national objectives through local and regional decision-making', discussions with policy-makers highlighted an uncertainty about the relationships between the centre and the regions. The role of the centre in relation to hydrogen was further developed through a strategic framework for hydrogen, in which a role for regions was only implicitly acknowledged.

A strategic framework for hydrogen

Following the White Paper, and in order to get an overview of existing (often fragmented) UK capabilities in relation to the hydrogen economy, the DTI commissioned E4Tech, Eoin Lees energy and ElementEnergy to produce a strategic framework, for the period to 2030, for hydrogen energy in the UK, addressing the question: 'How should the UK engage with hydrogen economy activities for maximum benefit?' (E4Tech et al, 2004: p8). The strategic framework concluded that 'hydrogen has the potential to make a significant contribution to the UK's priorities in transport, much less in electricity and heat'. The report identified five main areas of support needed to develop six main hydrogen options for transport by 2030, including support for R&D, support for demonstration, support for commercialization, the coordination of UK hydrogen activities and the creation of demand conditions for hydrogen (E4Tech et al, 2005: p15).

Although the report had an explicit national focus on the UK, there were a number of assumptions implicit in the report about different urban and regional contexts for the development of the hydrogen economy. First, the six hydrogen chains specifically assumed that 'the transition to hydrogen for each application will happen at different times and rates, and to different extents, in different places' (E4Tech et al, 2004: p16). For example: 'Remote communities may be renewable hydrogen-powered'; 'Urban areas could be predominantly electric, with a small amount of hydrogen' (E4Tech et al, 2004: p16). Second, an exercise in understanding 'selected UK actors in hydrogen energy' also had an implicit regional and local geography (E4 Tech et al, 2004: p87). For example:

> *The UK's oil and gas industry expertise could be combined with regional interests in hydrogen for the development of experimental hydrogen infrastructures featuring production systems. This could provide strong learning-by-doing benefits which could be developed into products and services for export.'(E4Tech et al, 2004: p90)*

Finally, the report recognized that the urban and regional possibilities of the hydrogen economy converge and diverge with national policy goals, in that: 'Numerous other applications for hydrogen have merit, though they do not meet major UK policy goals of energy security and CO_2 reduction.' These include, for example: 'Demonstrations and commercial application of vehicles for these reasons [low noise, low local emissions, etc.] give knowledge and revenue to support the development of the wider vehicle market – e.g. buses, forklifts' (E4Tech et al, 2004: p84). Consequently, a city attempting to develop hydrogen-fuelled buses for local contextual reasons may not explicitly resonate with immediate national policy goals.

Each of the frameworks says little directly about connecting their views of the production of the hydrogen economy with urban and regional contexts of appropriation. The next stage in our argument is to identify the key drivers of UK urban and regional hydrogen economies looked at from the local context, to assess the extent to which they inform or are informed by national and EU level drivers, and review the 'gaps' between the possibilities and manifestations of hydrogen economies. The interesting issue here is that supranational and national energy policy provides a context through which cities ,regions may appropriate national and European policies in a variety of different ways depending on how local partnerships are constituted in particular contexts, how they understand the possibilities of the hydrogen economy, and what their agenda is in developing partnerships and so on.

Connecting the hydrogen economy to urban and regional contexts

The foregoing analysis suggests that the role of cities and regions in the development of the hydrogen economy is currently inadequately conceptualized and poorly understood. At the same time, responsibility for key aspects of technology, innovation and competitiveness policy have been devolved from the nation state to city and regional scales. And at the city and regional scale, significant efforts are being made to strategically shape technological transitions through initiatives designed to systemically mediate relations between technological potentials and local context. Central to understanding these shifts are changes in the international economy, through the reconfiguration of national and international financial and political institutions (see Aglietta, 1979) over the last three decades, which have generated neo-liberal pressures for increased 'competitiveness', 'entrepreneurialism' and 'innovation'. The competitive state has a 'concern with technological change, innovation and enterprise and its attempt to develop new techniques of government and governance to these ends' (Jessop, 2002: p96). Consequently, new configurations of governance seek to create increasing international economic competitiveness, and respond to the competitiveness agenda, through encouraging (particularly technological) innovation at different scales. These structural shifts have three significant implications for our understanding of cities and regions in technological transitions.

The first of these is to highlight the pervasiveness of the notion of 'competitiveness' itself, and the ways in which this is manifest in wider pressures for city and regional transformation through science, technology and innovation. A closely aligned development in the UK context has been the establishment of Regional Development Agencies (RDAs) in 1999, and their identification with competitiveness of many of their local and regional economic governance concerns. This emphasis on narrowly defined features of economic governance has also become a central concern of many local authorities (see Fuller et al, 2004). What often follows is a 'race' for competitiveness and a constant search for transformation at the urban and regional scale. Cities and regions search for technological potentials to position themselves in the global race for economic competitiveness.

This leads to a second point. City and regional analyses need to take account of a complex interplay of relationships at various political scales. Critically, this requires 'an appreciation of the complex geometry of power and the political and cultural struggles through which societies assume their regional shape' (MacLeod and Jones, 2001: p670). A focus on the 'endogenous' city and region, and 'creating the conditions' for city and regional socio-technical innovation, often ignores what drives city and regional economies, and in doing so underplays the differential economic and political positions of places and the wider role of the nation-state in devolving responsibility (but often not power and resources) for technology and innovation strategies to city and regional development agencies (Ward and Jonas, 2004). Cities and regions have differential positions within existing social, political and economic relations, which affect their capacity to shape technological transitions.

Finally, new technology and innovation is both a product of, and produces political pressures for, institutional change. Seeing the city and regional level as merely responding, as reactive, ignores the specific set of existing social, political and economic relationships, which inform a city and regional response. It also ignores attempts to shape relationships across space with a variety of, for example, national, supranational, and other city and regional government departments and agencies. This highlights the importance of seeing city and regional development in relation to technological transitions not only through the lens of 'endogenous' institutional interrelationships, but also in terms of the influence of, and relationships with, the nation-state. Cities and regions actively and strategically work both internally and externally in developing the resources, networks and relationships to actively shape technological transitions.

Returning to the key question (what are the key 'drivers' for UK urban and regional hydrogen economy development?), the critical point is that attempts to understand hydrogen economy developments need to address not only its possibilities, but also the complex interpenetration of local, regional, national and international scales. This requires a focus on the importance of embedding and appropriating understandings of the hydrogen economy in particular regions. From a conceptual and theoretical approach we outlined previously (Hodson and Marvin, 2009), and also in relation to issues emerging from three regional case studies in London, Wales and Tees Valley (Hodson and Marvin, 2005, 2007; Hodson; 2008), we wish to outline key regional/urban and infrastructure 'drivers'. We do this through asking questions under three headings:

1. Why are cities and regions interested in developing hydrogen economies?
2. Who are the social interests involved and how do they work together?
3. What are the implications and consequences of these activities?

Tables 9.1, 9.2 and 9.3, and the accompanying discussion, summarize our responses to these questions.

Re-imagining cities and regions – the contextual 'drivers' of hydrogen economies

This section emphasizes the importance of representations or visions of regional hydrogen economy development, or the ways in which this may involve re-imagining the region. In this respect, it deals with the governance of representations. In doing this there is a focus on three sets of 'drivers' emerging from the regional case studies and then a detailing of a number of key common issues from looking across the cases (see Table 9.1).

Issues and problems

The first 'driver' underpinning moves towards the development of local hydrogen economies was related to issues or problems facing a city or region. There was a primary role in addressing issues of economic competitiveness, as well as systemic transport change, environmental and social equity agendas, in order to respond to various legacies of their local and regional social, political, economic and industrial history. For example, in London this led to a city-regional agenda that included not only city-level issues of air quality, social equity, and carbon emissions reduction, but also wider issues of economic competitiveness. The CUTE project – the development of a network of Europe-wide fuel cell buses – in London was explicitly related to the problems of managing uncertainty for multinational automobile and fuel corporations,

Table 9.1 *Re-imagining cities and regions*

Driver	*London*	*Wales*	*Teesside*
Issues problem facing context	Air quality, carbon emissions, social equity, and economy Management of uncertainty and testing potential for system change	Weak economic performance Job retention in automotive sector in South Wales	Decline of traditional industrial base in steel and chemicals
Possibilities and expectations	Preparing the conditions for a hydrogen economy in London. Fuel-cell bus demonstration in 'leading' cities as part of test-cycle	Exploring possibilities of hydrogen through networks and visions	Adapt existing infrastructure and skills to appropriate benefits of hydrogen
Contextual role	Preparatory city Test-bed city	Exploratory	Adaptable

and to the European Commission's DGTREN interests in systemic change in transport systems. In contrast, in Wales the problem was one of relatively poor economic performance both on an urban and rural Wales-wide basis. More specifically, it was about the retention of jobs and economic activity related to the 'global' automobile industry and its supply chains in south Wales. Whilst in the Tees Valley the dominant problem to be addressed was the decline of employment in its traditional industrial base, particularly chemicals and steel.

Possibilities and expectations

The second sets of drivers were the perceived possibilities and expectations of the development of a hydrogen economy in addressing these local issues and problems. In London this involved the 'preparation' of a 'necessary' social context favourable to the development of a London hydrogen economy. Additionally, for the CUTE project, fuel cell bus demonstration projects in highly visible 'leading' cities were seen as part of a 'test-cycle' informing corporate research and development, and understanding the 'transferability' of technologies to other cities. In the Welsh context the problem of relatively poor economic development resulted in a 'journey' of exploration of the possibilities of a hydrogen economy through the construction of networks and visions of perceived future economic potential. While in Tees Valley, responding to the decline of traditional sources of industrial employment was seen as requiring the adaptation of an existing physical and social infrastructure and skills base to appropriate the perceived benefits of hydrogen development.

Regional hydrogen relationships

The relationship between the issues and problems facing a city or region and the perceived possibilities of the development of a hydrogen economy in addressing them was inevitably mediated by the physical manifestation of the hydrogen technologies in the city and region. This took a number of different forms. In the CUTE project in the London city-region this involved the 'preparatory' creation of a social context, in which the city-region was viewed as a highly visible 'laboratory' or a 'test-bed' for a wider transformation of the city's transport system. In Wales, the relationship was seen as more 'exploratory', where there was to be an unfolding process of understanding the 'journey' and the production of manifest potentiality through the hydrogen economy in Wales. While in the Tees Valley the view of hydrogen technology and the region was a more 'adaptable' one of reconfiguring existing socio-technical networks and arrangements in respect of the perceived possibilities of the hydrogen economy.

Key issues

From these themes, four key issues become apparent:

- Primary importance in development of a regional hydrogen economy was given to addressing issues of economic competitiveness, as well as systemic transport change, environmental and social equity agendas. This was underpinned by particular views derived from local and regional social, political, economic and industrial history.

- There was often a lack of clarity and uncertainty – to varying degrees – as to the possibilities and potential of the hydrogen economy in addressing these issues. That is to say there were a number of responses to questions about the possibilities of the hydrogen economy, citing a variety of possible 'ends'.
- This clarity (or lack of it) links to the possibilities for mobilizing capacity and capability within local networks, the types and degree of local engagement, and influences whether such capacity and capability is made manifest or remains latent.
- This influences in turn how the relationships between hydrogen and fuel cell technology and regional contexts are viewed, ranging from 'experimental' (a 'test-bed'), which largely underplays the active role local and regional contexts may play, to 'preparatory' to 'exploratory', concerned with building capacity and visions, to 'adaptable', emphasizing local and regional adaptability.

Producing responses – key stakeholder and governance frameworks

The responses to the issues and problems facing a region emphasize the partial and negotiated way in which hydrogen economies are envisaged in specific regions. In particular, the emphasis is on who has the ability to generate such responses – in particular which institutions are involved? What types of relationships do they engage in with 'others' – including at a variety of political scales? This has important implications for the types of resources (financial, types of knowledge, political leverage etc.) which can be drawn upon (see Table 9.2).

Key institutions

Different institutions take the lead in a local hydrogen economy. The important issue with regard to hydrogen economy development is the level of resources – financial, forms of knowledge etc. – that are available to key institutions, the types of resource available to them in terms of relationships, and the ways in which institutional innovations are both informed by these resource issues and have consequences in terms of future resources which may be cultivated in terms of processes of learning through hydrogen economy developments. In the London city-region, for example, the Greater London Authority (GLA) was a key institution in informing a particular representation of the London hydrogen economy through the development of an 'inclusive' London Hydrogen Partnership (LHP). Also in London, a different form of key institution can be seen in the case of the London CUTE bus demonstration ,where DaimlerChrysler, BP and the European Commission through

Table 9.2 *Producing local responses*

Driver	*London*	*Wales*	*Teesside*
Key institutions	GLA and an inclusive London Hydrogen Partnership Multinational and DGTREN through a public private partnership	University driven with ERDF funding – H2 Wales Development Agency Hydrogen Valley Initiative	Local authority, Renew Tees Valley (sub-regional partnership, regional development agency and centre of excellence
Interrelationships	Wide variety institutions and interests in LHP – public, private, national government etc.	Ongoing journey through negotiation of ideas with multiple stakeholders	'Stitching-together' regionally
Scales of activity	Focus on coherent city-regional agenda – importance of proximity to national level and comparison with other cities	Confidence of newly devolved region looking outwards to Europe	Looking outwards to national government and attracting inward investors

DGTREN informed the production of a particular representation of the hydrogen economy from 'outside' of London through the use of a different form of institutional adaptability – the development of a public–private partnership (PPP).

From the context of a university, H2 Wales sought to draw on part-ERDF funding which provided an almost Wales-wide focus on the hydrogen economy, and thus the assembling of a large and wide-ranging network of 'stakeholders' in a Stakeholder Forum, with sub-networks of Demonstration Project Working Groups, guided by a Steering Group. Additionally, in Wales, the Welsh Development Agency was a key institution in pursuing the development of a hydrogen economy in a more specific area of industrial south Wales. In addressing this there were numerous similarities and, indeed, overlaps in terms of the network approach outlined on a Wales-wide basis by H2 Wales. In contrast, the key institution in addressing the Tees Valley hydrogen economy was a local authority, Redcar and Cleveland Borough Council. The institutional innovation was a specific strategic intervention – Renew Tees Valley – encompassing the Tees Valley Hydrogen Project underpinned by sub-regional funding. Additionally – through a 'stitched-together agenda' – a complementary centre of excellence, the Centre for Process Innovation, as part of the Regional Development Agency (RDA)'s science technology and innovation strategy, Strategy for Success, began to address the commercialization of fuel cell R&D through its Fuel Cell Application Facility.

Interrelationships

Second, this, in turn, links to a variety of network forms of interrelationships underpinning regional hydrogen economy development. These differ in size, the interests constituting them and degrees of alignment. It is the negotiations of such interrelationships, with their variety of aspirations, expectations and understandings of the possibilities of the hydrogen economy that informs the production of regional representations. So, for example in London, there was a wide variety of interests involved in the 'inclusive' LHP, including public, private, national government, and so on. This underpinned a lengthy process through which different understandings of the hydrogen economy, drawing on varieties of technical, environmental and business knowledge were negotiated in the production of the LHP's Action Plan. The interrelationships underpinning the CUTE project were narrower than this and reflected the fact that this was addressing a specific transport demonstration. There was a core network of multinational interests and the European Commission in a PPP, supplemented by more local level interests in London. The resources these actors were able to leverage (according to one source the costs of the initiative were split with DGTREN, contributing around €21m of the €60m total) informed a particular test-bed view of the city and its learning, to inform future wide-scale systemic transport change.

In contrast, in Wales the lack of clarity as to the specifics of how a hydrogen economy would address relatively poor economic performance, and the geographic scale of activities, led to a wide variety of interrelationships and produced an ongoing negotiation of various forms of knowledge – a circulation and negotiation of ideas – drawing on a variety of relationships and 'stakeholders' on the 'journey' to Wales' hydrogen economy. In the Tees Valley, interrelationships were underpinned by movements from the local level up and the regional level down to 'stitch-together' regionally a 'common' understanding of the hydrogen economy starting from different perspectives. Such a process involved drawing on forms of knowledge of the possibilities of economic regeneration, knowledge of the technical and market possibilities of fuel cell and hydrogen technologies, knowledge of regional economic strengths and attempts to strategically align these, and so on.

Scales of activity

Finally, these interrelationships are not territorially bounded. Local hydrogen economies are informed to different extents by a focus on different scales of political activity. Indeed, the entry of 'external' viewpoints into the development of regional hydrogen economies was a significant 'driver' in all cases. The importance of this – if one refers back to the views of the regions made, often implicitly, in a number of national and supranational contexts – is that this informs an ongoing negotiation between the often different expectations of regional hydrogen economy development across different scales and contexts of political activities. In London, through the GLA and the LHP, there was a focus on developing a coherent city-regional agenda, but in doing so they recognized the value of the enhanced visibility of the London initiative because of geographical proximity to national-level policy-makers. In terms of the CUTE project there was an attempt to develop interrelationships, which in many ways by-passed the national level to link the supranational and local and regional levels. There was also a focus on the comparative and competitive politics of 'world' and major cities both vying with one another and cooperating around common agendas.

In Wales the scales of political activity were both Wales-wide and south Wales specific in terms of the cultivation of networks, but also with specific project group networks developed at the local level. These views sought to position Wales in terms of the confidence of a newly devolved Wales looking 'outwards' to Wales in Europe, through the development of networks and the bidding for Framework projects. In Teesside the 'stitching-together' and aligning of agendas linked the local, sub-regional and regional scales together in informing a view of the adaptability of Teesside infrastructure, in creating jobs, economic competitiveness and informing regional economic, science, technology and innovation strategies. There was also an emphasis on looking 'outwards' to DTI, in positioning the Tees Valley as a place where a government uncertain about the possibilities of the hydrogen economy could come and 'play about' in an area of existing and adapted expertise.

Key issues

Again, the above themes highlight a number of key issues:

- That different institutions take the lead in regional hydrogen economy development – with a variety of views of roles within the region. The important issue with regard to hydrogen economy development is the level of resources (financial, forms of knowledge) that are available to key institutions, the types of resource available to them in terms of relationships (or 'social capital'), and the ways in which institutional innovations are both informed by these resource issues and have consequences in terms of future resources which may be cultivated in terms of processes of learning through hydrogen economy developments.
- This, in turn, links to a variety of network forms of interrelationships underpinning regional hydrogen economy development. These differ in size, interests constituting them and degrees of alignment, and it is the negotiations of such interrelationships, with their variety of aspirations, expectations and understandings of the possibilities of the hydrogen economy, which informs the production of regional representations.
- These interrelationships are not territorially bounded. Regional hydrogen economies are informed to different extents by a focus on different scales of political activity. Indeed, the entry of 'external' viewpoints into the development of regional hydrogen economies was a significant 'driver' in all cases. The importance of this – if one refers back to the views of the regions made, often implicitly, in a number of national and supranational contexts – is that this informs an *ongoing negotiation* between the often different expectations of regional hydrogen economy development across different scales and contexts of political activities.

Consequences and manifestations of urban and regional hydrogen economies

Having discussed the types of interests and motivations for developing regional hydrogen economies, the capability of these different interests to inform the symbolic meaning of what a regional hydrogen might look like and why, and the frameworks of governance which evolve or are generated, we now move to consider the role of intermediaries and the actual outcomes, and their transferability, that are produced (see Table 9.3).

The role of intermediaries

Intermediary organizations have a critical role in mediating between national, supranational and multinational corporation interests, and the regional and local levels. So, for example, the role of the LHP was in the generation of a wide-ranging network to produce a 'route-map', the know-how and know-who – the creation of a social context – to support a London hydrogen economy. In doing this the LHP positioned itself between the representations of the hydrogen economy in London and attempts to begin to create a social context for its 'realization'. The PPP underpinning the CUTE project was an 'outside'-driven network, appropriated and embedded in a particular place. There were interesting issues related to its role, which relied on very little apparent intermediation initially between local people and its MNC/DGTREN

Table 9.3 *Manifestations and consequences*

Driver	*London*	*Wales*	*Teesside*
Role of intermediary	LHP – generation of 'route-map' to support London HE PPP – external driven network embedded in locally context	H2 Wales – produce networks and seeking to embed projects in context HVI develop automotive supply change to remain global position	TVHP develop a series of demonstrations projects Fuel Cells Applications Facility – develop demonstration applications
Outcomes	Several small demonstration projects, educational and cultural events Relatively large-scale demonstration with local protects	A few demonstrations projects at planning or seeking funding	Visible demonstration projects, engaging through education, local providers, links with local R&D and market
Transferability	London-specific Test-bed developing transferable knowledge	Rolling out hydrogen economy across Wales, Wales as global showcase and Welsh technology in global cars.	Experimental Platform – come to Teesside to develop the HE Village Fete – know how to embed the HE in Teesside – first mover

agenda (Hodson and Marvin, 2007). In many senses the availability of relatively plentiful resources, underpinning the 'test-bed' view of technology, dominated to the detriment of local-level engagement.

The role of H2 Wales was as a university-led initiative, with the resource implications of this. The relatively limited level of resources, particularly financial, was an important motivation of Demonstration Project Working Groups and various sub-networks of the overall project to develop project proposals, in particular local contexts to attract financial support from a variety of funders. The Hydrogen Valley Initiative (HVI) acted as an 'intermediary' organization between the perceived competitiveness of the 'global' automobile industry and Welsh attempts to maintain their presence in such a sector, by encouraging the development of automobile industry supply chains in Wales. On Teesside, two different organizations were developed to generate practical manifestations of a hydrogen economy (Hodson, 2008). The first of these, the Tees Valley Hydrogen Project, sought to position itself between technology providers and a series of demonstration projects in different contexts. The second, the Fuel Cell Applications Facility, took a role 'connecting' fuel cell R&D to potential markets for 'application'.

Outcomes

It is important to recognize the limited scale of the actual hydrogen activities that took place in the three UK regions, in contrast to the rather grandiose visions of re-imagining regions that underpinned them. There is a large 'gap' between the possibilities and claims about regional hydrogen economies and events on the ground. The practical attempts to develop regional hydrogen economies were constrained by the opportunities of particular regional contexts and the available 'relevant' relationships and resources. Across the case studies, there were only a few small-scale demonstration projects and a range of cultural and educational events to 'educate' and 'inform' publics. This said, many demonstration projects were in the planning stage and reflected that the securing of financial resources was of key importance, but also that this needed some investment in terms of the development of a vision or representation and the cultivation of networks to underpin this. Of the few demonstration projects there was relatively high visibility in terms of the large-scale demonstration projects, driven through PPP, but which encountered local protests. It is interesting to note that the 'big boys' here suffered few of the financial resource issues of other initiatives, and therefore the perceived 'necessity' to 'prepare' and create a social context may not have figured as prominently, a consequence of which can be seen in terms of the bus refuelling station controversy related to the CUTE project. Where there were attempts to engage in demonstration projects, for example on Teesside, the important issues raised included an awareness and appreciation of a need to 'sell' the hydrogen economy in terms of the regional advantages to be gained. There was also recognition of the importance of engaging with the public through education. A series of design and safety issues were raised, as was the importance of visibility and being distinctive through demonstration projects. In addition, there was an emphasis on the importance of engaging local providers in training and also developing institutions to work between R&D and the market.

Transferability

Finally, there is a variability in understanding what may be 'transferable' from different regional and local contexts and to where. 'Transferability' was highlighted in terms of technological artefacts, know-how and processes, perceptions or images of regions. In many ways the city-regional agenda of the GLA was London-specific and not transferable. There was, however, a sense that perceptions of London in terms of it being a 'world' city and at the forefront of hydrogen economy developments was transferable. The CUTE project view of hydrogen economy development in terms of the test-bed suggests in many ways that it is the technology that is transferable between contexts where lessons are learned. In the Welsh case there was an unclear sense that through 'rolling-out' the hydrogen economy across Wales that technology was transferable. Furthermore, the notion of Wales as a 'global showcase' suggests the transferability of a particular vision of 'new', confident Wales, as well as attempting to position Wales as a technology exporter. This view of technology transfer also resonated with the HVI initiative relating Welsh technology and expertise to 'global' cars. In Teesside, transferability operated, through the notion of the 'experimental platform', in terms of the transferability of the message to DTI that Teesside is the place to prototype the hydrogen economy. If Teesside was then a 'first mover', the 'village fete' – the know-how and processes developed in Teesside – was seen as being transferable, in that it could be used to facilitate the embedding of the hydrogen economy in different regions.

Key issues

The key issues highlighted by these themes include:

- The importance of (understanding) the role of 'intermediary' organizations between the production of hydrogen and fuel cell technologies and the various contexts of appropriation, but also their role between the 'inside' and the 'outside' of the region; in other words, how the 'intermediary' organizations mediate between national, supranational and multinational corporation interests and the regional and local levels, and the role(s) that they might and do perform.
- The limited practical manifestations of the hydrogen economy compared to the visions of re-imagining regions.
- The variability in understanding what may be 'transferable' – in terms of technological artefacts, know-how and processes, perceptions or images of regions – from different regional and local contexts and to where.

Conclusion

Through a consideration of three regions in the UK, this chapter has outlined the importance of thinking about urban and regional hydrogen economies not only in terms of technical and economic possibilities, but also in respect of appreciating the local contexts within which such developments occur. It is important to acknowledge that such contexts are not bounded and fixed, but are best understood as a 'nested', fluid and complex interpenetration of scales of activity – including those of a variety of supranational, national, regional and local actors such as government departments, consultants, regional development agencies, local authorities, EU DGs, and so on. The importance of understanding not only technical and economic possibilities, but also how these relate to regional contexts, was stressed here in terms of a number of issues. The first of these was 'purpose', or why develop a regional hydrogen economy, and was understood through addressing the relationships between issues and problems facing a region, the possibilities of and response to the hydrogen economy, and how understandings of the relationship between regions and hydrogen technology were thought about. The second issue refers to relationships, or who was involved in regional hydrogen economy developments, how they were involved and with what resources. The third issue is the consequences of this activity in terms of material change, outcomes and forms of transferability of knowledge. The key point to note is that there is a gap between the visions and representations of the hydrogen economy outlined in the case studies, and the actual material production and manifestations to which they gave rise. Ongoing research is revisiting these regions to ascertain, five years later, the durability of the hydrogen developments undertaken there in an earlier period.

Note

1 https://www.hfpeurope.org/hfp/about_hfp. Accessed 6 May 2009.

References

Aglietta, M. (1979) *A theory of capitalist regulation: the US experience*, London, Verso

Bush, G. W. (2003) State of the Union address. Available at www.whitehouse.gov/news /releases/2003/01/20030128–19.html

DTI (2003) *Our Energy Future: Creating a Low Carbon Economy*, London, DTI

DTI (2004) *Creating a Low Carbon Economy: Progress on Regional Implementation of the Energy White Paper*, London, DTI

E4 Tech, ElementEnergy, Eoin Lees (2004) 'A Strategic Framework for Hydrogen Energy in the UK'. Available at http://www.dti.gov.uk/energy/sepn/hydrogen_framework_full.pdf

E4 Tech, ElementEnergy, Eoin Lees (2005) 'A Strategic Framework for Hydrogen Energy in the UK', Presentation by Adam Chase to ESRC Seminar Series

'Analysing Social Dimensions of Emerging Hydrogen Economies', Manchester, 24 February
Eames, M., McDowall, W., Hodson, M. and Marvin, S. (2006) 'Negotiating Generic and Place-Specific Expectations of the Hydrogen Economy', *Technology Analysis and Strategic Management*, vols 3–4, pp361–374
European Commission (2003) *Hydrogen Energy and Fuel Cells: A Vision of Our Future*, Brussels, European Commission
Fuller, C., Bennett, R. and Ramsden, M. (2004) 'Local government and the changing institutional landscape of economic development in England and Wales', *Environment and Planning* C, vol 22, pp317–347
Hodson, M. (2008) 'Old Industrial Regions, Technology and Innovation: Tensions of Obduracy and Transformation', *Environment and Planning* A, vol 40, no 5, pp1057–1075
Hodson, M. and Marvin, S. (2005) 'The "Journey" to Wales' Hydrogen Economy', Working Paper 5, SURF Centre, University of Salford, May
Hodson, M. and Marvin, S. (2006) 'Reconnecting the Technology Characterisation of the Hydrogen Economy to Contexts of Consumption', *Energy Policy*, vol 34, pp3006–3016
Hodson, M. and Marvin, S. (2007) 'Transforming London/Testing London: Understanding the role of the national exemplar in constructing "strategic glurbanisation"', *International Journal of Urban and Regional Research*, vol 31, no 2, June
Hodson, M. and Marvin, S. (2009) 'Cities mediating technological transitions: understanding visions, intermediation and consequences', *Technology Analysis & Strategic Management*, vol 21, no 4, May 2009, pp515–534
Jessop, B. (2002) *The future of the capitalist state*, Cambridge, Polity
MacLeod, G. and Jones M. (2001) 'Renewing the geography of regions', *Environment and Planning* D: Society and Space, vol 19, pp669–695
Mayor of London (2004) 'Green light to clean power: the mayor's energy strategy', London, Greater London Authority
POST (2002) 'Prospects for a Hydrogen Economy', London, Parliamentary Office of Science and Technology
Prodi, R. (2003) 'The energy vector of the future', Conference on the Hydrogen Economy, Brussels, 16 June. Available at http://europa.eu.int/rapid/start/cgi/guesten.ksh?p_action.gettxt=gt&doc=SPEECH/03/306|0|RAPID&lg=EN
Ward, K. and Jonas, A. (2004) 'Competitive city-regionalism as a politics of space: a critical reinterpretation of the new regionalism', *Environment and Planning* A, vol 36, pp2119–2139

10
Hydrogen Risks: A Critical Analysis of Expert Knowledge and Expectations

Miriam Ricci, Paul Bellaby and Rob Flynn

Introduction

The search for cleaner and more sustainable fuels has become a high priority in the global political agenda. Rising energy demand, coupled with increased concerns over climate change and energy security, are pressing national governments, international organizations and multinational companies to develop alternatives to oil-based fuels.

Among a plethora of innovative technologies, hydrogen (H_2) has been receiving significant attention as an attractive fuel and energy carrier (Dunn, 2002; Rifkin, 2002). Hydrogen, the most abundant and lightest element of the periodic table, can in principle be produced from any primary energy source, including renewables. When used in a fuel cell, hydrogen produces electricity without any noise and, most importantly, without emitting pollutants or greenhouse gases such as carbon dioxide (CO_2), thus potentially contributing to improved local air quality and helping to reduce carbon emissions.

The challenges for the development of a hydrogen economy, however, are daunting. They include overcoming outstanding technological problems (in particular, those associated with hydrogen storage) in developing sustainable production processes, establishing the necessary distribution and delivery infrastructures, and developing an adequate regulatory framework that would enable hydrogen-based technologies to be introduced into the market and compete with incumbent technologies.

What underpins all the efforts being made to overcome such challenges is the assumption that hydrogen would eventually provide at least the same level of safety as other conventional fuels and energy vectors. In this chapter we aim to critically analyse this assumption by spelling out what is known and what is relatively unknown or uncertain about the risks to safety, public health and the environment associated with hydrogen as an energy carrier. This will be the focus of the following section. We will then discuss the extent to which identified knowledge gaps are being addressed, by providing an overview of recent project developments both in the UK and abroad. We will also present selected evidence from qualitative fieldwork conducted within UKSHEC 1 in the North East of England, South Wales and Greater London, which illustrates the diversity of views expressed by representatives from industries and local authorities on the trade-off between hydrogen costs, benefits and risks, and how these could be managed. Finally, we will conclude the chapter by identifying and discussing key priorities for further research.

Hydrogen risks: the evidence base

When new technologies are being developed, and especially when these are capable of having far-reaching implications on society or the environment, a great deal of attention is often given to their prospective adverse effects. Notable examples in the UK include genetic engineering, in particular in relation to the development and commercialization of genetically modified foodstuffs, and nanotechnology. Both have spurred significant public debate and expert conflicts over the risks they might pose (The Royal Society and the Royal Academy of Engineering, 2004; Horlick-Jones et al, 2007; Stilgoe, 2007).

Although hydrogen energy is not (yet) at the centre of a public debate, the scientific, industrial and policy-making community promoting hydrogen as a future fuel and energy carrier is indeed concerned with risk perception issues, and appears eager to secure public confidence and support by showing that hydrogen will pose no greater risks than the fuels we use today.

The relevant question here is not whether this is true or not. Historical developments of other fuels and technologies have in fact shown that risks can be, and are, managed in a way that ensures the 'safe' operation of a certain technology, which means that the technology is routinely, and confidently, used by the lay public. What is important to ask here is on what precise grounds the assumption that hydrogen will be as safe as (or safer than) conventional fuels is based. Asking such a question means raising the following issues: what kind of evidence is there to help us understand and assess hydrogen risks? Is there any expert disagreement? Are there any knowledge gaps or uncertainties? In this section of the chapter we will attempt to address these questions.

To start, two key conceptual issues should be properly spelled out. The first one stems from the consideration that most accounts about hydrogen safety focus narrowly on hydrogen applications, chiefly vehicles where hydrogen could replace petrol and other commonly available fuels such as diesel and liquefied petroleum gas (LPG). What seems to be neglected is the complex system of technologies, processes and infrastructures associated with each step of the hydrogen supply chain. In other words, hydrogen cannot be equated to a 'technology' as such, but rather it should be conceptualized as the core of a 'technological system', defined as the set of associated technologies and infrastructures from the production stage through storage and distribution to end use. Each component of the hydrogen supply chain will involve different types of risk, according to the specific context in which exposure to a certain type of hazard might occur.

Secondly, safety issues are remarkably sparse in commentaries about hydrogen risks. Risks to public health – for instance, those associated with specific processes or substances used to manufacture hydrogen technologies – and to the environment have been touched upon very marginally, but deserve proper attention.

Hydrogen's hazards and safety risks: assessing the state of knowledge[1]

At ambient temperature, hydrogen is a gas and is widely used as a chemical feedstock across many industrial applications, including glass and steel manufacture, food processing, petroleum upgrading and ammonia production. It is also used as a coolant in large turbine generators. At –253°C hydrogen becomes liquid, and as such is used in the cryogenics industry and in research laboratories for the study of superconductivity. Its chemical and physical properties are well-known – the science of hydrogen is not new: hydrogen is colourless, odourless and tasteless. It is classified as non-toxic and non-carcinogenic, but can be asphyxiant if released in large amounts, as it can displace oxygen (NASA, 1997).

Like any other fuel, hydrogen can catch fire. If this occurs in a controlled reaction inside an internal combustion engine (ICE), power can be generated with very few noxious emissions – the German car company BMW is leading the way by demonstrating hydrogen-powered ICE vehicles (Madslien, 2006). Independent expert sources (see, for instance, Cadwallader and Herring, 1999; Lanz et al, 2001; Beeson and Woods, 2003) agree that accidental hydrogen leaks in confined spaces (such as the boot of a vehicle, a garage etc.) are potentially serious hazards, because hydrogen becomes combustible when mixed with air. In the presence of ignition sources, such as electric sparks, flames or high heat, hydrogen leaks can cause fire, which in turn may generate an explosion in specific circumstances, if no detection systems or venting are in place. Hydrogen flames, moreover, are almost invisible in daylight and emit less heat than other fuels, so that human senses alone are less able to detect them.

Hydrogen leaks, therefore, are generally considered very serious hazards. Having the smallest molecule of all substances, hydrogen has the greatest propensity to leak past seals and through tiny cracks. Because of this, hydrogen can also penetrate into the molecular structure of certain materials such as steel and plastic, and cause a severe loss of strength. This phenomenon, known as 'hydrogen embrittlement', can have adverse effects, such as leading to catastrophic ruptures of hydrogen containment systems. Liquid hydrogen entails different types of hazards to safety. Given the very low temperature at which it must be kept, an undesired spill of liquid hydrogen can lead to severe frostbite if it comes in contact with human skin.

However, hydrogen hazards are substantially different from those of conventional fuels. This also means that the circumstances under which hydrogen can become a 'risk' to safety (here we refer to the 'technological risk', which is defined as the product of the probability of an event and the magnitude, or severity, of such an event) are fundamentally different from those to which we are accustomed through the widespread use of petrol and other consumer fuels.

A general, straightforward comparative evaluation of hydrogen risks cannot be developed (Alcock et al, 2001). Risk assessment is highly dependent upon the precise context in which a certain hazard occurs. Claiming that hydrogen is safer or less safe than other fuels, without proper justification of the whole range of parameters used and the precise assumptions and circumstances of the study – as it is very common to find in hydrogen safety commentaries (see, for instance, Barbir, no date; Directed Technologies Inc. and Ford Motor Company, 1997; Doyle, 1998; Lanz et al, 2001; Shinnar, 2003) – is meaningless and also misleading (Ricci et al, 2006).

For instance, is an accidental hydrogen leak potentially more dangerous than that of conventional fuels? Knowledge of the chemical and physical properties of hydrogen alone cannot give much guidance on how to address such a question. Alcock et al (2001) reported that if hydrogen is stored at high pressure, it would leak 2.8 times faster than natural gas and 5.1 times faster than propane, on a volumetric basis. However, as hydrogen has a lower energy density, the energy leakage rate would be 0.88 times smaller than methane and 0.61 than propane. Without explicitly accounting for all the various characteristics of the 'risk scenario' – what technology is being used, by whom, how many people are present, what the surrounding environment is like etc. – any tentative inference from those numbers is pure conjecture.

Being significantly lighter than air, hydrogen gas is more diffusive and buoyant than conventional hydrocarbon fuels, so it disperses more rapidly when released, especially in open spaces. This argument is often used to claim that an accidental release of hydrogen in an open space would be less dangerous than other fuels. However, if cryogenic liquid hydrogen is released, the cold vapour cloud may initially be denser than the surrounding air. Buoyancy effects may be neglected at low concentration and high momentum releases, in which the orientation of the release can predict the direction of the cloud formation (Cadwallader and Herring, 1999).

In contrast, spilled petrol 'pools' in the vicinity of the leak, resulting in a protracted fire and explosion hazard. Propane gas is denser than air and it slowly accumulates in low spots, whereas methane disperses rapidly, though not as quickly as hydrogen (Lanz et al, 2001).

The much wider flammability range (4–75 per cent hydrogen concentration in air) and the lower minimum ignition energy of hydrogen raise safety concerns when compared with other fuels. The lower flammable limit (LFL), however, is similar to that of methane and higher than those of petrol and propane. There is general agreement that in many accidental situations the key parameter is the LFL, as ignition sources will ignite a fuel-air mixture as soon as a flammable concentration is reached. Moreover, the 4 per cent limit is valid for upward propagating flames, while for downward propagating flames the LFL is 9–10 per cent (Alcock et al, 2001).

The ignition energy is dependent on the fuel-air concentration (when plotted, it produces a U-shaped graph) and reaches a minimum at around the stoichiometric concentration (for hydrogen this is 29.5 per cent).[2] At the LFL, the ignition energy for hydrogen and methane is almost the same. Moreover, weak ignition sources, such as electrical equipment sparks, electrostatic sparks or sparks from striking objects, involve more energy than is required to ignite all the fuels. For instance, a weak electrostatic spark from the human body releases about 10mJ of energy, which is capable of setting fire to the majority of commonly used fuels.

Overall, therefore, the risks associated with hydrogen are highly specific to particular circumstances, and cannot be generalized in any simple or summary way.

Beneath the 'unspoken consensus'

Public communication about hydrogen and its associated technologies is sporadic if compared to other, often more controversial innovations. Hydrogen rarely makes the headlines, but whenever it receives coverage in the media, the message tends to be positive and to highlight the potential environmental benefits of a future hydrogen-based economy, especially in relation to its deployment in the transport system. Iconic images of quiet and clean vehicles consolidate the idea of a broad expert consensus around the development of hydrogen as a future fuel. Motor vehicle manufacturers in particular are keen to show the general public their achievements in turning hydrogen into a safe fuel, and often take advantage of many celebrities' willingness to be seen to be 'green'. For instance, Hollywood star Brad Pitt arrived in a BMW Hydrogen 7 prototype car at a movie premiere in 2007 (Temko, 2007), and actress Jamie Lee Curtis has recently leased a fuel-cell powered FCX Clarity from Honda (Ryan, 2008).

At least in relation to the type of information available to the general public, there seems to be an 'unspoken consensus' around hydrogen (Cherry, 2004). Extensive literature reviews (McDowall and Eames, 2006; Ricci, 2006) and a recent innovative stakeholder engagement exercise involving multi-criteria evaluation of hydrogen futures (McDowall and Eames, 2007), however, have shown that beneath this seeming consensus there is significant expert disagreement and ongoing debates on whether, and in what conditions, hydrogen will deliver its much-hyped promises of a better and more sustainable energy future. Equally, scientists and engineers are still struggling to overcome huge technical problems, not least the development of a better understanding of hydrogen's behaviour as a fuel.

The use of hydrogen as a consumer fuel is largely untested. This means that the range of situations in which hydrogen, or its associated technologies, might become harmful are poorly known and characterized. Despite the increasing number of demonstration projects involving different types of hydrogen technologies and vehicles, there still is a lack of basic knowledge and information, concerning, for instance, the failure rates for the components of the hydrogen infrastructure and for hydrogen tankers involved in transport accidents (Moonis et al, 2008). In contrast, hydrocarbon fuels are well known in this respect. Their long history of use has taught us how and in what circumstances they might become dangerous, so that prevention, detection and mitigation procedures could be developed.

A study by the US National Academy of Sciences (2004: p5) openly recognized that 'experts differ markedly in their views of the safety of hydrogen in a consumer-centred transportation system', although accumulated experience suggests 'that hydrogen can be manufactured and used in professionally managed systems with acceptable safety'. In particular, the study claimed that a 'salient and under-explored issue is that of leakage in enclosed structures, such as garages in homes and commercial establishments'.

Uncertainties and knowledge gaps become particularly evident when disastrous events involving hydrogen are considered, such as explosions with high-pressure gas. There are different types of explosions involving hydrogen gas (Cadwallader and Herring, 1999). A deflagration is a combustion event where the combustion wave front moves through the unreacted medium at subsonic speeds. The entire flammable range of hydrogen (4–75 per cent) can support a deflagration. Normally, a deflagration is characterized by modest timescale and energy release. The theoretical maximum 'overpressure' can be eight times greater than initial pressure, but lower values are generally observed. In particular conditions – depending on hydrogen concentration, the degree of space confinement, the presence of obstacles or conditions that promote turbulence in the gas, the strength of the ignition source and particular weather conditions, such as humidity, wind etc. – a deflagration may result in a detonation, a much more devastating event in which the combustion wave front moves at supersonic speeds and a 20-fold pressure increase can be reached.

Limited experience of these types of severe accidents has been accumulated so far, and mainly within industrial settings. Consequently, hydrogen's explosion behaviour following high-pressure releases, and the related likelihood of occurrence, is currently poorly understood. It must also be noted that some prospective power applications require hydrogen gas to be stored at much higher pressures than are conventionally required in current industrial applications. For example, Ross (2006) reports of advanced gas cylinders capable of storing hydrogen at 700 bar, when the current pressure for hydrogen gas cylinders is normally about 200 bar. Knowledge, skills and regulations in such an unfamiliar context are yet to be developed. According to EU-funded studies seeking to improve the knowledge base on hydrogen as a fuel (Dorofeev, 2003: p2): 'no solutions are available in terms of widely accepted standards, methodologies, mitigation techniques, and regulations'. Accumulated experience with hydrogen is presently limited to a number of industrial applications whose scale and proximity to the general public are small.

Similar claims were made in the first edition of the *Multi-Year Research, Development and Demonstration Plan* of the US Department of Energy's Hydrogen, Fuel Cells and Infrastructure Technologies Program (DoE, 2003). The programme set the ambitious goal of advancing research and development of hydrogen and associated technologies to facilitate their commercialization. Its founding document explicitly recognized the gap between the established set of safety practices associated with industrial uses of hydrogen, and the many 'unknowns' associated with the new uses of hydrogen as a fuel and energy vector.

The DoE document identified a number of challenges that needed to be addressed to develop a comprehensive safety plan for hydrogen as a fuel:

- a limited historical database for hydrogen components;
- lack of access to industry proprietary data;
- need for validation of old historical data related to safety parameters for the production, storage, transport and utilization of hydrogen;
- incomplete understanding of the fundamental limits of hydrogen systems;
- limited knowledge on past hydrogen safety incidents, in the absence of mandatory reporting requirements for these incidents.

The report also claimed that 'although hydrogen is listed as Class B hazard (defined as flammable and combustible material), some of the data used to classify hydrogen could not be reproduced in the DoE laboratories' (Section 3.7, p3).

Addressing the knowledge gaps

In October 2007 the DoE published an updated version of the *Multi-Year Plan*, outlining the progress made since the earlier report and the challenges that hydrogen research still faces (DoE, 2007). Among the achievements in improving the knowledge base, the DoE has developed a set of comprehensive information resources, which aim to collect the available safety technical data and promote the exchange and sharing of knowledge and experience of hydrogen energy systems. Examples include the Hydrogen Safety Best Practices Manual (http://h2bestpractices.org), a web-based resource collecting the wealth of practical knowledge on the safe handling and use of hydrogen in a variety of applications, and the Hydrogen Incident Reporting Database (http://www.h2incidents.org), a voluntary (and anonymous) reporting tool that allows learning from actual experience of hydrogen accidents in various contexts and circumstances.

In the European Union several projects have been funded through the various Framework Programmes for research, technological development and demonstration, with the aim of advancing knowledge and bridging the gap between hydrogen energy research and commercialization. For example, Hysafe (www.hysafe.org) is a Network of Excellence funded by the European Commission (EC) through the Sixth Framework Programme, bringing together 25 partners from 12 different countries, including research organizations, universities, governmental agencies and industry. The aim of the network is to consolidate and improve knowledge and actual experience of the safe use of hydrogen. Research conducted within the network has identified (and started to address) the following knowledge gaps:

- the compatibility of new compound materials used to store hydrogen under extremely high pressures (up to 800 bar) or very low temperatures;
- ignition behaviour of cold clouds;
- behaviour of liquid hydrogen following an accidental release;
- transitional phenomena, such as flame acceleration and deflagration to detonation transition in realistic scenarios;
- mitigation techniques.

The Hysafe network also developed a Hydrogen Incident and Accident Database (HIAD) covering the whole spectrum of hydrogen technologies, from production through storage and distribution to use.

A number of tests and simulations have been independently conducted to evaluate the comparative behaviour of hydrogen and hydrocarbon fuels on ignition (Swain et al, 2003; Parsons Brinckerhoff Inc, 2004), and to improve understanding of hydrogen explosive behaviour in realistic situations in vehicles, such as the engine compartment, the passenger compartment, the boot or the vicinity of the vehicle (Dorofeev et al, 2004).

In the UK, the Health and Safety Laboratory (HSL), an agency of the Health and Safety Executive (HSE), is working both at national and international level on a wide range of experimental and modelling activities addressing hydrogen safety and regulatory issues, which will be addressed later in this chapter.

One particularly crucial area that is still at the early stages of development is risk assessment of hydrogen systems. Risk assessments are frequently applied to flammable gases; however, there are few available for hydrogen. The European Integrated Hydrogen Project 2 (EIHP 2), a partnership between the European hydrogen industry supported by the EC, developed a semi-quantitative risk analysis methodology for several hydrogen applications, called Rapid Risk Ranking (RRR). The challenge of developing quantitative risk assessments for hydrogen systems lies in the highly provisional nature of most technologies associated with hydrogen, the lack of a harmonized set of standards and regulations and the fact that many necessary technical data are either non-existent or confidential (EIHP 2, 2004).

It is important to understand how hydrogen would interact with other gases and fuels. The EC-funded NaturalHy Integrated Project, for example, is attempting to develop a better knowledge-base on hydrogen–natural gas mixtures, in order to facilitate a transition to hydrogen by using the existing natural gas infrastructure. In fact, one of the possible ways in which hydrogen can be distributed is by mixing it with natural gas to use the same distribution network. Experiments showed that the addition of hydrogen to natural gas had substantial effects in overpressure generation in case of an explosion and warranted that further research was needed (Woolley et al, 2008).

In sum, there are many knowledge gaps concerning the new spectrum of infrastructure, technologies and materials that are likely to be deployed if hydrogen becomes an important player in the energy and transport systems. Some of these gaps have been acknowledged and are being addressed by several international collaborations seeking to foster the development of hydrogen as a 'safe' fuel. There are, however, additional knowledge gaps concerning other potential impacts of hydrogen's associated technologies and processes that have not attracted as much attention as issues related to safety. These will be the focus of the next section.

Beyond safety risks: exploring implications for public health and the environment

Unlike petrol, which is extremely polluting and toxic, hydrogen does not present any concern for medium- or long-term health implications (HSE, 2004). In fact, should hydrogen substitute for hydrocarbon fuels in the energy and transportation sectors – which currently are responsible for most air pollution – no noxious gases and fumes would be emitted at the point of use, thus improving local air quality and, consequently, benefiting public health.

Focusing only on end-of-pipe emissions, however, gives but one part of the whole picture. This becomes particularly evident when risks to the environment are also accounted for. As hydrogen needs to be produced by using an energy source, its potential beneficial effects to the environment at the point of use may be cancelled by harmful emissions at the production stage. For example, it has been estimated that a fuel cell car powered by hydrogen produced via electrolysis (through ordinary electricity from the grid) would increase CO_2 emissions by 17 per cent, compared to a conventional petrol-powered car (Wald, 2003). Sustainable hydrogen production and effective measures for reducing or eliminating greenhouse gas emissions, such as carbon capture and storage, should therefore be put in place. Most of the hydrogen used today is produced via steam-reforming of natural gas, which has its own carbon costs. Clearly, a future hydrogen-based economy would have to rely on more sustainable primary energy, such as renewables, to effectively tackle CO_2 emissions and climate change and improve energy security.

This again demonstrates that comprehensive assessments of health and environmental risks should take into account the whole technological system of which hydrogen will be part, as well as the entire life cycle of such a system. One important approach that seeks to identify and evaluate the environmental impacts of a certain technology or system of technologies is the so-called 'Life Cycle Assessment' (LCA), also known as 'well-to-wheel' or 'cradle-to-grave' analysis, according to the type of technology being studied. LCA is usually carried out in accordance to the ISO 14000 environmental management standards (International Organization for Standardization, 2006). However, at the time of writing, no comprehensive LCA for hydrogen has been reported. One of the reasons for that omission is that a wide array of established and new technologies will contribute to the production, storage, distribution and use of hydrogen. The complexity of such a system, combined with the uncertainty characterizing its future unfolding, does not allow easy predictions over the most appropriate sustainable pathway to producing and using hydrogen.

Any LCA, for example, must include the materials used throughout the energy chain. Storage materials, such as metal hydrides and carbon nanotubes, and various types of fuel cells components (such as electrolytes and catalysts) will be deployed across the hydrogen energy chain, in amounts which will depend upon the scale of hydrogen penetration in the economy and the relative adoption rates of different hydrogen technologies (based, for example, on different fuel cell types) (Hobbs, 2005). Increased production, diffusion and disposal of such materials, some of which may be totally newly engineered, may have risk implications for public health and the environment, and must be accounted for in any LCA.

Unlike hydrogen safety risks, long-term risks to public health and the environment have received comparably less attention. There are, however, a number of studies addressing these issues. Catalysts are essential components of fuel cells, accelerating the rate of chemical reactions involving hydrogen, and are usually made of mixtures of exotic metals, whose side-effects in the event of unintentional fires or during their disposal may raise safety, health and environmental concerns (Cherry, 2004). Other components of fuel cells, such as the electrolyte and the membrane, can also pose health concerns (Gaston et al, 2001). A common electrolyte used in alkaline fuel cells is potassium hydroxide, which is known to be harmful for all human tissue as it causes serious chemical burns. Sulphuric acid is corrosive and can oxidize certain materials. When burning it emits toxic fumes. The membrane used in proton exchange membrane (PEM) fuel cells contains fluorine, a substance that produces corrosive, toxic compounds when accidentally heated or set on fire. Lithium salts, present in molten carbonate (MC) fuel cells, do not pose toxicity dangers unless involved in a fire, when they produce toxic fumes.

A life cycle assessment (LCA) applied to PEM fuel cells (Pehnt, 2001) investigated the ecological impacts of the entire life cycle of the PEM fuel cell system, from manufacture to utilization. PEM fuel cells are becoming particularly important because of their modular structure, which allows considerable flexibility in portable, mobile and stationary energy applications. They can, in fact, be used in different power ranges by simply adding more stacks together. Car manufacturers are placing great expectations on PEM fuel cells as energy converters in future hydrogen-fuelled vehicles. The LCA concluded that the manufacturing phase had significant environmental impacts that could not be neglected. According to the results, the most significant environmental impacts of PEM fuel cells production were caused by the platinum group metals (PGM) materials used to fabricate the catalyst, followed by the materials and energy required to manufacture the graphitic flow field plates, which allow the feed of the fuel and oxidant, and conduct the electricity generated in the fuel cell. The study identified recycling and the use of clean primary energy sources as major requirements to achieve lower global warming emissions during both manufacture and utilization of PEM fuel cells.

LCA assessments allow those with an interest in hydrogen to understand how the different stages of the life cycle of a technological system contribute to the overall environmental impacts. Looking at the life cycle of a hydrogen PEM fuel cell vehicle, Hussain et al (2007) found that the impact of the fuel cycle only (in terms of primary energy consumption and greenhouse gas emissions) was worse for the fuel cell vehicle than for a conventional petrol vehicle. The study assumed that hydrogen would be produced by conventional steam-reforming of natural gas. Nevertheless, hydrogen vehicles were found to have a better overall impact on the environment.

Analysing alternative hydrogen production processes is of fundamental importance to identify and assess possible long-term risks to public health and the environment. Koroneos et al (2004) applied the LCA approach to determine and compare the environmental impacts of six different primary energy sources, which can be used to produce liquid hydrogen via electrolysis. In their study, they examine four categories of impacts having adverse consequences for health and the environment: greenhouse gas emissions; acidification emissions (those producing so-called 'acid rain'); eutrophication air emissions (responsible for the excessive enrichment with nutrients of water and soil); and winter smog effect emissions (solid particulate matter, sulphur dioxide etc.). The worst environmental performance is achieved through the use of photovoltaic energy, due to the negative impacts of the manufacturing process of photovoltaic modules and their low overall efficiency. Steam reforming of natural gas and biomass also produce high negative effects. The best choices among those investigated appear to be wind, hydropower and solar thermal energy.

The early stage of hydrogen-based technologies, such as fuel cells, means that for some of their components, especially those made of innovative, rare or toxic materials, there may be no established procedures for decommissioning and recycling. This emerged in particular in a multi-criteria life cycle assessment of molten carbonate fuel cells (Raugei et al, 2005), which concluded that there was considerable uncertainty in relation to the possible local health and environmental effects caused by the inherent toxicity of nickel and chromium compounds.

Hydrogen energy and climate change

Among the possible environmental impacts of the widespread use of hydrogen, there is one that deserves particular attention, not least because of the expert debate it sparked and the knowledge gaps it exposed. The high propensity of hydrogen to escape from where it is stored begs the question of whether small, but frequent, accidental hydrogen releases into the atmosphere would produce undesired effects on the global climate.

The Third Assessment Report of the Intergovernmental Panel on Climate Change (Houghton et al, 2001) indicated that hydrogen can negatively interfere with the atmospheric chemistry responsible for abating methane and other major greenhouse gases, although it did not consider molecular hydrogen a direct greenhouse gas. It clearly stated that 'in a possible fuel-cell economy, future (hydrogen) emissions may need to be considered as a potential climate perturbation' (p256).

To understand how this may happen, we need to consider the complex process by which hydrogen and other gases are produced and interact with one another, and with the whole 'climate system'. Molecular hydrogen is the simplest trace gas species in the atmosphere, produced by both natural and man-made sources. Hydrogen is present in the atmosphere at about 500ppb (parts per billion) as a mole fraction. According to the IPCC report, the total amount, or budget, of a trace gas is the result of a complex interplay of its global source, global sink (responsible for gas consumption) and atmospheric burden. The largest sources of hydrogen are direct emission into the atmosphere and atmospheric oxidation of methane and isoprene. The largest direct emission sources of atmospheric hydrogen are motor vehicle exhausts (due to incomplete combustion of fossil fuels) and biomass burning, followed by atmospheric chemistry processes (methane and isoprene oxidation). The hydrogen global sink comprises two major components: the soil, where microbes metabolize hydrogen to produce energy; and photochemical atmospheric reactions involving the radical OH.

According to evidence published in the Third Assessment Report, the current hydrogen budget is dominated by soil uptake, which accounts for the depletion of about two-thirds of the total hydrogen burden. This was also confirmed by further experimental discoveries (Rahn et al, 2003).

However, the extent to which a fully-fledged hydrogen economy would interfere with such a delicate balance and cause a climate perturbation is far from clear. A research group in atmospheric science at the California Institute of Technology (Tromp et al, 2003) predicted dramatic consequences of unintentional leaks of hydrogen on the stratosphere, the upper layer of the atmosphere situated between 10 and 50km above the Earth's surface. By drawing on a computer simulation of atmospheric chemistry, Tromp and colleagues argued that such leaks would potentially enhance global warming and jeopardize the ozone layer. Their predictions, however, were strongly dependent upon a number of assumptions based on guesses and uncertain scientific knowledge, as the authors explicitly admitted. These included the assumption that hydrogen-based technologies would replace all current fossil fuel-based technologies and that 10 to 20 per cent of hydrogen would be released into the atmosphere due to unintentional leaks. According to their calculations, such leaks would be four to eight times greater than current hydrogen emissions.

The paper received strong criticism. Kammen and Lipman (2003), Lehman (2003) and Lovins (2003) claimed that those assumptions were overly pessimistic and unrealistic, and suggested reasonable expected leaks of 1 to 3 per cent, for gaseous and liquid hydrogen delivery respectively. Instead of a total substitution of fossil fuels with hydrogen, they envisaged a less pervasive and more gradual diffusion of fuel cells into the economy.

Schultz et al (2003) attempted to provide quantitative estimates of the impact of a hydrogen-based economy, by assuming that 50 per cent of the current fossil fuel combustion would be replaced by hydrogen technology and hydrogen would be produced from renewable resources and nuclear energy. Their study, based on a model simulation of tropospheric air chemistry, concludes that 'a large-scale transition from fossil fuel combustion to hydrogen fuel cell technology can lead to substantially improved air quality and reduced climate forcing' (p626). Derwent (2004) estimated that if hydrogen completely replaced the current fossil fuel-based economy, a 1 per cent hydrogen leakage would give 0.6 per cent climate impact of actual fossil-fuel systems.

Despite being fundamentally divergent in their conclusions, all those papers recognized relevant gaps in the science base and areas where scientific knowledge and understanding is poor. These include estimates for the current budget of hydrogen, the mechanisms and variations of soil uptake of hydrogen, and the likely biosphere response to an increased flux of hydrogen. Last but not least, there are also great uncertainties concerning the extent to which hydrogen will displace carbon-rich fuels and what configurations a future hydrogen economy will have.

Regulations, codes and standards, and their implications in hydrogen risk assessment

When new technologies are commercialized, or when old technologies are used in substantially new settings, they need to follow a set of 'rules' which broadly ensure their safe production, delivery and operation, and make them compatible with other technologies with which they will interact and the systems in which they will be embedded. Such rules can be differentiated into regulations, codes and standards. According to the European Commission (European Commission, 2006: p11), regulations are 'legally enforceable documents emanating from governments or authorities to regulate conduct'; codes can be defined as 'any system or collection of rules or regulations'; and standards consist of 'documents established by consensus and approved by a recognized body, that provide, for common and repeated use, guidelines or characteristics for achievement of the optimum degree of order'.

Proper regulations, codes, standards and guidelines are key in enabling innovations to break through the market. This is particularly relevant when innovative technologies have to compete with incumbent technologies for which there is a well-established set of legislation and experience in practice. The actual energy and transport system is designed around and 'locked' into fossil fuels, and so are the institutional and regulatory frameworks. Hydrogen as a fuel does not fit into these frameworks, and will not do so unless they undergo fundamental changes. In addition, national and international bodies responsible for the regulation of hydrogen risks need appropriate regulations, codes and standards to be developed, which provide the basis for hazard identification and the consequent analysis, assessment and management of the associated risks.

Industrial standards and regulations covering the use of hydrogen as a chemical feedstock are well established, but they are not suitable when hydrogen is used as a fuel. In some cases, as the HSE has reported, they may even inhibit it (Moodie and Newsholme, 2003; Hawksworth, 2007). For example, the application of separation distances directly derived from industrial practice would not allow hydrogen to be used in realistic retail scenarios, and the current limitation on the quantity of bulk hydrogen that can be transported through tunnels (50kg) is likely to hamper the development of a large-scale infrastructure that will need increasing amounts of hydrogen to be distributed across the country by road and rail (Moonis et al, 2008).

Gaps in regulations, codes and standards are apparent in every step of the hydrogen supply chain. Hydrogen-fuelled road vehicles, for instance, cannot be tested in relation to emissions, fuel consumption and engine power according to the existing EC directives and regulations, which apply only to conventional fuels (European Commission, 2006). To overcome this gap in the EU regulatory framework, and to harmonize the standards and regulatory frameworks on a worldwide level, so-called *Global Technical Regulations for Hydrogen and Fuel Cell Vehicles* are being developed under the framework of the UN-ECE WP29 – World Forum for the Harmonization of Vehicle Regulations (http://www.unece.org/trans/doc/2007/wp29/ECE-TRANS-WP29-AC3–17e.pdf).

At European level, only very recently has the European Parliament voted in favour of an EC proposal, which seeks to simplify and harmonize the approval procedure of hydrogen-powered vehicles (European Commission, 2008). In the current fragmented approval system, a hydrogen vehicle obtaining national approval would not automatically be allowed in other member states. The procedure to obtain a Europe-wide approval is time-consuming and costly, which has the effect of discouraging the development of new cleaner vehicles and stifling the innovative potential of European car manufacturers. The proposed single approval, valid across all the member states, would significantly speed up the commercialization of hydrogen and fuel cell vehicles, by allowing car manufacturers to comply with a single uniform set of regulations. In relation to safety, the new approval procedure requires hydrogen fuelled vehicles to be at least as safe as those powered by conventional fuels. According to an EC study (European Commission, 2007), the proposed measure would also allow savings for the vehicle industry of up to €124m in approval costs, in the period 2017–25.

The HyApproval project (http://www.hyapproval.org), funded by the EC, attempts to overcome the lack of a simplified and harmonized set of approval procedures for hydrogen refuelling stations by building upon the experience gathered in demonstration projects around the world, including the UK. These projects include a number of EC-funded projects, such as Cleaner Urban Transport for Europe (CUTE) and the Iceland-based Ecological City Transport System (ECTOS), which involved the testing of hydrogen-powered buses, as well as demonstration projects in China, Japan and the US. One of the most important outputs of the project has been the development of a *Handbook for Hydrogen Refuelling Station Approval*, now publicly available on the project website (http://www.hyapproval.org/Publications/The_Handbook/HyApproval_Final_Handbook.pdf).

Looking at the broad spectrum of hydrogen and fuel cell technologies, the HarmonHy project (http://www.harmonhy.com) was concerned with the overall assessment of the state-of-the-art activities on regulations and standards on a worldwide level. The project, completed in 2006, identified a number of important actions to pursue, including the development of international standards on all appropriate technical matters (compliant with ISO and ICE, the International Electrical Committee) and the consequent development of globally accepted regulations referring to the standards.

In the UK, significant work is being done by the Health and Safety Executive in pre-normative research and identification of regulatory gaps and barriers. Two recent studies commissioned by the Department for Transport to the HSL (Pritchard et al, 2007; Moonis et al, 2008) identified major gaps in the UK regulatory framework, which might pose a barrier to the development of a fully-fledged hydrogen economy. Concerning in particular the dispensing of hydrogen, and possible on-site production and storage at hydrogen refuelling stations, there are crucial gaps in the available codes and standards that are required to identify the hazards and assess the risks in such specific settings. Among the areas that need addressing are the consequences of an accidental release of hydrogen, the specification of separation distances applicable to hydrogen refuelling stations, material compatibility and approval procedures (Pritchard et al, 2007).

Having summarized the principal features of hydrogen risks and recent developments in risk assessment and regulation, we now consider whether and how such risks are reflected in stakeholders' perceptions of hydrogen energy.

A stakeholder analysis of hydrogen risks, costs and benefits

As part of the UKSHEC 1 social research work, we conducted semi-structured, face-to-face interviews with a purposive sample of individuals, or small groups of individuals, working for different organizations in the private and public sector in the North East of England, South West Wales and Greater London. These areas had been identified as key localities in the UK, where hydrogen research programmes or demonstration projects were being developed (see Chapter 9 for a further description of these hydrogen places). The purpose of the interviews was to understand how hydrogen energy is represented across those geographical areas, each with a distinctive vision of how a 'local' hydrogen economy might be developed, and across different organizations and institutional bodies with distinctive interests in and connections to hydrogen and its associated technologies. The interview topic guide addressed stakeholders' perceptions of the benefits, costs and risks of hydrogen as an energy carrier; their perspectives on likely developments in hydrogen technologies; issues of public trust in science, industry and government; and views on whether and how the public should be involved in decisions about the future of energy and hydrogen in particular. More detailed description of both the methodology and key findings is provided in Ricci et al (2007a). An account of wider public perceptions of hydrogen is provided elsewhere in Chapter 11.

A total of 13 individuals from ten different organizations were interviewed. Table 10.1 presents a brief overview of the interviewees, their affiliations, and interests in and/or connection with hydrogen.

Table 10.1 *Description of interviewees for hydrogen stakeholder study*

Locality with H_2	*Role*	*Organization*	*Interest in/Connection*
Teesside	Technology Manager Supply-Chain Director Science Specialist	Industry – Petrochemicals	H_2 Producer/User H_2 Infrastructure management
	Commercial Director Contract Sales Manager	Industry – Ammonia Manufacturer	H_2 User
	Facility Manager	Industry – Gas Manufacturer	H_2 Producer
	Head of Regeneration	Local Authority	Economic regeneration
	Director	Fuel Cells Organization	FC stationary applications
	Chief Executive	Regional Regeneration Company	Renewable energy & recycling
South West Wales	Director Strategic Projects	Local Authority	Sustainable Development
	Manager	Local Energy Agency	Energy projects, EU funding
Greater London	Leader of Council	Local Authority	Sustainable Development
	Mayor	Local Authority	

Perceived advantages and disadvantages of hydrogen

Our research found that perceptions of and attitudes towards hydrogen as a possible future energy carrier and fuel varied substantially across stakeholders belonging to different types of organizations. Stakeholders working for regional and local development agencies, as well as representatives of local authorities, tended to stress the benefits that developing hydrogen applications would accrue to the specific region or locality under study, such as economic regeneration and growth, and job creation.

In Teesside, an area where the natural landscape is dominated by heavy industry installations (steel, chemicals etc.), hydrogen was represented as an opportunity to give new life to a declining industrial economy, whilst capitalizing on existing skills and infrastructures. An economic case for a local hydrogen development was also expressed by stakeholders in South Wales, where hydrogen energy was embedded in a wider vision aimed at reconfiguring an economy in transition by making the most of new technologies. In contrast, representatives of different Greater London boroughs identified environmental benefits as key drivers for the development and deployment of hydrogen technologies. They were especially interested in tackling air pollution, and talked about hydrogen as a component of a broader agenda addressing 'sustainable development', supported by the Mayor's Energy Strategy.

A very different picture emerged from interviews with industrial stakeholders (conducted in Teesside), which included both producers and users of industrial hydrogen. They looked at hydrogen from an exclusively commercial point of view – as a high-value feedstock for industrial uses – and tended to be sceptical about innovative uses of hydrogen as a fuel or energy carrier. One of them pointed out that virtually all hydrogen produced in Teesside was used in the local chemical industry, so that very little would be left for other applications, especially those of low commercial value.

Although all industrial stakeholders acknowledged the environmental benefits that hydrogen technologies could deliver in principle, they stressed that such benefits would be conditional upon the specific hydrogen production method. They also indicated that, in practice, hydrogen's prospective environmental benefits would entail huge investment costs. Moreover, as one stakeholder pointed out, hydrogen energy's added value might be realized in niche applications, such as in portable technologies, where the real environmental benefits, such as saved CO_2 emissions, would be minimal.

For these industrial stakeholders (admittedly a small sample), costs in setting up a nationwide hydrogen infrastructure, current costs of hydrogen-based technologies (such as fuel cells) and issues regarding safety and regulation were all highlighted as key challenges in developing a hydrogen-based economy in the UK.

Perspectives on hydrogen risks to safety

Most stakeholders indicated that safety would be a key factor in developing hydrogen technologies and assumed it would be the general public's primary concern. Several stakeholders believed that ordinary people would be afraid of hydrogen because of the Hindenburg zeppelin catastrophe.

However, opinions on how safety issues could be handled in a consumer market varied considerably. Some of our interviewees were lobbying for the development of a local hydrogen economy and this was clearly reflected in their narratives, which tended to highlight the benefits of hydrogen rather than its risks. In contrast, industrial stakeholders seemed to have more sceptical views, and stressed the difference between using hydrogen in a controlled environment like chemical complexes and a less controllable consumer environment. In their opinion, using hydrogen as energy carrier and fuel implies venturing out of the 'comfort zone', the rigorous regime of discipline, standards and regulation that the chemical industry has put in place.

Nevertheless, the majority of our interviewees agreed that all the risks attached to hydrogen energy would eventually be 'manageable' and believed that informing consumers about how to deal with such risks would increase their support towards hydrogen technologies.

Responsibility for action

Concerning issues of responsibility for action in relation to the development of hydrogen energy, stakeholders' agreed that it would be very unlikely that market forces alone would provide sufficient drive for a hydrogen economy to emerge. There was a general consensus on the need for clear leadership, and substantial financial support, from national and international governments.

When discussing issues around individual commitment in addressing energy and environmental problems, stakeholders expressed scepticism about whether people would make behavioural changes voluntarily, and doubts about whether people would be motivated by public good considerations – such as reducing carbon dioxide emissions for the sake of a better environment. Overall, our interviewees agreed that a particularly significant barrier would be the mismatch between people's awareness of energy and environmental problems, and their behaviour as energy consumers.

The representatives of two London boroughs thought responsibility for 'global' energy and environmental issues should be with the national government, whereas the role of local authorities would be to set the example with projects that bring 'tangible' benefits to the local community, such as lower energy prices, reduction in fuel poverty, better air quality and less congested roads.

Trust

Trust, and especially the lack of it, emerged as a crucial factor in all interviews. Stakeholders felt that there was widespread public distrust of political authorities (especially central government) and industry, and this would have negative implications for the development of public support around new energy technologies.

Representatives of local authorities and agencies, however, believed that their efforts to communicate and engage more actively with the local community would help strengthen public trust, and build consensus around hydrogen and, more generally, sustainable energy. The London stakeholders in particular pointed out that 'keeping the promises' in other fundamental policy areas, such as crime, housing and other community issues, could allow local authorities to consolidate the confidence of local communities and build public commitment and support for more ambitious programmes on energy and sustainability.

Discussion and conclusion

In this chapter we have critically reviewed and assessed the state of knowledge on hydrogen's risks to safety, public health and the environment. Through an extensive review of the available technical literature, we have shown that hydrogen, a chemical commodity that is widely used in many different sectors of industry and scientific research, is still largely unknown and untested as an energy carrier and fuel. As a consequence, hydrogen's risks associated with its prospective large-scale use in a consumer environment are not fully understood.

Perhaps not surprisingly, hydrogen supporters and lobby groups, including some of our interviewees, tend to present the public with a consensual optimistic view about an energy future based on hydrogen. Hydrogen has the potential of being a radical system innovation in the way energy is produced, distributed and used. Should it become a routine vehicle fuel, it would dramatically change the transport sector which today is tightly locked into oil-based fuels. Hydrogen has many potential benefits, but the tendency of the 'hydrogen economy movement' to focus only on these should not lead us to overlook its potential drawbacks.

In relation to hydrogen's risks to safety, hydrogen is known to be flammable and potentially explosive. The existing literature, however, suggests that the current scientific knowledge of hydrogen as a chemical feedstock is not sufficient to fully identify the various hazardous circumstances in which hydrogen would become a risk, when used as a fuel in vehicles or other types of energy applications. Risk identification, assessment and management all require a thorough knowledge of the precise circumstances in which hazards would occur and become harmful. Although risk analysis and assessment of various hydrogen applications are being developed, these are contingent upon the current state-of-the-art of hydrogen technologies, some of which are prototypes and likely to undergo fundamental changes.

Hydrogen's risks to public health and the environment are less frequently mentioned in the existing literature, and even less so in popular media. There are concerns about the toxicity of certain fuel cells' components for humans and ecosystems in general, and the lack of appropriate disposal procedures.

Life-cycle analyses of hydrogen systems are being carried out, but further research is needed.

There has been expert disagreement on whether and to what extent a hydrogen economy would negatively impact on the global climate. Despite not being a greenhouse gas itself, hydrogen has a key role in the complex atmospheric chemistry regulating the climate. Consequently, there have been concerns that frequent accidental releases of hydrogen in a fully-fledged hydrogen economy would cause a climate perturbation. Although the latest evidence seems to suggest that the overall effect would be positive – hydrogen may reduce, rather than aggravate, global warming thanks to its displacement of carbon-rich fuels – this must be put against a backdrop of lack of knowledge characterizing the extremely complex processes that govern the climate system and substantial uncertainties associated with climate models.

In our review of the technical literature, we have found that experts have rather distinctive views of the overall risks associated with hydrogen and, more broadly, of the wider advantages and disadvantages of hydrogen as an energy carrier. Likewise, our interviews with a range of hydrogen stakeholders found a wide range of opinions about its prospective risks, costs and benefits, which were highly dependent upon their professional knowledge of and experience with hydrogen and energy in general, and upon the overall 'mission' and 'vision' of the organization they were representatives of.

There are various demonstration projects and research programmes around the world seeking to advance knowledge of hydrogen as an energy carrier and fuel, some with the principal objective of improving the current understanding of the risks that might be associated with its use. Such projects and programmes are important for two sets of issues. On the one hand, they gradually test the technological building blocks of a future hydrogen economy – the 'hardware' – by developing new technologies and infrastructure, and testing whether they work in a real world situation. On the other hand, they contribute to build the 'software' of the hydrogen economy – practical knowledge, experience, skills and the suitable regulatory frameworks.

A particularly appropriate conceptualization of a hydrogen economy can be developed by using the insights provided by the 'socio-technical systems' framework (Bijker et al, 1987; Geels, 2004) being aware that there is no single 'hydrogen economy', but rather many different types of energy scenarios where hydrogen might play a role. An economy based on hydrogen would involve tangible and intangible components. To the first group belongs the complex set of technologies and infrastructure needed for the production, distribution and use of hydrogen, some of which are already available, while others are still at a very early stage of development. To the second group belong the human aspects of the technological system, which involve the knowledge of the practical contexts of production and use of hydrogen technologies, the symbolic meanings attached to them, and the institutional and regulatory frameworks in which they will be embedded.

Hydrogen is still very much an embryonic 'socio-technical system' and it is fundamentally uncertain whether and how it will develop. Certainly, until both the social and technical components have been further developed, the overall balance of its associated risks, costs and benefits will remain unclear and the subject of debate, while continuing uncertainties about the risks may lead to opposition to its more widespread deployment.

Notes

1 This section summarizes an extensive review of the technical scientific literature on hydrogen hazards and risks, whose findings are reported in greater details in Ricci (2005). See also Ricci et al (2006) and Ricci et al (2007b) for a critical discussion.
2 The stoichiometric concentration is the proportion of oxygen and the combustible gas that allows for the most complete combustion event in which no residual reactants remain.

References

Alcock, J. L., Shirvill, L. C. and Cracknell, R. F. (2001) 'Compilation of existing safety data on hydrogen and comparative fuels', European Integrated Hydrogen Project II, Work Package 5, ENK6-CT2000–00442

Barbir, F. (no date) 'Safety issues of hydrogen in vehicles'. Available at http://www.senternovem.nl/mmfiles/34660_tcm24–124264.pdf

Beeson, H. and Woods, S. (2003) *Guide for Hydrogen Hazards Analysis on Components and Systems*, NASA

Bijker, W. E., Hughes, P. T. and Pinch, T. (eds) (1987) *The Social Construction of Technological Systems*, Cambridge, MA, MIT Press

Cadwallader, L. C. and Herring, J. S. (1999) 'Safety issues with hydrogen as a vehicle fuel', INEEL/EXT-99–00522, Idaho Engineering and Environmental Laboratory, US Department of Energy

Cherry, R. S. (2004) 'A hydrogen utopia?', *International Journal of Hydrogen Energy*, vol 29, pp125–129

Derwent, D. (2004) 'Environmental impact of H_2', H2NET Summer Meeting, 14 July, CCLRC Rutherford Appleton Laboratory, UK

Directed Technologies Inc. and Ford Motor Company (1997) 'Direct-hydrogen-fuelled proton-exchange-membrane fuel cell system for transportation applications', Hydrogen safety report, Department of Energy, Office of Transportation Technologies

DoE (2003) *Hydrogen, Fuel Cells & Infrastructure Technologies Program – Multi-Year Research, Development and Demonstration Plan*, First Draft, US Department of Energy, Office of Energy Efficiency and Renewable Energy

DoE (2007) *Hydrogen, Fuel Cells & Infrastructure Technologies Program – Multi-Year Research, Development and Demonstration Plan*, US Department of Energy, Office of Energy Efficiency and Renewable Energy

Dorofeev, S. (2003) 'Safety aspects of hydrogen as an energy carrier', First European Hydrogen Energy Conference, 2–5 May, Grenoble, France

Dorofeev, S., Veser, A., Bielert, U., Breitung, W. and Kotchourko, A. (2004) 'Report on partially vented explosion tube (PET)', European Integrated Hydrogen Project – Phase II, WP 5, ENK6-CT2000–00442

Doyle, T. A. (1998) 'Technology Status of Hydrogen Road Vehicles', IEA Agreement on the Production and Utilisation of Hydrogen, IEA/H2/TRI-98

Dunn, S. (2002) 'Hydrogen futures: towards a sustainable energy system', *International Journal of Hydrogen Energy*, vol 27, issue 3, pp235–264

EIHP 2 (2004) 'Final Technical Report', European Integrated Hydrogen Project Phase 2, 30 April, Brussels, Belgium

European Commission (2006) 'Introducing Hydrogen as an energy carrier. Safety, regulatory and public acceptance issues', Directorate-General for Research – Sustainable Energy Systems, Brussels, Belgium

European Commission (2007) 'Annex to the Proposal for a Regulation of the European Parliament and of the Council', Commission Staff Working Document, SEC(2007) 1301, Brussels, Belgium

European Commission (2008) 'More hydrogen cars on EU roads', Press Release, 3 September, Brussels, Belgium, European Commission

Gaston, D., Chelhaoui, S. and Joly, C. (2001) 'Safety problems related to fuel cells', World Congress Safety of Modern Technical Systems, 12–14 September, Saarbruecken, Germany

Geels, F. W. (2004) 'From sectoral systems of innovation to socio-technical systems. Insights about dynamics and change from sociology and institutional theory', *Research Policy*, vol 33, pp897–920

Hawksworth, S. (2007) 'Hydrogen Safety Standards and the HyPER Project, HyPER Review Days', 10–11 October, Brussels, Belgium

Hobbs, J. (2005) 'The Hydrogen Economy – Evaluation of the materials science and engineering issues', Buxton, Health and Safety Laboratory

Horlick-Jones, T., Walls, J., Rowe, G., Pidgeon, N., Poortinga, W., Murdock, G. and O'Riordan, T. (2007) *The GM Debate: Risks, Politics and Public Engagement*, London, Routledge

Houghton, J. T., Ding, Y., Griggs, D. J., Noguer, M., van der Linden, P. J. and Xiaosu, D. (2001) 'Climate Change 2001: The Scientific Basis', Contribution of Working Group I to the Third Assessment Report of the Intergovernmental Panel on Climate Change, Cambridge University Press

HSE (2004) *Fuel cells. Understand the hazards, control the risks*, Health and Safety Executive Books

Hussain, M. M., Dincer, I. and Li, X. (2007) 'A preliminary life cycle assessment of PEM fuel cell powered automobiles', *Applied Thermal Engineering*, vol 27, pp2294–2299

International Organization for Standardization (2006) *ISO 14040. Environmental management – Life cycle assessment – Principles and framework*, Geneva, ISO

Kammen, D. M. and Lipman, T. E. (2003) 'Assessing the future hydrogen economy', Letter to the Editor, *Science*, 10 October, issue 302, p226

Koroneos, C., Dompros, A., Roumbas, G. and Moussiopulos, N. (2004) 'Life cycle assessment of hydrogen fuel production processes', *International Journal of Hydrogen Energy*, vol 29, pp1443–1450

Lanz, A., Heffel, J. and Messer, C. (2001) 'Hydrogen Fuel Cell Engines and Related Technologies', Palm Desert, CA, College of the Desert

Lehman, P. A. (2003) 'Assessing the future hydrogen economy', Letter to the Editor, *Science*, 10 October, issue 302, p227

Lovins, A. (2003) 'Assessing the future hydrogen economy', Letter to the Editor, *Science*, 10 October, issue 302, pp226–227

Madslien, J. (2006) 'BMW's hydrogen car: Beauty or beast', *BBC News*, 17 November. Available at http://news.bbc.co.uk/2/hi/business/6154212.stm

McDowall, W. and Eames, M. (2006) 'Forecasts, scenarios, visions, backcasts and roadmaps to the Hydrogen Economy: a review of the Hydrogen futures literature', *Energy Policy*, vol 34, issue 11, pp1236–1250

McDowall, W. and Eames, M. (2007) 'Towards a sustainable hydrogen economy; A multi-criteria sustainability appraisal of competing hydrogen futures', *International Journal of Hydrogen Energy*, vol 32, issue 18, pp4611–4626

Moodie, K. and Newsholme, G. (2003) 'The safe use of hydrogen as a fuel for transport', Health and Safety Executive

Moonis, M., Wilday, J., Wardman, M. and Balmforth, H. (2008) 'Assessing the safety of delivery and storage of hydrogen', Buxton, Health and Safety Laboratory

NASA (1997) 'Safety Standard for Hydrogen and Hydrogen Systems', Office of Safety and Mission Assurance, US

National Academy of Sciences (2004) 'The Hydrogen Economy: Opportunities, Costs, Barriers, and R&D Needs', Committee on Alternatives and Strategies for Future Hydrogen Production and Use, National Research Council, US

Parsons Brinckerhoff Inc. (2004) 'Support Facilities for Hydrogen-Fueled Vehicles', Technical Report, California Fuel Cell Partnership, US

Pehnt, M. (2001) 'Life-cycle assessment of fuel cell stacks', *International Journal of Hydrogen Energy*, vol 3026, pp91–101

Prather, M. J. (2003) 'An Environmental Experiment with H_2', *Science*, 24 October, issue 302, pp581–582

Pritchard, D. K., Fletcher, J. E. and Hobbs, J. W. (2007) 'A review of the regulatory framework around hydrogen refuelling', Buxton, Health and Safety Laboratory

Rahn, T., Eiler, J. M., Boering, K. A., Wennberg, P. O., McCarthy, M. C., Tyler, S. and Schauffler, S. (2003) 'Extreme deuterium enrichment in stratospheric hydrogen and the global atmospheric budget of H_2', *Nature*, 21 August, vol 424, issue 6951, pp918–921

Raugei, M., Bargigli, S. and Ulgiati, S. (2005) 'A multi-criteria life cycle assessment of molten carbonate fuel cells (MCFC) – a comparison to natural gas turbines', *International Journal of Hydrogen*, vol 30, pp123–130

Ricci, M. (2005) *Experts' assessments and representations of risks associated with hydrogen*, UKSHEC Social Science Working Paper 12, ISCPR, University of Salford. Available at http://www.psi.org.uk/ukshec/publications.htm#workingpapers

Ricci, M. (2006) 'Exploring public attitudes towards hydrogen energy: Conceptual and methodological challenges', UKSHEC Social Science Working Paper 13, ISCPR, University of Salford. Available at http://www.psi.org.uk/ukshec/publications.htm#workingpapers

Ricci, M., Newsholme, G., Bellaby, P. and Flynn, R. (2006) 'Hydrogen: too dangerous to base our future upon?', *Proceedings of Hazards XIX – Process Safety and Environmental Protection*, ICHEME NW Branch Symposium, 27–30 March, University of Manchester

Ricci, M., Bellaby, P. and Flynn, R. (2007a) 'Stakeholders' and Publics' Perceptions of Hydrogen Energy Technologies', in Flynn, R. and Bellaby, P. (eds) *Risk and the Public Acceptance of New Technologies*, Basingstoke, Palgrave Macmillan

Ricci, M., Newsholme, G., Bellaby, P. and Flynn, R. (2007b) 'The transition to hydrogen-based energy: combining technology & risk assessment and lay perspectives', *International Journal of Energy Sector Management*, vol 1, issue 1, pp34–50

Rifkin, J. (2002) *The Hydrogen Economy*, New York, Tarcher/Putnam

Ross, D. K. (2006) 'Hydrogen storage: The major technological barrier to the development of hydrogen fuel cell cars', *Vacuum*, vol 80, pp1084–1089

The Royal Society and the Royal Academy of Engineering (2004) 'Nanoscience and Nanotechnologies: Opportunities and Uncertainties', RS Policy Document 19/04, July, London

Ryan, C. (2008) 'Jamie Lee Curtis has a new Honda: Another fuel-cell star is born', *Los Angeles Times*, Los Angeles, 8 August. Available at http://latimesblogs.latimes.com/uptospeed/2008/08/fuel-cells-get.html

Schultz, M. G., Diehl, T., Brasseur, G. P. and Zittel, W. (2003) 'Air Pollution and Climate-Forcing Impacts of a Global Hydrogen Economy', *Science*, 24 October, issue 302, pp624–627

Shinnar, R. (2003) 'The hydrogen economy, fuel cells and electric cars', *Technology in Society*, vol 24, issue 4, pp455–476

Stilgoe, J. (2007) *Nanodialogues. Experiments in public engagement with science*, London, Demos

Swain, M. R., Filoso, P., Grilliot, E. S. and Swain, M. N. (2003) 'Hydrogen leakage into simple geometric enclosures', *International Journal of Hydrogen Energy*, vol 28, pp229–248

Temko, N. (2007) 'Stars back the clean green road machine', *The Observer*, London, 16 September. Available at http://www.guardian.co.uk/world/2007/sep/16/usa.ethicalliving

Tromp, T. K., Shia, R.-L., Allen, M., Eiler, J. M. and Yung, Y. L. (2003) 'Potential environmental impact of a hydrogen economy on the stratosphere', *Science*, 13 June, issue 300, pp1740–1742

Wald, M. L. (2003) 'Will Hydrogen Clean the Air? Maybe Not, Say Some', *The New York Times*, 12 November

Woolley, R. M., Fairweather, M., Falle, S. A. E. G. and Giddings J. R. (2008) 'Predictions of the consequences of natural gas-hydrogen explosions using a novel CFD approach', *Proceedings of ESCAPE 18*, 18th European Symposium on Computer Aided Process Engineering, 1–4 June, Lyon, France

11
Public Attitudes to Hydrogen Energy: Evidence from Six Case Studies in the UK

Miriam Ricci, Paul Bellaby, Rob Flynn, Simon Dresner and Julia Tomei

Introduction

The transition to a hydrogen economy will require a major transformation in technological systems, energy infrastructures, regulatory frameworks, and the overall development of appropriate energy and environmental policy. It also presumes the widespread acceptance and use of hydrogen technologies by members of the public. As discussed in the previous chapter, hydrogen is currently an industrial commodity, not a consumer fuel like petrol, or an ordinary energy vector like electricity. Expert knowledge of its characteristics as an energy carrier is still developing and many people are largely unaware of the distinctive properties of hydrogen and its prospective power applications. An increasing number of hydrogen demonstration projects around the world will certainly help bring hydrogen closer to the public, but so far there have been few signs of genuine, more participatory forms of public 'engagement' with hydrogen technologies and the potentially radical impact these may have on both the global energy order and people's daily lives.

The focus of this chapter is how to engage a cross-section of the public in an informed debate and deliberation about what achieving a transition to a 'hydrogen economy' might involve from their point of view. To do so, this chapter presents evidence from the two most recent studies conducted by the authors. These studies involved two complementary sets of case studies, each designed to engage the public in debate about the benefits, costs and risks of using hydrogen energy. One was part of the social research work of UKSHEC and focused on three areas of England and Wales – Teesside, South Wales and Greater London – in which there was embryonic development of hydrogen economies. The other was part of a subsequent project (Public Engagement with Future Hydrogen Infrastructure – PEwfH2, funded by the Department for Transport under the Horizons Research Programme) and covered three areas in England – Norwich, Sheffield and Southampton – that had no such developments.

It is important to engage the public because a shift to hydrogen energy is, as of now, a complex transition involving decisions at multiple levels of governance, not a simple economic decision for each individual consumer. Moreover, the changes in infrastructure required to supplant an economy based on fossil fuels with one in which hydrogen might be an energy vector are far-reaching. It could have major consequences, not only for producers and consumers, but also for those who seem merely on-lookers. If development is to proceed, consulting public opinion 'upstream' of its introduction may be prudent as well as democratic (Wilsdon and Willis, 2004). Finally, since public knowledge of hydrogen energy is very limited and the prospect of a hydrogen economy is quite distant and uncertain, one has to inform people about it in order to spur deliberation. In such circumstances, it is all too easy to shape opinion, rather than leave it open to people to offer their own views.

This chapter is organized as follows. First, it reviews the existing literature on public perceptions of and attitudes towards hydrogen, by critically discussing the available studies' methodology and findings. Then it presents the social research work carried out within UKSHEC and PEwfH2, which broadly consisted of a series of focus groups and a large questionnaire survey. A critical discussion of the results concludes the chapter and identifies further directions for research and policy implications.

Public perception of hydrogen: a review of existing studies

The development of hydrogen as an energy carrier is increasingly attracting the attention of natural and social scientists alike in relation to issues around 'public perception' and 'public acceptance'. Although studies addressing these issues are notably less numerous than studies addressing public perceptions of more controversial technologies (such as nuclear power and genetically modified food, for example), there is a growing recognition, especially among hydrogen promoters, of the need to discover the views that ordinary people have about this unfamiliar substance. A detailed critical review of hydrogen perception studies is provided by Ricci et al (2008), which this section briefly summarizes.

Arguably, most studies of public perceptions of hydrogen have been carried out in conjunction with demonstration projects (Altmann and Graesel, 1998; Maak et al, 2004; O'Garra, 2005; O'Garra et al, 2005; Haraldsson et al, 2006; Hickson et al, 2007; O'Garra et al, 2007; Sherry-Brennan et al, 2007) to gauge how people respond to seeing hydrogen 'in action', or in light of planned investments in hydrogen energy technologies (Cherryman et al, 2005; Schmoyer et al, 2006; Zachariah-Wolff and Hemmes, 2006), to help anticipate public sensitivities and concerns. With varying degrees of sophistication and depth in the study design, this has resulted in trying to understand whether 'the public' has positive or negative beliefs about hydrogen, which risks people perceive to be associated with hydrogen technologies (especially vehicles), whether people would accept a large-scale transition to hydrogen energy (such as the introduction of hydrogen transport) and whether they would be prepared to financially support such a transition, on the basis that it would bring collective goods like environmental benefits and air-quality improvements.

The majority of these studies were based on questionnaire surveys. Although straightforward comparisons of results are not possible due to significant differences in the questionnaire design, sampling technique and sample size and characteristics, there are some general findings that can be identified:

- Public awareness and knowledge of hydrogen, its associated technologies and demonstration programmes is generally low. In some cases, knowledge of hydrogen was found to be positively correlated with education levels and gender, with men more likely to know about hydrogen technologies than women (O'Garra, 2005; Zachariah-Wolff and Hemmes, 2006), and with interest in new technologies and positive environmental attitudes (O'Garra et al, 2005).
- While support for the development of hydrogen as a fuel appears to be high in principle, support for specific applications or infrastructures – for example, hydrogen refuelling stations – seems to be less enthusiastic and to be contingent upon the provision of more information.
- Concerns about risks to safety appear to be minimal. However, two studies (Haraldsson et al, 2006; Schmoyer et al, 2006) found that safety was ranked among the most important factors in people's choice of transport and energy options, while Zachariah-Wolff and Hemmes (2006) reported that perceptions of lower safety levels resulted in lower acceptance level.
- So-called willingness to pay (WTP) for the introduction of hydrogen as a fuel varies substantially across the surveyed population samples. Levels of WTP were quite low among the German students surveyed by Altmann and Graesel (1998) and the passengers on board the hydrogen bus in Stockholm (Haraldsson et al, 2006), moderate among Icelanders (Maak et al, 2004) and comparably higher in the cities participating in the AcceptH2 project (O'Garra, 2005).

From all these different studies important lessons can be learnt. First, there are significant limitations in what questionnaire-based studies can achieve when used to elicit opinion about complex issues that are rather remote from people's experience. Polls are widely used to test opinion and they undoubtedly have the merit of addressing large populations. However, the underlying assumption of polls is that those polled know enough about the topic to have an opinion. Evidence from the available studies on public perception of hydrogen, and from the research presented in this chapter, suggests that this is not the case. A poll of the lay public that covered the various whole systems in which hydrogen might be an energy vector in the future would be unlikely to get a valid response.

Second, it is important to acknowledge that different sections of the public understand and make sense of the 'unknowns' of hydrogen in different ways, and these cannot be fully conceptualized uniquely in terms of 'safety risk perception'. Safety does indeed appear to be important, but other criteria will also play a role in shaping opinions, attitudes and behaviours towards future hydrogen systems. The existing polls fail to provide an understanding of such broader issues.

Third, most studies tend to focus on perceptions of specific hydrogen applications, in particular cars and buses, thus neglecting the complex system of technologies and infrastructures that would be associated with a hydrogen economy, whatever this may be. Hydrogen needs to be produced, stored and distributed to the points and applications where it is used, and it is important to understand what people think about these complex (and rather uncertain) developments.

Finally, despite its attractive beneficial impacts – hydrogen's only by-product from fuel cells is water – not all hydrogen systems are sustainable. Most of the reviewed studies, however, fail to acknowledge this fact. Sustainability is itself a disputed concept, as it builds upon value judgements about the trade-off between current levels of preservation and consumption for the benefit of future generations. Like experts, who disagree in evaluating hydrogen futures (McDowall and Eames, 2007), lay members of the public are likely to have distinctive views on the overall 'sustainability' of hydrogen systems.

The case studies: research questions

Both research projects (UKSHEC and PEwfH2) had a two-fold purpose. They sought to discover the views that ordinary members of the public have about hydrogen as a fuel and energy carrier, and to allow some form of debate and deliberation about different hydrogen future scenarios. In particular, the studies carried out within UKSHEC addressed the following research questions:

- Are people aware of hydrogen energy in general and of hydrogen developments in their local area? What do they think about it?
- Are people aware of broader energy and environmental issues, which also have a bearing on the increasing interest in hydrogen? What are their beliefs, attitudes and behaviours in this respect?

- What do people think of hydrogen-based systems and technologies, when given more information about them? What criteria do people use to assess hydrogen energy?
- What concerns are raised, in which contexts are they discussed and what role do they play in shaping overall attitudes? How do people frame the risks of hydrogen and their relevance to their everyday lives?
- What are the values and beliefs that shape those concerns? How do public attitudes and concerns compare with those of interested parties, such as industrial and public sector stakeholders?
- Who should decide and act about developing hydrogen futures? Do people want to be involved in the debate and decisions about energy?

While the UKSHEC research addressed all possible energy systems in which hydrogen may be used, the PEwfH2 study focused in particular on the use of hydrogen as a fuel in transport. It sought to discover the views that members of the public have about the whole technological infrastructure – production, storage and distribution – that might be associated with hydrogen fuel, not just applications. It also attempted to understand the current attitudes and behaviours in relation to transport, especially private transport, and how these may be changed.

Method

The research methodology adopted in both research projects was partially informed by 'deliberative mapping' (DM) (www.deliberative-mapping.org). DM involves intensive discussion over a substantial period of time, informs participants as necessary step-by-step about the complexities of the issue, and provides opportunities for each group of participants to question experts. It does not assume that opinion is already formed and that participants know enough already to form an opinion.

However, DM is as intensive as the poll is extensive: that is, it can reach only a limited number of people. In the public engagement work reported in this chapter, we tried to strike a balance between the intensive and the extensive methods. Thus, we adapted DM to scale up the numbers of lay participants and also to accommodate the uncertainties of hydrogen technologies.

The social research carried out within UKSHEC was based on the use of focus groups, while PEwfH2 employed a combination of quantitative and qualitative methods. A large-scale questionnaire survey was used both to test lay opinion on hydrogen and to guide the recruitment of focus group participants. Focus groups consist of small groups of people, typically six to 12, who are gathered to discuss a specific topic in depth. Focus groups are widely used both in social and market research, as they are able to provide insights into how people form their beliefs and how these interact in a group discussion, where other points of views can be heard and new information can be provided (Morgan, 1997; Bloor et al, 2001; Rowe and Frewer, 2005).

UKSHEC involved two series of focus groups. The first, comprising nine groups, took place between June 2005 and March 2006. We conducted four groups in Teesside, two groups in South Wales and three groups in London. The second, involving seven groups (mostly reconvened focus groups from the first phase), was conducted between October and November 2006, and involved three groups in Teesside, two in South Wales and two in London. PEwfH2 involved a total of 12 focus groups, four in each case study area, between May and June 2007.

Our focus groups met for some 90 minutes at a time. The reduction in the time and resources required for DM (which usually involves a series of day-long meetings) enabled us to cover more participants in more groups and to vary the composition of these groups by social class and age (particularly in the PEwfH2 project). We concentrated on gathering qualitative responses to various hydrogen scenarios, rather than seeking to replicate the challenging and time-consuming multi-criteria appraisal that participants often undertake in DM studies.

Characterization of the case study areas

The three case study areas covered by the UKSHEC project were identified as localities involved, each in a distinctive way, in hydrogen energy developments. Teesside and South Wales are two areas characterized by a past tradition of heavy industries (chemicals, steels etc.), and now attempting to reconfigure their local economies with investment in new low-carbon technologies and processes by capitalizing on existing skills and infrastructures. Examples of this ongoing shift are the Centre for Process Innovation and the Fuel Cell Applications Facility at Wilton, Teesside, and Baglan Energy Park in South Wales. As already discussed in Chapter 9, in both areas hydrogen research programmes and demonstration projects are being formulated and implemented at different scales and towards different applications, but with the common objective of improving the local economy and quality of life, by creating better employment opportunities for an already skilled workforce. Greater London, in contrast, was chosen because it was hosting, together with other eight European cities, one of the largest hydrogen demonstration projects worldwide, Clean Urban Transport for Europe (CUTE), funded by the European Commission. This project involved the demonstration of hydrogen-fuelled buses on ordinary routes and the building of hydrogen supply and refuelling facilities.

Having a specific focus on hydrogen applications in transport, the PEwfH2 project sought to sample the population from areas with distinctive transport infrastructures and travel practices. Norwich – a city with a large rural hinterland – more than doubled its population in working hours with commuters in cars; Sheffield – a city with a predominantly local daytime population – maintained to some extent a tradition of using public transport; Southampton – a major transport hub, but overwhelmingly local in its daytime population – was a low user of public transport.

The context in which the focus groups were held often shaped how people framed their questions. We expected to find differences in levels of knowledge between participants in regional economies that had embryonic hydrogen development – Teesside, South Wales and London – and participants in those that did not do so – Norwich, Sheffield and Southampton. The areas have other differing characteristics that might have a bearing on how people respond.

A further source of difference in how participants approach the issues might cut across the areas: it lies in age, class and gender. It was only in the second of the two projects that a systematic attempt was made to vary the composition of focus groups by age group and social class, but in both projects gender was mixed. This is explained in more detail in the following section.

Recruitment of focus groups

In the UKSHEC research project, focus group members were recruited in each of the three case study areas by members of the research team, through existing local authority consultation panels, themselves a representative cross-section of the local population. In contrast, the PEwfH2 project used a baseline survey questionnaire, designed both to collect attitudinal data from samples of wider populations and to allow the recruitment of focus groups. A commercial market research company, BMRB, undertook the survey and the recruitment work for the focus groups. Telephone interviews were undertaken on a demographically representative survey of 1,003 people. The poll had to be concentrated geographically so that people could join focus groups in their vicinity. It contained mainly such questions as were necessary to differentiate groups by social class and age, and mix the membership of each by gender, transport uses and attitudes on environment and transport. Three areas, each approximating to a 'travel-to-work-area' for the majority of those who worked and also lived there, were selected. The populations had somewhat different transport needs, as explained earlier.

Composition and conduct of focus groups

Focus groups in the three areas covered by the UKSHEC project varied in size from eight to 13 participants in the first series and from three to nine in the second. The other 12 focus groups (four in each area, conducted in the three locations addressed by PEwfH2) involved eight to ten participants per group. In accordance with established good practice, each focus group in both projects was relatively homogeneous in terms of age, gender and social background. In particular, the poll provided a quota-sampling frame and gained permission from individuals that they could be approached to join a group. The four groups formed in each area differed in both social grade and age as follows: social grades A/B/C1 versus social grades C2/D/E, by ages 45 and over versus 21 to under 45. Each group included individuals of both genders. Each also had a systematic mix of people with different types of transport use and attitudes to the environment and transport, akin to that of the general population.

The groups were moderated by two members of the research team in the UKSHEC study (one also expert in the science of hydrogen to help with technical explanations), while an external facilitator, recruited by BRMB, was employed in PEwfH2. Participants were paid an incentive to attend and were given refreshments. All sessions were digitally audio-taped and subsequently transcribed for qualitative analysis.

Informing participants

We expected that most participants would not be familiar with hydrogen and its special characteristics, nor with its prospective uses as a fuel and energy carrier. We reasoned that information had to be provided gradually during the focus group meetings and in a way that did not pre-empt the topics of discussion, but rather empowered group members to engage in an open debate in which everyone felt comfortable to participate. Also, we avoided the use of expert jargon and categorizations and allowed participants to 'frame' the issues in their own terms.

In UKSHEC, the project team produced different types of stimulus material to be used in the groups. Participants in the first series of focus groups were shown, about half-way through the meetings, a Powerpoint presentation showing images of real hydrogen technologies, from production plants and high-pressure storage vessels to fuel cell cars and other mobile applications. The second focus group series, which reconvened most groups from the first series, involved a more informative presentation, with added images, diagrams and data, which aimed to provide an overall sense of what a 'hydrogen economy' might look like. In addition, we offered more detailed fact-sheets as supplementary material for those who expressed an interest in knowing more technical details about hydrogen. In advance of the meetings, participants in the reconvened groups were sent six postcards each illustrating different aspects of hydrogen – its molecular structure, how hydrogen is produced, stored and distributed, what the applications are, how a fuel cell works and what a global energy system involving hydrogen might look like. These postcards were intentionally designed to reproduce the information that is usually available to the general public in websites, popular science magazines and similar information sources. The aim was to test whether this type of information is useful to communicate the complexity of hydrogen systems, and whether members of the public could suggest any alternatives.

The PEwfH2 project built on the information material developed by the UKSHEC research team, but sought to use a different communication medium, a short documentary film, to convey information about hydrogen and stimulate debate. The project team worked with the sustainability communications firm Creative Concern to produce a high-quality, accessible digital video.

The DVD-based video was divided into chapters. There were pauses and question prompts for discussion at the end of each chapter. An ex-TV weather presenter (Fred Talbot) led viewers through the life cycle of hydrogen production, storage, distribution and use, pointing out some of the advantages and disadvantages of hydrogen, so that participants had balanced information on the topic. The options conveyed were based on a previous UKSHEC visioning exercise with expert stakeholders. The film script was written by the project team with the communications firm, and checked for scientific accuracy by a hydrogen science specialist.[1] In addition, an introductory fact sheet on hydrogen was compiled for use by the member of the project team, who attended only to answer technical questions.

The Powerpoint presentation in UKSHEC and the documentary film on DVD in PEwfH2 'informed' deliberation by the lay members of the focus groups, and also provoked questions that, as necessary, were answered by the 'second' to the moderator of each group.

Results and analysis

Transcripts from UKSHEC fieldwork were thematically analysed by different members of the research team and then validated by 'triangulation' (Barbour and Kitzinger, 1999; Bloor et al, 2001). Detailed analysis is reported in Ricci et al (2006), Dresner and Tomei (2007), Ricci et al (2007a), and Ricci et al (2007b). This chapter only focuses on a selection of key findings from both focus group series.

The PEwfH2 research team shared analysis of the data, both quantitative and qualitative, and checked each other's work. Quantitative data analysis was conducted on the poll of 1,003, using SPSS. This analysis was carried out by three of the team, seeking the patterns of opinion on wider environmental issues and on hydrogen energy in particular by gender, age, social grade and type of transport use. The three also benefited from the advice of a statistician.[2]

Detailed qualitative analysis was undertaken of the transcripts from focus groups conducted in each of the three travel-to-work areas, using a standardized thematic approach. The pattern was set for one area by an experienced analyst doubly qualified in physical and social sciences, and followed for the other two by an environmental scientist. A third analyst – a sociologist with no previous knowledge of the science, but extensive experience of analysing text qualitatively – independently analysed half the focus groups from each area. Full results are available in Bellaby and Upham (2007).

Poll results: knowledge of hydrogen prior to focus group participation

The poll of 1,003 people in Norwich, Sheffield and Southampton was dedicated wholly to the one set of issues – about transport use, perceptions of climate change and willingness to change behaviour to avert it, and included a test of elementary knowledge of hydrogen, prior to our providing any information. Eight questions were asked on this set of issues, the last focusing specifically on hydrogen. Table 11.1 compares the knowledge of hydrogen shown in the present survey with that of Zachariah-Wolff and Hemmes (2006).

The percentages of correct answers differ for some questions, but a Student's t-test suggests that overall there is no statistically significant difference at $p<0.05$. Individual items on hydrogen have been combined to form a scale of knowledge, ranging from 0 to 9, from getting none of the answers right to getting them all right. Responses are evenly distributed along the scale of values, as Table 11.2 shows.

The survey results suggest that the lay public as a whole is poorly informed about hydrogen. However, responses to the attitudinal questions reveal a generally positive stance and suggest most people would be prepared, in principle, to use hydrogen as a fuel. For example, on the assumption that hydrogen energy in cars might entail filling up twice as often as with petrol or diesel, there are more than six times the number of people who say they would be prepared to use such a car fuel than those who say they would not. Nearly half of the people questioned said they would definitely be prepared to fill up more often.

While the questionnaire results provide a general picture of the level of knowledge of and attitudes towards hydrogen as a fuel in transport, they obviously lack the depth and richness of detail that an informed reasoning can produce. Findings from the qualitative research work we have conducted, presented in the next section, complement those from the questionnaire and help identify the underlying beliefs and values that shape public perceptions of hydrogen.

Table 11.1 *Public knowledge of hydrogen characteristics: comparison of Zachariah-Wolff and Hemmes (2006) and Bellaby and Upham (2007)*

Hydrogen characteristics	*Correct answers (%) Zachariah-Wolff and Hemmes (2006), N = 612*	*Correct answers (%) Bellaby and Upham (2007), N = 1003*
Used as a fuel	75	67
Lighter than air at room temp	53	60
Liquid at room temp	56	49
Used as a fuel in cars	NA	73
Applied in airships	58	79
Applied in airplanes	45	39
Applied in buses	48	39
Car emissions as normal car	84	85
Car emissions are H_2O only	64	82

Table 11.2 *Distribution of correct answers*

Correct answers	*Percentage (%)*
0	16.0
1–2	22.3
3–5	22.2
6–7	21.6
8–9	17.9

Collated focus group findings

Though the PEwfH2 research project concentrated on applications of hydrogen energy to transport, while the social research in UKSHEC covered all uses currently envisaged, both treated hydrogen energy as a vector in a future 'whole system' of energy that involved a technological and institutional complex much greater than the hydrogen in vehicles quite familiar from the prestige advertising of some car manufacturers. Both also set hydrogen energy in the global context of energy insecurity and climate change and tested opinion on the process of public engagement itself. However, in what follows, it is what might become the everyday realities of hydrogen energy that take centre stage. These everyday realities have four facets: production of hydrogen from primary sources; storage and distribution of the hydrogen so produced; knowledge and understanding of various applications of hydrogen energy; and, more diffusely, risks associated with a future hydrogen economy, both physical and economic. The focus group results from the six case study areas are presented according to these four key themes, followed by conclusions as to how it can be made more publicly acceptable.

Attitudes towards hydrogen production processes

Most focus group participants were not aware of the very different ways in which hydrogen can be produced. After receiving information about this, they were able to ask cogent questions about the overall costs, operational performance and environmental implications of different hydrogen production processes. One man in Teesside made all these points together in one statement:

> *But which one [hydrogen production method] has the most potential? Because I think that is the one people want to know about, which is the one we should be going for because it is the cleanest, because it is reasonably cheap and less impact on the environment you know. (Man, Guisborough, Teesside)*

Some people were puzzled by and concerned about the additional step in the energy chain that is needed to produce hydrogen, and this led them to question the overall effectiveness of hydrogen in helping solve energy and environmental problems:

> *I think that by using it at present would be contributing to using more energy than less. And that to me seems a bit of a paradox. (Man, London)*

> *To me it's just another way, it's just another process in the chain that is going to cost money. It hasn't solved the problem yet. (Man, Guisborough, Teesside)*

Hydrogen production by fossil fuels, such as coal and gas, and nuclear energy (both via electrolysis and directly via thermo-chemical reactions) raised the most concerns across all six case study areas. Probably not surprisingly, widespread unease with nuclear energy was motivated by concerns in relation to safety, the (yet unsolved) issue of nuclear waste and the costs of decommissioning. Although opinions on nuclear energy were rather negative overall, there were a few participants who believed that nuclear should be considered part of the future 'energy portfolio', even as a 'last resort', due to its contribution to cutting carbon dioxide (CO_2) emissions:

> *If the alternative was that [nuclear] or the lights going out, then they'd have to put a nuclear power station in. (Man, Eston, Teesside)*

Similarly, people were not generally supportive of hydrogen production via steam reforming of natural gas (by which almost all current hydrogen supplies are produced) or via coal gasification, for two main reasons. First, fossil fuels in general were perceived as finite and shrinking resources, often located in and distributed across highly politically unstable areas of the world. Second, there was widespread awareness of the environmental impacts of using oil, gas and coal to produce electricity, which in some cases was enhanced by direct experience of local atmospheric pollution; for example, in London, Sheffield and Teesside. Additional concerns were voiced over the 'social sustainability' and health effects of coal mining in Sheffield and Norwich. The option of using geological carbon capture and storage (CCS) technology to dispose of the CO_2 emitted in the hydrogen production process, which otherwise would be pumped out in the atmosphere, raised substantial scepticism among participants, who questioned its long-term safety, health and environmental implications, as well as its cost-effectiveness in achieving carbon emissions reduction. CCS was largely unknown among most focus group participants.

Using renewable energy sources to produce hydrogen was generally favoured, but with fundamental differences according to the type of renewable energy and the context in which it would be developed. Not many people were aware of biomass and how it could be used to produce hydrogen. After the provision of more information, people were mostly neutral and cautious in their responses. The greatest concerns were raised in relation to growing 'energy crops' (such as willow) on dedicated pieces of land, which was seen as a threat to food security:

> *But have you seen what's happening to the price of food stocks round the world in the last six months since the Americans have said they want to use bio fuels? The price of many staple foods has gone up 40, 50 per cent, just because of supply and demand. If they start using that land which had previously been used*

> *to produce food and produce surplus and stock, effectively burning that surplus is going to put up the pressure on the price of food which is not exactly a moral thing to do. (Man, Sheffield, 21–44 ABC1)*

Similar comparisons with the negative effects of bio-fuels were made in Southampton, where one group pointed out the current environmental damage brought about by palm oil plantations to supply bio-fuels. In Norwich, however, one participant believed that biomass fitted well with the long-standing agricultural tradition of the region:

> *With biomass crops, particularly in Norfolk, you're going back to a historic way of managing the land. This is a willow-growing wetland area for at least two-thirds of the county so it fits with our environment, it fits with our wildlife, it fits with our heritage, and you can do it and do the wind turbines at the same time. (Woman, Norwich, 21–44 ABC1)*

Using sewage instead of crops to produce hydrogen received comparably more positive reactions, as it was perceived as an intelligent way of getting rid of waste as well, although a participant in Sheffield raised concerns over the potential odour (presumably from anaerobic digesters).

Attitudes towards wind power as a possible way of producing hydrogen were generally positive, but significant concerns with noise and aesthetics were voiced in all groups. Awareness of wind power was quite widespread across the groups in Norwich, an area where there are several onshore and offshore wind turbines. On more than one occasion, participants in all groups felt that renewable energy, such as wind and solar power, should receive more investment and government support. However, this must be put against concerns about how either a mass building of wind turbines or a major switch to renewable energy could be achieved without resorting to government intervention and the funding of the renewables through taxation. The use of taxation, in particular, raised questions over the distribution of costs and benefits and whether this would place additional financial burden on people, especially those on low incomes. The relative safety of wind power compared to nuclear gave it the advantage, particularly over the issue of nuclear waste. Though as several people appreciated, the merits of wind power had to be placed against the interests of those living near wind farms:

> *Like prisons, you don't want them near you, but you want more of them. (Woman, Sheffield, 21–44 ABC1)*

Solar energy was generally the most favoured across the groups in London, Teesside and South Wales (where it was explicitly addressed), but with some reservations over its overall viability in areas with not much sun. In general, the problem with 'natural' constraints associated with renewables (seasonality, intermittency, availability etc.) and their perceived high costs were always mentioned alongside their benefits across all groups.

Attitudes towards centralized/decentralized production

Overall, there was no real consensus about the suitability and desirability of either centralized or decentralized production. The group discussions, though, helped people to explicitly identify the advantages and disadvantages they attached to each option. Among the perceived advantages of centralized production, participants stressed the availability of existing infrastructure, for example in Teesside, and the ability to produce large amounts of hydrogen. Among the perceived disadvantages, people identified the potential problems with security of hydrogen supply, should a major disruption in production or a distribution network occur. Also, there were concerns with the physical magnitude of hydrogen production plants and the volumes of hydrogen they would store, and whether this had safety implications. The magnitude of large hydrogen production plants, in particular, generally raised similar concerns as those voiced over the visual effects of wind turbines:

> *That's all very well, but Teesside is the best place for it [large hydrogen production plant]. We don't want it in sunny Towyn and Carmarthen, do we? (Man, Carmarthen, South Wales)*

Localized production of hydrogen was perceived as improving local energy self-sufficiency for communities, but raised concerns over its efficiency and the overall safety risks associated with such a pervasive hydrogen production network, as the following remark suggests:

> *What's the relative explosive range of a hydrogen plant of that scale compared to a petrol station? I mean, 'cause we're thinking of something like Buncefield, that sent shock waves literally into the community. If you're going to have lots of decentralized sort of hydrogen producing facilities scattered around villages and towns, you know, are they actually community threats? (Man, Sheffield, 21–44 ABC1)*

Often, participants reasoned that a combination of localized and centralized production would be necessary according to the specific context, but admitted that hydrogen developments might be strongly shaped by economic forces and business interests.

Attitudes towards storage and distribution of hydrogen

As in the case of attitudes towards different levels of centralization as opposed to localization in hydrogen production, public opinions about different options for storing and distributing hydrogen were not clear-cut. The setting up of a hydrogen distribution infrastructure (either by expanding the natural gas pipeline network or the building of dedicated hydrogen pipelines), for example, was seen as costly, energy consuming, bringing about problems of security of supply and involving safety risks due to hydrogen's 'leaky' characteristics. However, in some cases (Sheffield) they were favoured over road tankers, which raised concerns about the consequences of increased traffic and accidents on roads. We found a general belief that people would adapt to a new infrastructure being put in place if they could be persuaded of its benefits, as the comment made by a Norwich group participant exemplifies:

> *People could be made to understand the necessity to have the energy. You know, people liked gas because it was convenient to them and if they can see the advantages to it in some way. I don't know how, but if they were to see the advantages, presumably eventually you'd want the hydrogen piped into their house in the same way as the gas is there. (Woman, Norwich, 21–44 C2DE)*

Storing hydrogen in underground caverns was an unfamiliar issue for most attending, so that people were reluctant to express definite opinions and preferred to ask questions over the risks it would involve, especially from undetected leaks.

Knowledge of hydrogen applications

A recurrent finding across all six case study areas was that people felt reluctant to express definitive judgements about different hydrogen applications, as they had no knowledge and experience of any of them. In the areas covered by the UKSHEC project, we sought to map attitudes towards the full range of hydrogen applications in portable (mobile phones, laptops and cameras), stationary (combined heat and power systems for homes) and mobile technologies (cars, motorbikes and buses). We found that awareness of these potential applications was generally low, with the exception of applications in transport, such as cars and buses, which most people claimed to be aware of thanks to articles in the newspaper or, more frequently, because they had seen it on television. Especially in Teesside, and to a lesser degree in South Wales, we found that awareness and knowledge of hydrogen as a chemical substance was comparably higher than in other areas, due to the pervasive presence of large chemical complexes. However, general levels of awareness of specific hydrogen demonstration projects and programmes in each of the three areas covered by the UKSHEC project were rather low, with few participants having already heard of the demonstrations or read about any hydrogen-related plans in their local areas.

In trying to make sense of and assess technologies and systems they had not seen before and had never used, people often resorted to their knowledge and experience of 'familiar' technologies and fuels. Five issues emerged as key factors in shaping the groups' appraisal of hydrogen systems, and applications in particular. These are safety, cost, environmental benefits, convenience and performance. Although it is not possible to rank them in order of importance, as this falls beyond the scope of our study, safety and cost were mentioned with particular frequency and concern. Safety emerged as a prerequisite attribute; to be able to use hydrogen technologies, people needed to be reassured that these would be at least as safe as other more conventional technologies, and that they would be affordable to everyone"

> *I think if people were thinking about putting hydrogen in their own back yard they would want it to be very very safe.* (Man, Guisborough, Teesside)

> *If you could be sure that this was going to be a) cheaper and b) safer than the existing fuels that we are using then I think people would think about it, but if it is going to be unsafe as in the case of accidents or a lot more expensive, then they would think twice.* (Woman, Guisborough, Teesside)

The current high costs associated with hydrogen technologies was generally regarded as a disincentive to adoption and also a potential cause of frustration for those people with 'good' environmental intentions:

> *[A]s unemployed people, you do have to go for the second-hand market and you have to get an old car. [There are] ... people who can afford new cars and other people who can go out say tomorrow, get one of these new hydrogen ones, but people like me can't do that, I can't suddenly say to someone oh yes I am going to buy a new car because it's greener.* (M 21–44 C2DE, Southampton)

> *It's like organic food, they're more expensive than these chemically grown ones, aren't they, so every time they have something good you can't afford it.* (Man, Middlesbrough, Teesside)

The practical aspects of using the new technology were particularly stressed and people asked relevant questions about the overall convenience of use and performance, including from an environmental point of view, of hydrogen applications. The main concern was that hydrogen would somehow entail a loss in comfort and ease of use in comparison with established technologies. This type of concern emerged especially in discussions about using hydrogen as a fuel in transport and in CHP systems in private homes. The comment made by a woman in one of the London groups illustrates the importance attached to preserving people's standards of living:

> *I don't care [about the type of fuel] as long as the buses run. I think that's what we care about, as long as your house is heated to a temperature that you like. (Woman, London, Group 1)*

In addition to the five issues discussed above, participants in the groups in Teesside and South Wales also suggested that improved job prospects and opportunities for regenerating otherwise derelict industrial sites or deprived areas would be seen as incentives to promote hydrogen developments in their localities. However, there was also an indication that hydrogen developments would not be accepted unconditionally and that hydrogen promoters would need to demonstrate the added value of hydrogen in each region:

> *I don't think I would say yes to it just because it was going to create a lot of jobs. You would have to give me a lot more than that. (Woman, Guisborough, Teesside)*

In discussing hydrogen vehicles, faced with the prospects of longer filling-up time, larger tank (with reduced boot space) and shorter range, most people thought that these would not be regarded as major inconveniences and expected that technologies would eventually be improved. However, there were concerns that longer filling-up times could lead to more frequent queues at refuelling stations. The beneficial features of hydrogen vehicles, such as the absence of noise and pollution, were generally acknowledged and considered attractive, particularly in the London groups, where many people appeared to be concerned with traffic congestion and air pollution.

Perception of risks attached to hydrogen

A wide range of issues emerged when people started to think critically about the risks hydrogen would involve, including whether silent vehicles would pose a safety risk for blind people, what kind of consequences collisions with a hydrogen vehicle would have and whether the widespread availability of hydrogen fuel would pose greater threats in case of deliberate misuse (e.g. vandalization or terrorist attacks). As noted earlier, questions about possible risks to safety were raised across all groups and concerned the whole hydrogen supply chain, not just applications.

The groups broadly agreed on the following key points. First, there was a broad acknowledgement that the distinctive nature of some of hydrogen's properties, such as its propensity to leak, flammability and explosive potential, could pose particular safety risks. However, this did not lead people to develop negative attitudes towards hydrogen developments, as the following comment indicates:

> *I do think historically hydrogen generally has bad press though. I mean, I had no idea that hydrogen could be used in the sort of way that, you know, would provide an efficient energy source.*

> *I just always assumed that hydrogen is bad and we should stay away from it. So in terms of safety then, you know, people need to be made aware that it can be safe, it can be manufactured safely. (Woman, Carmarthen, South Wales)*

Second, the consensus view emerging across all groups was that all technologies involve some degree of risk. This was frequently illustrated by reference to everyday technologies and fuels, like petrol and natural gas:

> *Well, gas and petrol are all dangerous, it's just usage isn't it, you become familiar with them. (Woman, Carmarthen, South Wales)*

As a consequence, most people expected that hydrogen technologies would be engineered to be safe before being commercialized, in the sense that people would be able to use them with the same degree of confidence as with ordinary technologies.

Third, participants in our groups agreed that people needed to understand how hydrogen would be handled by inexperienced users and what changes in their behaviour, as 'consumers' of the technology (car and bus users, pedestrians, residents etc.), would be required to deal with the different 'risk profiles' of hydrogen. The following comment illustrates the recurring need to understand to what extent hydrogen technologies would differ from ordinary ones:

> *I suppose what I'm asking is in terms of the risk assessment of the sort of accident that's likely to occur, say the turning over of a container, is the risk of harm more than we're used to or less than we're used to? (Woman, Norwich, 21–44 ABC1)*

Finally, in connection with the previous point, two different attitudes seemed to emerge in relation to the kind of reaction people would be likely to have to the novelty factor attached to hydrogen. A possible reaction, it was suggested, would be one of concern, and this would make people demand clear information about (and demonstrations of) the safety characteristics of the new technology. The remarks made by an older woman in relation to hydrogen-fuelled CHP systems summarize this attitude:

> *These units that you can have at the back or side of your house – what do they do? Is there anything to be afraid of, you know, will it blow up, will they let out a gas that will kill us all, you know I've no idea what they do, it's a box. And as far as I'm concerned I would want answers to that and I should imagine a lot of people would. Because when I had a big oil tank I knew what that was, you know, I knew it could catch fire so I kept it away from the house. (Woman, Eston, Teesside)*

Later she added:

> *Well I think people are scared of anything they don't know about and they don't understand, I know I am if I can't understand it I have to have it explained to me, once I could understand it I could take it in. (Woman, Eston, Teesside)*

The other view was that people would not mind the novelty of the technology, as long as its performance, ease of use and availability to the average consumer were comparable to those of conventional technologies:

> *I think in reality as long as you can buy it I don't think many people would care where it came from as long as it's there to use. (Man, London)*
>
> *And it's not too expensive. (Woman, London)*
>
> *As long as at point of use your cooker works and your fire works then 90 per cent of the population don't give a toss how it works. (Woman, Redcar, Teesside)*

Making hydrogen acceptable

As the previous section has made clear, there are a number of different criteria by which the overall 'acceptability' of hydrogen technologies, applications and infrastructures would be judged. How such different criteria, involving safety, cost, environmental benefits, performance and convenience of use, would play out in real world situations, however, is not clear. People themselves found it hard to express definitive assessments about a set of potentially radical technological innovations without being able to see them 'in action'. All groups commented on the importance of demonstration projects in promoting hydrogen and other new forms of energy, arguing that these would enable people to see how hydrogen would apply to their own everyday lives and understand whether it would provide significant and tangible benefits.

> *But this is the best form of advertising, isn't it. Something that is actually up and running, where they can actually say – This is run off hydrogen. (Man, Eston, Teesside)*

The groups also suggested that certain sections of the public might need role models they could associate hydrogen with, such as celebrities or respected public figures, or simply ordinary people that set an example everyone could follow. The need for role models also emerged as a key theme when groups discussed how to promote environmentally friendly behaviours:

You need the arguments presented with clarity, at the right level by somebody who you can trust. So you would have to find some kind of public figure that people would trust to put across the argument and you know could present it clearly. But you know you would have to make it interesting, you know not just have somebody talking to you. You would have to have ways of making it interesting and sort of presenting. (Man, Guisborough, Teesside)

When you see this kind of normal people instead of an eccentric with a house full of solar panels, I don't think people can relate to the eccentric, you know, who's driving, if there was one eccentric driving a hydrogen car then people would think – That's his little problem. But if, you know, normal people started driving hydrogen cars, then I just think that is how you change behaviour or change attitudes, if you see people that you can relate to doing it. (Woman, London)

Discussion and conclusion

Public engagement with hydrogen energy futures is still at its very beginning. Apart from the occasional ride in a hydrogen-powered demonstration bus, ordinary citizens have generally had very few opportunities to be able to see, experiment and scrutinize hydrogen technologies 'in action'. Engagement encompasses a wide range of different mechanisms and tools by which the public are brought closer to science and technology. At one extreme there is information provision, whereby people receive information on certain technological developments, but no real two-way dialogue or debate is established. At the other extreme there is genuine participation in technological development and decision-making on science and technology issues, whereby a section of the general public is able to express their views and frame the terms of the debate according to the issues they consider relevant, thus actively contributing to shape policy. An example of the latter type of engagement is the so-called Consensus Conference, established by the Danish Board of Technology and now widely used in various countries as a tool to make decision-making more democratic and open to debate (see, for instance, Einsidiel and Eastlick, 2000). In between these two extremes there are several mechanisms of 'consultation' with differing degrees of inclusion, impact on policy-making and openness of the debate.

The existing examples of public engagement with hydrogen energy that go beyond simple information provision are few in number and mostly consist of consultations on already framed topics, conducted via standardized questionnaires. Although our research work cannot claim to have moved public engagement with hydrogen to a substantially participatory level, it has nevertheless attempted to open the debate on hydrogen futures to public questioning and to offer an opportunity to challenge the mainstream, expert-based views on hydrogen to the ordinary members of the public who wished to be involved.

The research evidence presented in this chapter shows that, whilst in general people do not exhibit any significant objections to hydrogen on safety grounds, the public raise critically important questions about the relative costs and benefits of hydrogen as compared with other energy sources, and expect to be shown demonstrable gains in convenience, cost and practicality of everyday use. First, our research has demonstrated that public understanding of hydrogen cannot simplistically be conceptualized as 'risk perception', and that attitudes are likely to be shaped by the balance of opportunities and threats (such as increased risks and costs to consumers) attributed to hydrogen futures. Second, public attitudes to hydrogen are always related to context and are contingent on many factors, including the practical implications of living in a hydrogen-based world. Despite their initial lack of awareness and knowledge of the complex web of innovations that hydrogen might bring in the way energy is produced, distributed and used, participants in our groups were able and willing to ask relevant questions about the whole hydrogen supply chain, and demanded factual evidence on whether, and to what extent, hydrogen would deliver the much-trumpeted claims made for it.

Finally, it is clear that hydrogen promoters need to engage better with the general public, through demonstration projects that allow people to see what hydrogen would bring to them in their everyday lives, to understand how risks, costs and benefits would be distributed, and also how it would tackle the great challenges of climate change and energy security. Whether people will accept hydrogen as a fuel and energy carrier will mean different things according to the specific contexts and technological infrastructures involved. Acceptance cannot simply be equated to lack of opposition. Rather, our research has shown that there are many different criteria by which hydrogen developments might be judged, and different levels of acceptance across different social groups. Relying only, or predominantly, on the 'green' label that some hydrogen systems and applications are claimed to have might not be the most appropriate strategy.

Notes

1 Prof. Keith Ross, Institute for Materials Research, University of Salford.
2 Prof. Rose Baker, Centre for Operational Research and Statistics, University of Salford.

References

Altmann, M. and Graesel, C. (1998) 'The Acceptance of Hydrogen Technologies'. Available at http://www.HyWeb.de/accepth2

Barbour, R. S. and Kitzinger, J. (1999) *Developing Focus Group Research*, London, Sage
Bellaby, P. and Upham, P. (2007) 'Public Engagement with Hydrogen Infrastructures in Transport', Report for the Department for Transport, December, DfT Horizon Research Programme – Contract No. PPRO 4/54/2
Bloor, M., Frankland, J., Thomas, M. and Robson, K. (2001) *Focus Groups in Social Research,* London, Sage
Cherryman, S., King, S., Hawkes, F. R., Dinsdale, R. and Hawkes, D. L. (2005) *Public attitudes towards the use of hydrogen energy in Wales,* University of Glamorgan
Dresner, S. and Tomei, J. (2007) 'Public Acceptability of Hydrogen: Lessons for Policies and Institutions', UKSHEC Social Science Working Paper 31, Policy Studies Institute. Available at http://www.psi.org.uk/ukshec/pdf/31_Public%20 Acceptability_Lessons.pdf
Einsidiel, E. F. and Eastlick, D. L. (2000) 'Consensus Conferences as Deliberative Democracy', *Science Communication*, vol 21, issue 4, pp323–343
Haraldsson, K., Folkesson, A., Saxe, M. and Alvfors, P. (2006) 'A first report on the attitude towards hydrogen fuel cell buses in Stockholm', *International Journal of Hydrogen Energy*, vol 31, issue 3, pp317–325
Hickson, A., Phillips, A. and Morales, G. (2007) 'Public perception related to a hydrogen hybrid internal combustion engine transit bus demonstration and hydrogen fuel', *Energy Policy*, vol 35, issue 4, pp2249–2255
Maak, M., Nielsen, K. D., Torfason, H. T., Sverrisson, S. O. and Benediktsson, K. (2004) 'Assessment of Socio-Economic factors with emphasis on: Public Acceptance of Hydrogen as a fuel', ECTOS Deliverable 12. Available at http://www.ectos.is/newenergy/upload/files/utgefid_efni/ectos_12-assessement_of_socio-eco.pdf
McDowall, W. and Eames, M. (2007) 'Towards a sustainable hydrogen economy: A multi-criteria sustainability appraisal of competing hydrogen futures', *International Journal of Hydrogen Energy*, vol 32, issue 18, pp4611–4626
Morgan, D. L. (1997) *Focus Groups as Qualitative Research* (2nd edition), London, Sage
O'Garra, T. (2005) 'Comparative Analysis of the Impact of the Hydrogen Bus Trials on Public Awareness, Attitudes and Preferences: a Comparative Study of Four Cities', AcceptH2 Full Analysis Report. Available at http://www.accepth2.com
O'Garra, T., Mourato, S. and Pearson, P. (2005) 'Analysing awareness and acceptability of hydrogen vehicles: a London case study', *International Journal of Hydrogen Energy*, vol 30, issue 6, pp649–659
O'Garra, T., Mourato, S. and Pearson, P. (2007) 'Public Acceptability of Hydrogen Fuel Cell Transport and Associated Refuelling Infrastructure', in Flynn, R. and Bellaby, P. (eds) *Risk and the Public Acceptance of New Technologies*, Basingstoke, Palgrave Macmillan
Ricci, M., Flynn, R. and Bellaby, P. (2006) 'Public Attitudes towards Hydrogen Energy: Preliminary analysis of focus groups in London, Teesside and Wales', UKSHEC Social Science Working Paper 28, ISCPR, University of Salford, June 2006. Available at http://www.psi.org.uk/ukshec/pdf/28_attitudestohydrogen.pdf
Ricci, M., Bellaby, P. and Flynn, R. (2007a) 'Stakeholders' and Publics' Perceptions of Hydrogen Energy Technologies', in Flynn, R. and Bellaby, P. (eds) *Risk and the Public Acceptance of New Technologies*, Basingstoke, Palgrave Macmillan
Ricci, M., Flynn, R. and Bellaby, P. (2007b) 'Understanding the public acceptability of hydrogen energy – Key findings from focus groups in Teesside, SW Wales and London (October–November 2006)', UKSHEC Social Science Working Paper 33,

ISCPR, University of Salford, May 2007. Available at http://www.psi.org.uk/ukshec/pdf/33_Ricci_etal_PubAcceptfinal%20report.pdf

Ricci, M., Bellaby, P. and Flynn, R. (2008) 'What do we know about public perceptions and acceptance of hydrogen? A critical review and new case study evidence', *International Journal of Hydrogen Energy*, vol 33, issue 21, pp5868–5880

Rowe, G. and Frewer, L. (2005) 'A typology of public engagement mechanisms', *Science, Technology and Human Values*, vol 30, issue 2, pp251–290

Schmoyer, R. L., Truett, T. and Cooper, C. (2006) 'Results of the 2004 knowledge and opinions surveys for the baseline knowledge assessment of the U.S. Department of Energy Hydrogen Program', ORNL/TM-2006/417, Oak Ridge National Laboratory. Available at http://www1.eere.energy.gov/hydrogenandfuelcells/pdfs/survey_main_report.pdf

Sherry-Brennan, F., Devine-Wright, H. and Devine-Wright, P. (2007) 'Social Representations of Hydrogen Technologies: a Community-Owned Wind-Hydrogen Project', in Flynn, R. and Bellaby, P. (eds) *Risk and the Public Acceptance of New Technologies*, Basingstoke, Palgrave Macmillan

Wilsdon, J. and Willis, R. (2004) *See-Through Science: Why Public Engagement Needs to Move Upstream*, London, Demos. Available at http://www.demos.co.uk

Zachariah-Wolff, J. L. and Hemmes, K. (2006) 'Public Acceptance of Hydrogen in the Netherlands: Two Surveys That Demystify Public Views on a Hydrogen Economy', *Bulletin of Science, Technology & Society*, vol 32, issue 4, pp339–345

12
Hydrogen and Public Policy: Conclusions and Recommendations

Paul Ekins and Nick Hughes

This book has explored in some depth a range of hydrogen futures which might be regarded as including a 'hydrogen economy', defined as a (national) economic system in which hydrogen is the energy carrier that delivers 'a substantial fraction of the nation's energy-based goods and services' (NRC and NAE: p11). It has discussed the range of technologies of hydrogen production, distribution, storage and end-use, which these futures could involve, as well as the economics of these technologies, and modelled the role hydrogen could play in the energy system of a country like the UK if the technologies developed sufficiently to become competitive with current technology incumbents.

One of the striking characteristics of much of the literature on hydrogen is the seeming lack of special private performance characteristics of different hydrogen applications. Although (as discussed in Chapters 3 and 4) significant attention has been devoted by bodies such as the US DoE towards encouraging the development of hydrogen and fuel cell technologies with equal performance to equivalent incumbents, it hardly seems to be a serious prospect that hydrogen applications will actually deliver better *private* service than their conventional competitors. Of the various private performance characteristics, only cost is subject to systematic investigation (e.g. Padró and Putsche, 1999; E4Tech et al, 2004), and then in terms of what improvements are required for hydrogen applications to become competitive with established alternatives. Apart from cost, the technology is valued and desired almost entirely in relation to its public attributes (especially greenhouse gas emissions reductions and energy security). Despite this lack of obvious additional private benefits over incumbent technologies in mainstream (or 'regime') applications, there seems to be a hope that if fuel cells, for example, can be made to 'work' at 'competitive' cost (in itself a very considerable challenge), and if appropriate infrastructure can be provided at the right time (another very considerable challenge), then the technology can be diffused into end-markets, delivering the desired public benefits along the way. Because of the importance of these public attributes, it is appropriate to ask what public policies could help bring about both the development of the technologies and their infrastructure, and their diffusion.

The transition to a hydrogen economy: niche management or landscape engineering?

As discussed in Chapter 2, one of the ways in which new technologies can become more widely diffused is through their expansion out of niches, perhaps through a process of strategic niche management.

McDowall (2004) provides an overview of 'promising' hydrogen niches, and there have been surveys of fuel cell niches (e.g. EA Technology, 2000), and at least one attempt to identify a suitable niche for strategic niche management for hydrogen technologies (Farrell et al, 2001). McDowall starts by separating his niches into 'niche markets' (small but viable markets), 'technological niches' ('protected spaces') and 'bounded socio-technical experiments' (demonstration projects), but this distinction is not necessary for this discussion. All these phenomena are here called niches: for those involved in or promoting them, their attributes justify their existence, whether the attributes are particular performances not delivered by the mainstream market, or a time-bound desire for technology development or learning. Thus the European Commission's CUTE (Clean Urban Transport for Europe) project, whereby 33 fuel cell-powered buses, running and refuelled locally with locally produced hydrogen, were introduced into nine European cities, is classed as a 'bounded socio-technical experiment', but for its duration it can still be regarded as a niche for hydrogen buses, driven entirely by the public attribute of a desire to 'prove zero emission public transport is possible today when ambitious political will and innovative technology are combined'.[1]

McDowall identifies seven current niches for hydrogen technologies listed below, where 1–4 are classed as market niches, 5–6 as technological niches and 7 is a catch-all category of demonstrations, like the CUTE project:

1. Portable power for electronic and small electrical equipment.
2. Auxiliary power units (APUs) for vehicles.
3. Fuel cells for stationary power (in remote areas, or as premium or back-up power).
4. Fuel cells to propel 'niche vehicles', ranging from golf buggies to submarines.
5. Hydrogen-fuelled internal combustion vehicles.

6. Hydrogen/hydrocarbon fuel blends.
7. Demonstration projects and experiments.

Many of these niches have been discussed in earlier chapters. One of the interesting features about this list is that it does not even mention the hydrogen technology, road fuel cell vehicles (FCVs), in which there is the most interest from policy-makers and the automotive industry (see, for example, Foley, 2001; SMMT, 2002), although since McDowall's paper the Canadian government has set up the demonstration Vancouver Fuel Cell Vehicle Programme[2] (see Chapter 8), and doubtless there will be other initiatives. In any case, McDowall's listed niches were intended to represent a set of possible transition steps on a pathway towards the successful penetration of FCVs, recognizing that FCVs currently have no hope of competing with conventional internal combustion vehicles. These niches may well be relevant to the development of hydrogen technologies, and it may be the case that such hydrogen technologies could for various reasons successfully fulfil the particular requirements of these niche applications. Yet it is not necessarily the case that such niche applications will lead to a wider uptake of hydrogen technologies within the socio-technical regime, as part of a low-carbon energy system. Indeed, there is no suggestion in McDowall (2004) that they are necessarily appropriate targets for strategic niche management, for the purposes of bringing about a wider socio-technical transition to a low-carbon, hydrogen economy.

In themselves, the niches 1–4, all of which involve fuel cells, do not offer great opportunities for the reduction of emissions of carbon dioxide, in which policy-makers tend to be most interested:

1. Portable power packs generally replace batteries, not fossil fuels.
2. The main environmental motive behind the use of APUs would seem to be reduction of local air pollutants, rather than carbon dioxide.
3. A recent assessment of the prospects for stationary power considered that, even by 2030, 'the CO_2 savings from hydrogen to electricity chains do not appear to justify the additional costs over grid electricity' (E4Tech et al, 2004: p49). More generally, 'even if CO_2 and cost credit is given for heat generated in hydrogen fuel CHP plants, it is still more CO_2 and cost-effective to use the primary energy source directly for electricity production using a different technology' (E4Tech et al, 2004: p50).
4. CO_2 savings from niche vehicle markets will only become substantial to the extent that hydrogen expands out of those markets.

Of course, these rather sceptical points overlook the possibility that learning about and technological development of fuel cells through these niches may lead to the breakthroughs that are necessary for more potentially 'mainstream' technologies, such as FCVs, to achieve the significant improvements across a range of dimensions that are required for them to compete effectively with conventional fuel vehicles. Indeed, according to Levinthal, major technological changes occur when technologies that have been incubated within niches invade mainstream application domains: 'The phenomenon of creative destruction is associated with the "invasion" of the technological form that has evolved in the new domain of application into other domains' (Levinthal, 1998: p221).

However, if hydrogen technologies do succeed in capturing market share within niches such as those identified by McDowall (2004), it will be first because they perform with the particular characteristics which are satisfactory within the constraints of such a niche (e.g. weight, volume, power output), and second because they deliver sufficient benefits to the small, or 'niche', subset of consumers who use them (e.g. clean, silent or portable power).

It seems clear that breaking out of these niches will entail step changes in technological performance, which are by no means assured. As the NRC and NAE stress:

> *The challenge is to develop automotive fuel cell systems that are both lightweight and compact (i.e. have high power densities by both mass and volume), tolerant to rapid cycling and on-road vibration, reliable for 4000 to 5000 hours or so of non-continuous use in cold and hot weather, and able to respond rapidly to transient demands for power, and able to use hydrogen of varying purity. (NRC and NAE, 2004: p26)*

Each of these specifications represents a significant technical challenge to current hydrogen and fuel-cell technologies, but perhaps none more than storage:

> *No hydrogen storage system has yet been developed that is simultaneously lightweight, compact, inexpensive and safe. Further advances in hydrogen storage, so that FCVs can refuel quickly and have driving ranges comparable with those of conventional vehicles, thus constitute a key area for further development. (NRC and NAE 2004: p27)*

The cost challenges are no less demanding than those related to performance. E4Tech et al (2004: p98) estimated that the life-cycle energy costs of different fuel chains needed to improve by 40–70 per cent, and the cost of a fuel-cell vehicle powered by natural gas had to be reduced by more than a factor of ten, if the technology was to approach competitiveness with conventional vehicles by 2030.

On the second point, there remains a clear distinction between the kinds of benefits which are normally presumed to be associated with niche hydrogen technologies, and mainstream or regime ones. Niche hydrogen technologies of the kind listed by McDowall are usually presented as having clear direct benefits to the user, or *private* benefits. For example, Chapter 4 of this volume has discussed that the use of hydrogen-fuel forklift trucks is considered to be promising in part because the characteristic of zero emissions conveys a private benefit to users working within an enclosed warehouse environment. The use of a zero emissions vehicle within other applications, which do not operate within enclosed environments, cannot be said to deliver a *private* benefit in the same way. And, as noted above, there seems to be little anticipation that hydrogen and fuel-cell technologies will outcompete their rivals on private benefits alone.

NRC and NAE (2004: p27) state: 'For early fuel cell systems to succeed in the marketplace, they must have special appeal in some market niches, even if these niches are relatively small', and specifically identify zero-emission areas in cities and APUs as possible contexts within which FCVs and fuel cells respectively might become established. E4Tech et al (2004: p200) consider that 'use of other (i.e. non-road) fuel cell vehicles could provide a market for technologies needed for fuel cell cars, such as hydrogen storage, thus speeding their development'. However, it is clearly a tall order to expect these niches to contribute extensively to addressing the fundamental scientific and technical challenges which fuel cells will have to overcome for road FCV performance to come anywhere near that of conventional vehicles, which are, of course, improving all the time. Due to both the technical challenges, and the lack of significant additional private benefits of hydrogen and fuel-cell technologies in comparison to incumbents, the gap between the niches and the regime to be challenged seems unbridgeable in any manner that can be foreseen by market-pull attributes. This suggests, first, a continuing reliance for an extended period on basic and applied R&D, in order to try to generate the technical improvements which seem to be a prerequisite for a serious regime challenge.

It also suggests that if such a regime challenge is to be mounted by hydrogen technologies, some way will need to be found of enabling the almost entirely public benefits of hydrogen technologies to exert the kind of market pull for the technologies that is normally associated with technologies with more obvious private benefits (such as mobile phones, laptops, internet connections etc.). There is clearly an important role for policy at both of these levels, as will be expanded upon later in this chapter. But what is also clear is that the strategic management of niches, though potentially important, is unlikely *on its own* to bring about a major transition in the case of hydrogen.

Finally, it may be worth recognizing (as in Agnolucci and McDowall, 2007) that niches may often lead somewhere, but not necessarily to the endpoint desired or expected ex ante. For example, success of portable fuel cells could lead to the development of methanol as a major energy carrier, and divert attention from hydrogen. Successfully choosing specific 'strategic' niches within which to nurture a technology may be unrealistic, as it implies a degree of technological foresight that belies the indeterminate and uncertain nature of socio-technical change.

It is hard to avoid the conclusion that, in respect of the transition to a hydrogen economy, the strategic management of current hydrogen niches will itself be no more than a niche part of a broader strategy for transition management. The majority of the areas identified by E4Tech et al (2004) as having barriers that needed to be addressed by public policy involved basic scientific and technological issues related to the cost-effective supply of hydrogen, far removed from the demand-pull of end-use applications and likely only to be resolved, if at all, by R&D of a fairly fundamental kind. This R&D will only come about at the required level if the landscape processes and perceptions related to climate change and energy insecurity are given substantially higher political priority than at present. Current hydrogen niches should not be ignored, but it is pressures from the landscape of the energy system that currently seem far more important for the prospects of a hydrogen economy.

Hydrogen policy priorities

In the most detailed analysis yet carried out of the most appropriate hydrogen strategy for the UK, E4Tech et al (2004) identify six hydrogen chains as particularly relevant to the UK context. These are shown in Table 12.1, together with the areas which E4Tech et al suggest need to be addressed in order for the practical realization of these routes to hydrogen utilization to be achieved.

Table 12.1 may give the impression that the principal task to be accomplished for the establishment of 'a hydrogen economy' is the development of a range of different technologies, and there is no denying the essential role

Table 12.1 *Hydrogen chains appropriate for the UK, and areas to be addressed for them to become viable*

Hydrogen chains	*Areas to be addressed*
	1. Fuel cell road vehicles including storage*
	2. Other hydrogen and fuel cell vehicles*
	3. Hydrogen pipelines*
	4. Road transport of hydrogen*
	5. Refuelling infrastructure*
	Biomass and waste supply
Biomass gasification	6. Biomass gasification to hydrogen
	7. Hydrogen integration in biomass systems
Nuclear electricity	Nuclear electricity
Renewable electricity	Renewable electricity
	8. Hydrogen integration with renewable energy
	9. Electrolysers**
Novel H_2 technologies	10. Novel hydrogen production technologies
Natural gas with CCS	11. Natural gas reforming
	12. Hydrogen integration in natural gas systems
Coal with CCS	13. Coal gasification to hydrogen
	Carbon capture and storage (CCS)**

* Common to all chains

** Common to two chains

Note: The chains have been placed opposite the areas to which they are most closely related, but note that some areas are relevant to more than one chain, or to all chains. The numbered areas are those which are referred to in Table 12.3.

Source: E4Tech et al, 2004: p102

of technological development in this process. However, this is very much only part of what is required.

As was noted at the start of this book, the current energy system in industrial countries satisfies a wide range of consumer demands for energy services (heat, light, power, mobility), on the basis of an extensive, durable and expensive infrastructure. For hydrogen to become extensively used as an energy carrier, there will need to be a major transition away from the current energy system, which will require hydrogen technologies to compete effectively with fossil fuels and other alternatives. In particular, and as has been noted earlier, 'devices that use hydrogen (e.g. fuel cells) must compete successfully with devices that use competing fuels (e.g. hybrid propulsion systems)', and 'hydrogen must compete successfully with electricity and secondary fuels (e.g. gasoline, diesel fuel and methanol)' (NRC and NAE, 2004: p17). In addition to competing successfully economically, as has also been repeatedly noted, political and cultural factors will also be necessary to support and help drive any transition to hydrogen.

There is some scepticism in the literature as to whether hydrogen could realistically be expected to compete in this way, given the higher innate thermodynamic efficiency of using electricity to power electric vehicles (EVs), rather than to create hydrogen to power FCVs (Hammarschlag and Mazza, 2005; Mazza and Hammarschlag, 2005), and the fact that EV technology is significantly further advanced than FCV technology and the greater energy density compared to hydrogen of synthetic liquid hydrocarbons (Bossel et al, 2003). Moreover, as noted in Chapter 4, recent policy developments seem to suggest an increasing belief on the part of policy-makers in the greater near-term viability of electric vehicles, a tendency which could do as much to decide the winner of that particular 'race' as any technological development or breakthrough. How this technological competition will play out in coming decades is, of course, very uncertain. However, the modelling that was reported in Chapter 6 suggested that, under optimistic but not wholly unrealistic assumptions about the development of hydrogen technologies, it was quite possible to envisage it playing a cost-effective role in a future (e.g. 2050) energy system, whether there were tight carbon constraints or not.

Chapter 5 developed four different scenarios under which the kinds of development modelled in Chapter 6 might come about. What is apparent from these scenarios is that there are both differences and similarities across the characteristics of the different scenarios, and that different stories for the scenarios are possible (e.g. the Ubiquitous Hydrogen (UH) scenario could be driven by government, and the Centralized Hydrogen for Transport (CHT) scenario by business; or the drivers could be combined, with the transport component of UH being driven by business, but the technology then being taken into the residential and commercial sectors by innovative new small companies acting in 'policy networks' with government). However, what is clear in all these scenarios is that without concerted policy support for hydrogen, they are very unlikely to materialize.

Policies for hydrogen transitions

On the evidence to date, as presented in this book, market development and forces alone are unlikely to enable hydrogen technologies to break out of their current relatively limited uses. Indeed, there is no literature that suggests that the hydrogen economy will come to exist in the foreseeable future, if ever, without substantial and long-term public support. Even with the political will to give that support, the nature of what is being attempted should not be underestimated. Writing about the US, but with relevance for other industrialized countries, NRC and NAE (2004: p17) state:

> *In no prior case has the government attempted to promote the replacement of an entire, mature, networked energy infrastructure before market forces did the job. The magnitude of the change required if a meaningful fraction of the U.S. energy system is to shift to hydrogen exceeds by a wide margin that of previous transitions in which the government has intervened.*

To attain such a shift, strong public policy is likely to be required, applied consistently and systematically over an extended period.

It is worth exploring in a little more detail the cost implications of the kind of policy support that is being envisaged. Table 12.2 shows the extra system costs above the base from the modelling (reported in Chapter 6) of three scenarios of transition to a low-carbon economy.

It was noted in Chapter 6 that, even in the base case (a scenario with no carbon constraints), a significant use of hydrogen in 2050 (70 per cent of road fuels) was cost-optimal on the technological assumptions made. What public policy needs to achieve, if that level of hydrogen diffusion is to be delivered, is the improvement in the performance of hydrogen technologies embodied in the assumptions, which in turn will require sustained and high levels of public investment in hydrogen research and development. Of course, there is no guarantee that public investment in R&D will deliver the improved performance of hydrogen technologies that is envisaged. Such developments are inherently uncertain.

However, *if* the public R&D does deliver this enhanced performance of hydrogen technologies, then the modelling further shows that the achievement of the 60 per cent cut in carbon emissions by 2050 (from 2000 levels), as

Table 12.2 *Cost increases from the base scenario for different scenarios in 2050*

Increase above base of:	*Reference*	*CLT*	*UH*
System cost (£)	£4.8 bn	£8.0 bn	£41.1 bn
System cost (%)	1.48	2.47	12.63

Source: Table 6.4, Chapter 6

envisaged in the reference scenario, can be accomplished also with a significant use of hydrogen (about the same as in the base, but produced from carbon-free sources) at a relatively modest cost (£4.8 billion), and the costs of further increasing its use in transport (as in CLT) are also relatively small (about £8 billion). However, seeking to increase the hydrogen penetration into non-transport uses (as in UH) incurs a significant further cost penalty (to £41 billion).

Public policy, of course, needs to be justified in terms of the public benefits that it delivers. As has already been seen, in respect of hydrogen, the public benefits most often cited are of three kinds, which may be briefly recapitulated here. Two relate to air emissions, one to energy security. The potential air emission benefits are that, at the point of use, the use of hydrogen either in fuel cells or in combustion produces only water. Where this use substitutes for the combustion of fossil fuels (e.g. petrol/diesel in vehicles, coal in power stations), this means that the use of hydrogen can reduce emissions of carbon dioxide, and therefore contribute to climate change mitigation and to reducing local pollutants such as the oxides of sulphur and nitrogen, and therefore help to improve air quality. The delivery of these benefits is, of course, dependent on the means of production of the hydrogen (i.e. these means would have to involve low or no emissions themselves).

The potential benefits of energy security derive from being potentially able to substitute hydrogen for imported fuels (such as oil) that may suffer constraints in their supply, either because of scarcity or from political factors. Again, the delivery of these benefits will depend on the means of production of the hydrogen – for example, producing it from natural gas through SMR will do nothing to reduce dependence on imported gas.

A further possible perceived public benefit from the development of hydrogen technologies is economic. Some regions and countries which perceive that hydrogen technologies are likely to become important in the future consider that they will benefit economically from this development if they have created a local, regional or national capability in these technologies. Strictly, this is more a private benefit to the firms and employees concerned, but societies as a whole also stand to gain from successful technological developments of this kind; and, in fact, it is such industrial considerations that seem to be driving much of the current public support for hydrogen at regional level, as seen in Chapter 7. Of course, should hydrogen technologies fail to develop as foreseen, such benefits will fail to materialize, and the public subsidies that have been committed to them may well turn out to be effectively wasted.

Because of the importance of achieving technical improvements in hydrogen technologies, that deliver any or all of new functionalities, performance improvements and cost reductions, most public policy support for hydrogen is devoted to research and development (R&D). Hughes (2007) found that research in hydrogen technologies is mainly organized, coordinated and funded internationally and nationally. Important internationally are the International Partnership for a Hydrogen Economy (IPHE), and the work of the International Energy Agency (IEA) and the European Union (EU), while outside Europe individual countries with major hydrogen research programmes include the US, Japan, South Korea, Canada and Iceland, the last of which had a target to convert its economy entirely to hydrogen by 2030 (although this target may not survive the fall-out from the 2008–09 financial crisis, which hit Iceland particularly hard).

EU funding goes to support a number of research and demonstration projects, including the CUTE project which deployed 33 fuel cell buses in nine cities and has already been mentioned a number of times in this book, and networks and initiatives such as HyWays, which developed a hydrogen roadmap for the EU as a whole (HyWays, 2008). There is also a public–private collaboration called the European Hydrogen and Fuel Cells Technology Platform, which has ambitious targets for fuel cell commercialization in a range of uses, including vehicles.

An important source of EU funding for hydrogen activities at the sub-national level is through the European Regional Development Fund (ERDF), which is accessible to less prosperous EU regions or those undergoing industrial restructuring. It is clear from Hughes (2007) that most interest in hydrogen at a sub-national level, in the UK at least, is driven by the desire for economic development and regeneration, rather than the wider public benefits. Because economic development and regeneration is highly location-specific, it is not therefore surprising that different regions in the UK which have aspirations towards 'a hydrogen economy' have very different perceptions of what such an economy in their area would comprise, and how they might seek to move towards it (Hodson and Marvin, 2005a, 2005b, 2005c; and see Chapter 9). Hughes (2007), drawing heavily on this work by Hodson and Marvin, contrasts the differences in approach to this issue being taken in London, Teesside, Wales and Scotland. Two conclusions emerge from all of the regions studied. The first is the importance of the regional level (in England provided by the regional development agencies, in Wales and Scotland by the national governments) in providing impetus to activities on the ground. The regional level is large enough to be able to include a variety of relevant actors and interests, but small enough to be able to take account of local contexts, skills and enthusiasms. The second is for the need for these regional activities to be supported by and related to a clear national vision, policy framework and funding provision. As will become clear, it is this national–regional linkage which, in the UK at least, seems to be largely missing.

As seen earlier in this chapter, the Strategic Framework for hydrogen in the UK, developed by E4Tech et al (2004), identified six hydrogen chains as most promising in the UK context. However, all these chains were oriented exclusively towards the use of hydrogen in transport, and specifically in FCVs. This is in contrast with the main thrusts towards hydrogen coming from Scotland, Wales and Teesside, none of which are concerned with FCV development, and with 'the significant entrepreneurial activity in the UK from small companies developing stationary and portable fuel cells' (Hughes, 2007: p17).

As Hughes (2007: p34) later puts it:

> *High level policies and roadmaps should provide an aspirational drive to encourage local and regional actors to implement projects, supported with funding, whilst remaining flexible to regional interpretations of what a hydrogen or fuel cell economy means in each local context.*

UK policies and roadmaps would seem to leave quite a lot to be desired in this regard.

E4 Tech et al (2004) identify 33 measures to address the barriers to the development of hydrogen technologies in the UK, grouped according to the current ability of the UK to address them, alone or in international collaboration. Table 12.3 lists these measures (31 in number, because some have been combined for brevity). The numbers refer to the numbered areas to be addressed in Table 12.1. Many of these measures require the commitment of substantial resources. Their successful implementation would also require committed and knowledgeable actors and institutions at the regional and local levels. Perhaps the first policy priority is to connect the national perception of the priority of these measures (as opposed to others) with the realities of actors and institutions on the ground.

Table 12.3 confirms the point made above that a major focus of public policy support should be research, development and demonstration projects. However, of themselves, these are unlikely to mobilize the really large investments from private sources that will be necessary for the mass diffusion of hydrogen technologies, in terms of both applications and infrastructure and applications. This will require substantial policy measures of market enablement and incentives (such as feed-in tariffs, carbon pricing and fuel duty exemptions) that private investors believe to be long term. It is probably still too early for such measures – the markets to which they will need to be applied (e.g. FCVs) are still characterized by technologies that need further fundamental development. But policy-makers should keep in mind both the need for such measures in due course, and the desirability of targeting them appropriately and differently in line with the different developments at regional and local level.

Although one of the two key axes in the UKSHEC transition scenarios of Chapter 5 splits the scenarios according to whether they are characterized by a 'strong' or 'weak guiding vision' (see Table 5.1), nevertheless each of the scenarios is driven by decisive action on the part of at least one major actor, and, it could be argued, all are crucially dependent on strong government. In *Government Mission*, it is explicitly the Government which imposes strong policies to specifically bring about a hydrogen transition. *Corporate Race* is driven by large commercial interests, motivated by a growing culture of corporate social responsibility, but it is unlikely that this would be powerful enough unless it were also supported by government policy in the form of

Table 12.3 *Measures required to develop UK hydrogen options*

CREATE STRONG UK POSITION ALONE **Major Barriers** 1 Stimulate market for low-carbon transport in UK 4 Include road transport of H_2 in UK demonstrations 5 Demonstration of refuelling stations **Other Barriers** 3 Identify and focus UK pipeline capabilities 3 Evaluate and demonstrate undersea UK pipeline from UK remote renewables 7 Develop UK biomass policy to include H_2 8 Conduct feasibility studies on H_2 integration with renewable electricity 8 Policy development for H_2 and renewable electricity 8 Demonstration of H_2 with renewable electricity in the UK 11 Deploy large transformers and integrate with CCS in UK 13 Demonstrations of coal gasification with CCS	**UK LEAD IN INTERNATIONAL ACTIVITIES** **Major Barriers** 1 Lead international R&D effort on H_2 on-board storage **Other Barriers** 5 Create strong UK systems analysis position 10 Lead RD&D in non-nuclear novel H_2 production
NEED TO BUILD UK EXPERIENCE **Major Barriers** 2 Deployment of H_2 and other FC vehicles **Other Barriers** 3 Demonstrate urban pipeline network to supply refuelling stations in UK 3 Demonstrate trunk pipelines in UK 5 Cooperate in refuelling codes and standards development 7 Conduct UK systems studies and demonstration of biomass to UK 12 Plan for future natural gas demand for H_2	**UK COOPERATION IN INTERNATIONAL ACTIVITIES** **Major Barriers** 1 Cooperate in international R&D efforts on fuel cell stacks 1 Participate in international FCV design, demonstration and integration activities **Other Barriers** 2 Participate in international development efforts for other H_2 and FC vehicles 6 Participate in international R&D and demonstration on biomass gasification to H_2 7 Develop EU biomass policy to include H_2 9 Cooperate in international electrolyser R&D within areas of UK strength 9 Cooperate in international electrolyser demonstrations 10 Participate in international novel nuclear to H_2 RD&D 11 Demonstrate and commercialize reformers for energy applications in UK 12 Cooperate in studies and demonstration of H_2 use in pipelines 13 Conduct R&D on coal gasification, CO_2 separation, polygeneration and biomass co-firing

Source: E4Tech et al, 2004: p107

incentives or regulation, and would certainly require regulatory harmonization between countries of health and safety standards, for example. The other two transitions are characterized by a 'weak guiding vision', but even in these cases the notable absence of action in one area is compensated for by action from a large actor in another. In *Structural Shift*, there are no specifically hydrogen-directed policies, but it is nevertheless strong action on the part of government in terms of demanding high renewable energy targets which indirectly drives the need for hydrogen as an energy regulator. *Disruptive Innovation* is the transition which is least obviously driven by specific directed actions of government, with direct hydrocarbon fuel cells emerging for transport uses from portable niches. However, even here the developments in fuel-cell technology which enable the transfer from portable to automotive markets imply some significant levels of R&D on the part of companies within the automotive supply chains, and the Government is again broadly responsible for directing a move away from carbon-intensive fossil fuels through enforcing emissions reductions, incentivizing renewable transport fuels and stimulating the 'policy networks' and markets through which the knowledge generation and market development comes about.

Conclusions and recommendations

The main overall conclusion of this book is that there are a number of possible hydrogen futures, and transitions to a hydrogen economy, but realizing any of them will require substantial and sustained public policy support.

Beyond that, it is clear that not all hydrogen futures will be regarded as sustainable and desirable by everyone, so that public understanding and engagement will be required for them to gain public acceptance. Elements of possible hydrogen futures that may be contentious include the production of hydrogen from nuclear power, huge onshore wind farms, or fossil fuels with carbon capture and storage. Public familiarity with applications of hydrogen technologies and attitudes on safety, and the ability of hydrogen technologies to meet desired standards of cost, convenience and performance, are also likely to be important for its widespread diffusion. It is necessary for the public to be informed about the potential applications and implications of hydrogen technologies, and to be engaged in their early manifestations in different regions, if the diffusion of these technologies is to proceed smoothly when they are ready for mass marketing.

The transition to a hydrogen economy will require more than strategic niche management. Hydrogen and fuel-cell technologies are currently highly uneconomic, except for certain niche applications, in which particular features of hydrogen technologies are highly valued, where their market potential is greater. However, such applications, either because of their limited market size, or because any potential advantages of hydrogen or fuel cell technologies within them depend on large increases in energy demand, are unlikely on their own to represent a significant transition to a more sustainable energy economy. They may provide a 'stepping stone' to lowering costs of technologies through increased production. However, due to the variety of technical specifications to which different fuel cells are responding, there are significant technical distinctions between the technologies being used in the various niche applications. This imposes significant barriers on the potential for major technological transfer from niche to mass market, as such transfer has been characterized in case studies in the literature. Thus, in addition to the work of small- to medium-sized companies in designing fuel cells for niche applications, a major transition to the use of sustainable hydrogen energy in mass markets will require some significant and concerted efforts on the part of large-scale actors, including governments and major companies in the energy, automotive and other related sectors.

Early demonstrations of hydrogen and fuel-cell technologies are, almost by definition, likely to be on a small scale, embedded within policy and institutional arrangements, and promoted by actors operating at the particular location in which they are being developed. In other words, the regional dimension of governance is likely to be as crucial to the early development of hydrogen and fuel-cell technologies as the national scale. Given the relevance of a regional approach to hydrogen/fuel-cell development, there should be coordination between policies which operate at the regional level and national level incentives. The most likely potential public benefits of hydrogen/fuel cells are decarbonization and reduction of local pollution. The latter would be more likely to speak to a local agenda; however, the former could be a crucial long-term goal within the national context. The extent to which these different objectives should be prioritized or combined needs to be coordinated. Different groups in different regions may have different reasons for regarding hydrogen as potentially beneficial and may therefore wish to develop it in their regions in different ways. National roadmaps of hydrogen development should be sensitive to, and seek to support, these different regional aspirations, while providing an overall vision and rationale for moving towards a hydrogen economy which is both consistent with and makes wider sense of these different regional developments.

Policies should also be sensitive to the integrated nature of hydrogen production, storage, distribution and end-use systems, and view a potential system as an integrated whole. This includes consideration of how a hydrogen system could be integrated within the wider energy system. One of the most fundamental changes to the energy system over the next few decades is posed by the prospect of major decarbonization of electricity supply. This is almost certain to set the context for any development of hydrogen and fuel-cell technologies – it is possible indeed that it may open certain doors for their development, as hydrogen could be used as an energy vector to capture 'spare' electricity from inflexible low-carbon generation sources at times of low power demand, either to divert this energy to the transport sector or to feed it back to the grid when required. The wider energy system context is therefore crucial to consideration for hydrogen developments.

Whether large-scale hydrogen production will come about, and if so when, are matters of great uncertainty, but it is clear that the establishment of a hydrogen economy will require multiple reinforcing interactions between demand, investment and innovation. Public policy to stimulate the hydrogen economy should seek to promote the establishment of a virtuous circle of demand, investment and innovation in a coordinated way, as shown in Figure 12.1 (from Hughes, 2006).

The circularity in Figure 12.1 is rooted in the premise that the positive effect of a learning curve (cost reduction as a technology is more widely applied) is dependent on the number of units sold; however, if increasing numbers of units cannot be sold due to a high cost and lack of demand, progress down the learning curve will not be made. Conversely, if the price becomes acceptable to a significant number of consumers, the increased demand will stimulate increased production volumes, and progress down the curve will be much faster. For a technology such as hydrogen, government intervention in setting in motion this virtuous cycle is crucial. Figure 12.1 shows that government intervention could occur at two points, and these correspond to the two different kinds of intervention identified during the discussion on managing the transition from niche to mainstream for hydrogen technologies. On the one hand, basic R&D funding continues to be required as technologies are researched and fundamental technology breakthroughs sought. On the other hand, government policy can have a role through taxation or other means of giving incentives to render technologies financially attractive to the consumer, despite high manufacturing cost. The effect of such action is to turn an attribute – such as low emissions – which was previously only valued in certain niches into an attribute with value across the wider 'regime', through penalizing its opposite, high-emission technologies. This, for example, may help FCVs to broaden their initial niche market – where their high price might have limited their appeal to a narrow niche, incentives could widen their appeal to a wide enough consumer base to generate real economies of scale, which would in turn generate greater manufacturer confidence, investment and further increase economies of scale, producing lower cost and, in turn, even greater demand. Clearly, however, the beginning of this cycle is problematic. The greater the technical and economic gap between new technologies and incumbent 'regime' technologies, the greater the challenge for government policies which attempt to render new technologies attractive to the regime through penalizing the alternatives. In the case of hydrogen technologies, the gap between their current cost and performance and those of incumbent regime technologies is such that the required end-user focused policies would have to penalize incumbent technologies to such a degree that they would face major implementation challenges from the point of view of political and public acceptability. This is particularly the case when compared to the far more incremental progress in environmental standards, for example pertaining to the transport sector, which characterize recent and ongoing policy developments.

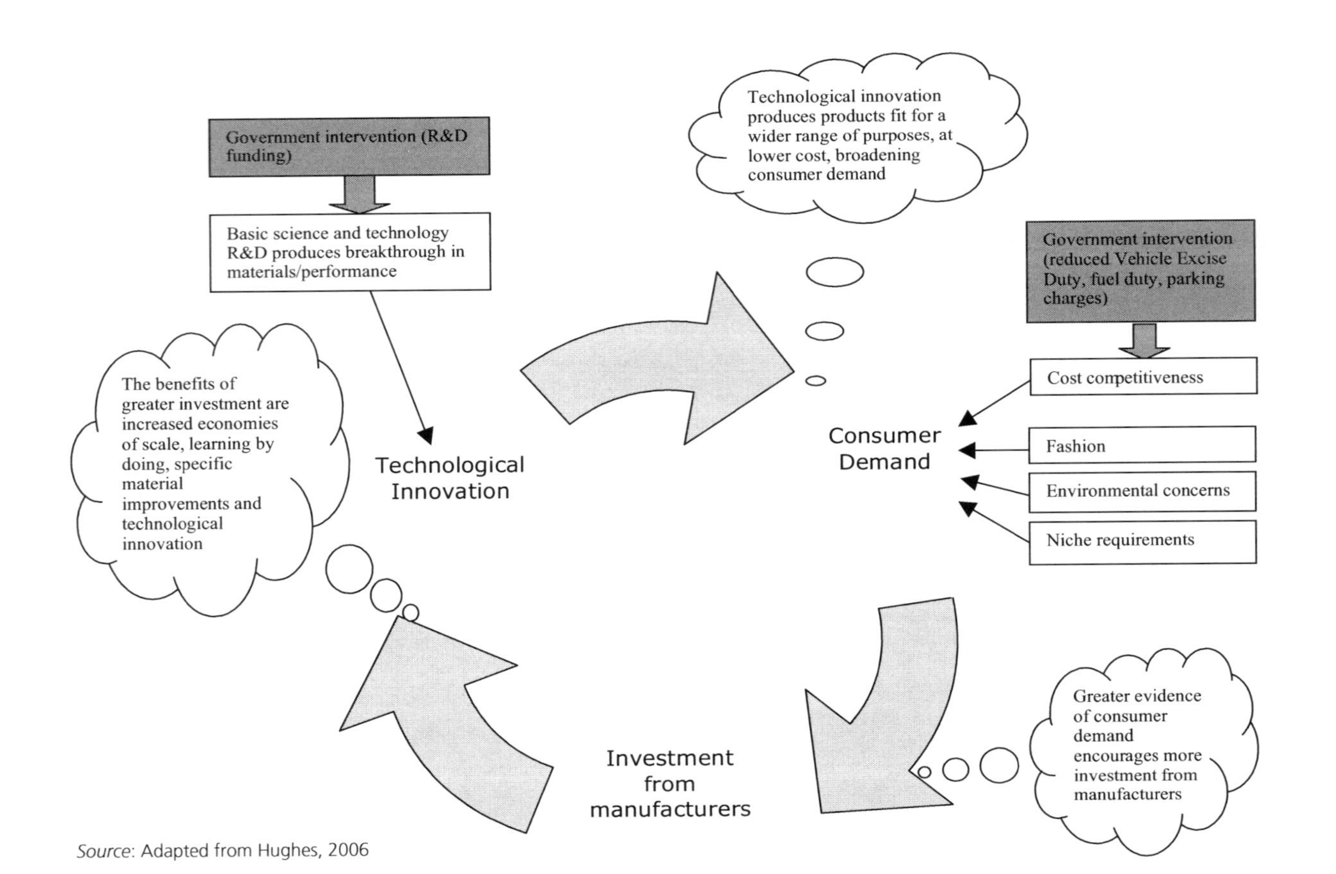

Source: Adapted from Hughes, 2006

Figure 12.1 *The circle of demand, investment and innovation*

If such policy measures are implemented, they should be coordinated to avoid giving conflicting signals both to consumers and potential manufacturers. For example, congestion charging and road pricing measures could emerge to be instruments of considerable power in stimulating the uptake of low-carbon vehicles (as discussed in Chapter 4, it appears that the success of the G-Wiz electric car in London is at least in part stimulated by the effect of the central London congestion charging zone). However, if such policies are to become a major lever for the long-term decarbonization of transport, clarity in aims and objectives will be crucial. Are they intended to actually reduce transport of *any* kind, or rather to stimulate low-carbon options? If the latter, should charges be graded according to the carbon intensity of the vehicle – that is, should petrol hybrids escape with less of a rebate than 'zero emission' electric or hydrogen vehicles? If so, would this purely be an 'exhaust pipe' judgement, or should such charges attempt to account for the potentially greatly differing well-to-wheels emissions of energy vectors such as electricity and hydrogen? Further, such policies which are aimed at affecting the economics of *operating* vehicles should be coordinated with those aimed at affecting the *purchase* of vehicles. A poor example of this was the policy announced in the 2009 Budget by the UK government whereby owners of old vehicles who trade them in for scrap would be rewarded with a £2,000 payment towards the purchase of a new vehicle (BERR, 2009). This was perceived as a measure to stimulate growth in the UK car manufacturing industry. However, it was apparently not considered that the payment could have been made available specifically for the purchase of low-emission vehicles. This could have stimulated the growth of a specialist sector of the auto-manufacturing industry which would be likely to have greater long-term prospects on UK shores than the conventional manufacturing plants currently operated by internationally mobile giants such as Vauxhall and Ford. It would also potentially have been better coordinated with possible future options for policies targeted at the use of vehicles, such as road pricing or congestion charging. As it stands, however, it would hardly be fair to effectively encourage consumers to buy carbon-intensive vehicles and then penalize them for using them.

Policies must also be constructed with long-term future pathways in mind, though with some sensitivity to the key areas of uncertainty. Extensive decarbonization requires both policies that realize near-term, relatively low-cost carbon reduction, and those that prepare the ground for longer-term, more expensive but potentially deeper cuts. Hydrogen technologies currently fall into this latter category. If long-term technologies such as hydrogen are to stand a chance of emerging from niche applications and prototypes to deploy widely in support of a major decarbonization of the economy, it is imperative that the signals deriving from coordinated policies such as those mentioned above must be consistent over the long term. An important aspect of this could increasingly be the clear advance signalling of intended future policy trajectories. This is important because, as mentioned in the discussion of Figure 12.1, the *immediate* implementation of policies of sufficient strength to improve the economics of hydrogen technologies, in comparison to incumbents, may face serious challenges of political and public acceptability. However, a signalling of the intention to introduce such strong policies at a future date could give both industry and the public a crucial window of opportunity in which to react. For industry in particular it would signal that the ramping-up of new supply chains to develop products, which would avoid the penalties of such future policies, would be a worthwhile endeavour. By setting strong policies in such long-term frameworks, they can cease to be seen simply as constrictions but also as opportunities. Whilst it might be argued that such long-term commitments are unrealistic in the context of normal electoral cycles, it may be that the UK's Climate Change Bill has broken an important precedent in this regard (DEFRA, 2008). The impact of policy decisions to support hydrogen should therefore be viewed in the context of fostering its long-term development, with an understanding of the different kinds of technologies and infrastructures different policies might be tuned to promoting, what kinds of transitions will be possible through these pathways, and what end goals might be achieved by each route.

The future of any kind of 'hydrogen economy' is far from assured, and doubtless there will be many false starts and hiccoughs along any of the routes that may be taken towards it. For example, one of the first acts of the new Obama Administration in the US (though this was later largely reversed by Congress) was to axe the substantial research programme for hydrogen fuel cell vehicles that had been put in place by President George W. Bush, on the grounds that the technology 'will not be practical over the next 10 to 20 years', and the new Administration 'preferred to focus on projects that would bear fruit more quickly' (Wald, 2009). However, countries have only just started in earnest considering how the necessary long-term cuts in carbon emissions are to be delivered if climate change is to be contained, and it is far too soon to know definitively which technologies will have the potential towards mid-century to achieve what is required. In our view, hydrogen technologies deserve very much to remain in the catalogue of possible major technological contributors to the mitigation of climate change, and to receive the targeted, internationally coordinated public support for research, development, demonstration and deployment that will be necessary if this possible contribution is ever to be realized.

Notes

1 See http://europa.eu.int/comm/energy_transport/en/prog_cut_en.html
2 See http://www.vfcvp.gc.ca/index_e.html

References

Agnolucci, P. and McDowall, W. (2007) 'Technological Change in Niches: Auxiliary Power Units and the Hydrogen Economy', *Technological Forecasting and Social Change*, vol 74, pp1394–1410

BERR (2009) 'Vehicle Scrappage Scheme'. Available at http://www.berr.gov.uk/whatwedo/sectors/automotive/scrappage/page51068.html, accessed 17 June 2009
Bossel, U., Eliasson, B. and Taylor, G. (2003) 'The Future of the Hydrogen Economy: Bright or Bleak?', Report E08, February, European Fuel Cell Forum, Lucerne. Available at http://www.efcf.com/reports/, accessed 7 August 2008
DEFRA (2008) 'Climate Change Act 2008'. Available at http://www.defra.gov.uk/environment/climatechange/uk/legislation/, accessed 17 June 2009
E4 Tech, Element Energy, Eoin Lees Energy (2004) 'A Strategic Framework for Hydrogen Energy in the UK: Final Report', London, E4 Tech. Available at http://www.dti.gov.uk/energy/sources/sustainable/hydrogen/strategic–framework/page26734.html
EA Technology (2000) 'Fuel Cells niche market applications and design studies', Report for the DTI managed by ETSU, London
Farrell, A., Keith, D. and Corbett, J. (2001) A strategy for introducing hydrogen into transportation', VIII Biennial Asilomar Conference: Transportation, Energy, and Environmental Policy, Asilomar, CA
Foley, J. (2001) 'H2: Driving the Future', Institute for Public Policy Research, London, IPPR
Hammarschlag, R. and Mazza, P. (2005) 'Questioning Hydrogen', *Energy Policy*, vol 33, pp 2039–2043
Hodson, M. and Marvin, S. (2005a) 'Re-Imagining Tees Valley in the Post-Industrial Age', UKSHEC Social Science Working Paper no 4, SURF Centre, University of Salford
Hodson, M. and Marvin, S. (2005b) 'The "Journey" to Wales' Hydrogen Economy', UKSHEC Social Science Working Paper no 5, SURF Centre, University of Salford
Hodson, M. and Marvin, S. (2005c) 'London's Hydrogen Economy: Negotiating the "Global", the "Regional" and the "Local"', UKSHEC Social Science Working Paper no 6, SURF Centre, University of Salford
Hughes, N. (2006) 'Summary of discussions from expert stakeholder workshops on the economics of hydrogen technologies', UKSHEC Social Science Working Paper no 27, London, Policy Studies Institute
Hughes, N. (2007) 'Actors, organizations and institutions relating to the development of hydrogen and fuel cell activities in the UK', UKSHEC Social Science Working Paper no 34, March, London, Policy Studies Institute
HyWays (2008) 'HyWays – The European Hydrogen Energy Roadmap'. Available at http://www.hyways.de/
Levinthal, D. (1998) 'The slow pace of rapid technological change: gradualism and punctuation in technological change', *Industrial and Corporate Change*, vol 7, pp217–247
Mazza, P. and Hammarschlag, R. (2005) 'Win-to-Wheel Energy Assessment', Report E18, European Fuel Cell Forum, Lucerne. Available at http://www.efcf.com/reports/, accessed 7 August 2008
McDowall, W. (2004) 'Promising Niches: a Survey of Early Markets for Hydrogen Technologies', October, mimeo, London, Policy Studies Institute
NRC and NAE (National Research Council and National Academy of Engineering) (2004) *The Hydrogen Economy: Opportunities, Costs, Barriers, and R&D Needs*, Washington, DC, The National Academies Press
Padró, C. and Putsche, V. (1999) 'Survey of the Economics of Hydrogen Technologies', National Renewable Energy Laboratory, Colorado. Available at http://www.nrel.gov/docs/fy99osti/27079.pdf

SMMT (Society of Motor Manufacturers and Traders) (2002) 'Towards a Shared Vision: Future Fuels and Sustainable Mobility', SMMT Future Fuels Strategy Group, London. Available at http://www.smmt.co.uk/publications/futurefuels.asp

Wald, M. (2009) 'U.S. Drops Research into Fuel Cells for Cars', 7 May, *The New York Times*

Index